Mind Readings

Introductory Selections on Cognitive Science

A Bradford Book
The MIT Press
Cambridge, Massachusetts
London, England

This book was set in Bembo on the Monotype "Prism Plus" PostScript Imagesetter by Asco Trade Typesetting Ltd., Hong Kong.

Printed and bound in the United States of America.

Library of Congress Cataloging-in-Publication Data

Mind readings: introductory selections in cognitive science / Paul
  Thagard, editor.
    p.   cm.
  "A Bradford book."
  Includes bibliographical references and index.
  ISBN 0-262-70067-0 (pbk.: alk. paper)
  1. Mental representation. 2. Intellect. 3. Thought and thinking.
4. Cognitive science. I. Thagard, Paul.
BF316.6.M55   1998
153—dc21   97-38748
                                                              CIP

To Mom, for teaching me to learn.

Contents

Guide for the Reader

This book is a collection of accessible readings on some of the most important topics in cognitive science. Anyone interested in the interdisiplinary study of mind should find these selections worth reading, but they work particularly well in company with my textbook *Mind: Introduction to Cognitive Science* (MIT Press, 1996). I have looked for up-to-date (less than a decade old) selections that provide further discussion of the major approaches and challenges to cognitive science that are discussed there. I have chosen selections that I hope will be comprehensible to people with little background in cognitive science. The table below displays the correspondences between the chapters in the textbook and those in this anthology. Chapters 1–8 of this anthology present the most important approaches to cognitive science from the perspective that thinking consists of computational procedures on mental representations. The remaining selections concern important challenges to the computational-representational understanding of mind. Together, *Mind* and *Mind Readings* provide all the material needed for an accessible one semester introductory course in cognitive science.

Mind chapter		*Mind Readings* chapter	
1	Representation and Computation	1	Simon
2	Logic	2	Johnson-Laird and Byrne
3	Rules	3	Anderson
		4	Pinker
4	Concepts	5	Medin
5	Analogies	6	Gentner and Markman
6	Images	7	Glasgow and Papadias
7	Connections	8	Rumelhart

Acknowledgments and Sources

I am very grateful to Kim Honeyford for her skilled and cheerful assistance in preparing the manuscript. Here is information on the original sources of the chapters:

1. Simon, H. A. (1992). What Is an "Explanation" of Behavior? *Psychological Science* 3: 150–161. © American Psychological Society. Reprinted with the permission of Cambridge University Press.
2. Johnson-Laird, P. N., and Byrne, R. M. (1991). The Cognitive Science of Deduction. Chapter 2 of *Deduction*. Hillsdale, NJ: Lawrence Erlbaum Associated, 17–40. Reprinted by permission of Erlbaum (UK), Taylor & Francis.
3. Anderson, J. R. (1993). Production Systems and the ACT-R Architecture. Chapter 1 of *Rules of the Mind*. Hillsdale, NJ: Erlbaum, 1–14. Reprinted with permission.
4. Pinker, S. (1991). Rules of Language. *Science* 253: 530–535. © 1991 American Association for the Advancement of Science. Reprinted with permission.
5. Medin, D. L. (1989). Concepts and Conceptual Structure. *American Psychologist* 44: 1469–1481. © 1989 by the American Psychological Association. Reprinted with permission.
6. Gentner, D., and Markman, A. B. (1997). Structure Mapping in Analogy and Similarity. *American Psychologist* 52: 45–56. © 1997 by the American Psychological Association. Reprinted with permission.
7. Glasgow, J., and Papadias, D. (1992) Computational Imagery. *Cognitive Science* 16: 355–394. © Cognitive Science Society Incorporated, used by permission.
8. Rumelhart, D. E. (1989). The Architecture of Mind: A Connectionist Approach. In M. I. Posner (ed.), *Foundation of Cognitive Science* (pp. 133–159). Cambridge, MA: The MIT Press. Reprinted with permission.
9. Oatley, K. (1992). The Structure of Emotions. From chapter 1 of *Best Laid Schemes: The Psychology of Emotions*. Cambridge, England: Cambridge, University Press. Reprinted with the permission of Cambridge University Press.

10. Flanagan, Owen (1992). A Unified Theory of Consciousness? Chapter 11 of *Consciousness Reconsidered*. Cambridge, MA: The MIT Press, 213–222. Reprinted with permission.
11. Mackworth, A. (1993). On Seeing Robots. In A. Basu and X. Li (eds.), *Computer Vision: Systems, Theory, and Applications* (pp. 1–13). Singapore: World Scientific. Reprinted with permission.
12. Durfee, E. H. (1992). What Your Computer Really Needs to Know, You Learned in Kindergarten. In *Proceedings of the Tenth International Conference on Artificial Intelligence* (pp. 858–864). Menlo Park, CA: AAAI Press/ The MIT Press. Reprinted with permission.
13. Eliasmith, C. (1996). The Third Contender: A Critical Examination of the Dynamicist Theory of Cognition. *Philosophical Psychology* 9: 441–463. Reprinted with permission of Carfax Publishing Company.

I am grateful to Windsor Viney and Poonan Dohutia for help with proofreading.

What Is an "Explanation" of Behavior?

Herbert A. Simon

The cognitive "revolution" in psychology introduced a new concept of explanation and somewhat novel methods of gathering and interpreting evidence. These innovations assume that it is essential to explain complex phenomena at several levels, symbolic as well as physiological; complementary, not competitive. As with the other sciences, such complementarity makes possible a comprehensive and unified experimental psychology. Contemporary cognitive psychology also introduced complementarity of another kind, drawing upon, and drawing together, both the behaviorist and the Gestalt traditions.

I would like to begin with two comments on contemporary cognitive psychology—on where we stand. The evidence supporting these observations is so overwhelming that I will not bore you by rehearsing it. But we have some conventional, customary ways of talking about psychology that fly in the face of what I think are the facts, and I would like to distance myself from these ways of speaking, which I believe are harmful to the continued rapid progress of our science.

How often have you heard that "some day we will understand the mind," or that "the human brain is a great mystery that we must seek to solve"? In fact, psychology exists not in the future, but in the present. By any reasonable metric, we know more about the human mind and brain than geophysicists know about the plate tectonics that move the continents over the globe, far more than particle physicists know about elementary particles, or biologists about the processes that transform a fertilized egg into a complex multicellular organism.

We discount our knowledge because some of it is so commonplace, so familiar from our everyday acquaintance with ourselves and other people. We discount it also because it often is insufficient to permit predictions of behavior in important matters that concern us. The former is a great blessing to us, for it allows us to learn easily facts of sorts that other sciences have to tease out with great effort. The latter is a true limitation that we share with meteorologists, evolutionary biologists, and all those physical or biological scientists who venture outside the laboratory into the complexity of real-world phenomena.

Hence, my first comment: In the year 1991, we know a great deal about human thinking, and especially about the symbolic processes, involving selective heuristic search and recognition of familiar cues, that people use to solve problems, to design artifacts and strategies, to make decisions, to communicate in natural language, and to learn. How people solve problems is no great mystery; we know enough about it to create computer programs that do it, and do it in a way that closely simulates human performance, step by step. By the same test, we know how people design strategies, and even how they learn language and make scientific discoveries.

In all these cases, we have examples of computer programs that perform these tasks in humanoid ways. If you want evidence for this claim, I can refer you, for starters, to standard sources like Anderson's (1990b) cognitive psychology textbook or the recent *Foundations of Cognitive Science*, edited by Posner (1989). Cognitive psychology is not some dream of the future; it exists, and it allows us to explain a vast range of phenomena. It is not a finished science, thank goodness (what science is?), but each year adds to its store of knowledge and understanding, and its powers of prediction.

My second comment: Histories of psychology are fond of talking about "schools of thought," and their rise and fall, attributing to the chronology of our field a circular course, rather than the helical one (at worst) attributed to other sciences. In the histories there is not just psychology, the science of human behavior; there is introspectionist psychology, and behaviorist psychology, and Gestalt psychology, and information processing psychology, and connectionist psychology—schools without end, and without cumulation, each school combating and destroying the previous one, to be consumed, in turn, by its successor.

This circular view of history is wholly counterfactual. The "cognitive revolution" (I even used the phrase in my opening summary) did not destroy either behaviorism or Gestalt psychology. It drew liberally upon both of them, both for experimental data and for concepts. The productions of information processing psychology are natural descendants of the familiar stimulus-response links of behaviorism (though not identical with them). Means–ends analysis, central to information processing theories of problem solving, was explored by Duncker (1945), and by Selz (1913) before him. The neural nets of current connectionist models have their origins in physiological probings of the nervous system, via the "cell assemblies" of Hebb (1949), and in notions, traceable back to Aristotle, of the associative structure of memory.

In the course of this paper, I refer to another currently fashionable novelty in psychology, so-called situated action and situated learning, and show that its antecedents are also very familiar. Psychology is as progressive and cumulative as any of the sciences, and we can today cite experiments of Ebbinghaus (1964), or Wundt (1902), or Hovland (1951), or Skinner (1938) as major sources of empirical support for contemporary theories.[1]

In our generation, we have discovered a mode of psychological theorizing that has greatly facilitated, and will continue to facilitate, the cumulation of knowledge and theory in psychology. Today we build computer models of both symbolic and connectionist systems. Instead of constructing microtheories for each phenomenon we observe (e.g., theories of retrospective inhibition), or macrostatements that are too simplistic and general to explain much (e.g., "forgetting follows a power law"), we construct computer programs that can be given complex cognitive tasks, identical to those given to our human subjects, and that will predict the temporal path of human behavior on those tasks (Newell and Simon, 1972).

Some cognitive psychologists today aspire to build "unified" models of this kind: The SOAR (Newell, 1990), ACT* (Anderson, 1983), and PDP (Rumelhart and McClelland, 1986) systems are familiar examples. Others of us aim at models of middle range: a GPS (Newell and Simon, 1972) to account for problem-solving phenomena; an EPAM (Feigenbaum and Simon, 1984) to account for verbal learning processes; an ISAAC (Novak, 1977) to explain how people understand problems described in natural language text, construct mental representations of those problems, and go on to solve them; and an INTERNIST (Miller, Pople, and Myers, 1982) or a MYCIN (Shortliffe, 1976) to describe the processes of expert medical diagnosis.

Whether comprehensive or not, such models enable cognitive psychology to organize large bodies of data around the mechanisms that produced them; and the availability and relevance of these large bodies of data provide powerful means to test adequacy of the models. This tying together and relating of disparate bodies of experimental data with hypotheses about the causal mechanisms greatly facilitates cumulation.

So much for these two debilitating myths: that the mind is something we will understand in the future and that the path of psychology is circular, each new "school" tearing down and replacing the one it succeeds. Neither myth bears the slightest resemblance to the true state of affairs, and it is time that we put them to rest and get on with advancing still further a science that has made great strides in this century.

Explaining a Conversation

The scene is a street in Singapore. A woman is talking to two other women, talking in Tamil, a Dravidian language that is spoken in a large region of southern India around Madras and in parts of Sri Lanka. We wish to explain her behavior.

What is there to explain? For one thing, why Tamil? Why not English, or Chinese, or Malayan, the predominant languages in Singapore? An explanation would describe the migrations that brought large numbers of Tamils from India to this distant port. This "simple" explanation still presupposes some vital theoretical underpinnings. It assumes that under some circumstances migrants will retain, for a generation or even beyond, the language of their ancestors. What are those circumstances, and what conditions in Singapore satisfied them? And when will this woman, probably multilingual, use Tamil, and when one of the other languages of Singapore?

The explanation by migration also assumes conditions that caused the migrants to leave their homeland, and historical "laws" that would explain migration as a response to such conditions. What were those conditions, and what is the nature of such laws?

Some social psychologists undertake to answer questions like these. For the rest, these questions are usually left to history, sociology, and the other social sciences. But insofar as they involve things stored in the human memory, they are also part of cognitive psychology. It is proper that they be welcomed back into our science, as is being done by those who are now focusing on the psychology of everyday life.

The Structure of a Dynamic Explanation

Even answers to all of these questions will only begin to explain our Tamil woman's behavior, but before continuing, let us ask what has already been revealed.

Our explanation has the form of a fugue, with two intertwined themes. First, to explain an event, we refer to antecedent events—initial conditions. To explain a Tamil-speaking woman's presence in Singapore, we find a migration from Madras. But that poses the new question of explaining the presence of Tamil-speaking people in southern India. So explanation by antecedent events takes us back to the explanation of those antecedents. If the data were available (they are not), they could take us step by step in an almost infinite regress to the cosmological Big Bang and beyond.

But—the second theme of the fugue—explanation by antecedent events also requires general laws to explain how each situation causes the succeeding one. What causes of migration can take people from one land to another? What laws determine the language that a person will speak in an ethnically foreign land, and when?

The natural sciences commonly employ this fuguelike structure of explanation. The differential equations of physics describe mechanisms that determine the next movements of the stars and planets, given the initial conditions: their present positions and velocities. The laws of genetics and Darwinian selection explain how a community of organisms (the initial conditions) evolves over years or millennia into a new and different community.

For systems that change through time, explanation takes this standard form: Laws acting on the current state of the system produce a new state—endlessly. Such explanations can be formalized as systems of differential equations or difference equations.

Explaining by Simulation

We return to our Tamil women, whom we left talking on the street. To understand their conversation, we must have some knowledge of the lexicon and syntax of their language. Tamil is one of about 20 highly inflected Dravidian languages spoken throughout southern

India. To characterize its syntax, we build a computer program that parses the speaker's sentences. Such a parser is also a set of difference equations, playing the same role as the differential equations in physics.

But we might go even further in explaining Tamil. We might build a diachronic story—conceptually, another set of difference equations—to explain how the contemporary Dravidian languages evolved from some common ancestral base. This means postulating laws of linguistic transformation that cause language evolution. Since Chomsky's revolution, or even since Grimm's, explanation in linguistics has become another exercise in building and testing difference equations (Chomsky, 1957).

Another approach to these questions is to write computer programs that are capable of using and understanding, even learning, language. A computer program is (literally, not metaphorically) a system of difference equations. For each possible state of the computer, combined with the input at that instant, the program determines the next state of the computer. The computer's memory holds the initial conditions (the current state) and the laws of behavior (the program). Its input devices convey to it the external stimulus, which may, as in the case before us, take the form of sentences in a natural language.

Since a computer program is a system of difference equations, a properly programmed computer can be used to explain the behavior of the dynamic system that it simulates. Theories can be stated as computer programs.

Controlled experiments can be performed on computer programs, altering specified program components to determine how such changes affect the performance of tasks. The architecture can thereby be modified to simulate the human performance better.

There is no epistemological difference between using a program incorporating Newton's laws to explain the movements of Mars and using a program incorporating linguistic laws to explain how speech is generated or understood. But perhaps you are not familiar with the computer programs that have these linguistic capabilities. One example is ISAAC, written by Novak (1977), which reads the English language statements of problems in physics textbooks, forms internal representations ("mental pictures") of the problem situations, and then proceeds to derive the applicable equations and to solve them.

Another such program is ZBIE, written by Siklóssy (1972), which reads a simple sentence in a natural language at the same time it inputs a diagrammatic representation of the scene described by the sentence (e.g., "The dog chases the cat."). ZBIE learns the meanings of the words in the sentences it reads (i.e., learns what objects or relations in the diagrams the words denote) and analyzes their grammatical structure. When it is later confronted with a scene it has not seen before, but one composed of familiar kinds of objects in familiar relations, it constructs an appropriate and grammatically correct sentence to describe the scene.[2]

A remarkable feature of programs like ZBIE is that they not only explain how natural language is understood, they also understand it. The linguistic symbols are not translated into an esoteric formal language; hence, we do not have to numericize or otherwise encode the sentences whose production or understanding we wish to explain. The programs use symbol structures that are isomorphic to those the human subject uses. All information processing theories of cognition have this property: They actually perform the tasks whose performance they explain.

Programs that simulate cognitive processes describe the processes in symbolic languages isomorphic to those being modeled, and hence, actually execute the processes. Consequently, they provide a rigorous test of the sufficiency of the hypothesized processes to perform the tasks of interest.

Neurophysiological Explanation

Simulating language behavior with a computer teaches us the properties an architecture must possess if it is to speak and listen, and what processes are employed by its program. It allows us to test, at the level of symbolic behavior, how closely these processes resemble those of human speakers or listeners. It does not tell us how the same structural conditions and programs are realized by the biological components known as neurons and the assemblages of components that make up the biological brain.

Explanation of cognitive processes at the information processing (symbolic) level is largely independent of explanation at the physiological (neurological) level that shows how the processes are implemented.

There is nothing mysterious about explaining phenomena at different levels of resolution. It happens all the time in the physical and biological sciences. A theory of genetics need not (fortunately) rely on a knowledge of quarks. As a matter of history, the former theory preceded the latter by many years. The theory of genetic processes was developed by Mendel, using genes as abstract primitive "atoms." Fifty years later, a microscopic foundation was provided for the theory by locating the genes in visible chromosomes. After another half century, the structure of chromosomes was elucidated in terms of the combinatorics of DNA, strands of four complex submolecules, nucleotides. Two levels of reduction and still no quarks! And no need of them, although we surely believe that nucleotides are made of atoms, which are made of neutrons and protons, which are made of quarks.

Explanation on different levels does not deny the possibility of reduction. Higher level theories use aggregates of the constructs at lower levels to provide parsimonious explanations of phenomena without explicit reference to the microconstructs. The lower level details do not show through to the higher level.

Of course, the higher level mechanisms are reducible to those of the lower level (at least in principle, although the computations can actually be carried out only in the simplest situations). But we do not require the reduction in order to explain the aggregate events at the higher level. We can write the system of difference equations for this higher level independently of any lower level explanation. Cognitive psychology (fortunately) does not have to stand still with breathless expectation until neurophysiology completes its work. As cognitive psychology has been doing, it can proceed with its task of explaining thought processes at the level of symbol systems.

Partitioning explanation into levels also points to a strategy for neurophysiological research. Neuropsychology has two main tasks. It must explain electrochemically how neurons and simple organizations of neurons store and transmit information. It must also help build the bridge theory that shows how the symbol structures and symbol-manipulating processes that handle information at a more aggregated level can be implemented by such neuronal structures and organizations. The bridge need not be built solely from one bank of the river; it can be constructed by cooperative effort of information processing psychologists with neuropsychologists. But if they are to cooperate, they must learn to read each other's blueprints.

This strategy relieves neuropsychology of the heroic, but impossible, task of climbing in a single step from neurons and nerve nets up to complex human behavior without inserting intermediate strata into the structure. Some neuropsychologists and connectionists do not yet accept the need for higher level aggregate theories, or the meaning of information processing programs as examples of such theories. Such misunderstanding forms a serious barrier to collaboration.

Nowadays, a discussion of neurophysiology necessarily raises the question of whether mental functions are to be modeled as parallel or serial systems. At the lowest level, the individual neuron demonstrably transmits signals longitudinally, in serial fashion. At the next level up, brain tissue forms a network of elements operating in parallel, and the same can be said of the eyes and ears. At the level of conscious reportable events, the bottleneck of attention and short-term memory again gives the mind the characteristics of a serial organization. It is worth pondering that the low-level anatomy of the conventional von Neumann "serial" computer looks every bit as parallel as a neural network; yet at the more aggregate, symbolic, level, it executes its processes sequentially, one or a few at a time.

From these observations, we can conclude, first, that at the level of the network of neurons, modeling will have to be largely parallel. It is not clear, as yet, how far we can abstract from the details of neural structure in our models, or how many structures the models will have to contain to simulate relevant events at this level.

Second, at the symbolic level—the level of events taking place in hundreds of milliseconds or more—modeling will continue to be largely serial, for the mind behaves like a serial system wherever the bottleneck of attention supervenes upon events. While most people can probably chew gum and walk at the same time, very few can carry on a technical conversation while maneuvering a car through heavy traffic.

Third, at the intermediate level of events milliseconds or tens of milliseconds in duration, the comparative advantages of parallel and serial modeling are not yet clear. This is the level of the EPAM program (Feigenbaum and Simon, 1984), which simulates learning and perception at the symbolic level, and the level of most connectionist systems. It is also the foundation level of SOAR (Newell, 1990), a unified control structure for cognition. Teasing out the respective roles of parallel and serial processors and their interface at or near this level is a major contemporary task for cognitive research.

Static Theories

Concern with architecture reminds us that not all theories take the form of difference equations. In fact, theories in psychology have traditionally had a quite different form. Typically, they make assertions such as "If the independent variable, x, increases, the dependent variable, y, will also increase." Laws of this form are very weak. They are also merely descriptive, not explanatory.

Much stronger claims are made by laws of the form "$y = 80x + 300$," where the parameters, 80 and 300, were known or estimated prior to the current experiment. If, in addition, these parameters describe structural characteristics of the system (e.g., the speed at which it can store or access information), then the law begins to explain as well as to describe. Let us call laws of this kind, with the numerical parameters taken seriously, *models*.

For example, Baddeley (1981) showed that the contents of short-term memory can be retained for only about 2 s without overt or covert rehearsal. This finding implies that the maximum capacity of short-term memory is whatever content can be rehearsed in this time. Other experiments have shown that it takes about 300 ms to recover a familiar "chunk" (e.g., a familiar word or phrase) from long-term memory, and about 80 ms per syllable to pronounce it. From these facts, there follows the law: $2,000 = 300C + 80S$, where C and S are the numbers of chunks and syllables, respectively, in the longest strings that can be retained in short-term memory. The law can be tested using the standard immediate recall paradigm (Zhang and Simon, 1985).

Some of the properties of systems can be captured in static laws, preferably models, which specify the relations among variables, qualitatively or numerically.

Explaining Thinking

Our Tamil women are still talking on the street in Singapore. So far, we do not know what they are saying. When we eavesdrop, we find that the speaker is explaining to her companions how to solve the Tower of Hanoi puzzle![3]

By now, we know exactly how to theorize about this kind of behavior. We construct a set of difference equations (a computer program in a symbol-processing language) that simulates human behavior in solving the Tower of Hanoi problem. In fact, programs of this kind have existed for some years (Simon, 1975). Notice that I refer to "programs" in the plural, for different people may solve the problem in different ways, using different strategies.

Heuristic Search

Heuristic search is too familiar to require lengthy description. Common to virtually all of the problem-solving strategies that people have been observed to use is a problem space and a search through this space until a solution is reached (Newell and Simon, 1972). The moves that change one situation into another in the Tower of Hanoi may be legal moves, as defined by the problem instructions, or they may be "wished-for" moves that change the current situation into a distant one in one step.

In some strategies, most of the problem solving takes place in the head, making use of symbolized goals and *mental models*, symbol structures describing the situation at each stage of the search. In other strategies, the subjects work directly from the physical Tower of Hanoi puzzle in front of them, using visual perception of the current arrangement of the disks to calculate a next move, and recording it by actually moving the disk. In currently fashionable terminology, the subjects who use the latter strategies are engaging in *situated action*.

There is a good deal of debate at present (under the rubric of situated action) as to whether problem solving requires the subject to create a mental problem space and to search in that space, or whether the search can be almost wholly external, with no significant problem representation in the head (Suchman, 1987; Winograd and Flores, 1986). Sometimes the debate is enlarged by challenging whether problem solving can be modeled at all by symbolic systems.

The best way to resolve the debate is to construct programs and observe what they can and cannot do. A running program is the moment of truth. This particular debate has been largely resolved by programs already written and tested. Some strategies that have been written for the Tower of Hanoi depend on search through an internal representation of the problem, or even initial search through an abstracted representation to find a plan for the more detailed search. Other strategies that have been written search externally, representing internally only the "affordances" provided by the external objects and their relations (Simon, 1975). Hence, it has been demonstrated constructively that both situated action and strategies requiring planning and internal representations are realizable by symbol-processing systems.

What has not been settled, and cannot be settled without extensive empirical study, is the extent to which, and the circumstances under which, human beings will use one or another kind of strategy. Our Tamil woman is not carrying a physical Tower of Hanoi puzzle with her. She has no alternative, if she is to explain the solution to her friends, but to form a mental representation of some sort—a problem space—and to describe the moves in that space. Her friends have no alternative for understanding the explanation but to translate the description into their own mental representations. If a physical Tower of Hanoi puzzle were present, matters might be quite different. But life does offer us a great deal of variety. So much for situated action.

Different people, or the same people in different situations, can employ different strategies for performing a given task. A theory of their performance would include a computer program describing the strategy they are using in a given instance together with a specification of the circumstance under which this particular strategy will be used. The specification can include a variety of elements, including the subjects' previous experience and learning.

Expert Behavior

Actually, I was joking about the Tower of Hanoi. That is not what the Tamil women are talking about at all. In fact, the speaker is telling about a new recipe she has learned; her friends regard her as an expert in preparing gourmet meals.

The conversation is not a monologue. The expert does most of the talking, but her friends ask frequent questions, and she usually replies promptly. One of them asks how long the dish should remain in the oven. The expert answers, then says, "Of course, I don't have any systematic rules for determining such things. I just use my intuition. It's all a matter of experience."

The expert has just stated, very succinctly, the theory of expert performance that has emerged in recent years from psychological research and modeling. In everyday speech, we use the word *intuition* to describe a problem-solving or question-answering performance that is speedy and for which the expert is unable to describe in detail the reasoning or other process that produced the answer. The situation has provided a cue; this cue has given the expert access to information stored in memory, and the information provides the answer. Intuition is nothing more and nothing less than recognition.

We do not have conscious access to the processes that allow us to recognize a familiar object or person. We recognize our friend, but we do not know what traits and features, what cues, enable that recognition to occur. Nor can we describe these traits and features to other people accurately enough to enable them to recognize the same person. We are aware of the *fact* of recognition, which gives us access to our knowledge about our friend; we are not aware of the *processes* that accomplish the recognition.

The process of recognition (i.e., intuition) is readily realized in computer programs by means of so-called *productions*. A production is an (if → then), or (condition → action), statement that, at least superficially, resembles a (stimulus → response) linkage. For our present purposes, we need note only that, while the stimuli of classical behaviorism are in the environment, not in the head, the conditions that have to be satisfied to trigger the action of a production may be (but need not be) symbol structures held in memory. Productions can implement either situated action or internally planned action, or a mixture of these.

Quite general programming languages (e.g., the language OPS5; Brownston, Farrell, and Martin, 1985) can be constructed entirely of productions. The execution of a production can be made to depend on a context by including among the conditions for execution one or more goal symbols. The production will then be activated only in contexts where the appropriate goal is present. Conditions can also reflect other elements of contexts besides goals.

Consider a (simplified) expert modeled as a production system. Cues in the environment that the expert encounters trigger information in memory, hence, initiate actions appropriate to the situations marked by these cues. In its simplest form, the model produces situated action.

When the doctor notices some symptoms, a diagnosis is triggered, or, alternatively, information that is accessed indicates certain additional tests should be performed to reach a definitive diagnosis (a departure from pure situated action). When the doctor has reached a diagnosis, another production accesses information in memory about the prognosis and about appropriate courses of treatment.

Information organized in a production system of this kind—a sort of indexed encyclopedia—can produce expert behavior. Expert systems may, in addition, have some capabilities for means-ends analysis or other forms of reasoning and heuristic search, but at their core is a production system capable of recognizing appropriate cues, hence, capable of acting intuitively.

There is no incompatibility between intuition and analysis. A chess master in a tournament does a good deal of analysis, of look-ahead to possible continuations of the game. The same chess master, playing simultaneously a number of weaker players, moves quickly, hardly analyzing ahead at all but selecting moves almost wholly on intuition in the form of recognition of weaknesses created by the opponents. This rapid play is weaker than the more analytic play of the tournament, but only a little weaker.

A large part of the chess master's expertise lies in his or her intuitive (recognition) capabilities, based, in turn, on large amounts of stored and indexed knowledge derived from training and experience. Under the conditions of rapid play, the chess master's behavior is a form of situated action; under tournament conditions, it is more planful.

Similarly, our expert Tamil gourmet, after a quick inventory of her refrigerator and kitchen cabinet, can rustle up a presentable and tasty meal in a hurry, relying on intuition—experience encapsulated in memory and evoked by the sight of familiar items of food. Of course, given some time to plan and prepare, she can usually produce an even more delicious meal.

The core of an expert system, in human or computer, is a system of productions that operates like an indexed encyclopedia. Cues in the situation (external or imagined) are recognized by the conditions of productions, triggering the actions associated with these conditions. The case in which the cues are predominantly external is sometimes called situated action.

The production system of an expert is generally associated also with reasoning (search) capabilities that support an adaptive system of analytic and intuitive responses.

Adaptivity of Behavior

The human mind is an adaptive system. It chooses behaviors in the light of its goals, and as appropriate to the particular context in which it is working. Moreover, it can store new knowledge and skills that will help it attain its goals more effectively tomorrow than yesterday: It can learn.

As a consequence of the mind's capacities for adaptation and learning, human behavior is highly flexible and variable, altered by both circumstances and experience.

Scientific laws, whether descriptive or explanatory, are supposed to capture the invariants of the phenomena, those underlying regularities that do not change from moment to moment. How does one find laws to describe or explain the behavior of an adaptive system?

The shape of a gelatin dessert cannot be predicted from the properties of gelatin, but only from the shape of the mold into which it was poured. If people were perfectly adaptable, psychology would need only to study the environments in which behavior takes place. Some of this viewpoint is reflected in the *affordances* of Gibson's (1979) theories of perception, and in the rational adaptation models of my colleague Anderson (1990a, 1991).

In its extreme form, this position eliminates the need to run laboratory experiments or to observe people. Merely examine the shape of the mold: Analyze the environment in which the behavior is to take place and the goals of the actor, and from these deduce logically and mathematically what the optimal behavior (and hence the actual behavior) must be.

Nowhere has this method of explaining human behavior been carried further than in modern neoclassical economics. The neoclassical theories also show the severe limits of the approach. First, the scheme works only if the actor's goals and the alternative behaviors available for choice are known in advance. Change either the goals or the alternatives and the optimal decision may change (Simon, 1991). Do we think that we can predict what the menu will be in the Singapore apartment tonight without knowing what is in the refrigerator, or what some of our gourmet's favorite recipes are? Can we predict it from a book on nutritionally optimal diets?

In most real choice situations, there is a multiplicity of goals, often partly conflicting and even incommensurable. A simple example is the trade-off between speed and accuracy: Unless we know their relative importance, we cannot select an optimal behavior.

Nor are the alternatives from which the actor might choose usually known in advance (even to the experimenter). Human beings spend much of their time inventing or discovering actions that fit the circumstances. The whole vast collection of human activities known as design—whether in architecture or engineering, or painting, or management—is aimed at synthesizing appropriate actions. In explaining or predicting behavior, whether optimal or not, we must know not only the design product (the alternative finally chosen) but the design process as well (Simon, 1981, chaps. 5 and 6).

The process of design is highly dependent on history and experience. Before Newton, designers did not use the calculus, and undoubtedly reached different solutions than in later ages when the calculus was available. So choice is always relativized to the current state of knowledge, and inventing new alternatives or even new processes for generating alternatives is very different from choosing among available and known alternatives.

Design does not aim at optimization. Almost always, the process must be halted and a solution selected long before all alternatives have been generated and compared. Even the idea of generating "all" alternatives is usually chimerical. Limits on human (and computer) calculation and incomplete information foreclose finding the best: Most often, a stop rule halts the search when a satisfactory alternative is found—one that meets a variety of criteria but maximizes none. So we should not expect the recipes of our expert gourmet cook to be optimal; but if she invites us to dinner at her Singapore home, the meal will be delicious; it will "satisfice."

The nonoptimality of behavior is obvious even in the simple Tower of Hanoi task discussed earlier. Many different strategies can be used to solve the problem; and even in identical circumstances, different subjects use different strategies, not all of which can be optimal. There is substantial empirical evidence that subjects also adopt a wide range of strategies, most of them suboptimal, in solving cryptarithmetic problems (Newell and Simon, 1972).

In complex adaptive behavior, the link between goals and environment is mediated by strategies and knowledge discovered or learned by the actor. Behavior cannot be predicted from optimality criteria alone without information about the strategies and knowledge agents possess and their capabilities for augmenting strategies and knowledge by discovery or instruction.

What constitutes an available alternative depends on the capabilities of the actor: such things as visual acuity, strength, short-term memory, reaction times, and speed and limits of computation and reasoning—to say nothing of expertise based on stored knowledge and skill. Before the exercise of optimizing can be carried out, all of these side conditions must be nailed down: goals, knowledge of immediately available alternatives, means for generating new alternatives, knowledge for predicting the outcomes these alternatives will produce, and limits on the ability of the actor to hold information in memory and to calculate.

The predictions of an optimizing theory depend as much on the postulated side conditions as on the optimization assumption. In fact, in most cases, if the correct side conditions are foreseen and predicted, the behavior can usually be predicted without any strict assumption of optimality; the postulate that people satisfice, look for "good enough" answers, is usually adequate to anticipate behaviors.

There is no way to determine a priori, without empirical study of behavior, what side conditions govern behavior in different circumstances. Hence, the study of the behavior of an adaptive system like the human mind is not a logical study of optimization but an empirical study of the side conditions that place limits on the approach to the optimum. Here is where we must look for the invariants of an adaptive system like the mind.

But does the point need to be belabored? Optimization is an ideal that can be realized only in (a) extremely simple worlds (if offered the choice, take a $10 bill in preference to a $1 bill) and (b) worlds having strong and simple mathematical structures that admit the computations required for optimization (e.g., worlds that can be described in terms of a linear objective function and linear constraints, so that solutions can be found by linear programming algorithms). These are not the worlds in which most human life is lived.

We would not think of trying to predict where the moon will be at midnight tomorrow night without knowing where it is tonight. In the same way, we should not presume to predict how a human being will solve a problem or learn a new skill without knowing what that human being already has stored in memory by way of relevant information and skills. Changing the information and skills will change the behavior. This principle is the basis for all of the differences observed between experts and novices.

To some extent, we can finesse this requirement for our research by restricting our study to the ubiquitous college sophomore, assuming that all college sophomores know roughly the same things, at least those that are relevant to the mainly contentless tasks we confront them with. When we want to go further to study individual differences in task performance or to study the effects of previous knowledge and skill on performance, we must face up to the boundary conditions outlined above.

Cognitive and Social Psychology

Since adaptive behavior is a function of strategies and knowledge, both largely acquired from the social environment, there can be no sharp boundary between cognitive psychology and social psychology. The context in which knowledge is acquired and used, an exogenous variable in cognitive psychology, provides the endogenous variables for social psychology and sociology.

Studying expert behavior immediately begins to dissolve the boundary between cognitive psychology, on the one side, and social psychology (to say nothing of social and intellectual history), on the other. It is not an accident that histories of science provide an important part of the data used to test cognitive theories of scientific discovery (Langley et al., 1987). The histories do not draw a boundary around individual investigators, but encompass the sources of an investigator's knowledge and, more broadly, the social processes that direct the production of scientific knowledge and its communication.

But we have already seen this point illustrated in the simple interaction among the Tamil women—their choice of language, their very presence in Singapore, the influence of their experience (itself a product of social environment) on what they can do and like to do.

As another example of this intermingling of the social with the cognitive, communication between different communities of experts involves translation, that is, understanding by members of one group of the language and concepts of the other. As Voss and his associates have shown, we can study one aspect of this phenomenon by observing how experts from different communities attack the same problem in quite different ways (Voss, Tyler, and Vengo, 1983). Another aspect, not yet much studied, would tell us how experts learn to translate from foreign dialects.

The flow between cognitive and social runs in both directions. Social psychologists have long been interested in how people form beliefs, or models, about other persons. Theories of person perception need to be integrated with cognitive theories about knowledge acquisition and formation of representations. There is no a priori reason to suppose that different processes are involved in the two cases.

Divide and Conquer

In trying to understand the behavior of three women on a street in Singapore, we have already set a dizzying array of tasks for psychology: to explain the migrations of peoples; the origins and changes in their languages; their development as individuals in society; their gradual acquisition of values, skills (including skills of social interaction), knowledge, and attitudes; the adaptation of their behavior to their goals; and the physiological underpinnings of all of these processes. It appears that we are going to have to build computer programs, systems of difference equations, of immense complexity to explain such behavior.

Forms of Subdivision

Fortunately, we do not have to explain everything at once, or within the boundaries of a single program. We have already seen that complex phenomena can usually be segmented into levels from macroscopic to microscopic, separated by both the spatial and the temporal scales of the events they describe. Provided that the phenomena are roughly hierarchical in structure, as most natural phenomena are, we can build explanatory theories at each level, and then bridging theories that link the aggregated physiological behavior to the units of explanation at the symbolic level just above.

Above the symbolic level, we can study more comprehensive social phenomena on a different time scale, without serious interaction between our theories of social history, say, and our theories of problem solving. Only aggregative properties of the symbolic processes will enter into the explanation of the larger scale social phenomena (Simon and Ando, 1961).

We can divide up the task of explanation in other ways. Difference equations explain actions and their consequences as functions of the initial conditions; they explain the moment after in terms of the moment before. For many purposes, we can take the system's initial conditions, the contents and organization of memory when our observations begin, as given, and leave to another day and another theory the explanation of how those initial conditions came about.

Thus, we can study the behavior of an accomplished expert and compare it with the behavior of a novice, while putting aside the explanation of how the expert became so. We can study how different strategies—plans versus situated action, say—lead to different behaviors, but study separately how strategies are acquired.

Similarly, we can factor, if only incompletely, the syntax of language from its semantics, and thereby study how speech strings are processed more or less independently of our study of how large structures of knowledge are organized when they are stored in the human brain.

Unified Theories

In pointing to the virtues and even necessities of the divide-and-conquer strategy, I am not denigrating the efforts of others to build unified theories of cognition: Anderson's (1983) ACT*, Newell's (1990) SOAR, or Rumelhart and McClelland's (1986) connectionist systems—just to mention the efforts of some colleagues. But we must understand the goal of those efforts. The goal is not to erect a single system representing the "whole man." Rather, it is to show how a single control structure can handle all of the cognitive processes of which the human mind is capable.

Perhaps the activity would be better understood if it were labeled "unified theories *of the control* of cognition." In any event, the effort to build such comprehensive control structures does not in any way make otiose or superfluous efforts to build explanatory theories of components of cognitive performances, and to build them at various levels of aggregation.

For a realistic conception of what *unified* might mean, we need to look over our shoulders at that most unified and parsimonious of sciences, physics, with its hundreds of pages of theory of specific phenomena at various levels of detail and resolution, all bound together rather shakily into the broader structures of quantum mechanics, relativity theory, and the still somewhat visionary unified field theories.

And if a look at physics does not persuade us that unified theories tell only a small part of the story, we can inspect chemistry, and biology, and geology, and genetics, where the point is even more glaringly obvious.

Methods for the Study of Behavior

Our methods for gathering data to test our theories must fit the formal shapes of the theories. I limit my remarks to theories of symbolic cognitive processes. What are appropriate methods for testing the fit of computer programs (difference equations) to human behavior? The programs predict the next action a system will take as a function of its present state and current input; that is to say, they predict what production will fire at each successive moment. The fineness of resolution of symbolic programs is of the order of tens or hundreds of milliseconds: The programs predict what the subject will do each few hundreds of milliseconds.

Contemporary technology largely limits us to observing subjects' visible and audible behaviors, and the richest streams of such behaviors are verbalizations and eye movements. Under most circumstances, we do not yet know how to interpret in detail the information we get from electrical measurements on the scalp.

We can obtain data for analyzing the behavior of the Tamil women because one of them, not wanting to miss any of the details of the recipes, is tape-recording their conversation. Unfortunately, the available technology does not permit us to record eye movements on a street in Singapore.

Data on eye movements and verbalizations are still too coarse to capture all the behavior at the symbolic level. In eye movements, we may detect a new saccade every 1/3 or 1/2 s. In verbalization, subjects may utter a clause or phrase equivalent to a proposition every 2 or 3 s, at best. Much of our inference from behavior to the underlying program has to be indirect.

But that is no cause for dismay. In this regard, cognitive psychology is not different from the other sciences, which are always inferring underlying theoretical processes from gross observed events. At that future time when we shall obtain direct evidence, say, electrochemical evidence, identifying precisely the sequence of processes being executed, the game will be over and we will need to look for new domains of research. But we need not hold our breaths while waiting for that to happen.

We now know the difference between verbal protocols, interpreted as behavior, and introspection (Ericsson and Simon, 1984). Over the past quarter century, we have gathered vast experience in encoding verbal protocols and eye movement records at a level of detail that permits us to test what productions are being executed. We should strive to improve these methodologies, and they will continue to improve, but we do not need to be unhappy with our current ability to test our theories of cognition.

Along one dimension at least, considerable unhappiness is still expressed. How can we test the significance of the discrepancies we find between our models and the observed human behavior? Computer programs are complex, having many degrees of freedom. By taking advantage of this freedom, cannot we simply adjust the program ad hoc to fit any data?

A sound caution underlies this objection. Our confidence in a theory grows, and should grow, with increase in the ratio of the number of data points explained to the number of degrees of freedom in the theory. A theory expressed as a computer program has many degrees of freedom. But a human thinking-aloud protocol, or a set of such protocols, contains a great many data points. It is the ratio that counts, and that ratio can be very large.

Standard procedures for evaluating the fit of computer programs to data are lacking today. The familiar tests of statistical significance are inappropriate. The percentage of variance explained is more useful, but does not take into account the number of degrees of freedom. I have no precise solution to offer to the problem, but the direction in which we should look for one is obvious.

Search for alternative ways of testing our theories brings us back to more conventional psychological experiments. Conventionally, we observe a few behaviors (latencies, accuracies) over some minutes, then average the data over tasks and subjects, then compare the averaged numbers between control and experimental conditions. While this standard procedure is often useful and valuable, it also suffers from severe limitations. Its temporal resolution is very low; it can seldom be used to study individual events of a few seconds' duration.

More serious, conventional experimental methods do not deal with the serial dependency of events on this temporal scale. Since the execution of each production of the cognitive system can change memory contents, hence, change the conditions that determine what production will fire next, it is hard to test an explanation of the behavior unless this temporal dependency can be captured in the data. In particular, averaging over subjects is bound to destroy sequential contingencies. Verbal protocols and eye movement records are almost the only forms of data that give us any means for capturing these contingencies.

A principal means for testing theories of cognition at the level of elementary symbolic processes is to compare the successive behaviors the theories predict with the successive behaviors of subjects revealed by thinking-aloud protocols and eye movement records. The procedures for testing goodness of fit are not yet standardized, but the underlying principle is to demand a high ratio of data points to numbers of productions in the simulation programs.

Conclusion

We have left our Tamil women standing on the street in Singapore, but I am sure that they will finish their conversation and return home before the heavy afternoon shower drenches them and refreshes the city. They have given us some hope that their behavior, as an example of the general run of human behavior, is explainable, and that today we already possess many important pieces of that explanation at the level of symbolic processes.

By way of summary, I recall here the main generalizations we reached along the way:

Computer Programs as Theories

For systems that change through time, explanation takes the form of laws acting on the current state of the system to produce a new state— endlessly. Such explanations can be formalized with differential or difference equations.

A properly programmed computer can be used to explain the behavior of the dynamic system that it simulates. Theories can be stated as computer programs.

Controlled experiments can be performed on computer programs to determine how such changes affect the performance of tasks. The programs can then be modified to simulate the human performance better.

Programs that simulate cognitive processes describe these processes in symbolic languages and actually execute the processes. Consequently, they test the sufficiency of the theory to perform the tasks.

Symbolic and Physiological Explanation

Explanation of cognitive processes at the information processing (symbolic) level is largely independent of explanation at the physiological (neurological) level.

Explanation on different levels does not deny the possibility of reduction. Higher level theories use aggregates of the constructs at lower levels. The lower level details do not show through to the higher level.

Some of the properties of systems can be captured in static laws that specify the relations among variables, qualitatively or numerically.

Dependence of Behavior on Knowledge

Different people, or the same people in different situations, can employ different strategies for performing a given task. A theory of their performance would describe their strategies and specify the circumstance under which each strategy will be used.

The core of an expert or expert system is a system of productions that operates like an indexed encyclopedia. External or imagined cues are recognized by the conditions of productions, triggering the associated actions. The case in which the cues are predominantly external is sometimes called situated action.

The production system of an expert is associated also with reasoning (search) capabilities that support an integrated system of analytic and intuitive responses.

Adaptive Systems

The human mind is an adaptive system that chooses behaviors in the light of its goals, and as appropriate to context. Moreover, it can store new knowledge and skills: It can learn.

The link between goals and environment is mediated by learned strategies and knowledge. Behavior cannot be predicted from optimality criteria without information about the strategies and knowledge agents possess or acquire.

The study of the behavior of an adaptive system is not a logical study of optimization but an empirical study of the side conditions that place limits on the approach to the optimum.

Cognitive and Social Psychology

Since strategies and knowledge are both largely acquired from the social environment, there can be no sharp boundary between cognitive psychology and social psychology. The context in which knowledge is acquired and used, an exogenous variable in cognitive psychology, provides the endogenous variables for social psychology and sociology.

Verbal Protocols as Data

Theories of cognition can be tested by comparing the behaviors they predict with the successive behaviors of subjects revealed by thinking-aloud protocols and eye movement records. Strictness demands a high ratio of data points to numbers of productions in the programs.

In summarizing at this high level of abstraction, I have left out all of the rich detail of the behavior we can explain: chess playing, medical diagnosis, problem solving in physics and mathematics, the use of diagrams in thinking, scientific discovery—yes, and even the Tower of Hanoi, and a conversation about cookery on a street in Singapore.

Acknowledgments

This article is in substance the author's Keynote Address to the Third Annual Convention of the American Psychological Society, Washington, DC, June 1991.

The research was supported by the Personnel and Training Programs, Psychological Sciences Division, Office of Naval Research, under Contract No. N00014-86-K-0768, and by the Defense Advanced Research Projects Agency, Department of Defense, ARPA Order 3597, monitored by the Air Force Avionics Laboratory under Contract F33615-81-K-1539. Reproduction in whole or in part is permitted for any purpose of the U.S. government. Approved for public release; distribution unlimited.

Notes

1. For example, see the uses of Ebbinghaus (1964) and Hovland (1951) in testing the EPAM theory of verbal learning (Feigenbaum and Simon, 1984).

2. Because the words in the sentences have denotations in the diagrams, ZBIE has a genuine understanding of the sentences it reads and those it constructs. It anticipates fully, and by a decade, the objections against machine understanding raised by Searle (1984) in his Chinese Room parable—and answers these objections decisively.

3. It is widely believed on the Carnegie-Mellon campus that I cannot give a talk without mentioning the Tower of Hanoi within the first 15 minutes. I contribute this new evidence to support that belief.

References

Anderson, J. R. (1983). *The architecture of cognition.* Cambridge, MA: Harvard University Press.

Anderson, J. R. (1990a). *The adaptive character of thought.* Hillsdale, NJ: Erlbaum.

Anderson, J. R. (1990b). *Cognitive psychology and its implications* (3rd ed.). New York: Freeman.

Anderson, J. R. (1991). The place of cognitive architectures in a rational analysis. In K. VanLehn (Ed.), *Architectures for intelligence* (pp. 1–24). Hillsdale, NJ: Erlbaum.

Baddeley, A. D. (1981). The concept of working memory. *Cognition, 10,* 17–23.

Brownston, L., Farrell, R., Kant, E., and Martin, N. (1985). *Programming expert systems in OPS5.* Reading, MA: Addison-Wesley.

Chomsky, N. (1957). *Syntactic structures.* The Hague: Mouton.

Duncker, K. (1945). On problem solving. *Psychological Monographs, 58* (Whole No. 270).

Ebbinghaus, H. (1964). *Memory: A contribution to experimental psychology.* New York: Dover.

Ericsson, K. A., and Simon, H. A. (1984). *Protocol analysis.* Cambridge, MA: MIT Press.

Feigenbaum, E. A., and Simon, H. A. (1984). EPAM-like models of recognition and learning. *Cognitive Science, 8,* 305–336.

Gibson, J. J. (1979). *The ecological approach to visual perception.* Boston: Houghton-Mifflin.

Hebb, D. O. (1949). *The organization of behavior.* New York: Wiley.

Hovland, C. I. (1951). Human learning and retention. In S. S. Stevens (Ed.), *Handbook of experimental psychology* (pp. 613–689). New York: Wiley.

Langley, P., Simon, H. A., Bradshaw, G., and Zytkow, J. (1987). *Scientific discovery.* Cambridge, MA: MIT Press.

Miller, R. A., Pople, H. E., and Myers, M. D. (1982). INTERNIST-1, an experimental computer-based diagnostic consultant for general medicine. *New England Journal of Medicine, 307,* 468–476.

Newell, A. (1990). *Unified theories of cognition.* Cambridge, MA: Harvard University Press.

Newell, A., and Simon, H. A. (1972). *Human problem solving.* Englewood Cliffs, NJ: Prentice-Hall.

Novak, G. (1977). Representation of knowledge in a program for solving physics problems. *Proceedings of the Fifth International Joint Conference on Artificial Intelligence,* pp. 286–291.

Posner, M. I. (Ed.). (1989). *Foundations of cognitive science.* Cambridge, MA: MIT Press.

Rumelhart, D. E., and McClelland, J. L. (1986). *Parallel distributed processing.* Cambridge, MA: Bradford Books.

Searle, J. R. (1984). *Minds, brains, and science.* Cambridge, MA: Harvard University Press.

Selz, O. (1913). *Ueber die Gezetze des Geordneten Denkverlaufs.* Stuttgart: Spemann.

Shortliffe, E. H. (1976). *Computer-based medical consultations: MYCIN.* New York: American Elsevier.

Siklóssy, L. (1972). Natural language learning by computer. In H. A. Simon and L. Siklóssy (Eds.), *Representation and meaning* (pp. 288–328). Englewood Cliffs, NJ: Prentice-Hall.

Simon, H. A. (1975). The functional equivalence of problem solving skills. *Cognitive Psychology, 7,* 268–288.

Simon, H. A. (1981). *The sciences of the artificial* (2nd ed.). Cambridge, MA: MIT Press.

Simon, H. A. (1991). Cognitive architectures and rational analysis: Comment. In K. VanLehn (Ed.), *Architectures for intelligence* (pp. 25–39). Hillsdale, NJ: Erlbaum.

Simon, H. A., and Ando, A. (1961). Aggregation of variables in dynamic systems. *Econometrica, 29,* 111–138.

Skinner, B. F. (1938). *The behavior of organisms.* New York: Appleton-Century-Crofts.

Suchman, L. A. (1987). *Plans and situated actions.* Cambridge, England: Cambridge University Press.

Voss, J. F., Tyler, S. W., and Vengo, L. A. (1983). Individual differences in the solving of social science problems. In R. Dillon and R. Smech (Eds.), *Individual differences in cognition* (pp. 205–232). New York: Academic Press.

Winograd, T., and Flores, F. (1986). *Understanding computers and cognition.* Norwood, NJ: Ablex.

Wundt, W. (1902). *Grundriss der psychologie.* Leipzig: Wilhelm Engelmann.

Zhang, G.-J., and Simon, H. A. (1985). STM capacity for Chinese words and idioms. *Memory and Cognition, 13,* 193–201.

The Cognitive Science of Deduction

Philip N. Johnson-Laird and Ruth M. J. Byrne

The late Lord Adrian, the distinguished physiologist, once remarked that if you want to understand *how* the mind works then you had better first ask *what* it is doing. This distinction has become familiar in cognitive science as one that Marr (1982) drew between a theory at the "computational level" and a theory at the "algorithmic level." A theory at the computational level characterizes what is being computed, why it is being computed, and what constraints may assist the process. Such a theory, to borrow from Chomsky (1965), is an account of human competence. And, as he emphasizes, it should also explain how that competence is acquired. A theory at the algorithmic level specifies how the computation is carried out, and ideally it should be precise enough for a computer program to simulate the process. The algorithmic theory, to borrow again from Chomsky, should explain the characteristics of human performance—where it breaks down and leads to error, where it runs smoothly, and how it is integrated with other mental abilities.

We have two goals in this chapter. Our first goal is to characterize deduction at the computational level. Marr criticized researchers for trying to erect theories about mental processes without having stopped to think about what the processes were supposed to compute. The same criticism can be levelled against many accounts of deduction, and so we shall take pains to think about its function: what the mind computes, what purpose is served, and what constraints there are on the process. Our second goal is to examine existing algorithmic theories. Here, experts in several domains of enquiry have something to say. Linguists have considered the logical form of sentences in natural language. Computer scientists have devised programs that make deductions, and, like philosophers, they have confronted discrepancies between everyday inference and formal logic. Psychologists have proposed algorithmic theories based on their experimental investigations. We will review work from these disciplines in order to establish a preliminary account of deduction—to show what it is, and to outline theories of how it might be carried out by the mind.

Deduction: A Theory at the Computational Level

What happens when people make a deduction? The short answer is that they start with some information—perceptual observations, memories, statements, beliefs, or imagined states of affairs—and produce a novel conclusion that follows from them. Typically, they argue from some initial propositions to a single conclusion, though sometimes merely from one proposition to another. In many practical inferences, their starting point is a perceived state of affairs and their conclusion is a course of action. Their aim is to arrive at a valid conclusion, which is bound to be true given that their starting point is true.

One long-standing controversy concerns the extent to which people are logical. Some say that logical error is impossible: deduction depends on a set of universal principles applying to any content, and everyone exercises these principles infallibly. This idea seems so contrary to common sense that, as you might suspect, it has been advocated by philosophers (and psychologists). What seems to be an invalid inference is nothing more than a valid inference from other premises (see Spinoza, 1677; Kant, 1800). In recent years, Henle (1962) has defended a similar view. Mistakes in reasoning, she claims, occur because people forget the premises, re-interpret them, or import extraneous material. "I have never found errors," she asserts, "which could unambiguously be attributed to faulty reasoning" (Henle, 1978). In all such cases, the philosopher L. J. Cohen (1981) has concurred, there is some malfunction of an information-processing mechanism. The underlying competence cannot be at fault. This doctrine leads naturally to the view that the mind is furnished with an inborn logic (Leibniz, 1765; Boole, 1854). These authors, impressed by the human invention of logic and mathematics, argue that people must think rationally. The laws of thought are the laws of logic.

Psychologism is a related nineteenth century view. John Stuart Mill (1843) believed that logic is a generalization of those inferences that people judge to be valid. Frege (1884) attacked this idea: logic may ultimately depend on the human mind for its discovery, but it is not a subjective matter; it concerns objective relations between propositions.

Other commentators take a much darker view about logical competence. Indeed, when one contemplates the follies and foibles of humanity, it seems hard to disagree with Dostoyevsky, Nietzsche, Freud, and those who have stressed the irrationality of the human mind. Yet this view is reconcilable with logical competence. Human beings may desire the impossible, or behave in ways that do not optimally serve their best interests. It does not follow that they are incapable of rational thought, but merely that their behaviour is not invariably guided by it.

Some psychologists have proposed theories of reasoning that render people inherently irrational (e.g. Erickson, 1974; Revlis, 1975; Evans, 1977). They may draw a valid conclusion, but their thinking is not properly rational because it never makes a full examination of the consequences of premises. The authors of these theories, however, provide no separate account of deduction at the computational level, and so they might repudiate any attempt to ally them with Dostoyevsky, Nietzsche, and Freud.

Our view of logical competence is that people are rational in principle, but fallible in practice. They are able to make valid deductions, and moreover they sometimes *know* that they have made a valid deduction. They also make invalid deductions in certain circumstances. Of course, theorists can explain away these errors as a result of misunderstanding the premises or forgetting them. The problem with this manoeuvre is that it can be pushed to the point where no possible observation could refute it. People not only make logical mistakes, they are even prepared to concede that they have done so (see e.g. Wason and Johnson-Laird, 1972; Evans, 1982). These metalogical intuitions are important because they prepare the way for the invention of self-conscious methods for checking validity. Thus, the development of logic as an intellectual discipline requires logicians to be capable of sound pre-theoretical intuitions. Yet, logic would hardly have been invented if there were never occasions where people were uncertain about the status of an inference. Individuals do sometimes formulate their own principles of reasoning, and they also refer to deductions in a meta-logical way. They say, for example: "It seems to follow that Arthur is in Edinburgh, but he isn't, and so I must have argued wrongly." These phenomena merit study like other forms of meta-cognition (see e.g. Flavell, 1979; Brown, 1987). Once the meta-cognitive step is made, it becomes possible to reason at the meta–meta-level, and so on to an arbitrary degree. Thus, cognitive psychologists and devotees of logical puzzles (e.g. Smullyan, 1978; Dewdney, 1989) can in turn make inferences about meta-cognition. A psychological theory of deduction therefore needs to accommodate deductive competence, errors in performance, and meta-logical intuitions (cf. Simon, 1982; Johnson-Laird, 1983; Rips, 1989).

Several ways exist to characterize deductive competence at the computational level. Many theorists—from Boole (1847) to Mac-namara (1986)—have supposed that logic itself is the best medium. Others, however, have argued that logic and thought differ. Logic is *monotonic*, i.e. if a conclusion follows from some premises, then no subsequent premise can invalidate it. Further premises lead mono-tonically to further conclusions, and nothing ever subtracts from them. Thought in daily life appears not to have this property. Given the premises:

Alicia has a bacterial infection.
If a patient has a bacterial infection, then the preferred treatment for the patient is penicillin.

it follows validly:

Therefore, the preferred treatment for Alicia is penicillin.

But, if it is the case that:

Alicia is allergic to penicillin.

then common-sense dictates that the conclusion should be withdrawn. But it still follows validly in logic. This problem suggests that some inferences in daily life are "non-monotonic" rather than logically valid, e.g. their conclusions can be withdrawn in the light of subsequent information. There have even been attempts to develop *formal* systems of reasoning that are non-monotonic (see e.g. McDermott and Doyle, 1980). We will show later in the book that they are unnecessary. Nevertheless, logic cannot tell the whole story about deductive competence.

A theory at the computational level must specify what is computed, and so it must account for what deductions people actually make. Any set of premises yields an infinite number of valid conclusions. Most of them are banal. Given the premises:

Ann is clever.
Snow is white.

the following conclusions are all valid:

Ann is clever and snow is white.
Snow is white and Ann is clever and snow is white.

They must be true given that the premises are true. Yet no sane individual, apart from a logician, would dream of drawing them. Hence, when reasoners make a deduction in daily life, they must be guided by more than logic. The evidence suggests that at least three extralogical constraints govern their conclusions.

The first constraint is *not* to throw semantic information away. The concept of semantic information, which can be traced back to medieval philosophy, depends on the proportion of possible states of affairs that an assertion rules out as false (see Bar-Hillel and Carnap, 1964; Johnson-Laird, 1983). Thus, a conjunction, such as:

Joe is at home and Mary is at her office.

conveys more semantic information (i.e. rules out more states of affairs) than only one of its constituents:

Joe is at home.

which, in turn, conveys more semantic information than the inclusive disjunction:

Joe is at home or Mary is at her office, or both.

A valid deduction cannot increase semantic information, but it can decrease it. One datum in support of the constraint is that valid deductions that do decrease semantic information, such as:

Joe is at home.

Therefore, Joe is at home or Mary is at her office, or both.

seem odd or even improper (see Rips, 1983).

A second constraint is that conclusions should be more parsimonious than premises. The following argument violates this constraint:

Ann is clever.

Snow is white.

Therefore, Ann is clever and snow is white.

In fact, logically untutored individuals declare that there is no valid conclusion from these premises. A special case of parsimony is not to draw a conclusion that asserts something that has just been asserted. Hence, given the premises:

If James is at school then Agnes is at work.

James is at school.

the conclusion:

James is at school and Agnes is at work.

is valid, but violates this principle, because it repeats the categorical premise. This information can be taken for granted and, as Grice (1975) argued, there is no need to state the obvious. The development of procedures for drawing parsimonious conclusions is a challenging technical problem in logic.

A third constraint is that a conclusion should, if possible, assert something new, i.e., something that was not explicitly stated in the premises. Given the premise:

Mark is over six feet tall and Karl is taller than him.

the conclusion:

Karl is taller than Mark, who is over six feet tall.

is valid but it violates this constraint because it assert nothing new. In fact, ordinary reasoners spontaneously draw conclusions that establish relations that are not explicit in the premises.

When there is no valid conclusion that meets the three constraints, then logically naive individuals say, "nothing follows" (see e.g. Johnson-Laird and Bara, 1984). Logically speaking, the response is wrong. There are always conclusions that follow from any premises. The point is that there is no valid conclusions that meets the three constraints. We do not claim that people are aware of the constraints or that they are mentally represented in any way. They may play no direct part in the process of deduction, which for quite independent reasons yields deductions that conform to them (Johnson-Laird, 1983, Ch. 3). In summary, our theory of deductive competence posits rationality, an awareness of rationality, and a set of constraints on the conclusions that people draw for themselves. *To deduce is to maintain semantic information, to simplify, and to reach a new conclusion.*

Formal Rules: A Theory at the Algorithmic Level

Three main classes of theory about the process of deduction have been proposed by cognitive scientists:

1. Formal rules of inference.
2. Content-specific rules of inference.
3. Semantic procedures that search for interpretations (or mental models) of the premises that are counterexamples to conclusions.

Formal theories have long been dominant. Theorists originally assumed without question that there is a mental logic containing formal rules of inference, such as the rule for modus ponens, which are used to derive conclusions. The first psychologist to emphasize the role of logic was the late Jean Piaget (see e.g. Piaget, 1953). He argued that children internalize their own actions and reflect on them. This process ultimately yields a set of "formal operations," which children are supposed to develop by their early teens. Inhelder and Piaget (1958, p. 305) are unequivocal about the nature of formal operations. They write:

No further operations need be introduced since these operations correspond to the calculus inherent to the algebra of propositional logic. In short, reasoning is nothing more than the propositional calculus itself.

There are grounds for rejecting this account: we have already demonstrated that deductive competence must depend on more than pure logic in order to rule out banal, though valid, conclusions.

Moreover, Piaget's logic was idiosyncratic (see Parsons, 1960; Ennis, 1975; Braine and Rumain, 1983), and he failed to describe his theory in sufficient detail for it to be modelled in a computer program. He had a genius for asking the right questions and for inventing experiments to answer them, but the vagueness of his theory masked its inadequacy perhaps even from Piaget himself. The effort to understand it is so great that readers often have no energy left to detect its flaws.

Logical Form in Linguistics

A more orthodox guide to logical analysis can be found in linguistics. Many linguists have proposed analyses of the logical form of sentences, and often presupposed the existence of formal rules of inference that enable deductions to be derived from them. Such analyses were originally inspired by transformational grammar (see e.g. Leech, 1969; Seuren, 1969; Johnson-Laird, 1970; Lakoff, 1970; Keenan, 1971; Harman, 1972; Jackendoff, 1972). What these accounts had in common is the notion that English quantifiers conform to the behaviour of logical quantifiers only indirectly. As in logic, a universal quantifier within the scope of a negation:

Not all of his films are admired.

is equivalent to an existential quantifier outside the scope of negation:

Some of his films are not admired.

But, unlike logic, natural language has no clear-cut devices for indicating scope. A sentence, such as:

Everybody is loved by somebody.

has two different interpretations depending on the relative scopes of the two quantifiers. It can mean:

Everybody is loved by somebody or other.

which we can paraphrase in "Loglish" (the language that resembles the predicate calculus) as:

For any x, there is some y, such that if x is a person then y is a person, and x is loved by y.

It can also mean:

There is somebody whom everybody is loved by.
(There is some y, for any x, such that y is a person and if x is a person, then x is loved by y.)

Often, the order of the quantifiers in a sentence corresponds to their relative scopes, but sometimes it does not, e.g.:

No-one likes some politicians.
(For some y, such that y is a politician, no x is a person and x likes y.)

where the first quantifier in the sentence is within the scope of the second.

Theories of logical form have more recently emerged within many different linguistic frameworks, including Chomsky's (1981) "government and binding" theory, Montague grammar (Cooper, 1983), and Kamp's (1981) theory of discourse representations. The Chomskyan theory postulates a separate mental representation of logical form (LF), which makes explicit such matters as the scope of the quantifiers, and which is transformationally derived from a representation of the superficial structure of the sentence (S-structure). The sentence, "Everybody is loved by somebody," has two distinct logical forms analogous to those above. The first corresponds closely to the superficial order of the quantifiers, and the second is derived by a transformation that moves the existential quantifier, "somebody," to the front—akin to the sentence:

Somebody, everybody is loved by.

This conception of logical form is motivated by linguistic considerations (see Chomsky, 1981; Hornstein, 1984; May, 1985). Its existence as a level of syntactic representation, however, is not incontrovertible. The phenomena that it accounts for might be explicable, as Chomsky has suggested (personal communication, 1989), by enriching the representation of the superficial structure of sentences.

Logical form is, of course, a necessity for any theory of deduction that depends on formal rules of inference. Kempson (1988) argues that the mind's inferential machinery is formal, and that logical form is therefore the interface between grammar and cognition. Its structures correspond to those of the deductive system, but, contrary to

Chomskyan theory, she claims that it is not part of grammar, because general knowledge can play a role in determining the relations it represents. For example, the natural interpretation of the sentence:

Everyone got into a taxi and chatted to the driver.

is that each individual chatted to the driver of his or her taxi. This interpretation, however, depends on general knowledge, and so logical form is not purely a matter of grammar. Kempson links it to the psychological theory of deduction advocated by Sperber and Wilson (1986). This theory depends on formal rules of inference, and its authors have sketched some of them within the framework of a "natural deduction" system.

One linguist, Cooper (1983), treats scope as a semantic matter, i.e. within the semantic component of an analysis based on Montague grammar, which is an application of model-theoretic semantics to language in general. A different model-theoretic approach, "situation semantics," is even hostile to the whole notion of reasoning as the formal manipulation of formal representations (Barwise, 1989; Barwise and Etchemendy, 1989a,b).

Formal Logic in Artificial Intelligence
Many researchers in artificial intelligence have argued that the predicate calculus is an ideal language for representing knowledge (e.g. Hayes, 1977). A major discovery of this century, however, is that there cannot be a full decision procedure for the predicate calculus. In theory, a proof for any valid argument can always be found, but no procedure can be guaranteed to demonstrate that an argument is invalid. The procedure may, in effect, become lost in the space of possible derivations. Hence, as it grinds away, there is no way of knowing if, and when, it will stop. One palliative is to try to minimize the search problem for valid deductions by reducing the number of formal rules of inference. In fact, one needs only a single rule to make any deduction, the so-called "resolution rule" (Robinson, 1965):

A or B, or both
C or not-B, or both
∴ A or C, or both.

The rule is not intuitively obvious, but consider the following example:

Mary is a linguist or Mary is a psychologist.
Mary is an experimenter or Mary is not a psychologist.
Therefore, Mary is a linguist or Mary is an experimenter.

Suppose that Mary is not a psychologist, then it follows from the first premise that she is a linguist; now, suppose that Mary is a psychologist, then it follows from the second premise that she is an experimenter. Mary must be either a psychologist or not a psychologist, and so she must be either a linguist or an experimenter.

Table 2.1 summarizes the main steps of resolution theorem-proving, which relies on the method of *reductio ad absurdum*, i.e. showing that the negation of the desired conclusion leads to a contradiction. Unfortunately, despite the use of various heuristics to speed up the search, the method still remains intractable: the search space tends to grow exponentially with the number of clauses in the premises (Moore, 1982). The resolution method, however, has become part of "logic programming"—the formulation of high level programming languages in which programs consist of assertions in a formalism closely resembling the predicate calculus (Kowalski, 1979). Thus, the language PROLOG is based on resolution (see e.g. Clocksin and Mellish, 1981).

No psychologist would suppose that human reasoners are equipped with the resolution rule (see also our studies of "double disjunctions" in the next chapter). But, a psychologically more plausible form of deduction has been implemented in computer programs. It relies on the method of "natural deduction," which provides separate rules of inference for each connective. The programs maintain a clear distinction between what has been proved and what their goals are, and so they are able to construct chains of inference working forwards from the premises and working backwards from the conclusion to be proved (see e.g. Reiter, 1973; Bledsoe, 1977; Pollock, 1989). The use of forward and backward chains was pioneered in modern times by Polya (1957) and by Newell, Shaw, and Simon (1963); as we will see, it is part of the programming language, PLANNER.

Table 2.1
A simple example of "resolution" theorem-proving

The deduction to be evaluated:
1. Mary is a psychologist.
2. All psychologists have read some books.
3. ∴ Mary has read some books.

Step 1: Translate the deduction into a *reductio ad absurdum*, i.e. negate the conclusion with the aim of showing that the resultant set of propositions is inconsistent:
1. (Psychologist Mary)
2. (For any x) (for some y)
            (Psychologist x & book y) → (Read x y)
3. (Not (For some z) (Book z & (Read Mary z)))

Step 2: Translate all the connectives into disjunctions, and eliminate the quantifiers. "Any" can be deleted: its work is done by the presence of variables. "Some" is replaced by a function (the so-called Skolem function), e.g. "all psychologists have read some books" requires a function, f, which, given a psychologist as its argument, returns a value consisting of some books:
1. (Psychologist Mary)
2. (Not (Psychologist x)) or (Read x (f x))
3. (Not (Read Mary (f Mary))

Step 3: Apply the resolution rule to any premises containing inconsistent clauses: it is not necessary for both assertions to be disjunctions. Assertion 3 thus cancels out the second disjunct in assertion 2 to leave:
1. (Psychologist Mary)
2. (Not (Psychologist Mary))

These two assertions cancel out by a further application of the resolution rule. Whenever a set of assertions is reduced to the empty set in this way, they are inconsistent. The desired conclusion follows at once because its negation had led to a *reductio ad absurdum*.

Formal Rules in Psychological Theories

Natural deduction has been advocated as the most plausible account of mental logic by many psychologists (e.g. Braine, 1978; Osherson, 1975; Johnson-Laird, 1975; Macnamara, 1986), and at least one simulation program uses it for both forward- and backward-chaining (Rips, 1983). All of these theories posit an initial process of recovering the logical form of the premises. Indeed, what they have in common outweighs their differences, but we will outline three of them to enable readers to make up their own minds.

Johnson-Laird (1975) proposed a theory of propositional reasoning partly based on natural deduction. Its rules are summarized in Table 2.2 along with those of the two other theories. The rule introducing disjunctive conclusions:

A

∴ A or B (or both)

leads to deductions that, as we have remarked, throw semantic information away and thus seem unacceptable to many people. Yet, without this rule, it would be difficult to make the inference:

If it is frosty or it is foggy, then the game won't be played.
It is frosty.
Therefore, the game won't be played.

Johnson-Laird therefore proposed that the rule (and others like it) is an auxiliary one that can be used only to prepare the way for a primary rule, such as modus ponens. Where the procedures for exploiting rules fail, then the next step, according to his theory, is to make a hypothetical assumption and to follow up its consequences.

Braine and his colleagues have described a series of formal theories based on natural deduction (see e.g. Braine, 1978; Braine and Rumain, 1983). At the heart of their approach are the formal rules presented in Table 2.2. They differ in format from Johnson-Laird's in two ways. First, "and" and "or" can connect any number of propositions, and so, for example, the first rule in Table 2.2 has the following form in their theory:

$P_1, P_2 \ldots P_n$
Therefore, P_1 and P_2 and $\ldots P_n$.

Second, Braine avoids the need for some auxiliary rules, such as the disjunctive rule above, by building their effects directly into the main rules. He includes, for example, the rule:

If A or B then C
A
Therefore, C

again allowing for any number of propositions in the disjunctive antecedent. This idea is also adopted by Sperber and Wilson (1986).

Table 2.2
The principal formal rules of inference proposed by three psychological theories of deduction

	Johnson-Laird	Braine	Rips
Conjunctions			
A, B ∴ A & B	+	+	+
A & B ∴ A	+	+	+
Disjunctions			
A or B, not-A ∴ B	+	+	+
A ∴ A or B	+		+
Conditionals			
If A then B, A ∴ B	+	+	+
If A or B then C, A ∴ C		+·	+
A ⊢ B ∴ If A then B	+	+	+
Negated conjunctions			
not (A & B), A ∴ B	+	+	
not (A & B) ∴ not-A or not-B			+
A & not-B ∴ not (A & B)	+		
Double negations			
not not-A ∴ A	+	+	
De Morgan's laws			
A & (B or C) ∴ (A & B) or (A & C)		+	
Reductio ad absurdum			
A ⊢ B & not-B ∴ not-A	+	+	+
Dilemmas			
A or B, A ⊢ C, B ⊢ C ∴ C		+	+
A or B, A ⊢ C, B ⊢ D ∴ C or D		+	
Introduction of tautologies			
∴ A or not-A		+	+

Notes
"+" indicates that a rule is postulated by the relevant theory.
"A ⊢ B" means that a deduction from A to B is possible. Braine's rules interconnect any number of propositions, as we explain in the text. He postulates four separate rules that together enable a *reductio ad absurdum* to be made. Johnson-Laird relies on procedures that follow up the separate consequences of constituents in order to carry out dilemmas.

   Braine, Reiser, and Rumain (1984) tested the theory by asking subjects to evaluate given deductions. The problems concerned the presence or absence of letters on an imaginary blackboard, e.g.:

If there is either a C or an H, then there is a P.
There is a C.
Therefore, there is a P.

The subjects' task was to judge the truth of the conclusion given the premises. The study examined two potential indices of difficulty— the number of steps in a deduction according to the theory, and the "difficulty weights" of these steps as estimated from the data. Both measures predicted certain results: the rated difficulty of a problem, the latency of response (adjusted for the time it took to read the problem), and the percentage of errors. Likewise, the number of words in a problem correlated with its rated difficulty and the latency of response.

   Rips (1983) has proposed a theory of propositional reasoning, which he has simulated in a program called ANDS (A Natural Deduction System). The rules used by the program—in the form of procedures—are summarized in Table 2.2. The program evaluates given conclusions and it builds both forward-chains and backward-chains of deduction, and therefore maintains a set of goals separate from the assertions that it has derived. Certain rules are treated as auxiliaries that can be used only when they are triggered by a goal, e.g.:

A, B
Therefore, A and B

which otherwise could be used *ad infinitum* at any point in the proof. If the program can find no rule to apply during a proof, then it declares that the argument is invalid. Rips assumes that rules of inference are available to human reasoners on a probabilistic basis. His main method of testing the theory has been to fit it to data obtained from subjects who assessed the validity of arguments. The resulting estimates of the availability of rules yielded a reasonable fit for the data as a whole. One surprise, however, was that the rule:

If A or B then C
A
Therefore, C

had a higher availability than the simple rule of modus ponens. It is worth nothing that half of the valid deductions in his experiment called for semantic information to be thrown away. Only one out of these 16 problems was evaluated better than chance. Conversely, 14 of the other 16 problems, which maintained semantic information, were evaluated better than chance.

A major difficulty for performance theories based on formal logic is that people are affected by the content of a deductive problem. Yet, formal rules ought to apply regardless of content. That is what they are: rules that apply to the logical form of assertions, once it has been abstracted from their content. The proponents of formal rules argue that content exerts its influence only during the interpretation of premises. It leads reasoners to import additional information, or to assign a different logical form to a premise. A radical alternative, however, is that reasoners make use of rules of inference that have a specific content.

Content-Specific Rules: A Second Theory at the Algorithmic Level

Content-specific rules of inference were pioneered by workers in artificial intelligence. They were originally implemented in the programming language PLANNER (Hewitt, 1971). It and its many descendants rely on the resemblance between proofs and plans. A proof is a series of assertions, each following from what has gone before, that leads to a conclusion. A plan is a series of hypothetical actions, each made possible by what has gone before, and leading to a goal. Hence, a plan can be derived in much the same way as a proof. A program written in a PLANNER-like language has a data-base consisting of a set of simple assertions, such as:

Mary is a psychologist.
Paul is a linguist.
Mark is a programmer.

which can be represented in the following notation:

(Psychologist Mary)
(Linguist Paul)
(Programmer Mark)

The assertion, "Mary is a psychologist," is obviously true with respect to this data base. General assertions, such as:

All psychologists are experimenters.

are expressed, not as assertions, but as rules of inference. One way to formulate such a rule is by a procedure:

(Consequent (x) (Experimenter x)
(Goal (Psychologist x)))

which enables the program to infer the consequent that x is an experimenter if it can satisfy the goal that x is a psychologist. If the program has to evaluate the truth of:

Mary is an experimenter

it first searches its data base for a specific assertion to that effect. It fails to find such an assertion in the data base above, and so it looks for a rule with a consequent that matches with the sentence to be evaluated. The rule above matches and sets up the following goal:

(Goal (Psychologist Mary))

This goal *is* satisfied by an assertion in the data base, and so the sentence, "Mary is an experimenter" is satisfied too. The program constructs backward-chains of inference using such rules, which can even be supplemented with specific heuristic advice about how to derive certain conclusions.

Another way in which to formulate a content-specific rule is as follows:

(Antecedent (x) (Psychologist x)
(Assert (x) (Experimenter x)))

Wherever its antecedent is satisfied by an input assertion, such as:

Mary is a psychologist.

the procedure springs to life and asserts that x is an experimenter:

Mary is an experimenter.

This response has the effect of adding the further assertion to the data base. The program can construct forward-chains of inference using such rules.

Content-specific rules are the basis of most expert systems, which are computer programs that give advice on such matters as medical diagnosis, the structure of molecules, and where to drill for minerals. They contain a large number of conditional rules that have been culled from human experts. From a logical standpoint, these rules are postulates that capture a body of knowledge. The expert systems, however, use them as rules of inference (see e.g. Michie, 1979; Duda, Gaschnig, and Hart, 1979; Feigenbaum and McCorduck, 1984). The rules are highly specific. For example, DENDRAL, which analyzes mass spectrograms (Lindsay, Buchanan, Feigenbaum, and Lederberg, 1980), includes this conditional rule:

If there is a high peak at 71 atomic mass units
and there is a high peak at 43 atomic mass units
and there is a high peak at 86 atomic mass units
and there is any peak at 58 atomic mass units
then there must be an N-PROPYL-KETONE3 substructure.

(see Winston, 1984, p. 196). Most current systems have an inferential "engine" which, by interrogating a user about a particular problem, navigates its way through the rules to yield a conclusion. The conditional rules may be definitive or else have probabilities associated with then, and the system may even use Bayes theorem from the probability calculus. It may build forward chains (Feigenbaum, Buchanan, and Lederberg, 1979), backward chains (Shortliffe, 1976), or a mixture of both (Waterman and Hayes-Roth, 1978).

Psychologists have also proposed that the mind uses content-specific conditional rules to represent general knowledge (e.g. Anderson, 1983). They are a plausible way of drawing inferences that depend on background assumptions. The proposal is even part of a seminal theory of cognitive architecture in which the rules (or "productions" as they are known) are triggered by the current contents of working memory (see Newell and Simon, 1972, and Newell, 1990). When a production is triggered it may, in turn, add new information to working memory, and in this way a chain of inferences can ensue.

A variant on content-specific rules has been proposed by Cheng and Holyoak (1985), who argue that people are guided by "pragmatic reasoning schemas." These are general principles that apply to a particular domain. For example, there is supposedly a permission schema that includes rules of the following sort:

If action A is to be taken then precondition B must be satisfied.

The schema is intended to govern actions that occur within a framework of moral conventions, and Cheng and Holyoak argue that it and other similar schemas account for certain aspects of deductive performance.

Content plays its most specific role in the hypothesis that reasoning is based on memories of particular experiences (Stanfill and Waltz, 1986). Indeed, according to Riesbeck and Schank's (1989) theory of "case-based" reasoning, human thinking has nothing to do with logic. What happens is that a problem reminds you of a previous case, and you decide what to do on the basis of this case. These theorists allow, however, that when an activity has been repeated often enough, it begins to function like a content-specific rule. The only difficulty with this theory is that it fails to explain how people are able to make valid deductions that do not depend on their specific experiences.

General knowledge certainly enters into everyday deductions, but whether it is represented by schemas or productions or specific cases is an open question. It might, after all, be represented by *assertions* in a mental language. It might even have a distributed representation that has no explicit symbolic structure (Rumelhart, 1989). Structured representations, however, do appear to be needed in order to account for reasoning about reasoning (see Johnson-Laird, 1988, Ch. 19).

Mental Models: A Third Theory at the Algorithmic Level

Neither formal rules nor content-specific rules appear to give complete explanations of the mechanism underlying deduction. On the one hand, the content of premises can exert a profound effect on the conclusions that people draw, and so a uniform procedure for extracting logical form and applying formal rules to it may not account for all aspects of performance. On the other hand, ordinary individuals are able to make valid deductions that depend solely on connectives and quantifiers, and so rules with a specific content would have to rely on some (yet to be formulated) account of purely logical competence. One way out of this dilemma is provided by a third sort of algorithmic theory, which depends on semantic procedures.

Consider this inference:

The black ball is directly behind the cue ball. The green ball is on the right of the cue ball, and there is a red ball between them. Therefore, if I move so that the red ball is between me and the black ball, the cue ball is to the left of my line of sight.

It is possible to frame rules that capture this inference (from Johnson-Laird, 1975), but it seems likely that people will make it by imagining the layout of the balls. This idea lies at the heart of the theory of mental models. According to this theory, the process of deduction depends on three stages of thought, which are summarized in Figure 2.1. In the first stage, comprehension, reasoners use their knowledge of the language and their general knowledge to understand the premises: they construct an internal model of the state of affairs that

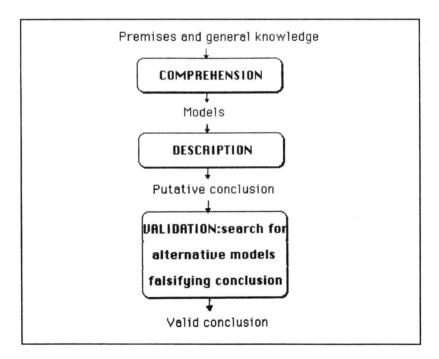

Figure 2.1
The three stages of deduction according to the model theory.

the premises describe. A deduction may also depend on perception, and thus on a perceptually-based model of the world (see Marr, 1982). In the second stage, reasoners try to formulate a parsimonious description of the models they have constructed. This description should assert something that is not explicitly stated in the premises. Where there is no such conclusion, then they respond that nothing follows from the premises. In the third stage, reasoners search for alternative models of the premises in which their putative conclusion is false. If there is no such model, then the conclusion is valid. If there is such a model, then prudent reasoners will return to the second stage to try to discover whether there is any conclusion true in all the models that they have so far constructed. If so, then it is necessary to search for counterexamples to it, and so on, until the set of possible models has been exhausted. Because the number of possible mental models is finite for deductions that depend on quantifiers and connectives, the search can in principle be exhaustive. If it is uncertain whether there is an alternative model of the premises, then the conclusion can be drawn in a tentative or probabilistic way. Only in the third stage is any essential deductive work carried out: the first two stages are merely normal processes of comprehension and description.

The theory is compatible with the way in which logicians formulate a semantics for a calculus. But, logical accounts depend on assigning an infinite number of models to each proposition, and an infinite set is far too big to fit inside anyone's head (Partee, 1979). The psychological theory therefore assumes that people construct a minimum of models: they try to work with just a single representative sample from the set of possible models, until they are forced to consider alternatives.

Models form the basis of various theories of reasoning. An early program for proving geometric theorems used diagrams of figures in order to rule out subgoals that were false (Gelernter, 1963). Although this idea could be used in other domains (see Bundy, 1983), there have been few such applications in artificial intelligence. Charniak and McDermott (1985, p. 363) speculate that the reason might be because few domains have counterexamples in the form of diagrams. Yet, as we will see, analogous structures are available for all sorts of deduction.

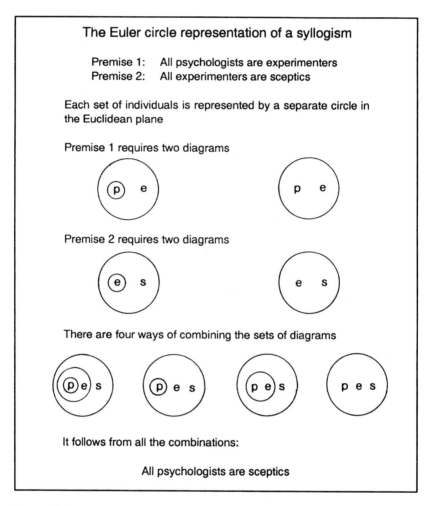

Figure 2.2
The Euler circle representation of a syllogism.

Deductions from singly-quantified premises, such as "All psy-chologists are experimenters," can be modelled using Euler circles (see Figure 2.2). Psychological theories have postulated such repre-sentations (Erickson, 1974) or equivalent strings of symbols (Guyote and Sternberg, 1981). These deductions can also be modelled using Venn diagrams (see Figure 2.3) or equivalent strings of symbols, and they too have been proposed as mental representations (Newell, 1981). A uniform and more powerful principle, however, is that *mental*

The Venn diagram representation of a syllogism

Premise 1:   All psychologists are experimenters
Premise 2:   All experimenters are sceptics

Each of the three sets is initially represented by one of three overlapping circles within a rectangle that represents the universe of discourse.

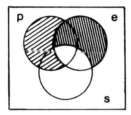

Premise 1 rules out the possibility of psychologists who are not experimenters, and so the corresponding portion of the circle representing psychologists is shaded out.
Premise 2 likewise rules out the possibility of experimenters who are not sceptics, and so the corresponding portion of the circle representing experimenters is shaded out. The resulting diagram establishes the conclusion:

All psychologists are sceptics.

Figure 2.3
The Venn diagram representation of a syllogism.

models have the same structure as human conceptions of the situations they represent (Johnson-Laird, 1983). Hence, a finite set of individuals is represented, not by a circle inscribed in Euclidean space, but by a finite set of mental tokens. A similar notion of a "vivid" representation has been proposed by Levesque (1986) from the standpoint of developing efficient computer programs for reasoning. But, there are distinctions between the two sorts of representation, e.g. vivid representations cannot represent directly either negatives or disjunctions (see also Etherington et al., 1989). The tokens of mental models may occur in a visual image, or they may not be directly accessible to consciousness. What matters is, not the phenomenal experience, but the structure of the models. This structure, which we will examine in detail in the following chapters, often transcends the perceptible. It can represent negation and disjunction.

The general theory of mental models has been successful in accounting for patterns of performance in various sorts of reasoning (Johnson-Laird, 1983). Errors occur, according to the theory, because people fail to consider all possible models of the premises. They therefore fail to find counterexamples to the conclusions that they derive from their initial models, perhaps because of the limited processing capacity of working memory (Baddeley, 1986).

The model theory has attracted considerable criticism from adherents of formal rules. It has been accused of being unclear, unworkable, and unnecessary. We will defer our main reply to critics until the final chapter, but we will make a preliminary response here to the three main charges that the theory is empirically inadequate:

1. Mental models do not explain propositional reasoning: "No clear mental model theory of propositional reasoning has yet been proposed" (Braine, Reiser, and Rumain, 1984; see also Evans, 1984, 1987; and Rips, 1986).
2. Mental models cannot account for performance in Wason's selection task. The theory implies that people search for counterexamples, yet they conspicuously fail to do so in the selection task (Evans, 1987). The criticism is based on a false assumption. The theory does not postulate that the search for counterexamples is invariably complete—far from it, as such an impeccable performance would be incompatible with observed errors. The theory explains performance in the selection task.
3. Contrary to the previous criticism, Rips (1986) asserts: "Deduction-as-simulation explains content effects, but unfortunately it does so at the cost of being unable to explain the generality of inference." He argues that a modus ponens deduction is not affected by the complexity of its content, and is readily carried out in domains for which the reasoner has had no previous exposure and thus no model to employ. However, the notion that reasoners cannot construct models for unfamiliar domains is false: all they need is a knowledge of the meaning of the connectives and other logical terms that occur in the premises. Conversely, modus ponens can be affected by its content.

Conclusion

We have completed our survey of where things stood at the start of our research. There were—and remain—three algorithmic theories of deduction. Despite many empirical findings, it had proved impossible to make a definitive choice among the theories.

References

Anderson, J. R. (1983). *The architecture of cognition*. Hillsdale, NJ: Lawrence Erlbaum Associates.

Baddeley, A. D. (1986). *Working memory*. Oxford: Clarendon Press.

Bar-Hillel, Y., and Carnap, R. (1964). An outline of a theory of semantic information. In Y. Bar-Hillel (Ed.) *Language and Information*. Reading, MA: Addison-Wesley.

Barwise, J. (1989). *The situation in logic*. Stanford: Center for the Study of Language and Information.

Barwise, J., and Etchemendy, J. (1989a). *A situation-theoretic account of reasoning with Hyperproof*. Unpublished paper. Center for the Study of Language and Information, Stanford University.

Barwise. J., and Etchemendy, J. (1989b). Model-theoretic semantics. In M. Posner (Ed.), *Foundations of cognitive science*. Cambridge, MA: Bradford Books, MIT Press.

Bledsoe, W. W. (1977). Non-resolution theorem proving. *Artificial Intelligence, 9*, 1–35.

Boole, G. (1847/1948). *The mathematical analysis of logic, being an essay towards a calculus of deductive reasoning*. Oxford: Basil Blackwell.

Boole, G. (1854). *An investigation of the laws of thought on which are founded the mathematical theories of logic and probabilities*. London: Macmillan.

Braine, M. D. S. (1978). On the relation between the natural logic of reasoning and standard logic. *Psychological Review, 85*, 1–21.

Braine, M. D. S., Reiser, B. J., and Rumain, B. (1984). Some empirical justification for a theory of natural propositional logic. *The psychology of learning and motivation* (Vol. 18). New York: Academic Press.

Braine, M. D. S., and Rumain, B. (1983). Logical reasoning. In J. H. Flavell and E. M. Markman (Eds.), *Carmichael's handbook of child psychology. Vol. III: Cognitive development* (4th Edition). New York: Wiley.

Brown, A. (1987). Metacognition, executive control, self-regulation, and other more mysterious mechanisms. In F. E. Weinert and R. Kluwe (Eds.), *Metacognition, motivation, and understanding*. Hillsdale, NJ: Lawrence Erlbaum Associates.

Bundy, A. (1983). *The computer modelling of mathematical reasoning*. London: Academic Press.

Charniak, E., and McDermott, D. (1985). *Introduction to artificial intelligence*. Reading, MA: Addison-Wesley.

Cheng, P. W., and Holyoak, K. J. (1985). Pragmatic reasoning schemas. *Cognitive Psychology, 17*, 391–416.

Chomsky, N. (1965). *Aspects of the theory of syntax*. Cambridge, MA: MIT Press.

Chomsky, N. (1981). *Lectures on government and binding.* Dordrecht: Foris.

Clocksin, W. and Mellish, C. (1981). *Programming in Prolog.* New York: Springer-Verlag.

Cohen, L. J. (1981). Can human irrationality be experimentally demonstrated? *Behavioral and Brain Sciences, 4,* 317–370.

Cooper, R. (1983). *Quantification and syntactic theory.* Dordrecht: Reidel.

Dewdney, A. K. (1989). People puzzles: Theme and variations. *Scientific American, 260,* 1 (January), 88–91.

Duda, R., Gaschnig, J., and Hart, P. (1979). Model design in the Prospector consultant system for mineral exploration. In D. Michi (Ed.), *Expert systems in the micro-electronic age.* Edinburgh: Edinburgh University Press.

Ennis, R. H. (1975). Children's ability to handle Piaget's propositional logic. *Review of Educational Research, 45,* 1–41.

Erickson, J. R. (1974). A set analysis theory of behavior in formal syllogistic reasoning tasks. In R. Solso (Ed.), *Loyola symposium on cognition* (Vol. 2). Hillsdale, NJ: Lawrence Erlbaum Associates.

Etherington, D. W., Borgida, A., Brachman, R. J., and Kautz, H. (1989). Vivid knowledge and tractable reasoning: Preliminary report. Mimeo, Murray Hill, NJ: AT&T Bell Laboratories.

Evans, J. St. B. T. (1977). Toward a statistical theory of reasoning. *Quarterly Journal of Experimental Psychology, 29A,* 297–306.

Evans, J. St. B. T. (1982). *The psychology of deductive reasoning.* London: Routledge & Kegan Paul.

Evans, J. St. B. T. (1984). Heuristic and analytic processes in reasoning. *British Journal of Psychology, 75,* 451–468.

Evans, J. St. B. T. (1987). Reasoning. In H. Beloff and A. M. Colman (Eds.), *Psychological Survey, 6,* 74–93.

Feigenbaum, E. A., Buchanan, B. G., and Lederberg, J. (1979). On generality and problem solving: a case study using the DENDRAL program. In D. Michi (Ed.), *Expert systems in the micro-electronic age.* Edinburgh: Edinburgh University Press.

Feigenbaum, E. A., and McCorduck, P. (1984). *The fifth generation: Artificial intelligence and Japan's computer challenge to the world.* London: Pan Books.

Flavell, J. H. (1979). Metacognition and cognitive monitoring: A new area of cognitive-developmental inquiry. *American Psychologist, 34,* 906–911.

Frege, G. (1884/1959). *The foundations of arithmetic.* Oxford: Basil Blackwell.

Gelernter, H. (1963). Realization of a geometry theorem-proving machine. In E. A. Feigenbaum and J. Feldman (Eds.), *Computers and thought.* New York: McGraw-Hill.

Grice, H. P. (1975). Logic and conversation. In P. Cole and J. L. Morgan (Eds.), *Syntax and semantics. Vol. 3: Speech acts.* New York: Seminar Press.

Guyote, M. J., and Sternberg, R. J. (1981). A transitive-chain theory of syllogistic reasoning. *Cognitive Psychology, 13,* 461–525.

Harman, G. (1972). Deep structure as logical form. In D. Davidson and G. Harman (Eds.), *Semantics of natural language.* Dordrecht: Reidel.

Hayes, P. (1977). In defense of logic. *Proceedings of the Fifth International Joint Conference on Artificial Intelligence,* 559–565.

Henle, M. (1962). The relation between logic and thinking. *Psychological Review, 69,* 366–378.

Henle, M. (1978). Foreward to Revlin, R. and Mayer, R. E. (Eds.), *Human reasoning.* Washington, D.C.. Winston.

Hewitt, C. (1971). PLANNER: A language for proving theorems in robots. *Proceedings of the Second Joint Conference on Artificial Intelligence.*

Hornstein, N. (1984). *Logic as grammar: An approach to meaning in language.* Cambridge, MA: Bradford Books, MIT Press.

Inhelder, B., and Piaget, J. (1958). *The growth of logical thinking from childhood to adolescence.* London: Routledge & Kegan Paul.

Jackendoff, R. (1972). *Semantic interpretation in generative grammar.* Cambridge, MA: MIT Press.

Johnson-Laird, P. N. (1970). The interpretation of quantified sentences. In G. B. Flores d'Arcais and W. J. M. Levelt (Eds.), *Advance in psycholinguistics.* Amsterdam: North-Holland.

Johnson-Laird, P. N. (1975). Models of deduction. In R. J. Falmagne (Ed.), *Reasoning: Representation and process in children and adults.* Hillsdale, NJ: Lawrence Erlbaum Associates.

Johnson-Laird, P. N. (1983). *Mental models: Towards a cognitive science of language, inference and consciousness.* Cambridge: Cambridge University Press.

Johnson-Laird, P. N. (1988). *The computer and the mind: An introduction to cognitive science.* London: Fontana.

Johnson-Laird, P. N. and Bara, B. (1984). Syllogistic inference. *Cognition, 16,* 1–61.

Kamp, J. A. W. (1981). A theory of truth and semantic representation. In J. Groenendijk, T. Janssen, and M. Stokhof (Eds.), *Formal methods in the study of language.* Amsterdam: Mathematical Centre Tracts.

Kant, I. (1800/1974). *Logic.* Trans. R. S. Hartman and W. Schwartz. New York: Bobbs-Merrill.

Keenan, E. L. (1971). Quantifier structures in English. *Foundations of Language, 7,* 255–284.

Kempson, R. M. (1988). Logical form: The grammar cognition interface. *Journal of Linguistics, 24*, 393–431.

Kowalski, R. A. (1979). *A logic for problem solving*. Amsterdam: Elsevier.

Lakoff, G. (1970). Linguistics and natural logic. *Synthese, 22*, 151–271.

Leech, G. N. (1969). *Towards a semantic description of English*. London: Longmans.

Leibniz, G. (1765/1949). *New essays concerning human understanding*. Trans. A. G. Langley. LaSalle, IL: Open Court.

Levesque, H. J. (1986). Making believers out of computers. *Artificial Intelligence, 30*, 81–108.

Lindsay, R., Buchanan, B. G., Feigenbaum, E. A., and Lederberg, J. (1980). *Applications of artificial intelligence for chemical inference: The DENDRAL project*. New York: McGraw-Hill.

Macnamara, J. (1986). *A border dispute: The place of logic in psychology*. Cambridge, MA: Bradford Books, MIT Press.

Marr, D. (1982). *Vision: A computational investigation into the human representation and processing of visual information*. San Francisco: W. H. Freeman.

May, R. (1985). *Logical form: Its structure and derivation*. Cambridge, MA: MIT Press.

McDermott, D., and Doyle, J. (1980). Non-monotonic logic. I. *Artificial Intelligence, 13*, 41–72.

Michie, D. (Ed.) (1979). *Expert systems in the micro-electronic age*. Edinburgh: Edinburgh University Press.

Mill, J. S. (1843). *A system of logic*. London: Longman.

Moore, R. C. (1982). Automatic deduction: A. Overview. In P. R. Cohen and E. A. Feigenbaum (Eds.), *The handbook of artificial intelligence* (Vol. 3). Los Altos, CA: William Kaufmann.

Newell, A. (1981). Reasoning, problem solving and decision processes: The problem space as a fundamental category. In R. Nickerson (Ed.), *Attention and performance* (Vol. 8). Hillsdale, NJ: Lawrence Erlbaum Associates.

Newell, A. (1990). *Unified theories in cognition*. Cambridge, MA: Harvard University Press.

Newell, A. and Simon, H. A. (1972). *Human problem solving*. Englewood Cliffs, NJ: Prentice-Hall.

Newell, A., Shaw, J. C., and Simon, H. A. (1963). Empirical explorations with the Logic Theory Machine. In E. A. Feigenbaum and J. Feldman (Eds.), *Computers and thought*. New York: McGraw-Hill.

Osherson, D. (1975). Logic and models of logical thinking. In R. J. Falmagne (Ed.), *Reasoning: Representation and process in children and adults*. Hillsdale, NJ: Lawrence Erlbaum Associates.

Parsons, C. (1960). Inhelder and Piaget's "The growth of logical thinking" II: A logician's viewpoint. *British Journal of Psychology, 51*, 75–84.

Partee, B. H. (1979). Semantics—mathematics or psychology? In R. Bäuerle, U. Egli, and A. von Stechow (Eds.), *Semantics from different points of view*. Berlin: Springer-Verlag.

Piaget, J. (1953). *Logic and psychology*. Manchester: Manchester University Press.

Pollock, J. (1989). *How to build a person: A prolegomenon*. Cambridge, MA: MIT Press Bradford Books.

Polya, G. (1957). *How to solve it* (2d ed.). New York: Doubleday.

Reisbeck, C. K., and Schank, R. C. (1989). *Inside case-based reasoning*. Hillsdale, NJ: Lawrence Erlbaum Associates.

Reiter, R. (1973). A semantically guided deductive system for automatic theorem-proving. *Proceedings of the Third International Joint Conference on Artificial Intelligence*. Pp. 41–46.

Revlis, R. (1975). Two models of syllogistic reasoning: Feature selection and conversion. *Journal of Verbal Learning and Verbal Behavior, 14*, 180–195.

Rips, L. J. (1983). Cognitive processes in propositional reasoning. *Psychological Review, 90*, 38–71.

Rips, L. J. (1986). Mental muddles. In M. Brand and R. M. Harnish (Eds.), *Problems in the representation of knowledge and belief*. Tucson: University of Arizona Press.

Rips, L. J. (1989). The psychology of knights and knaves. *Cognition, 31*, 85–116.

Robinson. J. A. (1965). A machine-oriented logic based on the resolution principle. *Journal of the Association for Computing Machinery, 12*, 23–41.

Rumelhart, D. E. (1989). Towards a microstructural account of human reasoning. In S. Vosniadou and A. Ortony (Eds.), *Similarity and analogical reasoning*. Cambridge: Cambridge University Press.

Seuren, P. A. M. (1969). *Operators and nucleus: A contribution to the theory of grammar*. Cambridge: Cambridge University Press.

Shortliffe, E. (1976). *MYCIN: Computer-based medical consultations*. New York: Elsevier.

Simon, H. A. (1982). *Models of bounded rationality* (Vols. 1 and 2). Cambridge, MA: MIT Press.

Smullyan, R. M. (1978). *What is the name of this book? The riddle of Dracula and other logical puzzles*. Englewood Cliffs, NJ: Prentice-Hall.

Sperber, D., and Wilson, D. (1986). *Relevance: Communication and cognition*. Oxford: Basil Blackwell.

Spinoza, B. (1677/1949). *Ethics*. Trans. W. H. White and Ed. by J. Gutmann. New York: Hafner.

Stanfill, C., and Waltz, D. (1986). Toward memory-based reasoning. *Communication of the Association for Computing Machinery, 29,* 1213–1228.

Wason, P. C., and Johnson-Laird, P. N. (1972). *Psychology of reasoning: Structure and content.* London: Batsford. Cambridge, MA: Harvard University Press.

Waterman, D. A., and Hayes-Roth, F. (Eds.) (1978). *Pattern directed inference systems.* New York: Academic Press.

Winston, P. H. (1984). *Artificial intelligence* (2d ed.). Reading, Massachusetts: Addison-Wesley.

3

Production Systems and the ACT-R Theory

John R. Anderson

3.1 Introduction

The work of most cognitive psychologists is driven by the same basic question: What is happening in the human head to produce human cognition? A great frustration of our field is that as we begin to search for an answer to what seems to be a straightforward question, we discover (a) that we may not be able to find an answer to the question, (b) that we are not sure what would constitute an answer, and, indeed, (c) that we are not even sure of what the question means. The goal of this book is to describe part of the answer to that question. Given the general uncertainty of our field, however, we must first define an interpretation of that question and specify what would constitute an answer to it. These are the primary goals of this chapter.

To avoid suspense, however, I offer here the partial answer that this chapter offers: Cognitive skills are realized by production rules. This is one of the most astounding and important discoveries in psychology and may provide a base around which to come to a general understanding of human cognition. I suspect, however, that most readers must be wondering what this statement really amounts to. What does it mean to say, "Cognitive skills are realized by production rules"? To help define this statement and place it in perspective this first chapter contains a brief discussion of foundational issues. Section 3.2 specifies what the theoretical status of the production system hypothesis is. Then, Section 3.3 identifies the basic features of the production rule theories of thought. Finally, Section 3.4 discusses the identifiability problems that haunt such proposals and how they are dealt with in the current approach. Each of these sections has as its goal placing the current work in proper relation to the relevant issues in cognitive science. The sections can be brief because they refer to fuller expositions of the issues elsewhere.

3.2 Frameworks, Theories, and Models

3.2.1 Levels of Specification

Cognitive psychology (and, indeed, psychology more generally) has had an almost fatal attraction to bold, general claims about human cognition (and human nature more generally). Here are a few examples:

1. There are two memory stores: a short-term store and a long-term store.
2. Knowledge is represented in terms of visual images and words.
3. People solve problems by means–ends analysis.
4. Syntactic knowledge and general world knowledge are encapsulated in different modules.
5. Human information processing is achieved by connectionist networks of neural-like elements.
6. Cognitive skills are realized by production rules.

Each of these assertions fails the most fundamental requirement of a scientific theory: empirical falsifiability. There are ways of construing each assertion such that it could be consistent with any empirical result. For instance, almost any form of the retention function could be made compatible with the distinction between long- and short-term memory by suitable auxiliary assumptions. Yet, these assertions are transparently not without meaning and, indeed, can be elaborated into predictions that *are* empirically falsifiable. To understand what is going on here requires reviewing the distinctions among frameworks, theories, and models (Anderson, 1983).[1]

Frameworks are composed of the bold, general claims about cognition. They are sets of constructs that define the important aspects of cognition. The distinction between long- and short-term memory, for example, would be a framework. Frameworks, however, are insufficiently specified to enable predictions to be derived from them, but they can be elaborated, by the addition of assumptions, to make them into *theories*, and it is these theories that can generate predictions. A single framework can be elaborated into many different theories. Certainly, many theories have been built around the distinction between long- and short-term memory; Atkinson and Shiffrin's

(1968) theory is, perhaps, the most famous. The details that one must specify in going from a framework to a theory may seem unimportant relative to the ideas that define the framework, but they are absolutely essential to creating a true theory. For instance, it may not seem very important to the concept of short-term memory to assume it is a buffer with a fixed number of slots, but this was essential to the predictive structure of the Atkinson and Shiffrin theory.

Even a precise theory like Atkinson and Shiffrin's, however, is not enough to make precise predictions about a specific situation, such as a particular free recall experiment. One must make additional auxiliary assumptions to define how the theory applies to that situation. For example, within Atkinson and Shiffrin's theory, different rehearsal strategies could be assumed. The theory, with assumptions about its application to a specific situation, defines a *model* for that situation. There are many models possible within a theory, each corresponding to one way a subject could approach the situation. It is a specific model that one actually tests, although sometimes one could argue that no model derivable from the theory would be consistent with the results. It has, for example, been argued that no version of the Atkinson-Shiffrin theory could produce effects associated with depth of processing (Craik and Lockhart, 1972).

Production rules constitute a particular framework for understanding human cognition, and by now many theories have been proposed as instantiations of that framework. In 1983, I proposed a particular theory called ACT*; here I propose a variant called ACT-R.[2] The details that define a specific production-rule theory, though perhaps insignificant compared to the features that are common to defining production rules in general, are essential if a claim that "cognitive skills are realized by production rules" is to be empirically falsifiable.

3.2.2 Cognitive Architectures

Production systems are particularly grand theories of human cognition because they are cognitive architectures. *Cognitive architectures* are relatively complete proposals about the structure of human cognition. In this regard, they contrast with theories, which address only an aspect of cognition, such as those involving the distinction between long- and short-term memory. Production systems are not unique as cognitive architectures. Popular, more recent alternatives are the various connectionist theories. To go back to an earlier era, Hullian theory (Hull, 1952) would constitute a cognitive architecture, although the adjective *cognitive* might seem a little misplaced.

The term *cognitive architecture* was brought into psychology by Newell, from his work on computer architectures (Bell and Newell, 1971). Just as an architect tries to provide a complete specification of a house (for a builder), so a computer or cognitive architecture tries to provide a complete specification of a system. There is a certain abstractness in the architect's specification, however, which leaves the concrete realization to the builder. So, too, there is an abstraction in a cognitive or computer architecture: One does not specify the exact neurons in a cognitive architecture, and one does not specify the exact computing elements in a computer architecture. This abstractness even holds for connectionist models that claim to be "neurally inspired." Their elements are in no way to be confused with real neurons.

The major assertion of this chapter—"Cognitive skills are realized by production rules"—is a general assertion about the architecture of human cognition. It is limited in its scope only insofar as cognitive skill does not encompass all of cognition. This book illustrates some of the scope of "cognitive skill." Along the way to making precise this general assertion, I define many more detailed assertions and present evidence for them.

A missing ingredient in the discussion so far is a specification of what constitutes a production system. The next section describes the concepts that define the production-system framework. The subsequent section addresses a fundamental indeterminacy that haunts such theoretical proposals. Although this indeterminacy is a problem for all cognitive architectures, this chapter focuses on its manifestation with respect to production systems.

3.3   Production-System Architecture

The basic claim of the ACT-R theory is that a cognitive skill is composed of production rules. The best way to understand what this might mean is to consider a production-system model for a common skill, such as multi-column addition.

3.3.1 An Example Production System for Addition

Production rules are if-then or *condition-action* pairs. The *if*, or *condition*, part specifies the circumstance under which the rule will apply. The *then*, or *action*, part of the rule specifies what to do in that circumstance. Table 3.1 lists a set of five production rules that are sufficient to perform a certain amount of multi-column addition. These production rules are informally stated. The next chapter deals with the issue of how to formally specify these rules and with the sticky issue of what we claim is in the human head when we propose such a set of production rules. For now it is sufficient just to get a sense of how these production rules work. These production rules operate on addition problems such as:

264
{+ 716

The production rules are organized around a set of goals. One goal is always active at any point in time. The first production rule, NEXT-COLUMN, focuses attention on the rightmost unprocessed column and will start by choosing the ones column.

The next production to apply is PROCESS-COLUMN. It responds to the goal of adding the column digits, but there are other elements in its condition. The second clause, "d1 and d2 are in that column," retrieves the digits. Its third clause, "d3 is the sum of d1 and d2," matches the sum of those digits. In its action, it sets the subgoal of writing out d3. The clauses in the condition of a production respond to elements that are said to be in working memory. *Working memory* refers to the knowledge that the system is currently attending to.

The production PROCESS-COLUMN illustrates the three major types of working memory elements. The first clause, "the goal is to solve an addition problem," matches a goal element in working memory. The second clause, "d1 and d2 are the digits in that column," matches part of the external problem representation. The third clause, "d3 is the sum of d1 and d2," matches a general fact from long-term memory. Often, goal information is distinguished from other working-memory information and *working memory* is used only to refer to non-goal information.

In this problem, the sum of the ones digits is 10 and so is greater than 9. The production that will fire in this situation is WRITE-

Table 3.1
Production Rules for Addition*

NEXT-COLUMN
IF	the goal is to solve an addition problem
	and c1 is the rightmost column without an answer digit
THEN	set a subgoal to write out an answer in c1

PROCESS-COLUMN
IF	the goal is to write out an answer in c1
	and d1 and d2 are the digits in that column
	and d3 is the sum of d1 and d2
THEN	set a subgoal to write out d3 in c1

WRITE-ANSWER-CARRY
IF	the goal is to write out d1 in c1
	and there is an unprocessed carry in c1
	and d2 is the number after d1
THEN	change the goal to write out d2
	and mark the carry as processed

WRITE-ANSWER-LESS-THAN-TEN
IF	the goal is to write out d1 in c1
	and there is no unprocessed carry in c1
	and d1 is less than 10
THEN	write out d1
	and the goal is satisfied

WRITE-ANSWER-GREATER-THAN-NINE
IF	the goal is to write out d1 in c1
	and there is no unprocessed carry in c1
	and d1 is 10 or greater
	and d2 is the ones digit of d1
THEN	write out d2
	and note a carry in the next column
	and the goal is satisfied

---

* c1, d1, d2, and d3 denote variables that can take on different values for different instantiations of each production.

Table 3.2
Trace of Production Rules for Addition

>>> Cycle 1: NEXT-COLUMN
Focusing on the next column.
>>> Cycle 2: PROCESS-COLUMN
Adding FOUR and SIX to get TEN.
>>> Cycle 3: WRITE-ANSWER-GREATER-THAN-NINE
Setting a carry in the next column.
Writing out ZERO and going to the next column.
>>> Cycle 4: NEXT-COLUMN
Focusing on the next column.
>>> Cycle 5: PROCESS-COLUMN
Adding SIX and ONE to get SEVEN.
>>> Cycle 6: WRITE-ANSWER-CARRY
Adding 1 for the carry to SEVEN to get EIGHT.
>>> Cycle 7: WRITE-ANSWER-LESS-THAN-TEN
Writing out EIGHT and going to the next column.
>>> Cycle 8: NEXT-COLUMN
Focusing on the next column.
>>> Cycle 9: PROCESS-COLUMN
Adding TWO and SEVEN to get NINE.
>>> Cycle 10: WRITE-ANSWER-LESS-THAN-TEN
Writing out NINE and going to the next column.

ANSWER-GREATER-THAN-NINE. It sets a carry in the next column and writes out d2, which is the difference between d1 and 10. In setting a carry in the next column, the production rule is placing in working memory some information that will be used by the next production rule. Just as all the clauses on the condition side are conceived of as testing working memory, so too, all the clauses on the action side can be considered to be adding to working memory. Table 3.2 provides a trace of the production system solving the problem. The listing shows the production rules in the order that they fire and a little protocol generated by each production rule.[3]

As I demonstrate in this book, we can understand and tutor skills like multicolumn addition by assuming that production rules like these are the embodiment of the skill. One sees compelling evidence for production models like the one in Table 3.1 by observing a child acquiring the skill of addition using just these sorts of rules. I discuss tutoring research that displays this power of production-rule models throughout the book.

3.3.2 Critical Features of a Production System

You should now have a sense of how production rules function. It is worth emphasizing their critical features:

• Each production rule is thought of as a *modular* piece of knowledge in that it represents a well-defined step of cognition.
• Complex cognitive processes are achieved by stringing together a sequence of such rules by appropriate setting of *goals* and other writing to *working memory*, and by reading from working memory.
• Essential to production rules are their *condition-action asymmetry*, which as seen in later chapters, is reflected in many asymmetries of human behavior.
• A final important feature of production rules is that they are *abstract* and can apply in multiple situations. Thus, the rules are not specific to adding the digits 4 and 6, for instance, but can apply to any pair of digits. This generality is achieved by use of variables in actual production-system formalism. In Table 3.1 this variable use is conveyed through terms like d1, but as shown in the next chapter, the informal specification in Table 3.1 underrepresents the variable use needed to get the correct generality for the rules.

There are a number of terms used to describe production system operation: *Pattern matching* refers to the process of determining if a production's conditions match the contents of working memory. Because multiple productions may match working memory, there arises the issue of deciding which of these will be performed. *Conflict resolution* is the term used to describe the process of determining which production rules to perform. When a production rule is performed it is said to *execute* or *fire*. The sequence of matching production rules, performing conflict resolution, and then firing a production is referred to as a *cycle*.

Corresponding to a production system is usually a computer program that actually simulates the behavior described by the production system. Writing a production-system model for a particular task usually takes the form of writing a set of production rules to perform the task. Indeed, production systems are often used as programming formalisms by people working in artificial intelligence who have no particular interest in cognitive modeling. Their status as programming languages has meant that production-system theories are precise and complete theories of particular tasks. This is a considerable virtue.

One problem with production-system theories has been that it is difficult to come to a deep understanding of a model without access to the actual running simulation, and access to other people's simulations has been hampered by a lack of access to appropriate machines and languages. This barrier has been substantially eliminated by advances in modern technology.

3.3.3   Alternative Production Systems

Over the years, multiple production systems that instantiate the general framework have been proposed. An informative overview of these production systems can be found in Klahr, Langley, and Neches (1987). Production systems can be traced back at least to Post's (1943) proposal for rewrite systems. They also constituted an important formalism in Newell and Simon's work, which culminated with the publication of their 1972 book, *Human Problem Solving*. Their early work involved production systems as a theoretical language, without a corresponding running program. The first production system that was implemented as a computer program was one called PSG, used by Newell as the basis for his original papers on production–system models of mind (1972, 1973). Figure 3.1 (taken from Klahr, Langley, and Neches, 1987) shows the lineage of production systems derived from this first implemented system. PSG was the inspiration for the ACTE production system, which was the basis for the cognitive theory proposed in Anderson (1976). Over the next 7 years, this evolved and matured into the ACT* production system reported in Anderson (1983). The ACT* production system was never completely implemented as a running computer system. GRAPES (Sauers and Farrell, 1982), shown in the figure, and PUPS (Anderson and Thompson, 1989), not shown, were partial implementations of the theory relevant to the acquisition of cognitive skills. One of the advantages of this book is the computer simulation that more completely corresponds to the theoretical statements in the book.

Other lines of production systems have evolved from PSG. Particularly significant among these are the OPS production systems, which evolved out of a concern for how to do pattern matching and conflict resolution more efficiently. OPS5 (Forgy, 1981) and OPS83 (Forgy, 1984) have served as the basis for development of some expert systems in artificial intelligence. The most well known of these expert systems is R1 (McDermott, 1982), which configures computer

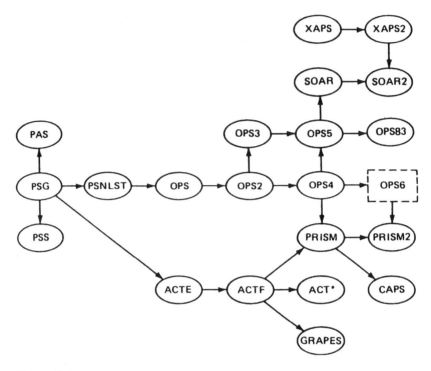

Figure 3.1
Development of production system architectures.

systems. Laird, Newell, and Rosenbloom (1987) produced a dramatic new system based in OPS called Soar, and Newell (1991) advanced Soar as a unified theory of cognition. A number of comparisons to Soar appear throughout this book.

Anderson (1983) referred to the PSG and OPS systems as *neo-classical production systems* to contrast them with the ACT production systems. Soar certainly differs from these earlier systems in many ways and is much closer to ACT* and ACT-R, but it does preserve one important feature of the earlier systems that contrasts it with the ACT theories. This is that it represents permanent knowledge only in production rules, whereas the ACT theories propose a separate declarative representation.

3.3.4 Evidence for Production Rules
It is worth describing at the outset the general kind of evidence that indicates production rules are psychologically real, although more

detailed evidence appears in later chapters. One line of evidence is simply the intuitive reasonableness of a rule set like that in Table 3.1 for describing the cognitive processes involved in a task like addition. The descriptive adequacy of a rule-based account has become apparent to most researchers in cognitive science—even those connectionists who oppose the symbol-manipulation paradigm. Thus, J. A. Anderson and Hinton (1981) acknowledged that "well-learned and regular interactions between patterns of activity can be captured as explicit rules governing manipulation of abstract symbols" (p. 31), and Smolensky (1986) recognized that "novices are described by productions with simple conditions and actions, and experts are described by complex conditions and actions" (p. 252).

Although the descriptive adequacy of such production rules has found ready acceptance, the critical question has been whether such rules are psychologically real. J. A. Anderson and Hinton went on to deny the plausibility of "models in which rules are added, deleted, or reordered" (p. 31), and Smolensky asserted that "productions are just descriptive entities" (p. 252). The critical question is what claim these rules have to psychological reality. A frequent view is that they are just descriptive approximations that obscure a deeper, underlying level where the significant psychological regularities lie. A major agenda of this book, therefore, is to show that the significant regularities in human behavior emerge at the level of production rules. It is only when a complex behavior is broken into subunits that correspond to production rules and these subunits are analyzed that we can see the detailed regularities of behavior, including the ones that connectionists are fond of. Thus, a production–rule analysis is actually critical to applying the connectionist program to complex behavior.

To establish the psychological reality of production rules, we have to commit to some theory of how production rules are executed. With ACT-R in place, I demonstrate the regularity in human performance and learning under a production–rule analysis.

In summary, the argument for the psychological reality of production rules involves two layers of evidence: One is the manifest appropriateness of rules in describing many aspects of skilled behavior. The second is the ability to predict the details of that behavior under a production–rule description.

3.4   Identifiability

Having explained what kind of theory ACT-R is, I come to the thorny issue of how we can know it is the correct theory. The answer might seem simple: The theory is correct if it corresponds to the available data. However, there are serious problems in using behavioral data to identify the correct theory of mind. The next subsections will explain these identifiability problems and the approach to them taken in ACT-R.

First, though, it is important to point out a tacit assumption made in the subsequent subsections. This is that the production-system framework is the right way to think about cognitive skill. The question addressed in the subsequent subsections is not how we know that there are production rules in the head, but rather, how we know ACT-R is the right production-system theory. This might well seem like we are focusing on the wrong question, but one cannot really argue for a framework because it is too poorly specified. The evidence for a framework always comes down to the success of the best theory specified within it. Thus, we have to be concerned with the details of the theory and how we know they are right. If we can get the details right, the framework will be established.

3.4.1   The Problems at the Implementation Level

For many theories, it is possible to make a distinction between an algorithm level and an implementation level (Anderson, 1987a, 1990b). That distinction is particularly well defined in the case of production systems. The *algorithm level* refers to a description of cognition in terms of the general steps of cognition. In the case of production systems, it is a description in terms of the production rules that are firing. The *implementation level* refers to a lower level description of cognition in terms of the factors that determine whether a specific production rule will fire and the speed with which it fires. The distinction is like the distinction between a high-level programming language like LISP and its machine-level implementation. Indeed, one can treat a production system as a programming language and simply ignore implementation issues. If we want a production system to be able to make psychological claims, however, we must be concerned with both the algorithm level and the implementation level.

As stated earlier, the details really matter when we make the claims that cognitive skills have a production-system base. Different production-system theories can differ in their details, at both the algorithm level and the implementation level. Distinguishing between different theories in terms of which production rules are actually at work (the algorithm level) is relatively unproblematic (as long as we do not get into empty debates about representation). This is because the rules that are firing have such a close connection to the observed behavior. For instance, one could claim, at the algorithm level, that there was a carrying production that augmented the lower digit in an addition problem. This would be a different production system than the one in Table 3.1. It would be confirmed or disconfirmed by the observable behavior of a subject, that is, by whether the lower digit was actually augmented or not.

In contrast, there are profound difficulties in identifying what is going on at the implementation level. These difficulties arise because the theoretical claims about the implementation level are very detailed relative to the empirical data that can be used to judge the theories. These identifiability problems manifest themselves in two different ways:

1. Uniqueness. Very different proposals about what is taking place can result in the same claims about the probability and speed of production firings. These identifiability problems are rampant. For example, one might have one theory that claimed that all the production rules in Table 3.1 were matched in parallel and another theory that claimed they were matched serially. In general, however, serial and parallel information-processing systems can be shown to be equivalent in their predictions about behavioral measures, such as processing time (Anderson, 1976; Townsend, 1974; Vosberg, 1977). Thus, behavioral data cannot distinguish between parallel and serial production matching. This is just one of the many ways that we face the fact that black boxes with very different internal structures can display identical external behavior in all respects.
2. Discovery. There is a huge space of possible implementation proposals and little guidance in finding the correct one. It sometimes seems impossible to discover one that is consistent with the data. It is like trying to find a needle in a haystack. The basic problem is that there are limitless ways to imagine the internal structure of a black box. Certainly, we have seen numerous proposals for production systems, and each has proven unsatisfactory in some regard.

One can question whether these problems really exist, and if they do whether they are peculiar to production-rule modeling. I have argued at length elsewhere (Anderson, 1976, 1987a, 1990b) that these are problems for all cognitive theorizing—not just for production systems—and it seems unnecessary to repeat the arguments. The news offered here is a way to approach these problems.

One can imagine the space of all possible cognitive theories, although infinite, as distinguishable into three ordered sets. First, there is the set of all theories. A subset of that is the set of theories consistent with the behavioral data collected so far. This subset is a tiny fraction of all theories. A much smaller subset of this subset is the set of all theories consistent with all behavioral data that could be collected. The discovery problem is that this final subset is such a tiny part of the set of theories. The uniqueness problem is that there is more than one theory in this final subset.

It needs to be emphasized that these are two independent problems. Even if we could recognize the right theory when we found it (i.e., solve the uniqueness problem), we would still have the problem of finding it. Even if we could find a theory consistent with the data (i.e., solve the discovery problem), we would face the fact that there are many equivalent theories. Thus, there are two separate problems, and they require two separate solutions. Although I cannot claim to have solved either problem completely, ACT-R reflects an approach to each problem that offers the hope of eventual solutions.

3.4.2   The Neural Approach to the Uniqueness Problem

The solution to the uniqueness problem that I have adopted is to commit to a particular style of implementation. Because cognition must be implemented in the human brain, it seems transparent that the implementation of ACT-R should be in terms of neural-like computations. Thus, the constraint used to choose among behaviorally equivalent proposals is that the mechanisms proposed correspond to what is known about neural processing. For instance, with respect to the parallel-serial issue, we know that neural computation is highly parallel. This tells us that many processes, such as memory retrieval, have to be parallel, including the matching of production rules.

The style of neural implementation assumed in ACT* and continued in ACT-R is activation based. Declarative memory structures vary in their level of activation, and this determines their availability.

Also, the rate of production-rule matching is determined by the activation levels of the declarative structures the rules match. Rules compete by inhibitory processes. A major component of learning is increasing the strength of declarative structures and production rules. Thus, when we dig below the surface of an ACT theory we find a system of computation that looks much like a connectionist system. However, in ACT, these connectionist computations at the implementation level are being used to support a system that is symbolic at the algorithm level. The computer analogy is that the primitive machine operations support the symbolic processing of LISP.

We have only partially acted on our commitment to a neural-style implementation of production systems. The activation-based computations described in subsequent chapters are only a gloss of the computations true connectionist would want to see specified in further detail.

Note, too, that the commitment to a neural-style implementation of a production system is no guarantee of a solution to the uniqueness problem. There may well be equivalent implementations consistent with what is known about neural processing. In such cases, we have to wait for more knowledge about what neural processing is like.

3.4.3 The Rational Approach to the Discovery Problem

The problem I had with the ACT* theory and other theories (even if they were neurally based) was that they do not solve the discovery problem: finding an implementation consistent with present and future data. There are an enormous number of ways to implement production systems in a neural-like system. Why believe one is more correct than another? One can try to find a theory consistent with the available data, but what reason is there to believe it will be consistent with the next empirical phenomenon? This is exactly what happened with ACT* (Anderson, 1983). No sooner had the theory been published than results came forth that seemed inconsistent with it. Such an occurrence is hardly unique to ACT*. Of course, one can always revise the theory slightly, to make it consistent. This is what happened in Anderson (1987b), and the same thing has happened with other theories.

An infinite number of theories that are consistent with any finite body of data will make different predictions about data yet to be collected. We need some reason to believe that when we commit to one of these theories it will hold up when the new data come in. As argued elsewhere (Anderson, 1983, 1990a), certain factors, such as parsimony, which help us choose among theories in some sciences, do not work that well in cognitive science. Biology in general and cognition in particular do not select systems on the basis of their parsimony.

It was this discovery problem that led to the rational analysis that was described in Anderson (1990a). In line with the arguments of Marr (1982), rational analysis seeks to provide some guidance in proposing the implementation details. Rational analysis was an attempt to understand cognition, based on the thesis that cognition is adapted to the structure of the environment. Anderson (1990a) was an attempt to explore this thesis with respect to the cognitive functions of memory, categorization, causal inference, and problem solving. In each case, it was argued that cognition seemed to maximize achievement of information-processing goals within the constraint of minimizing computational costs. The effort in the 1990 book was an attempt to show optimization with minimal commitment to mechanism, but rational analysis can be used to constrain the mechanisms that implement the production-system architecture. This is what happened with respect to ACT and has resulted in the new theory, ACT-R (with the R for rational).[4] The mechanisms in ACT* were tuned and slightly changed in ACT-R to yield adaptive processing under the 1990 rational analysis.

Notes

1. Deviating slightly from standard APA form, Anderson (without initials) refers throughout to J. R. Anderson.

2. The reader will note this is a step in the direction of parsimony. ACT* was pronounced act star. The current theory is pronounced act ar, deleting the consonant cluster *st*.

3. The actual production rule model is available in a file called Addition in the Examples folder on the accompanying disk.

4. When I wrote the 1990 book, I was not sure what the relationship between rational analysis and mechanistic theory was, although I did speculate that rational analysis could be used to guide mechanistic theory.

References

Anderson, J. A., and Hinton, G. E. (1981). Models of information processing in the brain. In G. E. Hinton and J. A. Anderson (Eds.), *Parallel models of associative memory* (pp. 9–48). Hillsdale, NJ: Lawrence Erlbaum Associates.

Anderson, J. R. (1976). *Language, memory, and thought*. Hillsdale, NJ: Lawrence Erlbaum Associates.

Anderson, J. R. (1983). *The architecture of cognition*. Cambridge, MA: Harvard University Press.

Anderson, J. R. (1987a). Methodologies for the study of human knowledge. *The Behavioral and Brain Sciences, 10*, 467–505.

Anderson, J. R. (1987b). Skill acquisition: Compilation of weak method problem solutions. *Psychological Review, 94*, 192–210.

Anderson, J. R. (1990a). *The adaptive character of thought*. Hillsdale, NJ: Lawrence Erlbaum Associates.

Anderson, J. R. (1990b). *Cognitive psychology and its implications* (3d ed.). New York: W. H. Freeman.

Anderson, J. R., and Thompson, R. (1989). Use of analogy in a production system architecture. In S. Vosniadou and A. Ortony (Eds.), *Similarity and analogical reasoning* (pp. 267–297). Cambridge, England: Cambridge University Press.

Atkinson, R. C., and Shiffrin, R. M. (1968). Human memory: A proposed system and its control processes. In K. Spence and J. Spence (Eds.), *The psychology of learning and motivation* (Vol. 2, pp. 89–105). New York: Academic Press.

Bell, C. G., and Newell, A. (1971). *Computer structures: Readings and examples*. New York: McGraw-Hill.

Craik, F. I. M., and Lockhart, R. S. (1972). Levels of processing: A framework for memory research. *Journal of Verbal Learning and Verbal Behavior, 11*, 671–684.

Forgy, C. L. (1981). *OPS5 user's manual* (Tech. Rep.). Pittsburgh, PA.: Carnegie Mellon University, Department of Computer Science.

Forgy, C. L. (1984). *The OPS83 report* (Tech. Rep.). Pittsburgh, PA.: Carnegie Mellon University, Department of Computer Science.

Hull, C. L. (1952). *A behavior system*. New Haven, CT: Yale University Press.

Klahr, D., Langley, P., and Neches, R. (Eds.). (1987). Implicit learning in patients with probable Alzheimer's disease. *Neurology, 37*, 784–788.

Laird, J. E., Newell, A., and Rosenbloom, P. S. (1987). Soar: An architecture for general intelligence. *Artificial Intelligence, 33*, 1–64.

Marr, D. (1982). *Vision*. San Francisco: W. H. Freeman.

McDermott, J. (1982). R1: A rule-based configurer of computer systems. *Artificial Intelligence, 19*, 39–88.

Newell, A. (1972). A theoretical exploration of mechanisms for coding the stimulus. In A. W. Melton and E. Martin (Eds.), *Coding processes in human memory* (pp. 373–434). Washington, DC: Winston.

Newell, A. (1973). Production systems: Models of control structures. In W. G. Chase (Ed.), *Visual information processing*. New York: Academic Press.

Newell, A. (1991). *Unified theories of cognition*. Cambridge, MA: Cambridge University Press.

Newell, A., and Simon, H. A. (1972). *Human problem solving*. Englewood Cliffs, NJ: Prentice-Hall.

Post, E. L. (1943). Formal reductions of the general combinatorial decision problem. *American Journal of Mathematics, 65*, 197–268.

Sauers, R., and Farrell, R. (1982). *GRAPES user's manual* (Tech. Rep.). Carnegie Mellon University, Department of Psychology.

Smolensky, P. (1986). Information processing in dynamical systems: Foundations of harmony theory. In D. E. Rumelhart and J. L. McClelland (Eds.), *Parallel distributed processing: Explorations in the microstructure of cognition* (Vol. 1, pp. 194–281). Cambridge, MA: MIT Press/Bradford Books.

Townsend, J. T. (1974). Issues and models concerning the processing of a finite number of inputs. In B. H. Kantowitz (Ed.), *Human information processing: Tutorials in performance and cognition* (pp. 133–186). Hillsdale, NJ: Lawrence Erlbaum Associates.

Vosberg, D. (1977). *On the equivalence of parallel and serial models of information processing*. Paper presented at the 10th Mathematical Psychology Meetings, Los Angeles, CA.

4

Rules of Language

Steven Pinker

Language and cognition have been explained as the products of a homogeneous associative memory structure or alternatively, of a set of genetically determined computational modules in which rules manipulate symbolic representations. Intensive study of one phenomenon of English grammar and how it is processed and acquired suggests that both theories are partly right. Regular verbs (walk-walked) are computed by a suffixation rule in a neural system for grammatical processing; irregular verbs (run-ran) are retrieved from an associative memory.

Every normal human can convey and receive an unlimited number of discrete messages through a highly structured stream of sound or, in the case of signed languages, manual gestures. This remarkable piece of natural engineering depends upon a complex code or grammar implemented in the brain that is deployed without conscious effort and that develops, without explicit training, by the age of four. Explaining this talent is an important goal of the human sciences.

Theories of language and other cognitive processes generally fall into two classes. Associationism describes the brain as a homogeneous network of interconnected units modified by a learning mechanism that records correlations among frequently co-occurring input patterns (1). Rule-and-representation theories describe the brain as a computational device in which rules and principles operate on symbolic data structures (2, 3). Some rule theories further propose that the brain is divided into modular computational systems that have an organization that is largely specified genetically, one of the systems being language (3, 4).

During the last 35 years, there has been an unprecedented empirical study of human language structure, acquisition, use, and breakdown, allowing these centuries-old proposals to be refined and tested. I will illustrate how intensive multidisciplinary study of one linguistic phenomenon shows that both associationism and rule theories are partly correct, but about different components of the language system.

Modules of Language

A grammar defines a mapping between sounds and meanings, but the mapping is not done in a single step but through a chain of intermediate data structures, each governed by a subsystem. Morphology is the subsystem that computes the forms of words. I focus on a single process of morphology: English past tense inflection, in which the physical shape of the verb varies to encode the relative time of occurrence of the referent event and the speech act. Regular past tenses marking (for example, *walk-walked*) is a rulelike process resulting in addition of the suffix *-d*. In addition there are about 180 irregular verbs that mark the past tense in other ways (for example, *hit-hit, come-came, feel-felt*).

Past tense inflection is an isolable subsystem in which grammatical mechanisms can be studied in detail, without complex interactions with the rest of language. It is computed independently of syntax, the subsystem that defines the form of phrases and sentences: The syntax of English forces its speakers to mark tense in every sentence, but no aspect of syntax works differently with regular and irregular verbs. Past tense marking is also insensitive to lexical semantics (5, 6): the regular–irregular distinction does not correlate with any feature of verb meaning. For example, *hit-hit, strike-struck*, and *slap-slapped* have similar meanings, but three different past tense forms; *stand-stood, stand me up-stood me up*, and *understand-understood*, have unrelated meanings but identical past tense forms. Past marking is also independent of phonology, which determines the possible sound sequences in a language: the three pronunciations of the regular suffix (in *ripped, ribbed*, and *ridded*) represent not three independent processes but a single suffix *-d* modified to conform with general laws of English sound patterning (5).

Rulelike Processes in Language

English inflection can illustrate the major kinds of theories used to explain linguistic processes. Traditional grammar offers the following first approximation: regular inflection, being fully predictable, is computed by a rule that concatenates the affix -d to the verb stem. This allows a speaker to inflect an unlimited number of new verbs, an ability seen both in adults, who easily create past forms for neologisms like *faxed*, and in preschoolers, who, given a novel verb like *to rick* in experiments, freely produced *ricked* (7). In contrast, irregular verb forms are unpredictable: compare *sit-sat* and *hit-hit*, *sing-sang* and *string-strung*, *feel-felt* and *tell-told*. Therefore they must be individually memorized. Retrieval of an irregular form from memory ordinarily blocks application of the regular rule, although in children retrieval occasionally fails, yielding "overregularization" errors like *breaked* (*8, 9, 10*).

The rule-rote theory, although appealingly straightforward, is inadequate. Rote memory, if thought of as a list of slots, is designed for the very rare verbs with unrelated past tense forms, like *be-was* and *go-went*. But for all other irregular verbs, the phonological content of the stem is largely preserved in the past form, as in *swing-swung* (*5, 11*). Moreover, a given irregular pattern such as a vowel change is typically seen in a family of phonetically similar items, such as *sing-sang*, *ring-rang*, *spring-sprang*, *shrink-shrank*, and *swim-swam*, or *grow-grew*, *blow-blew*, *throw-threw*, and *fly-flew* (*5, 9, 11*). The rote theory cannot explain why verbs with irregular past forms come in similarity families, rather than belonging to arbitrary lists. Finally, irregular pairs are psychologically not a closed list, but their patterns can sometimes be extended to new forms on the basis of similarity to existing forms. All children occasionally use forms such as *bring-brang* and *bite-bote* (*5, 9*). A few irregular past forms have entered the language historically under the influence of existing forms. *Quit, cost, catch* are from French, and *fling, sling, stick* have joined irregular clusters in the last few hundred years (*12*); such effects are obvious when dialects are compared [for example, *help-holp, rise-riz, drag-drug, climb-clome* (*13*)]. Such analogizing can be demonstrated in the laboratory: faced with inflecting nonsense verbs like *spling*, many adults produce *splung* (*6, 7, 14, 15*).

The partial systematicity of irregular verbs has been handled in opposite ways by modern rule and associationist theories. One version of the theory of Generative Phonology (*11*) posits rules for irregular verbs (for example, change *i* to *a*) as well as for regular ones.

The theory is designed to explain the similarity between verb stems and their past tense forms: if the rule just changes a specified segment, the rest of the stem comes through in the output untouched, by default, just as in the fully regular case. But the rule theory does not address the similarity among different verbs in the input set and people's tendency to generalize irregular patterns. If an irregular rule is restricted to apply to a list of words, the similarity among the words in the list is unexplained. But if a common pattern shared by the words is identified and the rule is restricted to apply to all and only the verbs displaying that pattern (for example, change *i* to *a* when it appears after a consonant cluster and precedes *ng*), the rule fails because the similarity to be accounted for is one of family resemblance rather than necessary or sufficient conditions (*5, 9, 14, 18*): such a rule, while successfully applying to *spring*, *shrink*, *drink*, would incorrectly apply to *bring-brought* and *fling-flung* and would fail to apply to *begin-began* and *swim-swam*, where it should apply.

Associationist theories also propose that regular and irregular patterns are computed by a single mechanism, but here the mechanism is an associative memory. A formal implementation in neural net terms is the "connectionist" model of Rumelhart and McClelland (*16*), which consists of an array of input units, an array of output units, and a matrix of modifiable weighted links between every input and every output. None of the elements or links corresponds exactly to a word or rule. The stem is represented by turning on a subset of input nodes, each corresponding to a sound pattern in the stem. This sends a signal across each of the links to the output nodes, which represent the sounds of the past tense form. Each output node sums its incoming signals and turns on if the sum exceeds a threshold; the output form is the word most compatible with the set of active output nodes. During the learning phase, the past tense form computed by the network is juxtaposed with the correct version provided by a "teacher," and the strengths of the links and thresholds are adjusted so as to reduce the difference. By recording and superimposing associations between stem sounds and past sounds, the model improves its performance and can generalize to new forms to the extent that their sounds overlap with old ones. This process is qualitatively the same for regular and irregular verbs: *stopped* is produced because input *op* units were linked to output *opped* units by previous verbs; *clung* is produced because *ing* was linked to *ung*. As a result such models can imitate people's analogizing of irregular patterns to new forms.

The models, however, are inadequate in other ways (*5, 17*). The precise patterns of inflectional mappings in the world's languages are unaccounted for: the network can learn input–output mappings found in no human language, such as mirror-reversing the order of segments, and cannot learn mappings that are common, such as reduplicating the stem. The actual outputs are often unsystematic blends such as *mail-membled* and *tour-tourder*. Lacking a representation of words as lexical entries, distinct from their phonological or semantic content, the model cannot explain how languages can contain semantically unrelated homophones with different past tense forms such as *lie-lied* (prevaricate) and *lie-lay* (recline), *ring-rang* and *wring-wrung*, *meet-met* and *mete-meted*.

These problems call for a theory of language with both a computational component, containing specific kinds of rules and representations, and an associative memory system, with certain properties of connectionist models (*5, 6, 10*). In such a theory, regular past tense forms are computed by a rule that concatenates an affix with a variable standing for the stem. Irregulars are memorized pairs of words, but the linkages between the pair members are stored in an associative memory structure fostering some generalization by analogy (*9, 14, 18*): although *string* and *strung* are represented as separate, linked words, the mental representation of the pair overlaps in part with similar forms like *sling* and *bring*, so that the learning of *slung* is easier and extensions like *brung* can occur as the result of noise or decay in the parts of the representation that code the identity of the lexical entry.

Because it categorically distinguishes regular from irregular forms, the rule-association hybrid predicts that the two processes should be dissociable from virtually every point of view. With respect to the psychology of language use, irregular forms, as memorized items, should be strongly affected by properties of associative memory such as frequency and similarity, whereas regular forms should not. With respect to language structure, irregular forms, as memory-listed words, should be available as the input to other word-formation processes, whereas regular forms, being the final outputs of such processes, should not. With respect to implementation in the brain, because regular and irregular verbs are subserved by different mechanisms, it should be possible to find one system impaired while the other is spared. The predictions can be tested with methods ranging from reaction time experiments to the grammatical analysis of languages to the study of child development to the investigation of brain damage and genetic deficits.

Language Use and Associative Laws

Frequency. If irregular verbs are memorized items, they should be better remembered the more they are encountered. Indeed, children make errors like *breaked* more often for verbs their parents use in the past tense forms less frequently (*9, 10, 19*). To adults, low-frequency irregular past tense forms like *smote, bade, slew,* and *strode* sound odd or stilted and often coexist with regularized counterparts such as *slayed* and *strided* (*5, 18, 20*). As these psychological effects accumulate over generations, they shape the language. Old English had many more irregular verbs than Modern English, such as *abide-abode, chide-chid, gild-gilt*; the ones used with lower frequencies have become regular over the centuries (*18*). Most surviving irregular verbs are used at high frequencies, and the 13 most frequent verbs in English—*be, have, do, say, make, go, take, come, see, get, know, give, find*—are all irregular (*21*).

Although any theory positing a frequency-sensitive memory can account for frequency effects on irregular verbs [with inverse effects on their corresponding regularized versions (*20*)], the rule-associative-memory hybrid model predicts that regular inflection is different. If regular past tense forms can be computed on-line by concatenation of symbols for the stem and affix, they do not require prior storage of a past tense entry and thus need not be harder or stranger for low-frequency verbs than higher ones (*22*).

Judgments by native English speakers of the naturalness of word forms bear this prediction out. Unlike irregular verbs, novel or low-frequency regular verbs, although they may sound unfamiliar in themselves, do not accrue any increment of oddness or uncertainty when put in the past tense: *infarcted* is as natural a past tense form of *infarct* as *walked* is of *walk* (*5*). The contrast can be seen clearly in idioms and clichés, because they can contain a verb that is not unfamiliar itself but that appears in the idiom exclusively in the present or infinitive form. Irregular verbs in such idioms can sound strange when put in the past tense: compare *You'll excuse me if I forgo the pleasure of reading your paper before it's published* with *Last night I forwent the pleasure of reading student papers*, or *I don't know how she can bear the guy* with *I don't know how she bore the guy*. In contrast, regular verbs in nonpast idioms do not sound worse when put in the past: compare *She doesn't suffer fools gladly* with *None of them ever suffered fools gladly*. Similarly, some regular verbs like *afford* and *cope* usually appear with *can't*, which requires the stem form, and hence have common stems but very low-frequency past tense forms (*21*). But the uncommon *I don't know how he afforded it* (*coped*) does not sound worse than *He can't afford it* (*cope*)

These effects can be demonstrated in quantitative studies (*20*): subjects' ratings of regular past tense forms of different verbs correlate significantly with their ratings of the corresponding stems ($r = 0.62$) but not with the frequency of the past form (-0.14, partialing out stem rating). In contrast, ratings of irregular past tense forms correlate less strongly with their stem ratings (0.32), and significantly with past frequency (0.29, partialing out stem rating).

Experiments on how people produce and comprehend inflected forms in real time confirm this difference. When subjects see verb stems on a screen and must utter the past form as quickly as possible, they take significantly less time (16- to 29-msec difference) for irregular verbs with high past frequencies than irregular verbs with low past frequencies (stem frequencies equated), but show no such difference for regular verbs (<2-msec difference) (*23*). When recognizing words, people are aided by having seen the word previously on an earlier trial in the experiment; their mental representation of the word has been "primed" by the first presentation. Presenting a regular past tense form speeds up subsequent recognition of the stem no less than presenting the stem itself (181- versus 166-msec reduction), suggesting that people store and prime only the stem and analyze a regular inflected form as a stem plus a suffix. In contrast, prior presentation of an irregular form is significantly less effective at priming its stem than presentation of the stem itself (39- versus 99-msec reduction), suggesting that the two are stored as separate but linked items (*24*).

Similarity. Irregular verbs fall into families with similar stems and similar past tense forms, partly because the associative nature of memory makes it easier to memorize verbs in such families. Indeed, children make fewer overregularization errors for verbs that fall into families with more numerous and higher frequency members (5, 8–10, 25). As mentioned above, speakers occasionally extend irregular patterns to verbs that are highly similar to irregular families (*brang*), and such extensions are seen in dialects (13). A continuous effect of similarity has been measured experimentally: subjects frequently (44%) convert *spling* to *splung* (based on *string*, *sling*, et cetera), less often (24%) convert *shink* to *shunk*, and rarely (7%) convert *sid* to *sud* (14).

The rule-associative-memory theory predicts that the ability to generate regular past tense forms should not depend on similarity to existing regular verbs: the regular rule applies as a default, treating all nonirregular stems as equally valid instantiations of the mental symbol "verb." Within English vocabulary, we find that a regular verb can have any sound pattern, rather than falling into similarity clusters that complement the irregulars (5): for example, *need-needed* coexists with *bleed-bled* and *feed-fed*, *blink-blinked* with *shrink-shrank* and *drink-drank*. Regular-irregular homophones such as *lie-lay*; *lie-lied*, *meet-met*; *mete-meted*, and *hang-hung*; *hang-hanged* are the clearest examples. Moreover verbs with highly unusual sounds are easily provided with regular pasts. Although no English verb ends in *-ev* or a neutral vowel (21), novel verbs with these patterns are readily inflectable as natural past tense forms, such as *Yeltsin out-Gorbachev'ed Gorbachev* or *We rhumba'd all night*. Children are no more likely to overregularize an irregular verb if it resembles a family of similar regular verbs than if it is dissimilar from regulars, suggesting that regulars, unlike irregulars, do not form attracting clusters in memory (10, 25). Adults, when provided with novel verbs, do not rate regular past forms of unusual sounds like *ploamphed* as any worse, relative to the stem, than familiar sounds like *plipped* (similar to *clip*, *flip*, *slip*, et cetera), unlike their ratings for irregulars (15, 26). In contrast, in associationist models both irregular and regular generalizations tend to be sensitive to similarity. For example the Rumelhart–McClelland model could not produce any output for many novel regular verbs that did not resemble other regulars in the training set (5, 15, 17).

Organization of Grammatical Processes

Grammars divide into fairly autonomous submodules in which blocks of rules produce outputs that serve (or cannot serve) as the input for other blocks of rules. Linguistic research suggests an information flow of lexicon to derivational morphology (complex word-formation) to regular inflection, with regular and irregular processes encapsulated within different subcomponents (*27, 28*). If irregular past tense forms are stored in memory as entries in the mental lexicon, then like other stored words they should be the input to rules of complex word formation. If regular past tense forms are computed from words by a rule acting as a default, they should be formed from the outputs of complex word formation rules. Two phenomena illustrate this organization.

A potent demonstration of the earlier point that regular processes can apply to any sound whatsoever, no matter how tightly associated with an irregular pattern, is "regularization-through-derivation": verbs intuitively perceived as derived from nouns or adjectives are always regular, even if similar or identical to an irregular verb. Thus one says *grandstanded*, not *grandstood*; *flied out* in baseball [from a fly (ball)], not *flew out*; *high-sticked* in hockey, not *high-stuck* (*5, 6, 28*). The explanation is that irregularity consists of a linkage between two word roots, the atomic sound-meaning pairings stored in the mental lexicon; it is not a link between two words or sound patterns directly. *High-stuck* sounds silly because the verb is tacitly perceived as being based on the noun root (*hockey*) *stick*, and noun roots cannot be listed in the lexicon as having any past tense form (the past tense of a noun makes no sense semantically), let alone an irregular one. Because its root is not the verb *stick* there is no data pathway by which *stuck* can be made available; to obtain a past tense form, the speaker must apply the regular rule, which serves as the default. Subjects presented with novel irregular-sounding verbs (for example, *to line-drive*) strongly prefer the regular past tense form (*line-drived*) if it is understood as being based on a noun ("to hit a line drive"), but not in a control condition for unfamiliarity where the items were based on existing irregular verbs ("to drive along a line"); here the usual irregular form is preferred (*6*).

The effect, moreover, occurs in experiments testing subjects with no college education (*6*) and in preschool children (*29*). This is consistent with the fact that many of these lawful forms entered the language from vernacular speech and were opposed by language mavens and guardians of "proper" style (*6, 13*). "Rules of grammar" in the psycholinguists' sense, and their organization into components, are inherent to the computational systems found in all humans, not just those with access to explicit schooling or stylistic injunctions. These injunctions, involving a very different sense of "rule" as something that ought to be followed, usually pertain to minor differences between standard written and nonstandard spoken dialects.

A related effect occurs in lexical compounds, which sound natural when they contain irregular noun plurals, but not regular noun plurals: Compare *mice-infested* with *rats-infested*, *teethmarks* with *claws-marks*, *men-bashing* with *guys-bashing* (*28*). Assume that this compounding rule is fed by stored words. Irregulars are stored words, so they can feed compounding; regulars are computed at the output end of the morphology system, not stored at the input end, so they do not appear inside lexical compounds. This constraint has been documented experimentally in 3- to 5-year-old children (*30*): when children who knew the word *mice* were asked for a word for a "monster who eats mice," they responded with *mice-eater* 90% of the time; but when children who knew *rats* were asked for a word for "monster who eats rats," they responded *rats-eater* only 2% of the time. The children could not have learned the constraint by recording whether adults use irregular versus regular plurals inside compounds. Adults do not use such compounds often enough for most children to have heard them: the frequency of English compounds containing any kind of plural is indistinguishable from zero (*21, 30*). Rather, the constraint may be a consequence of the inherent organization of the children's grammatical systems.

Developmental and Neurological Dissociations

If regular and irregular patterns are computed in different subsystems, they should dissociate in special populations. Individuals with undeveloped or damaged grammatical systems and intact lexical memory should be unable to compute regular forms but should be able to handle irregulars. Conversely, individuals with intact grammatical systems and atypical lexical retrieval should handle regulars properly but be prone to overregularizing irregulars. Such double dissociations, most clearly demonstrated in detailed case studies, are an important source of evidence for the existence of separate neural subsystems. Preliminary evidence suggests that regular and irregular inflection may show such dissociations.

Children. Most of the grammatical structure of English develops rapidly in the third year of life (*31*). One conspicuous development is the appearance of overregularizations like *comed*. Such errors constitute a worsening of past marking with time; for months beforehand, all overtly marked irregular past forms are correct (*10*). The phenomenon is not due to the child becoming temporarily overwhelmed by the regular pattern because of an influx of regular verbs, as connectionist theories (*16*) predict (*5, 10, 32*). Instead it accompanies the appearance of the regular tense marking process itself: overregularizations appear when the child ceases using bare stems like *walk* to refer to past events (*8, 10*). Say memorization of verb forms from parental speech, including irregulars, can take place as soon as words of any kind can be learned. But deployment of the rule system must await the abstraction of the English rule from a set of word pairs juxtaposed as nonpast and past versions of the same verb. The young child could possess memorized irregulars, produced probabilistically but without overt error, but no rule; the older child, possessing the rule as well, would apply it obligatorily in past tense sentences whenever he failed to retrieve the irregular, resulting in occasional errors.

Aphasics. A syndrome sometimes called agrammatic aphasia can occur after extensive damage to Broca's area and nearby structures in the left cerebral hemisphere. Labored speech, absence of inflections and other grammatical words, and difficulty comprehending grammatical distinctions are frequent symptoms. Agrammatics have trouble reading aloud regular inflected forms: *smiled* is pronounced as *smile*, *wanted* as *wanting*. Nonregular plural and past forms are read with much greater accuracy, controlling for frequency and pronounceability (*33*). This is predicted if agrammatism results from damage to neural circuitry that executes rules of grammar, including the regular rule necessary for analyzing regularly inflected stimuli, but leaves the lexicon relatively undamaged, including stored irregulars which can be directly matched against the irregular stimuli.

Specific language impairment (SLI). SLI refers to a syndrome of language deficits not attributable to auditory, cognitive, or social problems. The syndrome usually includes delayed onset of language, articulation difficulties in childhood, and problems in controlling grammatical features such as tense, number, gender, case, and person. One form of SLI may especially impair aspects of the regular inflectional process (*34*). Natural speech includes errors like "We're go take a bus; I play musics; One machine clean all the two arena." In experiments, the patients have difficulty converting present sentences to past (32% for SLI; 78% for sibling controls). The difficulty is more pronounced for regular verbs than irregulars. Regular past forms are virtually absent from the children's spontaneous speech and writing, although irregulars often appear. In the writing samples of two children examined quantitatively, 85% of irregular pasts but 30% of regular pasts were correctly supplied. The first written regular past tense forms are for verbs with past tense frequencies higher than their stem frequencies; subsequent ones are acquired one at a time in response to teacher training, with little transfer to nontrained verbs. Adults' performance improves and their speech begins to sound normal but they continue to have difficulty inflecting nonsense forms like *zoop* (47% for SLI; 83% for controls). It appears as if their ability to apply inflectional rules is impaired relative to their ability to memorize words: irregular forms are acquired relatively normally, enjoying their advantage of high frequencies; regular forms are memorized as if they were irregular.

SLI appears to have an inherited component. Language impairments have been found in 3% of first-degree family members of normal probands but 23% of language-impaired probands (*35*). The impairment has been found to be 80% concordant in monozygotic twins and 35% concordant in dizygotic twins (*36*). One case study (*34*) investigated a three-generation, 30-member family, 16 of whom had SLI; the syndrome followed the pattern of a dominant, fully penetrant autosomal gene. This constitutes evidence that some aspects of use of grammar have a genetic basis.

Williams syndrome. Williams syndrome (WS), associated with a defective gene expressed in the central nervous system involved in calcium metabolism, causes an unusual kind of mental retardation (*37*). Although their Intelligence Quotient is measured at around 50, older children and adolescents with WS are described as hyperlinguistic with selective sparing of syntax, and grammatical abilities are close to normal in controlled testing (*37*). This is one of several kinds of dissociation in which language is preserved despite severe cognitive impairments, suggesting that the language system is autonomous of many other kinds of cognitive processing.

WS children retrieve words in a deviant fashion (*37*). When normal or other retarded children are asked to name some animals, they say *dog, cat, pig*; WS children offer *unicorn, tyrandon, yak, ibex*. Normal children speak of *pouring water*; WS children speak of *evacuating a glass*. According to the rule-associative-memory hybrid theory, preserved grammatical abilities and deviant retrieval of high-frequency words are preconditions for overregularization. Indeed, some WS children overregularize at high rates (16%), one of their few noticeable grammatical errors (*37, 39*).

Conclusion

For hundreds of years, the mind has been portrayed as a homogeneous system whose complexity comes from the complexity of environmental correlations as recorded by a general-purpose learning mechanism. Modern research on language renders such a view increasingly implausible. Although there is evidence that the memory system used in language acquisition and processing has some of the properties of an associative network, these properties do not exhaust the computational abilities of the brain. Focusing on a single rule of grammar, we find evidence for a system that is modular, independent of real-world meaning, nonassociative (unaffected by frequency and similarity), sensitive to abstract formal distinctions (for example, root versus derived, noun versus verb), more sophisticated than the kinds of "rules" that are explicitly taught, developing on a schedule not timed by environmental input, organized by principles that could not have been learned, possibly with a distinct neural substrate and genetic basis.

References and Notes

1. D. Hume, *Inquiry Concerning Human Understanding* (Bobbs-Merril, Indianapolis, 1955); D. Hebb, *Organization of Behavior* (Wiley, New York, 1949); D. Rumelhart and J. McClelland, *Parallel Distributed Processing* (MIT Press, Cambridge, 1986).

2. G. Leibniz, *Philosophical Essays* (Hackett, Indianapolis, 1989); A. Newell and H. Simon, *Science* **134**, 2011 (1961).

3. J. Fodor, *Modularity of Mind* (MIT Press, Cambridge, 1983).

4. N. Chomsky, *Rules and Representations* (Columbia Univ. Press, New York, 1980); E. Lenneberg, *Biological Foundations of Language* (Wiley, New York, 1967).

5. S. Pinker and A. Prince, *Cognition* **28**, 73 (1988).

6. J. Kim, S. Pinker, A. Prince, S. Prasada, *Cognitive Science* **15**, 173 (1991).

7. J. Berko, *Word* **14**, 150 (1958).

8. S. Kuczaj, *J. Verb. Learn. Behav.* **16**, 589 (1977).

9. J. Bybee and D. Slobin, *Language* **58**, 265 (1982).

10. G. Marcus, M. Ullman, S. Pinker, M. Hollander, T. Rosen, F. Xu, *Ctr. Cog. Sci. Occ. Pap. 41* (Massachusetts Institute of Technology, Cambridge, 1990).

11. N. Chomsky and M. Halle, *Sound Pattern of English* (MIT Press, Cambridge, 1990).

12. O. Jespersen, *A Modern English Grammar on Historical Principles* (Allen and Unwin, London, 1961).

13. H. Mencken, *The American Language* (Knopf, New York, 1936).

14. J. Bybee and C. Moder, *Language* **59**, 251 (1983).

15. S. Prasada and S. Pinker, unpublished data.

16. D. Rumelhart and J. McClelland, in *Parallel Distributed Processing*, J. McClelland and D. Rumelhart, Eds. (MIT Press, Cambridge, 1986), pp. 216–271.

17. J. Lachter and T. Bever, *Cognition* **28**, 197 (1988). More sophisticated connectionist models of past tense formation employing a hidden layer of nodes have computational limitations similar to those of the Rumelhart-McClelland model (D. Egedi and R. Sproat, unpublished data).

18. J. Bybee, *Morphology* (Benjamins, Philadelphia, 1985).

19. In speech samples from 19 children containing 9684 irregular past tense forms (*10*), aggregate overregularization rate for 39 verbs correlated -0.37 with aggregate log frequency in parental speech. All correlations and differences noted herein are significant at $p = 0.05$ or less.

20. M. Ullman and S. Pinker, paper presented at the Spring Symposium of the AAAI, Stanford, 26 to 28 March 1991. Data represent mean ratings by 99 subjects of the naturalness of the past and stem forms of 142 irregular verbs and 59 regular verbs that did not rhyme with any irregular, each presented in a sentence in counterbalanced random order.

21. N. Francis and H. Kucera, *Frequency Analysis of English Usage* (Houghton Mifflin, Boston, 1982).

22. Such effects can also occur in certain connectionist models that lack distinct representations of words and superimpose associations between the phonological elements of stem and past forms. After such models are trained on many regular

verbs, any new verb would activate previously trained phonological associations to the regular pattern and could yield a strong regular form; the absence of prior training on the verb itself would not necessarily hurt it. However, the existence of homophones with different past tense forms (*lie-lay* versus *lie-lied*) makes such models psychologically unrealistic; representations of individual words are called for, and they would engender word familiarity effects.

23. S. Prasada, S. Pinker, W. Snyder, paper presented at the 31st Annual Meeting of the Psychonomic Society, New Orleans, 16 to 18 November 1990. The effects obtained in three experiments, each showing 32 to 40 subjects the stem forms of verbs on a screen for 300 msec and measuring their vocal response time for the past tense form. Thirty to 48 irregular verbs and 30 to 48 regular verbs were shown, one at a time in random order; every verb had a counterpart with the same stem frequency but a different past tense frequency (*21*). In control experiments, 40 subjects generated third person singular forms of stems, read stems aloud, or read past tense forms aloud, and the frequency difference among irregulars did not occur; this shows the effect is not due to inherent differences in access or articulation times of the verbs.

24. R. Stanners, J. Neiser, W. Hernon, R. Hall, *J. Verb. Learn. Verb. Behav.* **18**, 399 (1979); S. Kempley and J. Morton, *Br. J. Psychol.* **73**, 441 (1982). The effect was not an artifact of differences in phonological or orthographic overlap between the members of regular and irregular pairs.

25. For 17 of 19 children studied in (*10*), the higher the frequencies of the other irregulars rhyming with an irregular, the lower its overregulation rate (mean correlation −0.07, significantly less than 0). For the corresponding calculation with regulars rhyming with an irregular, no consistency resulted and the mean correlation did not differ significantly from zero.

26. Twenty-four subjects read 60 sentences containing novel verbs, presented either in stem form, a past form displaying an English irregular vowel change, or a past form containing the regular suffix. Each subject rated how good the verb sounded with a 7-point scale; each verb was rated in each of the forms by different subjects. For novel verbs highly similar to an irregular family, the irregular past form was rated 0.8 points worse than the stem; for novel verbs dissimilar to the family, the irregular past form was rated 2.2 points worse. For novel verbs resembling a family of regular verbs, the regular past form was rated 0.4 points better than the stem; for novel verbs dissimilar to the family, the regular past form was rated 1.5 points better. This interaction was replicated in two other experiments.

27. M. Aronoff, *Annu. Rev. Anthropol.* **12**, 355 (1983); S. Anderson, in *Linguistics: The Cambridge Survey* (Cambridge Univ. Press, New York, 1988), vol. 1, pp. 146–191.

28. P. Kiparsky, in *The Structure of Phonological Representations*, H. van der Hulst and N. Smith, Eds. (Foris, Dordrecht, 1982).

29. J. Kim, G. Marcus, M. Hollander, S. Pinker, *Pap. Rep. Child Lang. Dev.*, in press.

30. P. Gordon, *Cognition* **21**, 73 (1985). The effect is not an artifact of pronounceability, as children were willing to say *pants-eater* and *scissors-eater*, containing *s*-final nouns that are not regular plurals.

31. R. Brown, *A First Language* (Harvard Univ. Press, Cambridge, 1973).

32. The proportion of regular verb tokens in children's and parents' speech remains unchanged throughout childhood, because high frequency irregular verbs (*make, put, take,* et cetera) dominate conversation at any age. The proportion of regular verb types in children's vocabulary necessarily increases because irregular verbs are a small fraction of English vocabulary, but this growth does not correlate with overregularization errors (*3, 8*).

33. O. Marin, E. Saffran, M. Schwartz, *Ann. N.Y. Acad. Sci.* **280**, 868 (1976). For example, regular *misers, clues, buds* were read by three agrammatic patients less accurately than phonologically matched plurals that are not regular because they lack a corresponding singular, like *trousers, news, suds* (45% versus 90%), even though a phonologically well-formed stem is available in both cases. In another study, when verbs matched for past and base frequencies and pronounceability were presented to an agrammatic patient, he read 56% of irregular past forms and 18% of regular past forms successfully (G. Hickok and S. Pinker, unpublished data).

34. M. Gopnik, *Nature* **344**, 715 (1990); *Lang. Acq.* **1**, 139 (1990); M. Gopnik and M. Crago, *Cognition*, in press.

35. J. Tomblin, *J. Speech Hear. Disord.* **54**, 287 (1989); P. Tallal, R. Ross, S. Curtiss, *ibid.*, p. 167.

36. J. Tomblin, unpublished data.

37. U. Bellugi, A. Bihrle, T. Jernigan, D. Trauner, S. Doherty, *Am. J. Med. Genet. Suppl.* **6**, 115 (1990).

38. S. Curtiss, in *The Exceptional Brain*, L. Obler and D. Fein, Eds. (Guilford, New York, 1988).

39. E. Klima and U. Bellugi, unpublished data.

40. I thank my collaborators A. Prince, G. Hickok, M. Hollander, J. Kim, G. Marcus, S. Prasada, A. Senghas, and M. Ullman and thank T. Bever, N. Block, N. Etcoff, and especially A. Prince for comments. Supported by NIH grant HD18381.

Concepts and Conceptual Structure

Douglas L. Medin

Research and theory on categorization and conceptual structure have recently undergone two major shifts. The first shift is from the assumption that concepts have defining properties (the classical view) to the idea that concept representations may be based on properties that are only characteristic or typical of category examples (the probabilistic view). Both the probabilistic view and the classical view assume that categorization is driven by similarity relations. A major problem with describing category structure in terms of similarity is that the notion of similarity is too unconstrained to give an account of conceptual coherence. The second major shift is from the idea that concepts are organized by similarity to the idea that concepts are organized around theories. In this article, the evidence and rationale associated with these shifts are described, and one means of integrating similarity-based and theory-driven categorization is outlined.

What good are categories? Categorization involves treating two or more distinct entities as in some way equivalent in the service of accessing knowledge and making predictions. Take psychodiagnostic categories as an example. The need to access relevant knowledge explains why clinical psychologists do not (or could not) treat each individual as unique. Although one would expect treatment plans to be tailored to the needs of individuals, absolute uniqueness imposes the prohibitive cost of ignorance. Clinicians need some way to bring their knowledge and experience to bear on the problem under consideration, and that requires the appreciation of some similarity or relationship between the current situation and what has gone before. Although clinical psychologists may or may not use a specific categorization system, they must find points of contact between previous situations and the current context; that is, they must categorize. Diagnostic categories allow clinicians to predict the efficacy of alternative treatments and to share their experiences with other therapists. Yet another reason to categorize is to learn about etiology. People who show a common manifestation of some problem may share common precipitating conditions or causes. Ironically, the only case in which categorization would not be useful is where all individuals are treated alike; thus, categorization allows diversity.

More generally speaking, concepts and categories serve as building blocks for human thought and behavior. Roughly, a *concept* is an idea that includes all that is characteristically associated with it. A *category* is a partitioning or class to which some assertion or set of assertions might apply. It is tempting to think of categories as existing in the world and of concepts as corresponding to mental representations of them, but this analysis is misleading. It is misleading because concepts need not have real-world counterparts (e.g., unicorns) and because people may impose rather than discover structure in the world. I believe that questions about the nature of categories may be psychological questions as much as metaphysical questions. Indeed, for at least the last decade my colleagues and I have been trying to address the question of why we have the categories we have and not others. The world could be partitioned in a limitless variety of ways, yet people find only a minuscule subset of possible classifications to be meaningful. Part of the answer to the categorization question likely does depend on the nature of the world, but part also surely depends on the nature of the organism and its goals. Dolphins have no use for psychodiagnostic categories.

Given the fundamental character of concepts and categories, one might think that people who study concepts would have converged on a stable consensus with respect to conceptual structure. After all, Plato and Aristotle had quite a bit to say about concepts, medieval philosophers were obsessed with questions about universals and the essence of concepts, and concept representation remains as a cornerstone issue in all aspects of cognitive science. However, we have neither consensus nor stability. The relatively recent past has experienced at least one and probably two major shifts in thought about conceptual structure, and stability is the least salient attribute of the current situation. In the remainder of this article, I will briefly describe these shifts and then outline some ways of integrating the strong points of the various views.

The First Shift: Classical Versus Probabilistic Views

It is difficult to discuss concepts without bringing in the notion of similarity at some point. For example, a common idea is that our classification system tends to maximize within-category similarity relative to between-category similarity. That is, we group things into categories because they are similar. It will be suggested that alternative views of conceptual structure are associated with distinct (though sometimes implicit) theories of the nature of similarity.

The Classical View

The idea that all instances or examples of a category have some fundamental characteristics in common that determine their membership is very compelling. The classical view of concepts is organized around this notion. The classical view assumes that mental representations of categories consist of summary lists of features or properties that individually are necessary for category membership and collectively are sufficient to determine category membership. The category *triangle* meets these criteria. All triangles are closed geometric forms with three sides and interior angles that sum to 180 degrees. To see if something is a triangle one has only to check for these three properties, and if any one is missing one does not have a triangle.

What about other concepts? The classical view suggests that all categories have defining features. A particular person may not know what these defining features are but an expert certainly should. In our 1981 book, *Categories and Concepts*, Ed Smith and I reviewed the status of the classical view as a theory of conceptual structure. We concluded that the classical view was in grave trouble for a variety of reasons. Many of the arguments and counterarguments are quite detailed, but the most serious problems can be easily summarized:

1. *Failure to specify defining features.* One glaring problem is that even experts cannot come up with defining features for most lexical concepts (i.e., those reflected in our language). People may believe that concepts have necessary or sufficient features (McNamara and Sternberg, 1983), but the features given as candidates do not hold up to closer scrutiny. For example, a person may list "made of wood" as a necessary property for violins, but not all violins are made of wood. Linguists, philosophers, biologists, and clinical psychologists alike have been unable to supply a core set of features that all examples of a concept (in their area of expertise) necessarily must share.

2. *Goodness of example effects.* According to the classical view, all examples of a concept are equally good because they all possess the requisite defining features. Experience and (by now) a considerable body of research undermines this claim. For example, people judge a robin to be a better example of bird than an ostrich is and can answer category membership questions more quickly for good examples than for poor examples (Smith, Shoben,

and Rips, 1974). Typicality effects are nearly ubiquitous (for reviews, see Medin and Smith, 1984; Mervis and Rosch, 1981; Oden, 1987); they hold for the artistic style (Hartley and Homa, 1981), chess (Goldin, 1978), emotion terms (Fehr, 1988; Fehr and Russell, 1984), medical diagnosis (Arkes and Harkness, 1980), and person perception (e.g., Cantor and Mischel, 1977).

Typicality effects are not, in principle, fatal for the classical view. One might imagine that some signs or features help to determine the presence of other (defining) features. Some examples may have more signs or clearer signs pointing the way to the defining properties, and this might account for the difference in goodness of example judgments or response times. This distinction between identification procedures (how one identifies an instance of a concept) and a conceptual core (how the concept relates to other concepts) may prove useful if it can be shown that the core is used in some other aspect of thinking. It seems, however, that this distinction serves more to insulate the classical view from empirical findings, and Smith, Rips, and Medin (1984) argued that there are no sharp boundaries between core properties and those used for purposes of identification.

3. *Unclear cases.* The classical view implies a procedure for unambiguously determining category membership; that is, check for defining features. Yet there are numerous cases in which it is not clear whether an example belongs to a category. Should a rug be considered furniture? What about a clock or radio? People not only disagree with each other concerning category membership but also contradict themselves when asked about membership on separate occasions (Barsalou, 1989; Bellezza, 1984; McCloskey and Glucksberg, 1978).

These and other problems have led to disenchantment with the classical view of concepts. The scholarly consensus has shifted its allegiance to an alternative, the probabilistic view.

The Probabilistic View

The rejection of the classical view of categories has been associated with the ascendance of the probabilistic view of category structure (Wittgenstein, 1953). This view holds that categories are "fuzzy" or ill-defined and that categories are organized around a set of properties or clusters of correlated attributes (Rosch, 1975) that are only characteristic or typical of category membership. Thus, the probabilistic view rejects the notion of defining features.

The most recent edition of the *Diagnostic and Statistical Manual of Mental Disorders* (*DSM-IIIR*, American Psychiatric Association, 1987) uses criteria based on lists of characteristic symptoms or features to describe diagnostic categories and thereby endorses the probabilistic view. For example, a diagnosis of depression can be made if a dysphoric mood and any five of a set of nine symptoms are present nearly every day for a period of at least two weeks. Thus, two people may both be categorized as depressed and share only a single one of the nine characteristic symptoms!

The probabilistic view is perfectly at home with the typicality effects that were so awkward for the classical view. Membership in probabilistic categories is naturally graded, rather than all or none, and the better or more typical members have more characteristic properties than the poorer ones. It is also easy to see that the probabilistic view may lead to unclear cases. Any one example may have several typical properties of a category but not so many that it clearly qualifies for category membership.

In some pioneering work aimed at clarifying the structural basis of fuzzy categories, Rosch and Mervis (1975) had subjects list properties of exemplars for a variety of concepts such as *bird*, *fruit*, and *tool*. They found that the listed properties for some exemplars occurred frequently in other category members, whereas others had properties that occurred less frequently. Most important, the more frequently an exemplar's properties appeared within a category, the higher was its rated typicality for that category. The correlation between number of characteristic properties possessed and typicality rating was very high and positive. For example, robins have characteristic bird properties of flying, singing, eating worms, and building nests in trees, and they are rated to be very typical birds. Penguins have none of these properties, and they are rated as very atypical birds. In short, the Rosch and Mervis work relating typicality to number of characteristic properties put the probabilistic view on fairly firm footing.

1. Mental representations of probabilistic view categories If categories are not represented in terms of definitions, what form do our mental representations take? The term, probabilistic view, seems to imply that people organize categories via statistical reasoning. Actually, however, there is a more natural interpretation of fuzzy categories. Intuitively, probabilistic view categories are organized according to a *family resemblance* principle. A simple form of summary representation would be an example or ideal that possessed all of the characteristic features of a category. This summary representation is referred to as the *prototype*, and the prototype can be used to decide category membership. If some candidate example is similar enough to the prototype for a category, then it will be classified as a member of that category. The general notion is that, based on experience with examples of a category, people abstract out the central tendency or prototype that becomes the summary mental representation for the category.

A more radical principle of mental representation, which is also consistent with fuzzy categories, is the exemplar view (Smith and Medin, 1981). The exemplar view denies that there is a single summary representation and instead claims that categories are represented by means of examples. In this view, clients may be diagnosed as suicidal, not because they are similar to some prototype of a suicidal person, but because they remind the clinician of a previous client who was suicidal.

A considerable amount of research effort has been aimed at contrasting exemplar and prototype representations (see Allen et al., 1988; Estes, 1986a, 1986b; Medin, 1986; Medin and Smith, 1984; Nosofsky, 1987, 1988a; and Oden, 1987). Genero and Cantor (1987) suggested that prototypes serve untrained diagnosticians well but that trained diagnosticians may find exemplars to be more helpful. For my present purposes, however, I will blur over this distinction to note that both prototype and exemplar theories rely on roughly the same similarity principle. That is, category membership is determined by whether some candidate is sufficiently similar either to the prototype or to a set of encoded examples, where similarity is based on matches and mismatches of independent, equally abstract, features.

2.   **Probabilistic view and similarity**   To give meaning to the claim that categorization is based on similarity, it is important to be specific about what one means by similarity. Although the consensus is not uniform, I believe that the modal model of similarity with respect to conceptual structure can be summarized in terms of the four assumptions as follows: (a) Similarity between two things increases as a function of the number of features or properties they share and decreases as a function of mismatching or distinctive features. (b) These features can be treated as independent and additive. (c) The features determining similarity are all roughly the same level of abstractness (as a special case they may be irreducible primitives). (d) These similarity

principles are sufficient to describe conceptual structure, and therefore, a concept is more or less equivalent to a list of its features. This theory of similarity is very compatible with the notion that categories are organized around prototypes. Nonetheless, I will later argue that each of these assumptions is wrong or misleading and that to understand conceptual structure theories of similarity are needed that reject each of these assumptions. Before outlining an alternative set of similarity assumptions, however, I will first describe a set of observations that motivate the second, still more recent, shift in thinking concerning conceptual structure.

Problems for Probabilistic View Theories

Problems for Prototypes

Although the general idea that concepts are organized around prototypes remains popular, at a more specific, empirical level, prototype theories have not fared very well. First of all, prototype theories treat concepts as context-independent. Roth and Shoben (1983), however, have shown that typicality judgments vary as a function of particular contexts. For example, tea is judged to be a more typical beverage than milk in the context of secretaries taking a break, but this ordering reverses for the context of truck drivers taking a break. Similarly, Shoben and I (Medin and Shoben, 1988) noted that the typicality of combined concepts cannot be predicted from the typicality of the constituents. As an illustrative example, consider the concept of *spoon*. People rate small spoons as more typical spoons than large spoons, and metal spoons as more typical spoons than wooden spoons. If the concept *spoon* is represented by a prototypic spoon, then a small metal spoon should be the most typical spoon, followed by small wooden and large metal spoons, and large wooden spoons should be the least typical. Instead, people find large wooden spoons to be more typical spoons than either small wooden spoons or large metal spoons (see also Malt and Smith, 1983). The only way for a prototype model to handle these results is to posit multiple prototypes. But this strategy creates new problems. Obviously one cannot have a separate prototype for every adjective noun combination because there are simply too many possible combinations. One might suggest that there are distinct subtypes for concepts like *spoon*, but one would need a theory describing how and when subtypes are created. Current prototype models do not provide such a theory. A third problem for prototype theories grows out of Barsalou's work (1985, 1987) on goal-derived categories such as "things to take on a camping trip" and "foods to eat while on a diet." Barsalou has found that goal-derived categories show the same typicality effects as other categories. The basis for these effects, however, is not similarity to an average or prototype but rather similarity to an ideal. For example, for the category of things to eat while on a diet, typicality ratings are determined by how closely an example conforms to the ideal of zero calories.

Laboratory studies of categorization using artificially constructed categories also raise problems for prototypes. Normally many variables relevant to human classification are correlated and therefore confounded with one another. The general rationale for laboratory studies with artificially created categories is that one can isolate some variable or set of variables of interest and unconfound some natural correlations. Salient phenomena associated with fuzzy categories are observed with artificially constructed categories, and several of these are consistent with prototype theories. For example, one observes typicality effects in learning and on transfer tests using both correctness and reaction time as the dependent variable (e.g., Rosch and Mervis, 1975). A striking phenomenon, readily obtained, is that the prototype for a category may be classified more accurately during transfer tests than are the previously seen examples that were used during original category learning (e.g., Homa and Vosburgh, 1976; Medin and Schaffer, 1978; Peterson, et al., 1973).

Typicality effects and excellent classification of prototypes are consistent with the idea that people are learning these ill-defined categories by forming prototypes. More detailed analyses, however, are more problematic. Prototype theory implies that the only information abstracted from categories is the central tendency. A prototype representation discards information concerning category size, the variability of the examples, and information concerning correlations of attributes. The evidence suggests that people are sensitive to all three of these types of information (Estes, 1986b; Flannagan, Fried, and Holyoak, 1986; Fried and Holyoak, 1984; Medin, Altom, Edelson, and Freko, 1982; Medin and Schaffer, 1978). An example involving correlated attributes pinpoints part of the problem. Most people have the intuition that small birds are much more likely to sing than large birds. This intuition cannot be obtained from a single summary prototype for birds. The fact that one can generate large numbers of such correlations is a problem for the idea that people reason using prototypes. More generally, prototype representations seem to discard too much information that can be shown to be relevant to human categorizations.

Yet another problem for prototypes is that they make the wrong predictions about which category structures should be easy or difficult to learn. One way to conceptualize the process of classifying examples on the basis of similarity to prototypes is that it involves a summing of evidence against a criterion. For example, if an instance shows a criterial sum of features (appropriately weighted), then it will be classified as a bird, and the more typical a member is of the category, the more quickly the criterion will be exceeded. The key aspect of this prediction is that there must exist some additive combination of properties and their weights that can be used to correctly assign instances as members or nonmembers. The technical term for this constraint is that categories must be linearly separable (Sebestyn, 1962). For a prototype process to work in the sense of accepting all members and rejecting all nonmembers, the categories must be linearly separable.

If linear separability acts as a constraint on human categorization, then with other factors equal, people should find it easier to learn categories that are linearly separable than categories that are not linearly separable. To make a long story short, however, studies employing a variety of stimulus materials, category sizes, subject populations, and instructions have failed to find any evidence that linear separability acts as a constraint on human classification learning (Kemler-Nelson, 1984; Medin and Schwanenflugel, 1981; see also Shepard, Hovland, and Jenkins, 1961).

The cumulative effect of these various chunks of evidence has been to raise serious questions concerning the viability of prototype theories. Prototype theories imply constraints that are not observed in human categorization, predict insensitivity to information that people readily use, and fail to reflect the context sensitivity that is evident in human categorization. Rather than getting at the character of human conceptual representation, prototypes appear to be more of a caricature of it. Exemplar models handle some of these phenomena, but they fail to address some of the most fundamental questions concerning conceptual structure.

Exemplar-Based Theories

The problems just described hold not only for prototype theories in particular but also for any similarity-based categorization model that assumes that the constituent features are independent and additive. To give but one example, one could have an exemplar model of categorization that assumes that, during learning, people store examples but that new examples are classified by "computing" prototypes and determining the similarity of the novel example to the newly constructed prototypes. In short, the central tendency would be abstracted (and other information discarded) at the time of retrieval rather than at the time of storage or initial encoding. Such a model would inherit all the shortcomings of standard prototype theories.

Some exemplar storage theories do not endorse the notion of feature independence (Hintzman, 1986; Medin and Schaffer, 1978), or they assume that classification is based on retrieving only a subset of the stored examples (presumably the most similar ones or, as a special case, the most similar one). The idea that retrieval is limited, similarity-based, and context-sensitive is in accord with much of the memory literature (e.g., Tulving, 1983). In addition, these exemplar models predict sensitivity to category size, instance variability, context, and correlated attributes. It is my impression that in head-to-head competition, exemplar models have been substantially more successful than prototype models (Barsalou and Medin, 1986; Estes, 1986b; Medin and Ross, 1989; Nosofsky, 1988a, 1988b; but see Homa, 1984, for a different opinion).

Why should exemplar models fare better than prototype models? One of the main functions of classification is that it allows one to make inferences and predictions on the basis of partial information (see Anderson, 1988). Here I am using classification loosely to refer to any means by which prior (relevant) knowledge is brought to bear, ranging from a formal classification scheme to an idiosyncratic reminding of a previous case (which, of course, is in the spirit of exemplar models; see also Kolodner, 1984). In psychotherapy, clinicians are constantly making predictions about the likelihood of future behaviors or the efficacy of a particular treatment based on classification. Relative to prototype models, exemplar models tend to be conservative about discarding information that facilitates predictions. For instance, sensitivity to correlations of properties within a category enables finer predictions: from noting that a bird is large, one can predict that it cannot sing. It may seem that exemplar models do not discard any information at all, but they are incomplete without assumptions concerning retrieval or access. In general, however, the pairs of storage and retrieval assumptions associated with exemplar models preserve much more information than prototype models. In a general review of research on categorization and problem-solving, Brian Ross and I concluded that abstraction is both conservative and tied to the details of specific examples in a manner more in the spirit of exemplar models than prototype models (Medin and Ross, 1989).

Unfortunately, context-sensitive, conservative categorization is not enough. The debate between prototype and exemplar models has taken place on a platform constructed in terms of similarity-based categorization. The second shift is that this platform has started to crumble, and the viability of probabilistic view theories of categorization is being seriously questioned. There are two central problems. One is that probabilistic view theories do not say anything about why we have the categories we have. This problem is most glaringly obvious for exemplar models that appear to allow any set of examples to form a category. The second central problem is with the notion of similarity. Do things belong in the same category because they are similar, or do they seem similar because they are in the same category?

Does Similarity Explain Categorization?

1. **Flexibility** Similarity is a very intuitive notion. Unfortunately, it is even more elusive than it is intuitive. One problem with using similarity to define categories is that similarity is too flexible. Consider, for example, Tversky's (1977) influential contrast model, which defines similarity as a function of common and distinctive features weighted for salience or importance. According to this model, similarity relationships will depend heavily on the particular weights

given to individual properties or features. For example, a *zebra* and a *barber pole* would be more similar than a *zebra* and a *horse* if the feature "striped" had sufficient weight. This would not necessarily be a problem if the weights were stable. However, Tversky and others have convincingly shown that the relative weighting of a feature (as well as the relative importance of matching and mismatching features) varies with the stimulus context, experimental task (Gati and Tversky, 1984; Tversky, 1977), and probably even the concept under consideration (Ortony et al., 1985). For example, common properties shared by a pair of entities may become salient only in the context of some third entity that does not share these properties.

Once one concedes that similarity is dynamic and depends on some (not well-understood) processing principles, earlier work on the structural underpinnings of fuzzy categories can be seen in a somewhat different light. Recall that the Rosch and Mervis (1975) studies asked subjects to list attributes or properties of examples and categories. It would be a mistake to assume that people had the ability to read and report their mental representations of concepts in a veridical manner. Indeed Keil (1979, 1981) pointed out that examples like *robin* and *squirrel* shared many important properties that almost never show up in attribute listings (e.g., has a heart, breathes, sleeps, is an organism, is an object with boundaries, is a physical object, is a thing, can be thought about, and so on). In fact, Keil argued that knowledge about just these sorts of predicates, referred to as ontological knowledge (Sommers, 1971), serves to organize children's conceptual and semantic development. For present purposes, the point is that attribute listings provide a biased sample of people's conceptual knowledge. To take things a step further, one could argue that without constraints on what is to count as a feature, any two things may be arbitrarily similar or dissimilar. Thus, as Murphy and I (Murphy and Medin, 1985) suggested, the number of properties that plums and lawn mowers have in common could be infinite: Both weigh less than 1000 Kg, both are found on earth, both are found in our solar system, both cannot hear well, both have an odor, both are not worn by elephants, both are used by people, both can be dropped, and so on (see also Goodman, 1972; Watanabe, 1969). Now consider again the status of attribute listings. They represent a biased subset of stored or readily inferred knowledge. The correlation of attribute listings with typicality judgments is a product of such knowledge and a variety of processes that operate on it. Without a theory of that knowledge and those processes, it simply is not clear what these correlations indicate about mental representations.

The general point is that attempts to describe category structure in terms of similarity will prove useful only to the extent that one specifies which principles determine what is to count as a relevant property and which principles determine the importance of particular properties. It is important to realize that the explanatory work is being done by the principles which specify these constraints rather than the general notion of similarity. In that sense similarity is more like a dependent variable than an independent variable.

2. **Attribute Matching and Categorization**   The modal model of similarity summarized in Table 5.1 invites one to view categorization as attribute matching. Although that may be part of the story, there are several ways in which the focus on attribute matching may be misleading. First of all, as Armstrong, Gleitman, and Gleitman (1983) emphasized, most concepts are not a simple sum of independent features. The features that are characteristically associated with the concept *bird* are just a pile of bird features unless they are held together in a "bird structure." Structure requires both attributes and *relations* binding the attributes together. Typical bird features (laying eggs, flying, having wings and feathers, building nests in trees, and singing) have both an internal structure and an external structure based on interproperty relationships. Building nests is linked to laying eggs, and building nests in trees poses logistical problems whose solution involves other properties such as having wings, flying, and singing. Thus, it makes sense to ask why birds have certain features (e.g., wings and feathers). Although people may not have thought about various interproperty relationships, they can readily reason with them. Thus, one can answer the question of why birds have wings and feathers (i.e., to fly).

In a number of contexts, categorization may be more like problem solving than attribute matching. Inferences and causal attributions may drive the categorization process. Borrowing again from work by Murphy and me (1985), "jumping into a swimming pool with one's

Table 5.1
Comparison of Two Approaches to Concepts

Aspect of conceptual theory	Similarity-based approach	Theory-based approach
Concept representation	Similarity structure, attribute lists, correlated attributes	Correlated attributes plus underlying principles that determine which correlations are noticed
Category definition	Various similarity metrics, summation of attributes	An explanatory principle common to category members
Units of analysis	Attributes	Attributes plus explicitly represented relations of attributes and concepts
Categorization basis	Attribute matching	Matching plus inferential processes supplied by underlying principles
Weighting of attributes	Cue validity, salience	Determined in part by importance in the underlying principles
Interconceptual structure	Hierarchy based on shared attributes	Network formed by causal and explanatory links, as well as sharing of properties picked out as relevant
Conceptual development	Feature accretion	Changing organization and explanations of concepts as a result of world knowledge

clothes on" in all probability is not associated directly with the concept *intoxicated*. However, observing this behavior might lead one to classify the person as drunk. In general, real world knowledge is used to reason about or explain properties, not simply to match them. For example, a teenage boy might show many of the behaviors associated with an eating disorder, but the further knowledge that the teenager is on the wrestling team and trying to make a lower weight class may undermine any diagnosis of a disorder.

3. Summary   It does not appear that similarity, at least in the form it takes in current theories, is going to be at all adequate to explain categorization. Similarity may be a byproduct of conceptual coherence rather than a cause. To use a rough analogy, winning basketball teams have in common scoring more points than their opponents, but one must turn to more basic principles to explain why they score more points. One candidate for a set of deeper principles is the idea that concepts are organized around theories, and theories provide conceptual coherence. In the next section, I will briefly summarize some of the current work on the role of knowledge structures and theories in categorization and then turn to a form of rapprochement between similarity and knowledge-based categorization principle.

The Second Shift: Concepts as Organized by Theories

Knowledge-Based Categorization

It is perhaps only a modest exaggeration to say that similarity gets at the shadow rather than the substance of concepts. Something is needed to give concepts life, coherence, and meaning. Although many philosophers of science have argued that observations are necessarily theory-labeled, only recently have researchers begun to stress that the organization of concepts is knowledge-based and driven by theories about the world (e.g., Carey, 1985; S. Gelman, 1988; S. Gelman and Markman, 1986a, 1986b; Keil, 1986, 1987; Keil and Kelly, 1987; Lakoff, 1987; Markman, 1987; Massey and R. Gelman, 1988; Murphy and Medin, 1985; Oden, 1987; Rips, 1989; Schank, Collins, and Hunter, 1986; and others).

The primary differences between the similarity-based and theory-based approaches to categorization are summarized in Table 5.1, taken from Murphy and Medin (1985). Murphy and Medin suggested that the relation between a concept and an example is analogous to the relation between theory and data. That is, classification is not simply based on a direct matching of properties of the concept with those in the example, but rather requires that the example have the right "explanatory relationship" to the theory organizing the concept. In the case of a person diving into a swimming pool with his or her clothes on, one might try to reason back to either causes or predisposing conditions. One might believe that having too much to drink impairs judgment and that going into the pool shows poor judgment. Of course, the presence of other information, such as the fact that another person who cannot swim has fallen into the pool, would radically change the inferences drawn and, as a consequence, the categorization judgment.

One of the more promising aspects of the theory-based approach is that it begins to address the question of why we have the categories we have or why categories are sensible. In fact, coherence may be achieved in the absence of any obvious source of similarity among examples. Consider the category comprised of children, money, photo albums, and pets. Out of context the category seems odd. If one's knowledge base is enriched to include the fact that the category represents "things to take out of one's house in case of a fire," the category becomes sensible (Barsalou, 1983). In addition, one could readily make judgments about whether new examples (e.g., personal papers) belonged to the category, judgments that would not be similarity based.

Similarity effects can be overridden by theory-related strategies even in the judgments of young children. That fact was very nicely demonstrated by Gelman and Markman (1986a) in their studies of induction. Specifically, they pitted category membership against perceptual similarity in an inductive inference task. Young children were taught that different novel properties were true of two examples and then were asked which property was also true of a new example that was similar to one alternative but belonged to a different category, and one that was perceptually different from the other examples but belonged to the same category. For example, children might be taught that a (pictured) flamingo feeds its baby mashed-up food and that a (pictured) bat feeds its baby milk, and then they might be asked how a (pictured) owl feeds its baby. The owl was more perceptually similar to the bat than to the flamingo, but even four-year-olds made inferences on the basis of category membership rather than similarity.

Related work by Susan Carey and Frank Keil shows that children's biological theories guide their conceptual development. For example, Keil has used the ingenious technique of describing transformations or changes such as painting a horse to look like a zebra to examine the extent to which category membership judgments are controlled by superficial perceptual properties. Biological theories determine membership judgments quite early on (Keil, 1987; Keil and Kelly, 1987). Rips (1989) has used the same technique to show that similarity is neither necessary nor sufficient to determine category membership. It even appears to be the case that theories can affect judgments of similarity. For example, Medin and Shoben (1988) found that the terms *white hair* and *grey hair* were judged to be more similar than *grey hair* and *black hair*, but that the terms *white clouds* and *grey clouds* were judged as less similar than *grey clouds* and *black clouds*. Our interpretation is that white and grey hair are linked by a theory (of aging) in a way that white and grey clouds are not.

The above observations are challenging for defenders of the idea that similarity drives conceptual organization. In fact, one might wonder if the notion of similarity is so loose and unconstrained that we might be better off without it. Goodman (1972) epitomized this attitude by calling similarity "a pretender, an imposter, a quack" (p. 437). After reviewing some reasons to continue to take similarity seriously, I outline one possible route for integrating similarity-based and theory-based categorization.

The Need for Similarity

So far I have suggested that similarity relations do not provide conceptual coherence but that theories do. Because a major problem with similarity is that it is so unconstrained, one might ask what constrains theories. If we cannot identify constraints on theories, that is, say something about why we have the theories we have and not others, then we have not solved the problem of coherence: It simply has been shifted to another level. Although I believe we can specify some general properties of theories and develop a psychology of explanation (e.g., Abelson and Lalljee, 1988; Einhorn and Hogarth, 1986; Hilton and Slugoski, 1986; Leddo, Abelson, and Gross, 1984), I equally believe that a constrained form of similarity will play an important role in our understanding of human concepts. This role is not to provide structure so much as it is to guide learners toward structure.

The impact of more direct perceptual similarity on the development of causal explanations is evident in the structure of people's naive theories. Frazer's (1995) cross-cultural analysis of belief systems pointed to the ubiquity of two principles, homeopathy and contagion. The principle of homeopathy is that causes and effects tend to be similar. One manifestation of this principle is homeopathic medicine, in which the cure (and the cause) are seen to resemble the symptoms.

In the Azande culture, for example, the cure for ringworm is to apply fowl's excrement because the excrement looks like the ringworm. Schweder (1977) adduced strong support for the claim that resemblance is a fundamental conceptual tool of everyday thinking in all cultures, not just so-called primitive cultures.

Contagion is the principle that a cause must have some form of contact to transmit its effect. In general, the more contiguous (temporally and spatially similar) events are in time and space, the more likely they are to be perceived as causally related (e.g., Dickinson, Shanks, and Evenden, 1984; Michotte, 1963). People also tend to assume that causes and effects should be of similar magnitude. Einhorn and Hogarth (1986) pointed out that the germ theory of disease initially met with great resistance because people could not imagine how such tiny organisms could have such devastating effects.

It is important to recognize that homeopathy and contagion often point us in the right direction. Immunization can be seen as a form of homeopathic medicine that has an underlying theoretical principle to support it. My reading of these observations, however, is not that specific theoretical (causal) principles are constraining similarity but rather that similarity (homeopathy and contagion) acts as a constraint on the search for causal explanations. Even in classical conditioning studies, the similarity of the conditioned stimulus and the unconditioned stimulus can have a major influence on the rate of conditioning (Testa, 1974). Of course, similarity must itself be constrained for terms like homeopathy to have a meaning. Shortly, I will suggest some constraints on similarity as part of an effort to define a role for similarity in conceptual development.

Similarity is likely to have a significant effect on explanations in another way. Given the importance of similarity in retrieval, it is likely that explanations that are applied to a novel event are constrained by similar events and their associated explanations. For example, Read (1983) found that people may rely on single, similar instances in making causal attributions about behaviors. Furthermore, Ross (1984) and Gentner and Landers (1985) have found that superficial similarities and not just similarity with respect to deeper principles or relations play a major role in determining the remindings associated with problem solving and the use of analogy.

In brief, it seems that similarity cannot be banished from the world of theories and conceptual structures. But it seems to me that a theory of similarity is needed that is quite different in character from the one summarized in Table 5.1. I will suggest an alternative view of similarity and then attempt to show its value in integrating and explanation with respect to concepts.

Similarity and Theory in Conceptual Structure

A Contrasting Similarity Model

The following are key tenets of the type of similarity theory needed to link similarity with knowledge-based categorization: (a) Similarity needs to include attributes, relations, and higher-order relations. (b) Properties in general are not independent but rather are linked by a variety of interproperty relations. (c) Properties exist at multiple levels of abstraction. (d) Concepts are more than lists. Properties and relations create depth or structure. Each of the four main ideas directly conflicts with the corresponding assumption of the theory of similarity outlined earlier. In one way or another all of these assumptions are tied to structure. The general idea I am proposing is far from new. In the psychology of visual perception, the need for structural approaches to similarity has been a continuing, if not major, theme (e.g., Biederman, 1985, 1987; Palmer, 1975, 1978; Pomerantz, Sager, and Stoever, 1977). Oden and Lopes (1982) have argued that this view can inform our understanding of concepts: "Although similarity must function at some level in the induction of concepts, the induced categories are not 'held together' subjectively by the undifferentiated 'force' of similarity, but rather by structural principles" (p. 78). Nonindependence of properties and simple and higher-order relations add a dimension of depth to categorization. Depth has clear implications for many of the observations that seem so problematic for probabilistic view theories. I turn now to the question of how these modified similarity notions may link up with theory-based categorization.

Psychological Essentialism

Despite the overwhelming evidence against the classical view, there is something about it that is intuitively compelling. Recently I and my colleagues have begun to take this observation seriously, not for its metaphysical implications but as a piece of psychological data (Medin and Ortony, 1989; Medin and Wattenmaker, 1987; Wattenmaker, Nakamura, and Medin, 1988). One might call this framework "psychological essentialism." The main ideas are as follows: People act as if things (e.g., objects) have essences or underlying natures that make them the thing that they are. Furthermore, the essence constrains or generates properties that may vary in their centrality. One of the things that theories do is to embody or provide causal linkages from deeper properties to more superficial or surface properties. For example, people in our culture believe that the categories *male* and *female* are genetically determined, but to pick someone out as male or female we rely on characteristics such as hair length, height, facial hair, and clothing that represent a mixture of secondary sexual characteristics and cultural conventions. Although these characteristics are more unreliable than genetic evidence, they are far from arbitrary. Not only do they have some validity in a statistical sense, but also they are tied to our biological and cultural conceptions of *male* and *female*.

It is important to note that psychological essentialism refers not to how the world is but rather to how people approach the world. Wastebaskets probably have no true essence, although we may act as if they do. Both social and psychodiagnostic categories are at least partially culture specific and may have weak if any metaphysical underpinnings (see also Morey and McNamara, 1987).

If psychological essentialism is bad metaphysics, why should people act as if things had essences? The reason is that is may prove to be good epistomology. One could say that people adopt an *essentialist heuristic*, namely, the hypothesis that things that look alike tend to share deeper properties (similarities). Our perceptual and conceptual systems appear to have evolved such that the essentialist heuristic is very often correct (Medin and Wattenmaker, 1987; Shepard, 1984). This is true even for human artifacts such as cars, computers, and camping stoves because structure and function tend to be correlated. Surface characteristics that are perceptually obvious or are readily produced on feature listing tasks may not so much constitute the core of a concept as point toward it. This observation suggests that classifying on the basis of similarity will be relatively effective much of the time, but that similarity will yield to knowledge of deeper principles.

Thus, in the work of Gelman and Markman (1986a) discussed earlier, category membership was more important than perceptual similarity in determining inductive inferences.

Related Evidence

The contrasting similarity principles presented earlier coupled with psychological essentialism provide a framework for integrating knowledge-based and similarity-based categorization. Although it is far short of a formal theory, the framework provides a useful perspective on many of the issues under discussion in this article.

1. Nonindependence of Features Earlier I mentioned that classifying on the basis of similarity to a prototype was functionally equivalent to adding up the evidence favoring a classification and applying some criterion (at least X out of Y features). Recall also that the data ran strongly against this idea. From the perspective currently under consideration, however, there ought to be two ways to produce data consistent with prototype theory. One would be to provide a theory that suggests the prototype as an ideal or that makes summing of evidence more natural. For example, suppose that the characteristic properties for one category were as follows: it is made of metal, has a regular surface, is of medium size, and is easy to grasp. For a contrasting category the characteristic properties were: it is made of rubber, has an irregular surface, is of small size, and is hard to grasp. The categories may not seem sensible or coherent but suppose one adds the information that the objects in one category could serve as substitutes for a hammer. Given this new information, it becomes easy to add up the properties of examples in terms of their utility in supporting hammering. In a series of studies using the above descriptions and related examples, Wattenmaker et al. (1986) found data consistent with prototype theory when the additional information was supplied, and data inconsistent with prototype theory when only characteristic properties were supplied. Specifically, they found that linearly separable categories were easier to learn than nonlinearly separable categories only when an organizing theme was provided (see also Nakamura, 1985).

One might think that prototypes become important whenever the categories are meaningful. That is not the case. When themes are provided that are not compatible with a summing of evidence, the data are inconsistent with prototype theories. For instance, suppose that the examples consisted of descriptions of animals and that the organizing theme was that one category consisted of prey and the other of predators. It is a good adaptation for prey to be armored and to live in trees, but an animal that is both armored and lives in trees may not be better adapted than an animal with either characteristic alone. Being armored and living in trees may be somewhat incompatible. Other studies by Wattenmaker et al. using directly analogous materials failed to find any evidence that linear separability (and, presumably, summing of evidence) was important or natural. Only some kinds of interproperty relations are compatible with a summing of evidence, and evidence favoring prototypes may be confined to these cases.

The above studies show that the ease or naturalness of classification tasks cannot be predicted in terms of abstract category structures based on distribution of features, but rather requires an understanding of the knowledge brought to bear on them, for this knowledge determines interproperty relationships. So far only a few types of interproperty relationships have been explored in categorization, and much is to be gained from the careful study of further types of relations (e.g., see Barr and Caplan, 1987; Chaffin and Hermann, 1987; Rips and Conrad, 1989; Winston, Chaffin, and Hermann, 1987).

2. Levels of Features   Although experimenters can often contrive to have the features or properties comprising stimulus materials at roughly the same level of abstractness, in more typical circumstances levels may vary substantially. This fact has critical implications for descriptions of category structure (see Barsalou and Billman, 1988). This point may be best represented by an example from some ongoing research I am conducting with Glenn Nakamura and Ed Wisniewski. Our stimulus materials consist of children's drawings of people, a sample of which is shown in Figure 5.1. There are two sets of five drawings, one on the left and one on the right. The task of the participants in this experiment is to come up with a rule that could be used to correctly classify both these drawings and new examples that might be presented later.

Figure 5.1
Children's drawings of people used in the rule induction studies by Nakamura, Wisniewski, and Medin.

One of our primary aims in this study was to examine the effects of different types of knowledge structures on rule induction. Consequently, some participants were told that one set was done by farm children and the other by city children; some were told that one set was done by creative children and the other by noncreative children; and still others were told that one set was done by emotionally disturbed children and the other by mentally healthy children. The exact assignment of drawings was counterbalanced with respect to the categories such that half the time the drawings on the left of Figure 5.1 were labeled as done by farm children and half the time the drawings on the right were labeled as having been done by farm children.

Although we were obviously expecting differences in the various conditions, in some respects the most striking result is one that held across conditions. Almost without exception the rules that people gave had properties at two or three different levels of abstractness. For example, one person who was told the drawings on the left were done by city children gave the following rule: "The city drawings use more profiles, and are more elaborate. The clothes are more detailed, showing both pockets and buttons, and the hair is drawn in. The drawings put less emphasis on proportion and the legs and torso are off." Another person who was told the same drawings were done by farm children wrote: "The children draw what they see in their normal life. The people have overalls on and some drawings show body muscles as a result of labor. The drawings are also more detailed. One can see more facial details and one drawing has colored the clothes and another one shows the body under the clothes." As one can see, the rules typically consist of a general assertion or assertions coupled with either an operational definition or examples to illustrate and clarify the assertion. In some cases these definitions or examples extend across several levels of abstractness.

One might think that our participants used different levels of description because there was nothing else for them to do. That is, there may have been no low-level perceptual features that would separate the groups. In a followup study we presented examples one at a time and asked people to give their rule after each example. If people are being forced to use multiple levels of description because simple rules will not work, then we should observe a systematic increase in the use of multiple levels across examples. In fact, however, we observed multiple levels of description as the predominant strategy from the first example on. We believe that multiple levels arise when people try to find a link between abstract explanatory principles or ideas (drawings reflect one's experience) and specific details of drawings.

There are several important consequences of multilevel descriptions. First of all, the relation across levels is not necessarily a subset, superset, or a part–whole relation. Most of the time one would say that the lower level property "supports" the higher level property; for example, "jumping into a swimming pool with one's clothes on" supports poor judgment. This underlines the point that categorization often involves more than a simple matching of properties. A related point is that features are ambiguous in the sense that they may support more than one higher level property. When the drawings on the right were associated with the label *mentally healthy*, a common description was "all the faces are smiling." When the label for the same drawing was *noncreative*, a common description was "the faces show little variability in expression." Finally, it should be obvious that whether a category description is disjunctive (e.g., pig's nose or cow's mouth or catlike ears) or conjunctive or defining (e.g., all have animal parts) depends on the level with respect to which the rule is evaluated.

3. Centrality If properties are at different levels of abstraction and linked by a variety of relations, then one might imagine that some properties are more central than others because of the role they play in conceptual structure. An indication that properties differ in their centrality comes from a provocative study by Asch and Zukier (1984). They presented people with trait terms that appeared to be contradictory (e.g., kind and vindictive) and asked participants if these descriptions could be resolved (e.g., how could a person be both kind and vindictive?). Participants had no difficulty integrating the pairs of terms, and Asch and Zukier identified seven major resolution strategies. For present purposes, what is notable is that many of the resolution strategies involve making one trait term more central than the other one. For example, one way of integrating *kind* and *vindictive* was to say that the person was fundamentally evil and was kind only in the service of vindictive ends.

In related work, Shoben and I (Medin and Shoben, 1988) showed that centrality of a property depends on the concept of which it is a part. We asked participants to judge the typicality of adjective noun pairs when the adjective was a property that other participants judged was not true of the noun representing the concept. For example, our participants judged that all bananas and all boomerangs are curved. Based on this observation, other participants were asked to judge the typicality of a straight banana as a banana or a straight boomerang as a boomerang. Other instances of the 20 pairs used include *soft knife* versus *soft diamond* and *polka dot fire hydrant* versus *polka dot yield sign*. For 19 of the 20 pairs, participants rated one item of a pair as more typical than the other. Straight banana, soft knife, and polka dot fire hydrant were rated as more typical than straight boomerang, soft diamond, and polka dot yield sign. In the case of boomerangs (and probably yield signs), centrality may be driven by structure–function correlations. Soft diamonds are probably rated as very atypical because hardness is linked to many other properties and finding out that diamonds were soft would call a great deal of other knowledge into question.

Most recently, Woo Kyoung Ahn, Joshua Rubenstein, and I have been interviewing clinical psychologists and psychiatrists concerning their understanding of psychodiagnostic categories. Although our project is not far enough along to report any detailed results, it is clear that the *DSM-IIIR* guidebook (American Psychiatric Association, 1987) provides only a skeletal outline that is brought to life by theories and causal scenarios underlying and intertwined with the symptoms that comprise the diagnostic criteria. Symptoms differ in the level of abstractness and the types and number of intersymptom relations in which they participate, and as a consequence, they differ in their centrality.

Conclusions

The shift to a focus on knowledge-based categorization does not mean that the notion of similarity must be left behind. But we do need an updated approach to, and interpretation of, similarity. The mounting evidence on the role of theories and explanations in organizing categories is much more compatible with features at varying levels linked by a variety of interproperty relations than it is with independent features at a single level. In addition, similarity may not so much constitute structure as point toward it. There is a dimension of depth to categorization. The conjectures about psychological essentialism may be one way of reconciling classification in terms of perceptual similarity or surface properties with the deeper substance of knowledge-rich, theory-based categorization.

Acknowledgment

The research described in this chapter was supported in part by National Science Foundation Grant No. BNS 84-19756 and by National Library of Medicine Grant No. LM 04375. Brian Ross, Edward Shoben, Ellen Markman, Greg Oden, and Dedre Gentner provided helpful comments on an earlier draft of the article.

References

Abelson, R. P., and Lalljee, M. G. (1988). Knowledge-structures and causal explanation. In D. J. Hilton (Ed.), *Contemporary science and natural explanation: Commonsense conceptions of causality* (pp. 175–202). Brighton, England: Harvester Press.

Allen, S. W., Brooks, L. R., Norman, G. R., and Rosenthal, D. (1988, November). *Effect of prior examples on rule-based diagnostic performance.* Paper presented at the meeting of the Psychonomic Society, Chicago.

American Psychiatric Association. (1987). *Diagnostic and statistical manual of mental disorders* (rev. ed.). Washington, DC: Author.

Anderson, J. R. (1988). The place of cognitive architectures in a rational analysis. In *The Tenth Annual Conference of the Cognitive Science Society* (pp. 1–10). Montreal, Canada: University of Montreal.

Arkes, H. R., and Harkness, A. R. (1980). Effect of making a diagnosis on subsequent recognition of symptoms. *Journal of Experimental Psychology: Human Learning and Memory, 6,* 568–575.

Armstrong, S. L., Gleitman, L. R., and Gleitman, H. (1983). What some concepts might not be. *Cognition, 13,* 263–308.

Asch, S. E., and Zukier, H. (1984). Thinking about persons. *Journal of Personality and Social Psychology, 46,* 1230–1240.

Barr, R. A., and Caplan, L. J. (1987). Category representations and their implications for category structure. *Memory and Cognition, 15,* 397–418.

Barsalou, L. W. (1983). Ad hoc categories. *Memory and Cognition, 11*, 211–227.

Barsalou, L. W. (1985). Ideals, central tendency, and frequency of instantiation as determinants of graded structure in categories. *Journal of Experimental Psychology: Learning, Memory and Cognition, 11*, 629–654.

Barsalou, L. W. (1987). The instability of graded structure: Implications for the nature of concepts. In U. Neisser (Ed.), *Concepts and conceptual development: The ecological and intellectual factors in categorization* (pp. 101–140). Cambridge, England: Cambridge University Press.

Barsalou, L. W. (1989). Intra-concept similarity and its implications for inter-concept similarity. In S. Vosniadou and A. Ortony (Eds.), *Similarity and analogical reasoning* (pp. 76–121). Cambridge, England: Cambridge University Press.

Barsalou, L. W., and Billman, D. (1988, April). *Systematicity and semantic ambiguity*. Paper presented at a workshop on semantic ambiguity, Adelphi University.

Barsalou, L. W., and Medin, D. L. (1986). Concepts: Fixed definitions or dynamic context-dependent representations? *Cahiers de Psychologie Cognitive, 6*, 187–202.

Bellezza, F. S. (1984). Reliability of retrieval from semantic memory: Noun meanings. *Bulletin of the Psychonomic Society, 22*, 377–380.

Biederman, I. (1985). Human image understanding: Recent research and a theory. *Computer Vision, Graphics, and Image Processing, 32*, 29–83.

Biederman, I. (1987). Recognition-by-components: A theory of human image understanding. *Psychological Review, 94*, 115–147.

Cantor, N., and Mischel, W. (1977). Traits as prototypes: Effects on recognition memory. *Journal of Personality and Social Psychology, 35*, 38–48.

Carey, S. (1985). *Conceptual change in childhood*. Cambridge, MA: MIT Press.

Chaffin, R., and Herrmann, D. J. (1987). Relation element theory: A new account of the representation and processing of semantic relations. In D. Gorfein and R. Hoffman (Eds.), *Learning and memory: The Ebbinghaus centennial conference* (pp. 221–245). Hillsdale, NJ: Erlbaum.

Dickinson, A., Shanks, D., and Evenden, J. (1984). Judgment of act-outcomes contingency: The role of selective attribution. *Quarterly Journal of Experimental Psychology, 36A*(1), 29–50.

Einhorn, J. H., and Hogarth, R. M. (1986). Judging probable cause. *Psychological Bulletin, 99*, 3–19.

Estes, W. K. (1986a). Memory storage and retrieval processes in category learning. *Journal of Experimental Psychology: General, 115*, 155–175.

Estes, W. K. (1986b). Array models for category learning. *Cognitive Psychology, 18*, 500–549.

Fehr, B. (1988). Prototype analysis of the concepts of love and commitment. *Journal of Personality and Social Psychology, 55*, 557–579.

Fehr, B., and Russell, J. A. (1984). Concepts of emotion viewed from a prototype perspective. *Journal of Experimental Psychology: General, 113*, 464–486.

Flannagan, M. J., Fried, L. S., and Holyoak, K. J. (1986). Distributional expectations and the induction of category structure. *Journal of Experimental Psychology: Learning, Memory and Cognition, 12*, 241–256.

Frazer, J. G. (1959). *The new golden bough*, New York: Criterion Books.

Fried, L. S., and Holyoak, K. J. (1984). Induction of category distribution: A framework for classification learning. *Journal of Experimental Psychology: Learning, Memory and Cognition, 10*, 234–257.

Gati, I., and Tversky, A. (1984). Weighting common and distinctive features in perceptual and conceptual judgments. *Cognitive Psychology, 16*, 341–370.

Gelman, S. A. (1988). The development of induction within natural kind and artifact categories. *Cognitive Psychology, 20*, 65–95.

Gelman, S. A., and Markman, E. M. (1986a). Categories and induction in young children. *Cognition, 23*, 183–209.

Gelman, S. A., and Markman, E. M. (1986b). Young children's inductions from natural kinds: The role of categories and appearances. *Child Development, 58*, 1532–1541.

Genero, N., and Cantor, N. (1987). Exemplar prototypes and clinical diagnosis: Toward a cognitive economy. *Journal of Social and Clinical Psychology, 5*, 59–78.

Gentner, D., and Landers, R. (1985). *Analogical reminding: A good match is hard to find*. Paper presented at the International Conference of Systems, Man and Cybernetics, Tucson, AZ.

Goldin, S. E. (1978). Memory for the ordinary: Typicality effects in chess memory. *Journal of Experimental Psychology: Human Learning and Memory, 4*, 605–616.

Goodman, N. (1972). Seven strictures on similarity. In N. Goodman (Ed.), *Problems and projects*. New York: Bobbs-Merrill.

Hartley, J., and Homa, D. (1981). Abstraction of stylistic concepts. *Journal of Experimental Psychology: Human Learning and Memory, 7*, 33–46.

Hilton, D. J., and Slugoski, B. R. (1986). Knowledge-based causal attribution: The abnormal conditions focus model. *Psychological Review, 93*, 75–88.

Hintzman, D. L. (1986). "Schema abstraction" in a multiple-trace memory model. *Psychological Review, 93*, 411–428.

Homa, D. (1984). On the nature of categories. In G. Bower (Ed.), *The psychology of learning and motivation* (Vol. 18, pp. 49–94). New York: Academic Press.

Homa, D., and Vosburgh, R. (1976). Category breadth and the abstraction of prototypical information. *JEP: Human Learning and Memory, 2*, 322–330.

Keil, F. C. (1979). *Semantic and conceptual development: An ontological perspective*. Cambridge, MA: Harvard University Press.

Keil, F. C. (1981). Constraints on knowledge and cognitive development. *Psychological Review*, *88*, 197–227.

Keil, F. C. (1986). The acquisition of natural kind and artifact terms. In W. Demopoulos and A. Marras (Eds.), *Language learning and concept acquisition* (pp. 133–153). Norwood, NJ: Ablex.

Keil, F. C. (1987). Conceptual development and category structure. In U. Neisser (Ed.), *Concepts and conceptual development: Ecological and intellectual factors in categorization* (pp. 175–200). Cambridge, England: Cambridge University Press.

Keil, F. C., and Kelly, M. H. (1987). Developmental changes in category structure. In S. Harnad (Ed.), *Categorical perception: The groundwork of cognition* (pp. 491–510). Cambridge, England: Cambridge University Press.

Kemler-Nelson, D. G. (1984). The effect of intention on what concepts are acquired. *Journal of Verbal Learning and Verbal Behavior*, *23*, 734–759.

Kolodner, J. L. (1984). *Retrieval and organizational structures in conceptual memory: A computer model*. Hillsdale, NJ: Erlbaum.

Lakoff, G. (1987). *Women, fire, and dangerous things: What categories tell us about the nature of thought*. Chicago: University of Chicago Press.

Leddo, J., Abelson, R. P., and Gross, P. H. (1984). Conjunctive explanation: When two explanations are better than one. *Journal of Personality and Social Psychology*, *47*, 933–943.

Malt, B. C., and Smith, E. E. (1983). Correlated properties in natural categories. *Journal of Verbal Learning and Verbal Behavior*, *23*, 250–269.

Markman, E. M. (1987). How children constrain the possible meanings of words. In U. Neisser (Ed.), *Concepts and conceptual development: The ecological and intellectual factors in categorization* (pp. 256–287). Cambridge, England: Cambridge University Press.

Massey, C. M., and Gelman, R. (1988). Preschoolers' ability to decide whether a photographed unfamiliar object can move itself. *Developmental Psychology*, *24*, 307–317.

McCloskey, M., and Glucksberg, S. (1978). Natural categories: Well-defined or fuzzy sets? *Memory and Cognition*, *6*, 462–472.

McNamara, T. P., and Sternberg, R. J. (1983). Mental models of word meaning. *Journal of Verbal Learning and Verbal Behavior*, *22*, 449–474.

Medin, D. L. (1986). Commentary on "Memory storage and retrieval processes in category learning." *Journal of Experimental Psychology: General*, *115*(4), 373–381.

Medin, D. L., Altom, M. W., Edelson, S. M., and Freko, D. (1982). Correlated symptoms and simulated medical classification. *Journal of Experimental Psychology: Learning, Memory and Cognition*, *8*, 37–50.

Medin, D. L., and Ortony, A. (1989). Psychological essentialism. In S. Vosniadou and A. Ortony (Eds.), *Similarity and analogical reasoning* (pp. 179–195). New York: Cambridge University Press.

Medin, D. L., and Ross, B. H. (1989). The specific character of abstract thought: Categorization, problem-solving, and induction. In R. J. Sternberg (Ed.), *Advances in the psychology of human intelligence* (Vol. 5, pp. 189–223). Hillsdale, NJ: Erlbaum.

Medin, D. L., and Schaffer, M. M. (1978). A context theory of classification learning. *Psychological Review, 85,* 207–238.

Medin, D. L., and Schwanenflugel, P. J. (1981). Linear separability in classification learning. *Journal of Experimental Psychology: Human Learning and Memory, 7,* 355–368.

Medin, D. L., and Shoben, E. J. (1988). Context and structure in conceptual combination. *Cognitive Psychology, 20,* 158–190.

Medin, D. L., and Smith, E. E. (1984). Concepts and concept formation. In M. R. Rosenzweig and L. W. Porter (Eds.), *Annual Review of Psychology, 35,* 113–118.

Medin, D. L., and Wattenmaker, W. D. (1987). Category cohesiveness, theories, and cognitive archeology. In U. Neisser (Ed.), *Concepts and conceptual development: The ecological and intellectual factors in categories* (pp. 25–62). Cambridge, England: Cambridge University Press.

Mervis, C. B., and Rosch, E. (1981). Categorization of natural objects. In M. R. Rosenzweig and L. W. Porter (Eds.), *Annual Review of Psychology, 32,* 89–115.

Michotte, A. (1963). *Perception of causality.* London: Methuen.

Morey, L. C., and McNamara, T. P. (1987). On definitions, diagnosis, and DSM-III. *Journal of Abnormal Psychology, 96,* 283–285.

Murphy, G. L., and Medin, D. L. (1985). The role of theories in conceptual coherence. *Psychological Review, 92,* 289–316.

Nakamura, G. V. (1985). Knowledge-based classification of ill-defined categories. *Memory and Cognition, 13,* 377–384.

Nosofsky, R. M. (1987). Attention and learning processes in the identification and categorization of integral stimuli. *Journal of Experimental Psychology: Learning, Memory, and Cognition, 13,* 87–108.

Nosofsky, R. M. (1988a). Exemplar-based accounts of relations between classification, recognition, and typicality. *Journal of Experimental Psychology: Learning, Memory, and Cognition, 14,* 700–708.

Nosofsky, R. M. (1988b). Similarity, frequency, and category representations. *Journal of Experimental Psychology: Learning, Memory, and Cognition, 14,* 54–65.

Oden, G. C., (1987). Concept, knowledge, and thought. In M. R. Rosenzweig and L. W. Porter (Eds.), *Annual Review of Psychology, 38,* 203–227.

Oden, G. C. and Lopes, L. (1982). On the internal structure of fuzzy subjective categories. In R. R. Yager (Ed.), *Recent developments in fuzzy set and possibility theory* (pp. 75–89). Elmsford, NY: Pergamon Press.

Ortony, A., Vondruska, R. J., Foss, M. A., and Jones, L. E. (1985). Salience, similes, and the asymmetry of similarity. *Journal of Memory and Language, 24,* 569–594.

Palmer, S. E. (1975). Visual perception and world knowledge. In D. A. Norman and D. E. Rumelhart (Eds.), *Explorations in cognition* (pp. 279–307). San Francisco: W. H. Freeman.

Palmer, S. E. (1978). Structural aspects of visual similarity. *Memory and Cognition, 6,* 91–97.

Peterson, M. J., Meagher, R. B., Jr., Chait, H., and Gillie, S. (1973). The abstraction and generalization of dot patterns. *Cognitive Psychology, 4,* 378–398.

Pomerantz, J. R., Sager, L. C., and Stoever, R. G. (1977). Perception of wholes and their component parts: Some configural superiority effects. *Journal of Experimental Psychology: Human Perception and Performance, 3,* 422–435.

Read, S. J. (1983). Once is enough: Causal reasoning from a single instance. *Journal of Personality and Social Psychology, 45,* 323–334.

Rips, L. (1989). Similarity, typicality, and categorization. In S. Vosniadou and A. Ortony (Eds.), *Similarity and analogical reasoning* (pp. 21–59). New York: Cambridge University Press.

Rips, L. J., and Conrad, F. G. (1989). The folk psychology of mental activities. *Psychological Review, 96,* 187–207.

Rosch, E. (1975). Cognitive representations of semantic categories. *Journal of Experimental Psychology: General, 104,* 192–233.

Rosch, E., and Mervis, C. B. (1975). Family resemblances: Studies in the internal structure of categories. *Cognitive Psychology, 7,* 573–605.

Ross, B. H. (1984). Remindings and their effects in learning a cognitive skill. *Cognitive Psychology, 16,* 371–416.

Roth, E. M., and Shoben, E. J. (1983). The effect of context on the structure of categories. *Cognitive Psychology, 15,* 346–378.

Schank, R. C., Collins, G. C., and Hunter, L. E. (1986). Transcending induction category formation in learning. *The Behavioral and Brain Sciences, 9,* 639–686.

Schweder, R. A. (1977). Likeness and likelihood in everyday thought: Magical thinking in judgments about personality. *Current Anthropology, 18,* 4.

Sebestyn, G. S. (1962). *Decision-making processes in pattern recognition.* New York: Macmillan.

Shepard, R. H. (1984). Ecological constraints on internal representation: Resonant kinematics of perceiving, imagining, thinking, and dreaming. *Psychological Review, 19,* 417–447.

Shepard, R. N., Hovland, C. I., and Jenkins, H. M. (1961). Learning and memorization of classifications. *Psychological Monographs, 75,* (13, Whole No. 517).

Smith, E. E., and Medin, D. L. (1981). *Categories and concepts.* Cambridge, MA: Harvard University Press.

Smith, E. E., Rips, J. J., and Medin, D. W. (1984). A psychological approach to concepts: Comments on Rey's "Concepts and stereotypes." *Cognition, 17,* 265–274.

Smith, E. E., Shoben, E. J., and Rips, J. J. (1974). Structure and processes in semantic memory: A featural model for semantic decisions. *Psychological Review, 81,* 214–241.

Sommers, F. (1971). Structural ontology. *Philosophia, 1,* 21–42.

Testa, T. J. (1974). Causal relationships and the acquisition of avoidance responses. *Psychological Review, 81,* 491–505.

Tulving, E. (1983). *Elements of episodic memory.* New York: Oxford University Press.

Tversky, A. (1977). Features of similarity. *Psychological Review, 84,* 327–352.

Watanabe, S. (1969). *Knowing and guessing: A formal and quantitative study.* New York: Wiley.

Wattenmaker, W. D., Dewey, G. I., Murphy, T. D., and Medin, D. L. (1986). Linear separability and concept learning: Context, relational properties, and concept naturalness. *Cognitive Psychology, 18,* 158–194.

Wattenmaker, W. D., Nakamura, G. V., and Medin, D. L. (1988). Relationships between similarity-based and explanation-based categorization. In D. Hilton (Ed.), *Contemporary science and natural explanation: Commonsense conceptions of causality* (pp. 205–241). Brighton, England: Harvester Press.

Winston, M. E., Chaffin, R., and Herrmann, D. (1987). A taxonomy of part–whole relations. *Cognitive Science, 11,* 417–444.

Wittgenstein, L. (1953). *Philosophical investigations* (G. E. M. Anscombe, trans.). Oxford, England: Blackwell.

6

Structure Mapping in Analogy and Similarity

Dedre Gentner and Arthur B. Markman

Analogy and similarity are often assumed to be distinct psychological processes. In contrast to this position, the authors suggest that both similarity and analogy involve a process of structural alignment and mapping, that is, that similarity is like analogy. In this article, the authors first describe the structure-mapping process as it has been worked out for analogy. Then, this view is extended to similarity, where it is used to generate new predictions. Finally, the authors explore broader implications of structural alignment for psychological processing.

Analogy and similarity are central in cognitive processing. They are often viewed as quite separate: Analogy is a clever, sophisticated process used in creative discovery, whereas similarity is a brute perceptual process that we share with the entire animal kingdom. This view of similarity has important implications for the way we model human thinking, because similarity is demonstrably important across many areas of cognition. We store experiences in categories largely on the basis of their similarity to a category representation or to stored exemplars (Smith and Medin, 1981). In transfer, new problems are solved using procedures taken from prior similar problems (Bassok, 1990; Holyoak and Koh, 1987; Keane, 1988; Kolodner, 1993; Novick, 1988, 1990; Ross, 1987, 1989; Winston, 1980), and inferences about people are influenced by their similarity to other known individuals (Andersen and Cole, 1990; Read, 1984). Even the way we respond affectively to a situation may be based in part on our responses to previous similar situations (Kahneman and Miller, 1986). Thus, an understanding of similarity processing may provide general insight into human thinking.

In our research, we have taken a very different route from the "stars above, mud below" view of analogy and similarity. We suggest that the process of carrying out a comparison is the same in both cases. The general idea is summarized by the slogan "similarity is like analogy" (Gentner and Markman, 1995; Markman and Gentner, 1993a; Medin, Goldstone, and Gentner, 1993). We summarize recent evidence suggesting that the process involved in both similarity and analogy comparisons is one of structural alignment and mapping between mental representations (Falkenhainer, Forbus, and Gentner, 1989; Gentner, 1983, 1989; Gentner and Markman, 1993, 1994, 1995; Goldstone, 1994b; Goldstone and Medin, 1994; Goldstone, Medin, and Gentner, 1991; Markman and Gentner, 1993a, 1993b; Medin, Goldstone, and Gentner, 1993). We begin with creative analogy and then turn to similarity.

Analogy

Johannes Kepler was a great discoverer and a prolific analogizer. He was an early champion of Copernicus's (1543/1992) proposal that the earth and other planets moved, rather than the sun. In 1596, in the course of trying to work out the laws of planetary motion, Kepler found himself asking a seemingly simple question: Why is it that the outermost planets move slower than the innermost planets? According to the best existing models, the planets' motion was caused by planetary spirits or souls that impelled the planets on their courses. As Kepler noted, one possibility was that the spirits that moved the outer planets just happened to be weaker than the spirits that moved the inner planets; but he proposed instead the radical idea that there is one spirit or power emanating from the sun that moves all the planets: that is, that the sun causes the motion of the planets.[1] Kepler had hit upon a major idea, an important precursor of gravity. But there was a seemingly fatal objection. For the sun to move the planets would require action at a distance, an abhorrent notion to any physical scientist (including Newton, when he developed the full theory of gravity some 80 years later).

Kepler's response to this self-posed challenge was to consider an analogy to light. In his *Astronomia Nova* (*The New Astronomy*, 1609/ 1992), Kepler developed this analogy between the motive power and light (see Gentner et al., in press, for details):

But lest I appear to philosophize with excessive insolence, I shall propose to the reader the clearly authentic example of light, since it also makes its nest in the sun, thence to break forth into the whole world as a companion to this motive power. Who, I ask, will say that light is something material? Nevertheless, it carries out its operations with respect to place, suffers alteration, is reflected and refracted, and assumes quantities so as to be dense or rare, and to be capable of being taken as a surface wherever it falls upon something illuminable. Now just as it is said in optics, that light does not exist in the intermediate space between the source and the illuminable, this is equally true of the motive power. (*Astronomia Nova*, p. 383)

If light can travel undetectably on its way between the source and destination, yet illuminate its destination, then so too could the motive force be undetectable on its way from sun to planet, yet affect the planet's motion once it arrives at the planet. But Kepler was not content with a mere proof of possibility. He pushed the analogy further. He used it to state why the motive power diminishes with distance: Just as the light from a lamp shines brighter on near objects than on further ones, so it is with the sun's motive power, and for the same reason: The motive power (like the light) is not lost as it disperses but is spread out over a greater area. Because nothing is lost as the emission spreads from the source, Kepler (1609/1992) argued, "The emission, then, in the same manner as light, is immaterial, unlike odours, which are accompanied by a diminution of substance, and unlike heat from a hot furnace, or anything similar which fills the intervening space" (p. 381). Here, odors and heat are used as "near-misses" (Winston, 1980)—potential analogs that differ with respect to the key behavior and serve to sharpen the parallel between light and the motive power.

Kepler's analogical model faced further challenges. He had to explain why, given this power emanating from the sun, the planets moved closer and further on their orbits instead of maintaining a constant distance from the sun. To meet these challenges, he again turned to analogy. For example, he invoked a "boatman" analogy to explain the in-and-out motion of the planets. He postulated that the sun rotated around its axis, creating a whirling circular river of motive power that pushed the planets around.[2] Then, as a ferryman can steer his boat (the planet) back and forth orthogonally to the river's current, so the planets could move in and out with only a constant sidewise current of motive power. But although Kepler worked this analogy for decades, he was never satisfied with it; it seemed to require a degree of sentience on the part of the planets to sense how to steer. In another much explored analogy, he likened the sun and planet to two magnets that approach or repel each other depending on which poles are proximate.

Kepler's writings demonstrate the central features of analogy. First, analogy is a device for conveying that two situations or domains share relational structure despite arbitrary degrees of difference in the objects that make up the domains (Gentner, 1983). The magnet analogy, for example, will stand or fall according to whether the causal relations between two magnets are the same as those between the sun and planet, and not according to the resemblance between a magnet and the sun. Common relations are essential to analogy; common objects are not. This promoting of relations over objects makes analogy a useful cognitive device, for physical objects are normally highly salient in human processing—easy to focus on, recognize, encode, retrieve, and so on.

But this is still not specific enough. There is, in general, an indefinite number of possible relations that an analogy could pick out (Goodman, 1972), and most of these are ignored. For example, we may find a spiderweb and a fishing net analogous because both trap their prey, both remain stationary while their prey enters, and so on. But it would not contribute to the analogy to note that "Both are smaller than the Taj Mahal," or "Both are smaller than the Kremlin." How do we select which common relations to pay attention to? The major goal of this article is to demonstrate that the process of comparison—both in analogy and in similarity—operates so as to favor interconnected systems of relations and their arguments.

As the above discussion shows, to capture the process of analogy, we must make assumptions not only about the processes of comparison, but about the nature of typical conceptual cognitive representations and how representations and processes interact (Palmer, 1978). In particular, we must have a representational system that is sufficiently explicit about relational structure to express the causal dependencies that match across the domains. We need a representational scheme capable of expressing not only objects but also the relationships and bindings that hold between them, including higher order relations such as causal relations.[3] One clarification is in order here. To discuss alignment processes, we need to take representation seriously, but this should not be taken to imply a commitment to any particular representation as the best or only possible representation of a situation. (Logically, such a position would be indefensible.) Rather, we assume that the comparison process operates over a person's current representations, however they are derived. Thus, to predict the outcome of a comparison, we should know the person's current psychological construal of the things being compared, including goals and contextual information as well as long-term knowledge.

Structural Alignment View of Analogy and Similarity

The defining characteristic of analogy is that it involves an alignment of relational structure. There are three psychological constraints on this alignment. First, the alignment must be *structurally consistent*: In other words, it must observe parallel connectivity and one-to-one correspondence. *Parallel connectivity* requires that matching relations must have matching arguments, and *one-to-one correspondence* limits any element in one representation to at most one matching element in the other representation (Falkenhainer, Forbus, and Gentner, 1986, 1989; Gentner, 1983, 1989; Gentner and Clement, 1988; Holyoak and Thagard, 1989). For example, in Kepler's (1609/1992) analogy, the planet corresponds to the boat and the sun's power to the river's current, because they play similar roles in a common relational structure. This also shows a second characteristic of analogy, namely, *relational focus*: As discussed above, analogies must involve common relations but need not involve common object descriptions (e.g., it does not detract from the analogy that the planet does not look like a boat). The final characteristic of analogy is *systematicity*: Analogies tend to match connected systems of relations (Gentner, 1983, 1989). A matching set of relations interconnected by higher order constraining relations makes a better analogical match than an equal number of matching relations that are unconnected to each other. The systematicity principle captures a tacit preference for coherence and causal predictive power in analogical processing. We are not much interested in analogies that capture a series of coincidences, even if there are a great many of them.

A particularly striking example of structural dominance in analogy is that of cross-mapping. A *cross-mapping* is a comparison in which two analogous scenarios contain similar or identical objects that play different relational roles in the two scenarios (Gentner and Toupin, 1986; see also Gentner and Rattermann, 1991; Goldstone and Medin, 1994; Markman and Gentner, 1993b; Ross, 1987, 1989). A simple example of a cross-mapping is this simple proportional analogy:

$1:3::3:9.$

The obvious possibility of matching the two identical 3s is dismissed because to do so would misalign the relational roles of the terms. Instead, the object correspondences are $1 \rightarrow 3$ and $3 \rightarrow 9$, preserving the relational commonality (the identical ratio) across the pair.

Given an alignment of structure, further inferences can often be made from the analogy. The implicit preference for systematicity—for aligning of connected systems of knowledge—is crucial here. It is what permits us to generate spontaneous inferences. When we have aligned a system in the base domain with a (typically less complete) system in the target domain, then further statements (*candidate inferences*) connected to the base system in the base can be projected into the target. These candidate inferences are only guesses: Their factual correctness must be checked separately. This uncertainty is appropriate: Any process capable of producing novel true inferences is also capable of generating false inferences.

This kind of spontaneous analogical inference abounds in Kepler's writings. He followed his initial analogy establishing that the motive power (like light) can operate at a distance with a series of further projections (that the motive power [like light] spreads out through space, that it becomes diffused without diminishing in total quantity, etc.). He even asked whether it could undergo an eclipse (he decided not and used this disanalogy to conclude that the motive power cannot be the same thing as the sun's light).

Similarity Is Like Analogy

Kepler's analogical feats are nothing short of amazing. Reflecting on his powers makes it clear why the ability to form analogies has been taken as a sign of intelligence, making the four-term analogy problem a staple of aptitude tests. But consider the following more prosaic example:

Lucas, a 25-month-old child, plays with a new toy that has six colored doors. Each door has its own key—a red key for a red door, a blue key for a blue door, and so on. Lucas opens each door with the key of the corresponding color. Then he sees a seventh white key. He carefully inspects the toy from top to bottom. Then he turns to his parents and asks, "Where the white door?"

Child development is full of these moments, as in the example of Aaron's analogy from self to other discussed in the article by Holyoak and Thagard (1997) or this example contributed by Lise Menn (personal communication, February 1995): Her two-year-old son watched fascinated as some pet ducklings ate. Then he held his arms to his sides and bent down and up like the ducklings. Finally he announced, pointing at the ducklings, "Have no hands!" He had figured out why they ate so differently from him. These kinds of comparison-based discoveries are so commonplace that they are hardly noticeable as anything special, and yet they contain the same essential characteristics of analogical processing that marks Kepler's use of analogy.

In a fundamental sense, similarity is like analogy, in that both involve an alignment of relational structure (Gentner and Markman, 1995). The difference between them is that in analogy, only relational predicates are shared, whereas in literal similarity, both relational predicates and object attributes are shared. In Kepler's analogy, there is no physical resemblance between a boat on a river and a planet revolving around the sun. In Lucas's similarity comparison, each key and door pair is similar to every other, making it easy for Lucas to align the pairs. This contrast between analogy and literal similarity is in fact a continuum, not a dichotomy. Yet it is an important continuum psychologically, because overall similarity comparisons are far easier to notice and map than purely analogical comparisons, especially for novices like Lucas (Gentner, Rattermann, and Forbus, 1993; Holyoak and Koh, 1987; Keane, 1988; Ross, 1989).

Figure 6.1 places this distinction between analogy and similarity within a similarity space defined by the degree of attributional similarity and the degree of relational similarity. *Analogy* occurs when comparisons exhibit a high degree of relational similarity with very

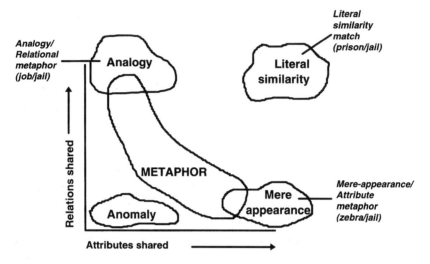

Figure 6.1
Similarity space, showing different kinds of matches in terms of the degree of relational versus object-description overlap.

little attribute similarity. As the amount of attribute similarity increases, the comparison shifts toward literal similarity. *Mere-appearance matches* share object descriptions but not relations. For example, comparing a planet with a round ball would constitute a mere-appearance match. Mere-appearance matches are, in a sense, the opposite of analogies. Such matches are of course sharply limited in their predictive utility. Nonetheless, they are important to consider, because they often occur among children and other novices and may interfere with their learning. The bottom left corner of the space is anomalous comparisons, which share no significant attribute or relational commonalties. Finally, Figure 6.1 shows that metaphors span the range from relational comparisons (e.g., "two lovers like twin compasses") to attribute comparisons (e.g., "a moon like a silver coin").

Process Model of Alignment and Mapping: The Structure-Mapping Engine

We have argued that the comparison process involves a rather sophisticated process of structural alignment and mapping over rich complex representations. A skeptical reader might justifiably inquire at this point whether there is any plausible real-time mechanism that could compute such a structural alignment. This problem is not trivial, and some early models made the assumption that the top-level conclusion or goal of the analogy was known in advance to ease the computational burden (Greiner, 1988; Holyoak, 1985; see Gentner and Clement, 1988, for a discussion). However, these solutions are limited, because people can process analogies without advance knowledge of their meaning. When you read "Philosophy is language idling," you probably understand its meaning without a prior goal context (although a relevant prior context would of course facilitate comprehension). Thus, a process model of comparison should be able to operate without advance knowledge of the final interpretation.

The structure-mapping engine (SME; Falkenhainer et al., 1986, 1989; Forbus, Gentner, and Law, 1995) uses a local-to-global alignment process to arrive at a structural alignment of two representations.[4] Figure 6.2 shows SME's three stages of mapping. In the first stage, SME begins blind and local by matching all identical predicates and subpredicates in the two representations.[5] This initial mapping is typically inconsistent, containing many-to-one matches. In the second phase, these local matches are coalesced into structurally consistent connected clusters (called *kernals*). Finally, in the third stage, these kernals are merged into one or a few maximal structurally consistent interpretations (i.e., mappings displaying one-to-one correspondences and parallel connectivity). SME then produces a structural evaluation of the interpretation(s), using a kind of cascade-like algorithm in which evidence is passed down from predicates to their arguments. This method favors deep systems over shallow systems, even if they have equal numbers of matches (Forbus and Gentner, 1989). Finally, predicates connected to the common structure in the base, but not initially present in the target, are proposed as *candidate inferences* in the target. Thus, structural completion can lead to spontaneous unplanned inferences.

SME has the psychologically appealing feature that it can derive more than one interpretation for an analogy. It normally produces two or three best interpretations of an analogy—that is, interpretations receiving the highest structural evaluations. For example, suppose we asked SME to interpret another of Kepler's analogical conjectures, namely, that the earth might impel the moon just as the sun does the earth:

Base   **Target**

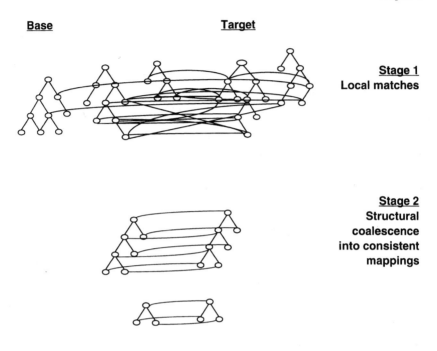

Stage 1
Local matches

Stage 2
Structural
coalescence
into consistent
mappings

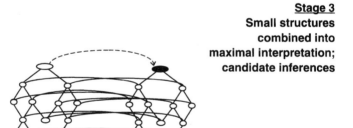

Stage 3
Small structures
combined into
maximal interpretation;
candidate inferences

Figure 6.2
Overview of the algorithm used by the structure-mapping engine.

1. CAUSE [TRAVEL (motive power, sun, earth), REVOLVE AROUND (earth, sun)]
2. CAUSE [TRAVEL (motive power, earth, moon), REVOLVE AROUND (moon, earth)].

Given this cross-mapped pair, SME would produce a relational interpretation in which the earth in Sentence 1 corresponds to the moon in Sentence 2, as well as an object-based interpretation in which the earth corresponds to the earth. Because of its preference for deeply connected relational structure, the relational interpretation would receive a higher structural evaluation and would win over the object interpretation.

A good explanatory analogy can often be extended, as in Kepler's analogical extensions. Computational models have tried to capture this propensity with the notion of *incremental mapping*. For example, SME can extend an existing analogical mapping by adding further connected material from the base domain (either drawn from current context or from long-term memory [Forbus, Ferguson, and Gentner, 1994; see also Burstein, 1988; Keane, Ledgeway, and Duff, 1994]). These models operate on the assumption (which we discuss later) that extending a connected mapping is easier than creating a new mapping.

Structure Mapping at Work

Commonalities and Differences

The experience of comparison is selective: Only certain commonalities are highlighted. We have suggested that a central factor controlling what information is considered in a comparison is *systematicity*: the presence of higher order connections between lower order relations (Clement and Gentner, 1991; Forbus and Gentner, 1989; Gentner, 1983). For example, comparing the pictures in Figure 6.3A and 6.3B highlights the commonality that both show a child looking at a pet. In contrast, comparing Figure 6.3A with 6.3C highlights the commonality that both show an animal being frightened by another animal (Markman and Gentner, in press). In both cases, the information highlighted by the comparison forms a connected relational system, and commonalities not connected to the matching system (such as the fact that there are dressers in both 3A and 3B) seem to recede in importance. This pattern has also been demonstrated using

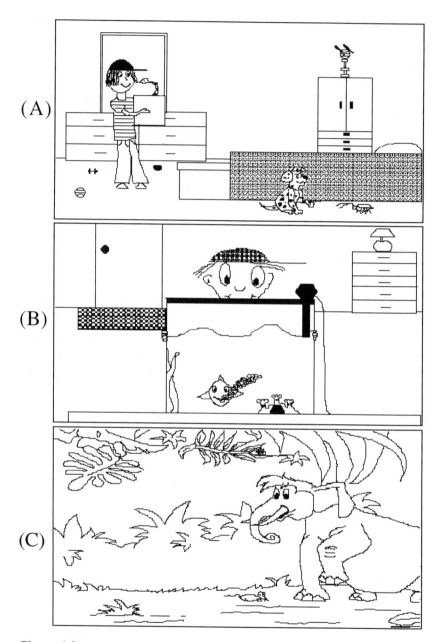

Figure 6.3
The role of commonalities and differences in similarity.

passages (Clement and Gentner, 1991). In this study, people who were given analogous stories judged that corresponding sentences were more important when the corresponding sentence pairs were part of a matching relational system than when they were not.

More surprisingly, structural alignment also influences what differences are psychologically salient. For example, when comparing Figure 6.3A and 6.3B, we notice that it is a snake that the boy is looking at in one picture and a fish in the other. Both the snake and the fish play the same role in the matching structure. Differences that are connected to the common system (like the fish–snake difference) we call *alignable differences* (Gentner and Markman, 1994; Markman and Gentner, 1993b, 1996). Alignable differences can be contrasted with *nonalignable differences*, which are aspects of one situation that have no correspondence at all in the other situation. For example, in the comparison of Figures 6.3A and 6.3B, the dog in Figure 6.3A has no correspondence with anything in Figure 6.3B, and hence it is a nonalignable difference.

Just as commonalities gain in importance when they are part of a matching system, so too do differences. That is, alignable differences are more salient than nonalignable differences. Intuitively, this focus on alignable differences makes sense, for it leads to a focus on those differences that are relevant to the common causal or goal structure that spans the situations. However, if we follow this logic a few steps further, we arrive at the rather intriguing prediction that there should be more salient differences for high-similar than for low-similar pairs (because in general, high-similarity pairs will have larger common systems and more alignable differences). For example, if you imagine listing all possible differences for the pair *hotel–motel* and contrast that with listing all possible differences for the pair *magazine–kitten*, you will probably find that it is much easier to list differences for the first, high-similarity pair. Experimental results bear out this observation. Participants who were asked to list differences between *hotel* and *motel* readily listed (alignable) differences: "Hotels are in cities, motels are on the highway"; "you stay longer in hotels than in motels"; "hotels have many floors, motels only one or two"; and so on. When given a low-similarity pair like *magazine–kitten*, participants tended to list nonalignable differences, such as "You pet a kitten, you don't pet a magazine," or "kittens have fur and magazines don't." This finding of a greater number of alignable differences for high-similarity pairs has been obtained in empirical studies involving both word pairs (Markman and Gentner, 1993b; Markman and Wisniewski, in press) and picture pairs (Markman and Gentner, 1996). An informal observation is that participants often expressed confusion or irritation over the low-similarity pairs, perhaps reflecting their feeling that it makes no sense to talk about differences in the absence of a meaningful alignment.

If the comparison process focuses on alignable differences rather than on nonalignable differences, then alignable differences should be listed more fluently than nonalignable differences. This means that people should find it easier to list differences for pairs of similar items than for pairs of dissimilar items, because high-similarity pairs have many commonalties and, hence, many alignable differences. Such a prediction runs against the commonsense view—and the most natural prediction of feature-intersection models—that it should be easier to list differences the more of them there are to list—that is, the more dissimilar the two items are. In a study by Gentner and Markman (1994), participants were given a page containing 40 word pairs, half similar and half dissimilar, and were given five minutes to list one difference for as many different pairs as they could. They were told that they would not have time to do all 40 pairs, and so they should do the easiest pairs first. The results provided strong evidence for the alignability predictions: Participants listed many more differences for similar pairs ($M = 11.4$) than for dissimilar pairs ($M = 5.9$). Furthermore, this difference was concentrated in the alignable differences. Over twice as many alignable differences were given for similar pairs ($M = 9.0$) than for dissimilar pairs ($M = 3.9$).

Because people focus on alignable differences rather than on nonalignable differences when making comparisons, alignable differences have a greater impact on people's perception of similarity than do nonalignable differences. Thus, all else being equal, alignable differences count more against similarity than nonalignable differences. One way to test this prediction is to pit comparisons involving a given alignable difference against comparisons involving the same contrast as a nonalignable difference. For example, in the top figure of

Nonalignable difference choice   Alignable difference choice

Figure 6.4
The importance of alignable and nonalignable differences in similarity.

the triad in Figure 6.4, the man shoots an arrow at a target. In the nonalignable-difference option, the man shoots an arrow at a target, but there is also a bird (a nonalignable difference) in the picture. In the alignable-difference option, the man shoots an arrow at a bird (an alignable difference); the target has been moved to the tree behind the man. When asked which option is most similar to the target, participants chose the nonalignable-difference option, suggesting that the alignable difference decreased the similarity of the pair more than did the nonalignable difference (Markman and Gentner, 1996).[6]

In summary, the process of structural alignment leads to a focus on matching relational systems. This focus determines both which commonalities are salient and which differences are salient. This last may seem paradoxical: Why should the common alignment determine which differences are important? Yet, if we reflect that most pairs of items in the world are dissimilar, this pattern seems functionally sensible. Intuitively, it is when a pair of items is similar that their differences are likely to be important.

Analogical Inference

Analogies can lead to new inferences, as Kepler's (1609/1992) example demonstrates, and the same is true of similarity comparisons. As in analogy, when there is a match between a base and target domain, facts about the base domain that are connected to the matching information may be proposed as candidate inferences (Falkenhainer, Forbus, and Gentner, 1986, 1989). For example, imagine you have a friend with a sarcastic sense of humor that makes her difficult to get along with but a helpful temperament that wins her the loyalty of her friends. If you met a new person and discovered that he had a sarcastic sense of humor, then based on his similarity to your other friend, you would probably be more willing to suppose that he is difficult to get along with than to infer that he has a helpful temperament that wins him loyal friends.

This point was demonstrated in a study by Clement and Gentner (1991). They asked people to read pairs of analogous stories. The base story had two key facts, each of which was connected to a causal antecedent. Neither of these key facts was stated in the target story. However, the target story did have a fact that corresponded to one of the causal antecedents from the base. When participants were given the analogy and asked to make a new prediction about the target story, they predicted the key fact that was connected to the matching causal antecedent more than twice as often as they predicted the other key fact. Convergent findings have been obtained by Read (1984), Spellman and Holyoak (in press), and Markman (1996). Likewise, Lassaline (1996) showed that people's willingness to infer new facts in a category-induction task increased when these facts were connected to shared causal relations. These results show how structural alignment and mapping allow people to predict new information from old.

Connectivity and Asymmetry

People often find comparisons much more similar in one direction than the other, as Tversky (1977) noted in his seminal treatise on similarity. For example, we prefer "A scanner is like a copy machine" to "A copy machine is like a scanner." As Tversky pointed out, this directionality is at odds with the pervasive intuition that similarity is a symmetric relation (after all, if A is similar to B, then shouldn't B be equally similar to A?). Structure mapping offers a natural explanation: We propose that asymmetries typically arise when one of the comparison items is more systematic than the other (Bowdle and Gentner, 1996; Gentner and Bowdle, 1994). According to structure-mapping theory, inferences are projected from the base to the target. Thus, having the more systematic and coherent item as the base maximizes the amount of information that can be mapped from base to target. Consistent with this claim, Bowdle and Gentner found that when participants were given pairs of passages varying in their causal coherence, they (a) consistently preferred comparisons in which the more coherent passage was the base and the less coherent passage was the target, (b) generated more inferences from the more coherent passage to the less coherent one, and (c) rated comparisons with more coherent bases as more informative than the reverse comparisons.

Extended Mapping

One particularly interesting use of analogy is in extended mappings. They arise in creative thinking, as when Kepler explored the implications of analogies between the motive power and light or magnetism. Extended analogies are used in instruction as well: for example, when electric current and voltage are described in terms of water flow and pressure (Gentner and Gentner, 1983). They also arise in ordinary language, with metaphoric systems like "Marriage is a journey" that can be extended (e.g., "You have to slog through the rough spots but eventually the road will get smoother" [Gibbs, 1994; Lakoff and Johnson, 1980]. We have found, consistent with the structure-mapping account, that it is easier to extend an existing domain mapping than to initiate a new one [Boronat and Gentner, 1996; Gentner and Boronat, 1992]). People who read passages containing extended metaphors one sentence at a time were faster to read the final sentence when it was a consistent extension of the metaphor of the passage, as in Example A (below), than when it utilized a different metaphor, as in Example B (below). For example, one passage described a debate in terms of a race:

A. Dan saw the big debate as a race. . . . He knew that he had to steer his course carefully in the competition. His strategy was to go cruising through the initial points and then make his move. . . . He revved up as he made his last key points. His skill left his opponent far behind him at the finish line.

B. Dan saw the big debate as a war.... He knew that he had to use every weapon at his command in the competition. He mapped out his strategy to ensure that he established a dominant position.... He intensified the bombardment as he made his last key points. His skill left his opponent far behind him at the finish line.

If extending an existing connected mapping is easier than creating a new mapping, then people should be faster to read the final sentence in Example A than in Example B. This is exactly what happened. This finding fits with the computational notion of *incremental mapping*, in which metaphoric passages can be understood by adding to an initial mapping (Forbus, Ferguson, and Gentner, 1994; Keane et al., 1994). Interestingly, this result held only for novel metaphors and not for conventional metaphors. It is possible that conventional metaphors have their metaphoric meanings stored lexically, making it unnecessary to carry out a domain mapping (Bowdle and Gentner, 1996; Gentner and Wolff, 1996).

Connectivity and Pure Mapping

Learners are often called on to map information from one situation to another. For example, when we buy a new VCR, climb into a rental car, or fire up an update of Windows, we must decide which aspects of our prior knowledge apply to the new situation. To study the determinants of this mapping process, Gentner and Schumacher (1986; Schumacher and Gentner, 1988) taught participants how to pilot a ship using a simulated device panel. A game-like task was used in which participants could directly manipulate certain parameters (such as engine thrust or coolant valve opening) that controlled other parameters (such as velocity or engine temperature). If they performed correctly, the ship made port in time; otherwise, they lost the game. After the first device had been well learned, participants were transferred to a second analogous device panel, and the number of trials to reach criterion on the new panel was measured. Participants' speed of learning was affected both by transparency—participants learned the new panel faster when there were physical resemblances between structurally corresponding elements—and by systematicity—participants learned the new panel faster when they had learned a causal explanation for the procedures.

Consistent with these patterns, both Ross (1987, 1989) and Reed (1987) have found transparency effects. They have shown that participants are better at transferring algebraic solutions when corresponding base and target objects are similar. Reed measured the transparency of the mapping between two analogous algebra problems by asking participants to identify pairs of corresponding concepts. He found that transparency was a good predictor of their ability to notice and apply solutions from one problem to the other. Ross (1989) found that participants' ability to transfer the problem-solving solution correctly was disrupted when cross-mapped correspondences were used. Research with children shows early effects of transparency and somewhat later effects of systematicity (Gentner and Toupin, 1986). We suspect that to derive the benefits of systematic explanations may require possessing some degree of domain knowledge.

Three generalizations emerge from the transfer studies. First, transparency makes analogical mapping easier. Close, literal similarity matches are the easiest sort of mapping and the kind for which participants are least likely to make errors. Second, possessing a systematic higher order structure can permit transfer even under adverse transparency conditions. Having a strong causal model can enable a learner to transfer even when the objects mismatch perceptually. A third point, on which we expand below, is that different kinds of similarity may enter into different subprocesses of transfer.

Further Implications

Ubiquity of Alignment

Our structure-mapping abilities constitute a rather remarkable talent. In creative thinking, analogies serve to highlight important commonalities, to project inferences, and to suggest new ways to represent the domains. Yet, it would be wrong to think of analogy as esoteric, the property of geniuses. On the contrary, we often take analogy for granted, as in examples like the following from Hofstadter (1995, p. 76).

Shelley: I'm going to pay for my beer now.
Tim: Me, too [Tim had a coke.]

Tim does not mean that he too is going to pay for Shelley's beer (the nonanalogical interpretation), nor even that he too is going to pay for his own beer, but rather that he is going to pay for what in his situation best corresponds to Shelley's beer: namely, his coke. This ability to carry out fluent, apparently effortless, structural alignment and mapping is a hallmark of human cognitive processing.

Plurality of Similarity

We have reviewed evidence that similarity is a process of structural alignment and mapping over articulated representations. However, similarity does not always appear so structurally discerning. A particularly striking case occurs in similarity-based retrieval. Several findings suggest that similarity-based retrieval from long-term memory is based on overall similarity, with surface similarity heavily weighted, rather than by the kind of structural alignment that best supports inference (Gentner, 1989; Holyoak and Koh, 1987; Keane, 1988; Ross, 1989; Seifert et al, 1986). For example, Gentner, Rattermann, and Forbus (1993) gave participants a memory set of stories and later probed them with stories that were similar in various ways. The greater the surface similarity between the probe and a target in memory (in terms of shared objects and characters), the more likely the target was to be retrieved. In contrast, the greater the degree of shared higher order relational structure (such as shared causal structure), the higher the rated inferential soundness and similarity of the pair. Thus, the kind of similarity that most reliably led to remindings was not the kind participants most valued in making inferences. In fact, participants often rated their own remindings as low in both soundness and similarity.

Findings like this suggest that similarity is pluralistic (Gentner, 1989; Goldstone, 1994a; Medin, Goldstone, and Markman 1993). Indeed, a parallel disassociation has been found in problem-solving transfer: Retrieval likelihood is sensitive to surface similarity, whereas likelihood of successful problem solving is sensitive to structural similarity (Keane, 1988; Ross, 1987, 1989; but see Hammond, Seifert, and Gray, 1991). This suggests that different kinds of similarity may have different psychological roles in transfer. The simulation "Many are called—but few are chosen" (MAC-FAC; Forbus, Ferguson, and

Gentner, 1995) models this phenomenon with a two-stage system: The first stage (MAC) is an indiscriminate, computationally cheap search for any kinds of similarities in memory, and the second stage (FAC) carries out a structure mapping of the candidates from the first stage.

Another way in which similarity is pluralistic is that different kinds of similarity emerge at different points in processing. Response deadline studies of relational comparisons suggest that when participants are required to respond quickly (under 700 ms or under 1,000 ms, depending on the task and materials), they base their sense of similarity on local matches (even cross-mapped object matches) rather than on relational matches (Goldstone and Medin, 1994; Ratcliff and McKoon, 1989). At longer response deadlines, this pattern is reversed. This time course of similarity has been successfully modeled for processing features conjoined into objects by Goldstone and Medin's (1994) Similarity, Interactive Activation, and Mapping (SIAM) model, using a local-to-global process like that of SME. Overall, the difference between early and late processing seems to be a shift from local matches to global structural alignment.

Implications for Other Cognitive Processes

Categorization Structural alignment and mapping can provide insight into other cognitive processes (see Figure 6.5). As one example, similarity is often given a central role in categorization (Hampton, 1995; Rosch, 1975; Smith and Medin, 1981). It is common to assume that objects can be categorized on the basis of perceptual, behavioral, or functional commonalities with the category representation (e.g., robins are seen as birds because of their perceptual and behavioral similarity to a prototype bird or to many other birds that have been encountered). However, many researchers have pointed out cases in which rated similarity and probability of category membership are dissociated (Gelman and Wellman, 1991; Keil, 1989; Rips, 1989). For example, bats have the perceptual and behavioral characteristics of birds (they are similar to birds in this sense), but they are classified as mammals, because of important (though nonobvious) properties, such as giving birth to live young. On the basis of examples like this, similarity's role in categorization has been challenged; it has been argued

Alignment and mapping processes are used in

**perceiving similarity
(alignment)**

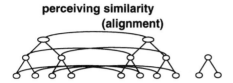

perceiving differences

**categorizing
(selecting best match from memory)**

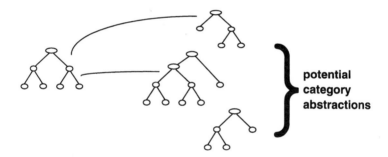

}
**potential
category
abstractions**

**discovering new category
(abstracting common system)**

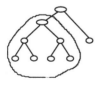   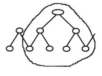

Figure 6.5
Some uses of comparison in cognitive processing.

that category membership judgments are theory based rather than similarity based (Keil, 1989; Murphy and Medin, 1985).

The process of alignment and mapping points the way to a reconciliation of similarity-based and theory-based accounts (see also Goldstone, 1994a). If we focus purely on perceptual similarity among objects, we are led to conclude that bats should be categorized with birds. On this view, theory-based knowledge (such as why bats are mammals) must intervene from elsewhere to overrule this assignment. However, if the similarity computation is assumed to be that of structural alignment, then the similarity between two instances will be based not only on object-level commonalities but also on common relations such as common causal relations and common origins. Assuming that our representations include information about theory-based relations, such as that bats bear live young, as well as information about features, then the schism between similarity-based and theory-based categorization may be more apparent than real.

Developmentally, if we assume that theoretical knowledge is acquired gradually, this view would account for the characteristic-to-defining shift (Keil and Batterman, 1984) in children's interpretations of word meaning from local object features (e.g., a taxi is bright yellow and has a checkered sign) to deeper relational commonalities (e.g., a taxi is a vehicle that may be hired to transport people).

Choice and decision Structural alignment also sheds light on the processes underlying choice behavior. Medin, Goldstone, and Markman (1995) reviewed parallels between phenomena in decision processing and phenomena in comparison processing that suggest an important role for structural alignment in decision making. Structural alignment influences which features to pay attention to in choice options. Research suggests that alignable differences are given more weight in choice situations than are nonalignable differences (Lindemann and Markman, 1996; Markman and Medin, 1995; Slovic and MacPhillamy, 1974). For example, Markman and Medin (1995) asked participants to choose between video games and to justify their choices. Their justifications were more likely to contain alignable differences than nonalignable differences. As another example, Kahneman and Tversky (1984) described to participants a hypothetical store in which a jacket could be bought for $125 and a calculator for

$15. They offered participants the opportunity to go to another store and save $5 on the total purchase. Participants who were offered a jacket for $125 and a calculator for $10 were more willing to make the effort to go to another store than those offered a jacket for $120 and a calculator for $15. Even though the monetary reward for going to the other store was the same for both groups, participants were influenced by the alignable difference.

Conclusions

Comparison processes foster insight. They highlight commonalities and relevant differences, they invite new inferences, and they promote new ways of construing situations. This creative potential is easiest to notice when the domains compared are very different, as in Kepler's analogies or John Donne's metaphors. But even prosaic similarity comparisons can lead to insights. Sometimes these insights are so obvious that we might fail to notice them, as when two-year-old Lucas noticed the repeated pattern of keys opening doors; or Aaron (in Holyoak and Thagard's article, 1997) spontaneously switched roles in the kiss-and-make-better schema; or when a six-year-old realized that tulips must need water, because people do (Inagaki and Hatano, 1987). At first glance, these mundane examples might seem to have nothing in common with the bold analogies of scientific discovery. But let us close with our own analogy. Analogies are like comets, flashing through our awareness and riveting our attention. Literal similarity is like planetary motion: steady, predictable, and prosaic. But the planets are central to the behavior of the solar system, and (like literal similarity comparisons) they are always with us. Finally, both planets and comets are governed by the same fundamental laws.

Notes

1. This causal interpretation, which went well beyond Copernicus's original proposal, also accounted for another regularity Kepler noted, namely, that each individual planet moves faster in its orbit the closer it is to the sun.

2. In Kepler's pre-Newtonian physics, the sun was required to push the planets around in their orbits, not merely to attract them.

3. Formally, the elements of our representations are objects (or *entities*), object descriptors (called *attributes*), *functions* (which express dimensional information),

and *relations* between representational elements. Attributes and relations are predicates with truth values. Functions differ from predicates in that they map from a set of arguments onto values other than truth values. For example, a function like **color** (ball) = red may be used to represent the dimension of color. The same assertion could be represented using color as an attribute, as in **red** (ball), or using color as a relation, as in **color** (ball, red). We assume that how a property is represented will affect the way it is processed.

4. Similar algorithms have been incorporated into other computational models of analogy (Burstein, 1988; Goldstone, 1994b; Goldstone and Medin, 1994; Holyoak and Thagard, 1989; Keane, Ledgeway, and Duff, 1994).

5. We make the theoretical assumption that similarity of relational predicates can be expressed as partial identity. The idea is that when two situations are analogous, they must have some system of identical relations. This identicality applies to the underlying concepts; the actual surface words used to express the relation need not be identical, for example, "Jupiter travels slower than Mercury" is analogous to "Jupiter moves slower than Mercury" or "Jupiter's rate of motion is lower than Mercury's" (see Gentner and Clement, 1988).

6. In the triad in Figure 6.4, the manipulation of alignable- and nonalignable-difference options also involves moving the target, which could be a confound. See Markman and Gentner (1996) for another variant of the study that escapes this problem.

References

Andersen, S. M., and Cole, S. W. (1990). "Do I know you?": The role of significant others in general social perception. *Journal of Personality and Social Psychology, 59*, 384–399.

Bassok, M. (1990). Transfer of domain-specific problem-solving procedures. *Journal of Experimental Psychology: Learning, Memory and Cognition, 16*, 522–533.

Boronat, C., and Gentner, D. (1996). *Metaphors are (sometimes) processed as generative domain mappings.* Manuscript in preparation.

Bowdle, B. F., and Gentner, D. (1996). *Informativity and asymmetry in similarity.* Manuscript in preparation.

Burstein, M. H. (1988). Incremental learning from multiple analogies. In A. Prieditis (Ed.), *Analogica* (pp. 37–62). Los Altos, CA: Morgan Kaufmann.

Copernicus, N. (1992). *De revolutionibus orbium caelestium* (Edward Rosen, Trans.). Baltimore: Johns Hopkins University Press. (Original work published 1543)

Clement, C. A., and Gentner, D. (1991). Systematicity as a selection constraint in analogical mapping. *Cognitive Science, 15*, 89–132.

Falkenhainer, B., Forbus, K. D., and Gentner, D. (1986). The structure-mapping engine. In *Proceedings of the fifth national conference on artificial intelligence* (pp. 272–277). Los Altos, CA: Morgan Kaufmann.

Falkenhainer, B., Forbus, K. D., and Gentner, D. (1989). The structure-mapping engine: Algorithm and examples. *Artificial Intelligence, 41,* 1–63.

Forbus, K. D., Ferguson, R. W., and Gentner, D. (1994). Incremental structure-mapping. In A. Ram and K. Eiselt (Eds.), *Proceedings of the sixteenth annual conference of the Cognitive Science Society* (pp. 313–318). Hillsdale, NJ: Erlbaum.

Forbus, K. D., and Gentner, D. (1989). Structural evaluation of analogies: What counts? In *The proceedings of the eleventh annual conference of the Cognitive Science Society* (pp. 341–348). Hillsdale, NJ: Erlbaum.

Forbus, K. D., Gentner, D., and Law, K. (1995). MAC/FAC: A model of similarity-based retrieval. *Cognitive Science, 19,* 141–205.

Gelman, S. A., and Wellman, H. M. (1991). Insides and essences: Early understandings of the non-obvious. *Cognition, 38,* 213–244.

Gentner, D. (1983). Structure-mapping: A theoretical framework for analogy. *Cognitive Science, 7,* 155–170.

Gentner, D. (1989). The mechanisms of analogical learning. In S. Vosniadou and A. Ortony (Eds.), *Similarity and analogical reasoning* (pp. 199–241). London: Cambridge University Press.

Gentner, D., and Boronat, C. B. (1992). *Metaphors are (sometimes) processed as generative domain-mappings.* Unpublished manuscript.

Gentner, D., and Bowdle, B. F. (1994). The coherence imbalance hypothesis: A functional approach to asymmetry in comparison. In A. Ram and K. Eiselt (Eds.), *The sixteenth annual meeting of the Cognitive Science Society* (pp. 351–356). Hillsdale, NJ: Erlbaum.

Gentner, D., Brem, S., Ferguson, R., Markman, A. B., Levidow, B. B., Wolff, P., and Forbus, K. D. (in press). Conceptual change via analogical reasoning: A case study of Johannes Kepler. *Journal of the Learning Sciences.*

Gentner, D., and Clement, C. (1988). Evidence for relational selectivity in the interpretation of analogy and metaphor. In G. H. Bower (Ed.), *The psychology of learning and motivation* (pp. 307–358). San Francisco: Academic Press.

Gentner, D., and Gentner, D. R. (1983). Flowing waters or teeming crowds: Mental models of electricity. In D. Gentner and A. L. Stevens (Eds.), *Mental models* (pp. 99–129). Hillsdale, NJ: Erlbaum.

Gentner, D., and Markman, A. B. (1993). Analogy—Watershed or Waterloo? Structural alignment and the development of connectionist models of analogy. In S. J. Hanson, J. D. Cowan, and C. L. Giles (Eds.), *Advances in neural information processing systems 5* (pp. 855–862). San Mateo, CA: Morgan Kaufmann.

Gentner, D., and Markman, A. B. (1994). Structural alignment in comparison: No difference without similarity. *Psychological Science, 5,* 152–158.

Gentner, D., and Markman. A. B. (1995). Similarity is like analogy. In C. Cacciari (Ed.), *Similarity* (pp. 111–148). Brussels, Belgium: BREPOLS.

Gentner, D., and Rattermann, M. J. (1991). Language and the career of similarity. In S. A. Gelman and J. P. Byrnes (Eds.), *Perspectives on thought and language: Interrelations in development* (pp. 225–277). London: Cambridge University Press.

Gentner, D., Rattermann, M. J., and Forbus, K. D. (1993). The roles of similarity in transfer: Separating retrievability from inferential soundness. *Cognitive Psychology, 25*, 524–575.

Gentner, D., and Schumacher, R. M. (1986). Use of structure mapping theory for complex systems. In *Proceedings of the 1986 IEEE international conference on systems, man, and cybernetics* (pp. 252–258). New York: IEEE.

Gentner, D., and Toupin, C. (1986). Systematicity and surface similarity in the development of analogy *Cognitive Science, 10*, 277–300.

Gentner, D., and Wolff, P. (1996). Metaphor and knowledge change. In A. Kasher and Y. Shen (Eds.), *Cognitive aspects of metaphor: Structure, comprehension and use*. Manuscript in preparation.

Gibbs, R. W. (1994). *The poetics of mind*. New York: Cambridge University Press.

Goldstone, R. L. (1994a). The role of similarity in categorization: Providing a groundwork. *Cognition, 52*, 125–157.

Goldstone, R. L. (1994b). Similarity, interactive activation, and mapping. *Journal of Experimental Psychology: Learning, Memory and Cognition, 20*, 3–28.

Goldstone, R. L., and Medin, D. L. (1994). The time course of comparison. *Journal of Experimental Psychology: Learning, Memory and Cognition, 20*, 29–50.

Goldstone, R. L., Medin, D. L., and Gentner, D. (1991). Relational similarity and the non-independence of features in similarity judgments. *Cognitive Psychology, 23*, 222–262.

Goodman, N. (1972). *Problems and prospects*. Indianapolis, IN: Bobbs-Merrill.

Greiner, R. (1988). Learning by understanding analogies. *Artificial Intelligence, 35*, 81–125.

Hammond, K. J., Seifert, C. M., and Gray, K. C. (1991). Functionality in analogical transfer: A hard match is good to find. *The Journal of the Learning Sciences, 1*, 111–152.

Hampton, J. A. (1995). Testing the prototype theory of concepts. *Journal of Memory and Language, 34*, 686–708.

Hofstadter, D. (1995). *Fluid concepts and creative analogies*. New York: Basic Books.

Holyoak, K. J. (1985). The pragmatics of analogical transfer. In G. H. Bower (Ed.), *The psychology of learning and motivation: Advances in research and theory* (pp. 59–87). New York: Academic Press.

Holyoak, K. J., and Koh, K. (1987). Surface and structural similarity in analogical transfer. *Memory and Cognition, 15*, 332–340.

Holyoak, K. J., and Thagard, P. (1989). Analogical mapping by constraint satisfaction. *Cognitive Science, 13*, 295–355.

Holyoak, K. J., and Thagard, P. (1997). The analogical mind. *American Psychologist, 52*, 35–44.

Inagaki, K., and Hatano, G. (1987). Young children's spontaneous personification as analogy. *Child Development, 58*, 1013–1020.

Kahneman, D., and Miller, D. T. (1986). Norm theory: Comparing reality to its alternatives. *Psychological Review, 93*, 136–153.

Kahneman, D., and Tversky, A. (1984). Choices, values, and frames. *American Psychologist, 39*, 341–350.

Keane, M. T. (1988). Analogical mechanisms. *Artificial Intelligence Review, 2*, 229–250.

Keane, M. T., Ledgeway, T., and Duff, S. (1994). Constraints on analogical mapping: A comparison of three models. *Cognitive Science, 18*, 387–438.

Keil, F. C. (1989). *Concepts, kinds and cognitive development*. Cambridge, MA: MIT Press.

Keil, F. C., and Batterman, N. (1984). A characteristic-to-defining shift in the development of word meaning. *Journal of Verbal Learning and Verbal Behavior, 23*, 221–236.

Kepler, J. (1992). *The new astronomy* (W. H. Donahue, Trans.). Cambridge, England: Cambridge University Press. (Original work published 1609)

Kolodner, J. (1993). *Case-based reasoning*. San Mateo, CA: Morgan Kaufmann.

Lakoff, G., and Johnson, M. (1980). *Metaphors we live by*. Chicago: University of Chicago Press.

Lassaline, M. E. (1996). Structural alignment in induction and similarity. *Journal of Experimental Psychology: Learning, Memory and Cognition, 22*, 754–770.

Lindemann, P. G., and Markman, A. B. (1996). Alignability and attribute importance in choice. In G. Cottrell (Ed.), *Proceedings of the eighteenth annual meeting of the Cognitive Science Society* (pp. 358–363). Hillsdale, NJ: Erlbaum.

Markman, A. B. (1996). *Constraints on analogical inference*. Manuscript in preparation.

Markman, A. B., and Gentner, D. (1993a). Splitting the differences: A structural alignment view of similarity. *Journal of Memory and Language, 32*, 517–535.

Markman, A. B., and Gentner, D. (1993b). Structural alignment during similarity comparisons. *Cognitive Psychology, 25*, 431–467.

Markman, A. B., and Gentner, D. (1996). Commonalities and differences in similarity comparisons. *Memory and Cognition, 24*, 235–249.

Markman, A. B., and Gentner, D. (in press). The effects of alignability on memory. *Psychological Science*.

Markman, A. B., and Medin, D. L. (1995). Similarity and alignment in choice. *Organizational Behavior and Human Decision Processes, 63,* 117–130.

Markman, A. B., and Wisniewski, E. J. (in press). Similar and different: The differentiation of basic level categories. *Journal of Experimental Psychology: Learning, Memory and Cognition.*

Medin, D. L., Goldstone, R. L., and Gentner, D. (1993). Respects for similarity. *Psychological Review, 100,* 254–278.

Medin, D. L., Goldstone, R. L., and Markman, A. B. (1995). Comparison and choice: Relations between similarity processing and decision processing. *Psychonomic Bulletin and Review, 2,* 1–19.

Murphy, G. L., and Medin, D. L. (1985). The role of theories in conceptual coherence. *Psychological Review, 92,* 289–315.

Novick, L. R. (1988). Analogical transfer, problem similarity and expertise. *Journal of Experimental Psychology: Learning, Memory and Cognition, 14,* 510–520.

Novick, L. R. (1990). Representational transfer in problem solving. *Psychological Science, 1,* 128–132.

Palmer, S. E. (1978). Fundamental aspects of cognitive representation. In E. Rosch and B. B. Lloyd (Eds.), *Cognition and categorization* (pp. 259–303). Hillsdale, NJ: Erlbaum.

Ratcliff, R., and McKoon, G. (1989). Similarity information versus relational information: Differences in the time course of retrieval. *Cognitive Psychology, 21,* 139–155.

Read, S. J. (1984). Analogical reasoning in social judgment: The importance of causal theories. *Journal of Personality and Social Psychology, 46,* 14–25.

Reed, S. K. (1987). A structure-mapping model for word problems. *Journal of Experimental Psychology: Learning, Memory and Cognition, 13,* 124–139.

Rips, L. J. (1989). Similarity, typicality, and categorization. In S. Vosniadou and A. Ortony (Eds.), *Similarity and analogical reasoning* (pp. 21–59). New York: Cambridge University Press.

Rosch, E. (1975). Cognitive representations of semantic categories. *Journal of Experimental Psychology: General, 104,* 192–233.

Ross, B. H. (1987). This is like that: The use of earlier problems and the separation of similarity effects. *Journal of Experimental Psychology: Learning, Memory and Cognition, 13,* 629–639.

Ross, B. H. (1989). Distinguishing types of superficial similarities: Different effects on the access and use of earlier examples. *Journal of Experimental Psychology: Learning, Memory and Cognition, 15,* 456–468.

Schumacher, R. M., and Gentner, D. (1988). Remembering causal systems: Effects of systematicity and surface similarity in delayed transfer. In *Proceedings of the Human Factors Society 32nd annual meeting* (pp. 1271–1275). Santa Monica, CA: Human Factors Society.

Seifert, C. M., McKoon, G., Abelson, R. P., and Ratcliff, R. (1986). Memory connection between thematically similar episodes. *Journal of Experimental Psychology: Learning, Memory and Cognition, 12,* 220–231.

Slovic, P., and MacPhillamy, D. (1974). Dimensional commensurability and cue utilization in comparative judgment. *Organizational Behavior and Human Performance, 11,* 172–194.

Smith, E. E., and Medin, D. L. (1981). *Categories and concepts.* Cambridge, MA: Harvard University Press.

Spellman, B. A., and Holyoak, K. J. (in press). Pragmatics in analogical mapping. *Cognitive Psychology.*

Tversky, A. (1977). Features of similarity. *Psychological Review, 84,* 327–352.

Winston, P. H. (1980). Learning and reasoning by analogy. *Communications of the Association for Computing Machinery, 23,* 689–703.

Computational Imagery

Janice Glasgow and Dimitri Papadias

After many years of neglect, the topic of mental imagery has recently emerged as an active area of research and debate in the cognitive science community. This article proposes a concept of computational imagery, which has potential applications to problems whose solutions by humans involve the use of mental imagery. Computational imagery can be defined as the ability to represent, retrieve, and reason about spatial and visual information not explicitly stored in long-term memory.

The article proposes a knowledge representation scheme for computational imagery that incorporates three representations: a long-term memory, descriptive representation and two working-memory representations, corresponding to the distinct visual and spatial components of mental imagery. The three representations, and a set of primitive functions, are specified using a formal theory of arrays and implemented in the array-based language Nial. Although results of studies in mental imagery provide initial motivation for the representations and functionality of the scheme, our ultimate concerns are expressive power, inferential adequacy, and efficiency.

Numerous psychological studies have been carried out and several, often conflicting, models of mental imagery have been proposed. This article does not present another computational model for mental imagery, but instead treats imagery as a problem-solving paradigm in artificial intelligence (AI). We propose a concept of computational imagery, which has potential applications to problems whose solutions by humans involve the use of mental imagery. As a basis for computational imagery, we define a knowledge representation scheme that brings to the foreground the most important visual and spatial properties of an image. Although psychological theories are used as a guide to these properties, we do not adhere to a strict cognitive model: Whenever possible, we attempt to overcome the limitations of the human information-processing system. Thus, our primary concerns are efficiency, expressive power, and inferential adequacy.

Computational imagery involves tools and techniques for visual–spatial reasoning, where images are generated or recalled from long-term memory and then manipulated, transformed, scanned, associated with similar forms (constructing spatial analogies), pattern matched, increased or reduced in size, distorted, and so on. In particular, we are concerned with the reconstruction of image representations to facilitate the retrieval of visual and spatial information that was not explicitly stored in long-term memory. The images generated to retrieve this information may correspond to representations of real physical scenes or to abstract concepts that are manipulated in ways similar to visual forms.

The knowledge representation scheme for computational imagery separates visual from spatial reasoning and defines independent representations for the two modes. Whereas visual thinking is concerned with *what* an image looks like, spatial reasoning depends more on *where* an object is located relative to other objects in a scene (complex image). Each of these representations is constructed, as needed, from a descriptive representation stored in long-term memory. Thus, our scheme includes three representations, each appropriate for a different kind of processing:

• An image is stored in long-term memory as a hierarchically organized, descriptive, *deep representation* that contains all the relevant information about the image.
• The *spatial representation* of an image denotes the image components symbolically and preserves relevant spatial properties.
• The *visual representation* depicts the space occupied by an image as an occupancy array. It can be used to retrieve information such as shape, relative distance, and relative size.

While the deep representation is used as a permanent store for information, the spatial and visual representations act as working (short-term) memory stores for images.

A formal theory of arrays provides a meta-language for specifying the representations for computational imagery. Array theory is the mathematics of nested, rectangularly arranged data objects (More, 1981). Several primitive functions, which are used to retrieve, construct, and transform representations of images, have been specified in the theory and mapped into the functional programming language, Nial (Jenkins, Glasgow, and McCrosky, 1986).

The knowledge representation scheme for computational imagery provides a basis for implementing programs that involve reconstructing and reasoning with image representations. One such system, currently under investigation, is a knowledge-based system for molecular scene analysis. Some of the concepts presented in this article will be illustrated with examples from that application area.

Research in computational imagery has three primary goals: a cognitive science goal, an AI goal, and an applications goal. The *cognitive science goal* addresses the need for computational models for theories of cognition. We describe a precise, explicit language for specifying, implementing, and testing alternative, and possibly conflicting, theories of cognition. The *AI goal* involves the development of a knowledge representation scheme for visual and spatial reasoning with images. Finally, the *applications goal* involves incorporating the knowledge representation scheme for computational imagery into the development of programs for solving real-world problems.

The article begins with an overview of previous research in mental imagery, which serves as a motivation for the representations and processes for computational imagery. This is followed by a detailed description of the deep, visual, and spatial representations for imagery, and the primitive functions that can be applied to them. It concludes with a summary of the major contributions of computational imagery to the fields of cognitive science, AI, and knowledge-based systems development, and a discussion of the relationship between our scheme and previous research in the area.

Mental Imagery

In vision research, an image is typically described as a projection of a visual scene of the back of the retina. However, in theories of mental imagery, the term "image" refers to an internal representation used by the human information-processing system to retrieve information from memory.

Although no one seems to deny the existence of the phenomenon called "imagery," there has been a continuing debate about the structure and the function of imagery in human cognition. The imagery debate is concerned with whether images are represented as *descriptions* or *depictions*. It has been suggested that descriptive representations contain symbolic, interpreted information, whereas depictive representations contain geometric, uninterpreted information

(Finke, Pinker, and Farah, 1989). Others debate whether or not images play any causal role in the brain's information processing (Block, 1981). According to Farah (1988a), in depictive theories the recall of visual objects consists of the top-down activation of perceptual representation, but in descriptive theories visual recall is carried out using representations that are distinct from those in vision, even when it is accompanied by the phenomenology of "seeing with the mind's eye." Further discussions on the imagery debate can be found in various sources (e.g., Anderson, 1978; Block, 1981; Kosslyn and Pomerantz, 1977).

This article does not attempt to debate the issues involved in mental imagery, but to describe effective computational techniques for storing and manipulating image representations. To accomplish this, however, requires an understanding of the broad properties of representations and processes involved in mental imagery.

Research Findings in Mental Imagery

Many psychological and physiological studies have been carried out in an attempt to demystify the nature of mental imagery. Of particular interest to our research are studies that support the existence of multiple image representations and describe the functionality of mental imagery processes. In this section we overview relevant results from such studies, and based on these results, propose some important properties of mental imagery, which we use to motivate our representation scheme for computational imagery.

Several experiments provide support for the existence of a visual memory, distinct from verbal memory, in which recognition of verbal material is inferior. Paivio's (1975) dual-code theory suggests that there is a distinction between verbal and imagery processing. This theory leaves the exact nature of mental images unspecified, but postulates two interconnected memory systems—verbal and imaginal—operating in parallel. The two systems can be independently accessed by relevant stimuli but they are interconnected in the sense that nonverbal information can be transformed into verbal and vice versa. Furthermore, it has been indicated that visual memory may be superior in recall (Standing, 1973).

The issue of visual memory is an important one for computational imagery. What it implies to us is the need for separate descriptive and depictive representations. This is reinforced by the experiments carried out by Kosslyn (1980) and his colleagues, who concluded that images preserve the spatial relationships, relative sizes, and relative distances of real physical objects. Pinker (1988) suggested that image scanning can be performed in two- and three-dimensional space, providing support for Kosslyn's proposal that mental images capture the spatial characteristics of an actual display. Pinker also indicated that images can be accessed using either an object-centered or a world-centered coordinate system.

A series of experiments suggest that mental images are not only visual and spatial in nature, but also structurally organized in patterns, that is, they have a hierarchical organization in which subimages can occur as elements in more complex images (Reed, 1974). Some researchers propose that under certain conditions images can be reinterpreted: They can be reconstructed in ways that were not initially anticipated (Finke, Pinker, and Farah, 1989). Experiments also support the claim that creative synthesis is performed by composing mental images to make creative discoveries (Finke and Slayton, 1988).

The relationship between imagery and perception was considered by Brooks (1968), who demonstrated that spatial visualization can interfere with perception. Farah (1988a) also suggested that mental images are visual representations in the sense that they share similar representations to those used in vision, but noticed that this conclusion does not imply that image representations are depictive because both imagery and perception might be descriptive. Farah argued, from different evidence, however, that they are in fact spatial.

Findings, provided by the study of patients with visual impairments, point toward distinct visual and spatial components of mental imagery. Mishkin, Ungerleider, and Macko (1983) showed that there are two distinct cortical visual systems. Their research indicated that the temporal cortex is involved in recognizing *what* objects are, whereas the parietal cortex determines *where* they are located. Further studies have verified that there exists a class of patients who often have trouble localizing an object in the visual field, although their ability to recognize the object is unimpaired (De Renzi, 1982). Other patients show the opposite patterns of visual abilities: They cannot recognize visually presented objects, although they can localize them in space (Bauer and Rubens, 1985). Such patients are able to recognize objects by touch or by characteristic sounds. It has also been suggested that the preserved and impaired aspects of vision in these patients are similarly preserved or impaired in imagery (D. Levine, Warach, and Farah, 1985). In experimental studies, subjects with object identification problems were unable to draw or describe familiar objects despite being able to draw and describe in detail the locations of cities on a map, furniture in a house, and landmarks in a city. Patients with localization problems were unable to describe relative locations, such as cities on a map, although they could describe from memory the appearance of a variety of objects. Such findings have been interpreted by some researchers (e.g., Kosslyn, 1987) as suggesting two distinct components of mental imagery, the spatial and the visual, where the spatial component preserves information about the relative positions of the meaningful parts of a scene and the visual component preserves information about how (e.g., shape, size) a meaningful part of a scene looks.

Although there are varying strategies for retrieving spatial information and solving problems concerning spatial relations, research has suggested that humans typically use mental imagery for spatial reasoning (Farah, 1988b). Experimental results also support an isomorphism between physical and imaged transformations (Shepard and Cooper, 1982). A premise of Kritchevsky (1988) is that behavior can be divided into spatial and nonspatial components. For example, determining the color of an object is a nonspatial behavior, whereas determining relative positions of objects is a spatial behavior. Kritchevsky assumed that the spatial component of behavior is understood in terms of elementary spatial functions. Furthermore, these functions are independent of any particular sensory modality (Ratcliff, 1982).

Although individually the results described previously do not imply a particular approach to computational imagery, collectively they infer several properties that we wish to capture in our approach. Most importantly, an image may be depicted and reasoned with visually or spatially, where a visual representation encodes what the image looks like and the spatial representation encodes relative location of objects within an image. As well, images are inherently three-dimensional and hierarchically organized. This implies that computational routines must be developed that can decompose, reconstruct, and reinterpret image representations. Results from studies comparing imagery and vision imply that the representations and processes of imagery may be related to those of high-level vision. Thus, we should also consider the representations and functionality of object recognition when defining computational imagery. Finally, we must be able to consider an image from either an object-centered or a viewer-centered perspective.

The numerous experiments that have been carried out in mental imagery not only suggest properties for the representation scheme, but also support the premise that mental imagery is used extensively to reason about real-world problems. Thus, computational imagery is an important topic to investigate in relation to AI problem solving.

The subjective nature of mental imagery has made it a difficult topic to study experimentally. Qualities like clarity, blurring, and vividness of images are not directly observable and may differ from one person to another. Furthermore, it has been argued by some researchers that it is impossible to resolve the imagery debate experimentally because depictive and descriptive representations do not have distinct properties from which behavioral consequences can be predicted (Anderson, 1978). As a result, several alternative accounts have been proposed to explain the findings mentioned previously. The most important of these are tacit knowledge, experimenter bias, eye movements, and task-induced characteristics (Intons-Peterson, 1983). These difficulties involved in experimental studies emphasize the need for computer models for mental imagery. Although the knowledge representation scheme for computational imagery is not meant to model a particular theory of imagery, it does provide the tools specifying, testing, and formally analyzing a variety of theories, and thus can contribute to resolving the imagery debate.

Theories and Principles of Mental Imagery

Pylyshyn (1981), a forceful proponent of the descriptive view, argued that mental imagery simply consists of the use of general thought processes to simulate perceptual events, based on tacit knowledge of how these events happened. Pylyshyn disputed the idea that mental images are stored in a raw uninterpreted form resembling mental photographs, and argued for an abstract format of representation called propositional code. Kosslyn's (1980) model of mental imagery is based on a depictive theory, which claims that images are quasi-pictorial, that is, they resemble pictures in several ways but lack some of their properties. According to Kosslyn's model, mental images are working memory, visual representations generated from long-term memory, deep representations. A set of procedures, which is referred to as the "mind's eye," serves as an interface between the visual representations and the underlying data structures, which may be decidedly nonpictorial in form. Hinton (1979) disputed the picture metaphor for imagery and claimed that images are more like generated constructions. In this approach, as in Marr and Nishihara's (1978) 3D model, complex images can be represented as a hierarchy of parts.

Finke (1989) took a different approach to the imagery debate. Instead of proposing a model, Finke defined five "unifying principles" of mental imagery:

- The principle of *implicit encoding* states that imagery is particularly useful for retrieving information about physical properties of objects and relations among objects whenever this information was not previously, explicitly encoded.
- The principle of *perceptual equivalence* states that similar mechanisms in the visual system are activated when objects or events are imagined, as when the same objects or events are actually perceived.
- The principle of *spatial equivalence* states that the spatial relations between objects are preserved, although sometimes distorted, in mental images.
- The principle of *structural equivalence* states that the structure of images corresponds to that of perceived objects, in the sense that the structure is coherent, well organized, and can be reinterpreted.
- The principle of *transformational equivalence* states that imagined and physical transformations exhibit similar dynamic characteristics and follow the same laws of motion.

These principles provide a basis for evaluating the representations and functions for computational imagery; in the development of our scheme we have attempted to address each of the underlying principles for mental imagery.

Stages of Image Representations

The hypothesis of multiple representations for mental imagery can explain several experimental results that cannot be explained independently by either a propositional, a spatial, or a visual representation. For instance, after a series of experiments, Atwood (1971) concluded that memory for high-image phrases is disrupted if followed by a task requiring the subject to process a visually presented digit in contrast to abstract phrases. Although other researchers found difficulty in replicating Atwood's experiments, Jannsen (1976) succeeded consistently over several experiments and claimed that other failures stemmed from using an interfering task that is spatial rather than visual. Baddeley and Lieberman (1980) interpreted these results as pointing towards distinct visual and spatial components of mental imagery.

When images are retrieved, it is possible to recall information about which objects constitute a scene and their spatial relationships with other objects without remembering what the object looks like. Furthermore, we are able to recognize objects independent of any context. Distinct spatial and visual components for imagery can explain such phenomena, where the spatial component can be considered as an index that connects visual images to create a scene.

Intuitively, we can distinguish between visual and spatial representations by considering the type of information we wish to retrieve. Consider, for example, answering the following questions: *How many windows are there in your home? What city is farther north, Seattle or Montreal? What objects are sitting on top of your desk? Who was sitting beside Mary in class?* These questions can typically be answered without constructing an explicit visual image, that is, you could possibly recall that John was sitting beside Mary without knowing what John looked like or what clothes he was wearing. Each of these questions does rely on knowing the relative locations of objects within a recalled image, information that is embodied in a spatial representation. Now consider questions such as: *What is the shape of your dog's ears? What does a particular image look like if you rotate it ninety degrees? What is larger, a rabbit or a racoon? Is Montreal or Toronto closer to Ottawa?* To answer these questions you may need to reconstruct a representation that preserves information such as size, shape, or relative distance, information that is embodied in a visual representation.

From the computational point of view, a single representational system cannot always effectively express all the knowledge about a given domain; different representational formalisms are useful for different computational tasks (Sloman, 1985). In perceptual systems, for instance, multiple representations have been proposed to derive cognitively useful representations from a visual scene. For computational imagery, we propose three stages of image representation, each appropriate for a different type of information processing (Papadias and Glasgow, 1991). The deep representation stores structured, descriptive information in terms of a semantic network, long-term memory model. The working-memory representations (spatial and visual) are consciously experienced and generated as symbolic and occupancy arrays, as needed, using information stored in the deep representation. Details about the computational advantages of each of the image representations involved in the scheme will be presented in the following section.

Knowledge Representation Scheme

Research in AI has long been concerned with the problem of knowledge representation. AI programs rely on the ability to store descriptions of a particular domain and formally manipulate these descriptions to derive new knowledge. Traditional approaches to knowledge representation include logic representations, which denote the objects and relations in the world in terms of axioms, and structural knowledge representation schemes, which denote concepts and relations in terms of structural hierarchies.

In addition to general schemes, there exist specialized schemes concerned with the representation of the visual representation of images. In discrimination trees, objects are sorted by discriminating on their coordinates, as well as other quantitative and qualitative discriminators (McDermott and Davis, 1984). A simple way of describing volume or shape is with occupancy arrays, where cells of the array denote objects filling space. For computer vision applications, an occupancy array is often called a gray-level description, because the values of the cells encode the intensity of light on a gray scale from white to black. For our molecular scene analysis application, we use three-dimensional occupany arrays that correspond to electron density maps resulting from X-ray diffraction experiments. The values of the cells in such maps correspond to the electron density in a unit cell of a crystal.

According to Biederman (1987), the visual representation for objects can be constructed as a spatial organization of simple primitive volumes, called geons. Other researchers have proposed alternative primitive volumes, like generalized cones, spheres, and so forth. A major contribution in representational formalisms for images is the progression of primal sketch, $2\frac{1}{2}$D sketch, and 3D sketch (Marr and Nishihara, 1978). The primal sketch represents intensity changes in a 2D image. The $2\frac{1}{2}$D sketch represents orientation and depth of surface from a particular viewer perspective. Finally, the 3D sketch represents object-centered spatial organization.

The representation schemes discussed before are not suggested as structures for representing human knowledge and do not necessarily commit to addressing questions about mental processes. Whereas many AI researchers believe that the best way to make true thinking machines is by getting computers to imitate the way the human brain works (Israel, 1987), research in knowledge representation often is more concerned with expressiveness and efficiency, rather than explanatory and predictive power. Thus, although our knowledge representation scheme attempts to preserve the most relevant properties of imagery, whenever possible we try to overcome the limitations of the human information-processing system. For example, theories of divided attention argue that attention can be concentrated on, at most, a few mental processes at a time. Our proposed scheme has the capability of relatively unrestrictive parallel processing of spatial images. Furthermore, although the resolution of mental images is limited by the capabilities of the human mind, in the knowledge representation scheme the resolution restrictions are imposed by the implementation architecture.

A theory of arrays provides a formalism for the representations and functions involved in computational imagery. Array theory (More, 1981) is the mathematics of nested, rectangularly arranged collections of data objects. Similar to set theory, array theory is concerned with the concepts of nesting, aggregation, and membership. Array theory is also concerned with the concept of data objects having a spatial position relative to other objects in a collection. Thus, it provides for a multidimensional, hierarchical representation of images, in which spatial relations are made explicit.

We consider computational imagery as the ability to represent, retrieve, and reason about information not explicitly stored in long-term memory. In particular, we are concerned with visual and spatial information. Recall that the visual component of imagery specifies how an image looks and is used to retrieve information such as shape, size, and volume, whereas the spatial component of imagery denotes where components of an image are situated relative to one another and is used to retrieve information such as neighborhoods, adjacencies, symmetry, and relative locations. As illustrated in Figure 7.1, the long-term memory representation is implemented as a description of the image, and the working-memory representations correspond to representations that make explicit the visual and spatial properties of an image. In the remainder of this section, we describe each of the representations in detail and discuss the primitive functions that operate on them. First, though, we overview the theory of arrays that provides the basis for describing and implementing the representations and functions for computational imagery.

Array Theory
Results of empirical studies suggest that images may be organized using both a hierarchical and a spatial structure. Components of an image may be grouped into features and stored based on their topological relations, such as adjacency or containment, or their spatial relations, such as *above, beside, north-of*, and so on. Because of the relevance of storing and reasoning about such properties of an image, we base the development of the knowledge representation scheme for computational imagery on a theory of arrays. This mathematical theory allows for a multidimensional, hierarchical representation of images in which spatial relations are made explicit. Furthermore, functions can be defined in array theory for constructing, manipulating, and retrieving information from images represented as arrays. For example, functions that compose, translate, juxtapose, and compare images have been defined within the theory.

The development of array theory was motivated by efforts to extend the data structures of APL and has been influenced by the search for total operations that satisfy universal equations (More, 1981). In this theory, an array is a collection of zero or more items held at positions in a rectangular arrangement along multiple axes. Rectangular arrangement is the concept of data objects having a position relative to other objects in the collection. The interpretation of this structure can be illustrated using nested, box diagrams. Consider

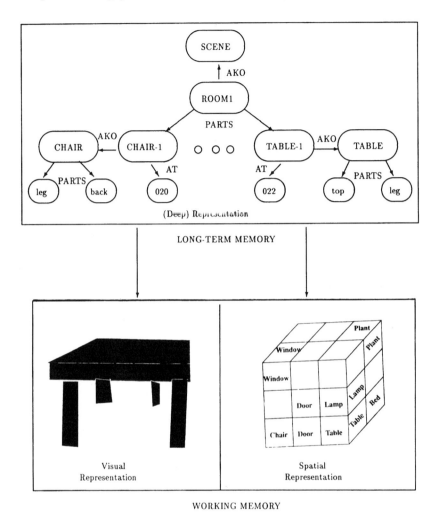

Figure 7.1
Representations for computational imagery.

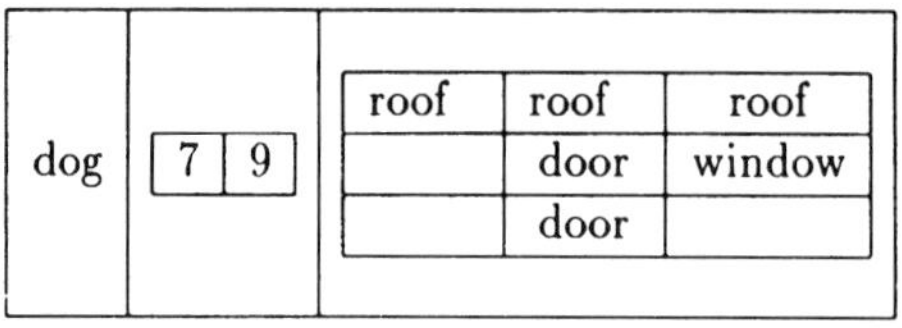

dog	7	9	roof	roof	roof
				door	window
				door	

Figure 7.2
Example of nested array diagram.

the array diagram in Figure 7.2. In this array the pair formed from 7 and 9 is an array nested within the larger array. Nesting is the concept of having the objects of a collection be collections themselves. This is an important concept in array theory because it is the power of aggregating arbitrary elements in an array that gives the theory much of its expensive power. The third element of the array is a symbolic array, which denotes an image of a house containing three parts. The indexing of the array allows us to make explicit such properties as *above(roof, door)* and *left-of(door, window)* in a notation that is both compact and accessible.

Array theory has provided a formal basis for the development of the *N*ested *I*nteractive *A*rray *L*anguage, *Nial.* This multiparadigm programming language combines concepts from APL, Lisp, and FP with conventional control mechanisms (Jenkins, Glasgow, and McCrosky, 1986). The primitive functions of array theory have all been implemented in Q'Nial (Jenkins and Jenkins, 1985), a commercially available, portable interpreter of Nial developed at Queen's University.

Operations in array theory are functions that map arrays to arrays. A large collection of total, primitive operations are described for the theory. They are chosen to express fundamental properties of arrays. Nial extends array theory by providing several syntactic forms that describe operations, including composition, partial evaluation of a left argument, and a lambda form. Array theory also contains second-order functions called transformers that map operations to operations.

It has previously been shown that the syntactic constructs of array theory facilitate both sequential and parallel computations (Glasgow, et al., 1989). This is an important feature when considering computational imagery as a basis for specifying cognitive processes, which themselves may be sequential or parallel. The potential parallelism in array theory comes from three sources: inherent parallelism in the primitive operations, parallelism expressed by syntactic constructs, and parallelism in operation application controlled by primitive transformers. The potential parallelism of the primitive operations results from treating an entire array as a single value; each array takes an array as a single argument and returns an array as its result. Array theory includes transformers that allow expression of the parallel application of an operation to subparts of an array.

The software development associated with AI problem solving in general, and with computational imagery in particular, differs from traditional computer applications. AI problems are solved at the conceptual level, rather than a detailed implementation level. Thus, much of the programming effort is spent on understanding how to represent and manipulate the knowledge associated with a particular problem, or class of problems. This imposes certain features on a programming language, including interactive program development, operations for symbolic computation, dynamically created data structures, and easy encoding of search algorithms. Although Lisp and Prolog both address capabilities such as these, they provide very different and complementary approaches to problem solving. The language Nial is an attempt to find an approach to programming that combines the logic and functional paradigms of Prolog and Lisp (Glasgow and Browse, 1985; Jenkins, Glasgow, and McCrosky, 1986). It has been demonstrated that array theory and Nial can provide a foundation for logic programming (Glasgow, et al., in press), as well as other descriptive knowledge representation techniques (Jenkins, Glasgow, and McCrosky, 1988). These techniques have been implemented and tested on a variety of knowledge-based applications.

Deep (Long-Term Memory) Representation

The deep representation for computational imagery is used for the long-term storage of images. Earlier work has suggested that there exists a separate long-term memory model that encodes visual information descriptively (Kosslyn, 1980; Pinker, 1984). This encoding can then be used to generate depictive representations in working memory. As pointed out in Marschark et al., (1987), most of the research in vision and imagery has focused on the format of the on-line conscious representations, excluding long-term storage considerations. Our point of view is that the deep representation falls more in the limits of research in long-term memory than imagery, and we base its implementation on the hierarchical network model of semantic memory (Collins and Quillian, 1969). This model is suitable for storing images because they have a structured organization in which subimages can occur as elements in more complex images.

The deep representation in our scheme is implemented using a frame language (Minsky, 1975), in which each frame contains salient information about an image or class of images. This information includes propositional and procedural knowledge. There are two kinds of image hierarchies in the scheme: the AKO (a kind of) and the PARTS. The AKO hierarchy provides property inheritance: Images can inherit properties from more generic image frames. The PARTS hierarchy is used to denote the structural decomposition of complex images. The deep representation for imagery can be characterized as nonmonotonic because default information (stored in specific slots, or inherited from more generic frames) is superseded as new information is added to a frame.

A frame corresponding to the image of a map of Europe and part of the semantic network for a map domain is illustrated in Figure 7.3. Each node in the network corresponds to an individual frame and the links describe the relationships among frames. The AKO slot in the frame of the map of Europe denotes that the frame is an instance of the concept "Map-of-Continent." The PARTS slot contains the meaningful parts that compose the map, along with an index value that specifies their relative locations. The POPULATION slot contains a call to a procedure that calculates the population of Europe, given the populations of the countries. As well, the frame could incorporate several other slots, including ones used for the generation of the spatial and visual representations.

For the molecular scene analysis application, the frame hierarchy is more complex than the simple map example. The structure of a protein is described in terms of a crystal, which consists of a regular three-dimensional arrangement of identical building blocks. The structural motif for a protein crystal can be described in terms of aggregate (complex or quaternary), three-dimensional structures.

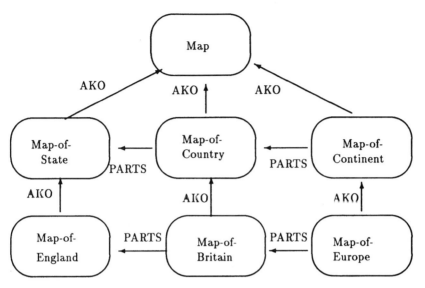

a) Semantic network representation

FRAME	Map-of-Europe
AKO	Map-of-Continent
PARTS	Sweden (0 4) Britain (1 0) ...
POPULATION	'find-population'
...	...

b) Frame representation

Figure 7.3
Example of deep representation.

Similarly, tertiary structures can be decomposed into secondary structures, and so on. Each level in this decomposition hierarchy corresponds to a conceptual frame denoting a molecular fragment at a meaningful level of abstraction. If we consider a fully determined crystal as a molecular scene, there exist databases containing over 90,000 images of small molecules and over 600 images of protein structures (Allen, Bergerhoff, and Sievers, 1987). These databases include the three-dimensional geometry of the molecular scenes that forms a basis for our long-term memory model for molecular images.

Semantic networks and frames have previously been suggested as representations for images in vision research. One example of this deals with the interpretation of natural scenes (M. Levine, 1978). In Levine's system, the spatial relations are represented as arcs such as *left-of*, *above*, or *behind*. A classic example of the use of semantic networks is the work of Winston (1975) on structural descriptions. In that study on scene understanding, common structures, such as arches and pedestals, are represented in terms of their decomposition into parts and a description of the spatial relations among the parts. Although this approach may be useful for some applications, we argue later that explicitly representing spatial relations in terms of an indexed array provides increased computation efficiency for spatial reasoning.

Our implementation of the deep representation has several attractive properties. First, it provides a natural way to represent knowledge because all the information about an image (or a class of images) can be stored in a single frame, and the structure of images is captured by the PARTS hierarchy. It is assumed that a property is stored at the most general level possible (highest level in the conceptual hierarchy) and is shared by more specific levels, thus providing a large saving in space over propositional or database formulations of property relations. The deep representation also incorporates the psychological concept of semantic networks in an implementation that provides features such as procedural attachment. The nonmonotonic feature of the frame allows for reasoning with incomplete information; default information can be stored in conceptual frames and inherited and used for depicting or reasoning about subconcepts or instances of images. Despite its attractive properties, however, the deep representation is not the most suitable representation for all of the information processing involved in imagery. Thus, we require alternative representations to facilitate the efficiency of the scheme.

Working-Memory Representations

Mental images are not constantly experienced. When an image is needed, it is generated on the basis of stored information. Thus, unlike the deep representation, which is used for the permanent storage of information, the working-memory representations of an image exist only during the time that the image is active, that is, when visual or spatial information processing is taking place.

The distinct working-memory representations were initially motivated by results of cognitive studies that suggest distinct components in mental imagery (Kosslyn, 1987). More importantly, separate visual and spatial representations provide increased efficiency in information retrieval. The visual representation is stored in a format that allows for analysis and retrieval of such information as shape and relative distance. Because the spatial representation makes explicit the important features and structural relationships in an image while discarding irrelevant features such as shape and size, it provides a more compact and efficient depiction for accessing spatial and topological properties.

Visual Representation The visual representation corresponds to the visual component of imagery, and it can either be reconstructed from the underlying deep representation or generated from low-level perceptual processes. Similar to Kosslyn's (1980) skeletal image, this representation is depictive and incorporates geometric information. Unlike Kosslyn's approach, we assume that the visual representation can be three-dimensional and viewer-independent.

For the current implementation of the visual representation we use *occupancy arrays*. An occupancy array consists of cells, each mapping onto a local region of space and representing information such as volume, lightness, texture, and surface orientation about this region. Objects are depicted in the arrays by patterns of filled cells isomorphic in surface area to the objects. Figure 7.4 illustrates depictions of three-dimensional occupancy arrays corresponding to a molecular fragment at varying levels of resolution. These arrays were constructed using geometric coordinates and radii of the atomic components of the molecule.

Representing occupancy arrays explicitly in long-term memory can be a costly approach. As a result, other approaches to storing or generating this information (like generalized shapes) have been developed. Such approaches can be incorporated into an application of the scheme for computational imagery.

Spatial Representation A primary characteristic of a good formalism for knowledge representation is that it makes relevant properties explicit. Although an occupancy array provides a representation for

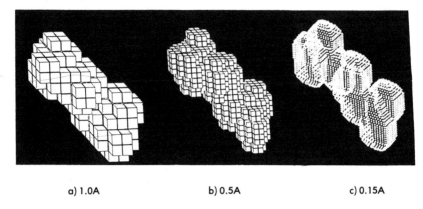

a) 1.0A   b) 0.5A   c) 0.15A

Figure 7.4
Example of occupancy arrays for visual representations.

the visual component of imagery, it is basically uninterpreted. For the spatial component of imagery we are best served by a representation that explicitly denotes the spatial relations between meaningful parts of an image, corresponding to the mental maps created by humans. Thus, we use a multidimensional symbolic array to depict the spatial structure of an image, where the symbolic elements of the array denote its meaningful parts (Glasgow, 1990). The symbolic array preserves the spatial and topological relationships of the image features, but not necessarily relative sizes or distances. The arrays can be interpreted in different ways depending on the application. If, for example, we use the scheme to reason about geographic maps, interpretations could include predicates such as *north, east, south,* and *west*; if the array is used to represent the image of a room, then the interpretation would involve predicates such as *above, behind, left-of, beside,* and so on. For molecular scene analysis we are more concerned with properties such as *symmetry* and *adjacency* (bonding), which are made explicit by a symbolic array. The spatial representation can also denote nonspatial dimensions. For example, the symbolic array could be used to index features such as height or speed.

The symbolic array representation for the spatial component of imagery is generated, as needed, from information stored explicitly in the frame representation of an image. For example, in Figure 7.3 the PARTS slot contains the indices needed to reconstruct the spatial representation for a simplified map of Europe. Figure 7.5 illustrates this

				Sweden	
Britain			Denmark		
		Holland	Germany	Germany	
		Belgium			
	France	France	Italy	Yugoslavia	Yugoslavia
Portugal	Spain		Italy		Greece

Figure 7.5
Example of symbolic array for spatial representation.

glass	water	glass
glass	glass	glass

Figure 7.6
Symbolic array depiction of inside relation.

symbolic array. Note that some parts occupy more than one element in an array (e.g., Italy, France). This is necessary to capture all the spatial relationships of the parts of an image. We may also wish to denote more complex relations, such as one object being "inside" another. This is illustrated in Figure 7.6, which displays a spatial image of a glass containing water.

According to Pylyshyn (1973), images are not raw, uninterpreted, mental pictures, but are organized into meaningful parts that are remembered in terms of their spatial relations. Furthermore, we can access the meaningful parts, that is, we are able to focus attention on a specific feature of an image. Nested symbolic arrays capture these properties by representing images at various levels of abstraction as prescribed by the PART hierarchy of the deep representation; each level of embedding in an array corresponds to a level of structural decomposition in the frame hierarchy. For instance, focusing attention on Britain in the array of Figure 7.5 would result

				Sweden	
Wales | Scotland / England			Denmark		
		Holland	Germany	Germany	
		Belgium			
	France	France	Italy	Yugoslavia	Yugoslavia
Portugal	Spain		Italy		Greece

Figure 7.7
Embedded symbolic array representation.

in a new array in which the symbol for Britain is replaced by its spatial representation (see Figure 7.7). This subimage is generated using the PARTS slot for the frame of Britain in the deep representation.

It has been suggested that people can reconstruct and reinterpret mental images (Finke, 1989). The proposed scheme also provides the capability to combine and reconstruct images, using special functions that operate on the symbolic array representations. For instance, we can combine a portion of the array of Figure 7.5 with a portion of the array that corresponds to the map of Africa and create a new array containing Mediterranean countries.

Recall that Pinker (1988) pointed out that images are represented and manipulated in three dimensions. Similar to the visual representation, a symbolic array can be two- or three-dimensional, depending on the application. In the domain of molecular scenes, fragments of molecules are represented as three-dimensional symbolic arrays at varying levels of abstraction, corresponding to the level of decomposition in the frame hierarchy. For example, a protein can be represented as a three-dimensional array of symbols denoting high-level structures, which can he decomposed into nested arrays of symbols denoting progressively more detailed substructures. Because of the size and complexity of molecular structures, it is essential to be

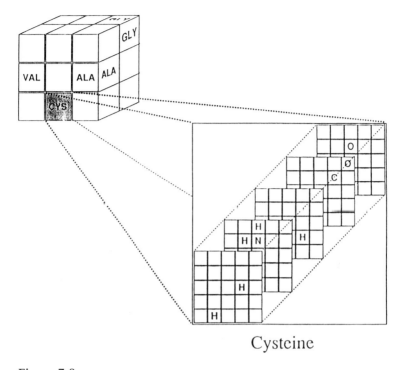

Cysteine

Figure 7.8
Symbolic array of molecular fragment.

able to reason at multiple levels of abstraction when analyzing a particular molecular scene. Figure 7.8 depicts a three-dimensional image of a fragment of a protein secondary structure, and an embedded amino acid residue substructure containing symbols denoting atoms. Bonding at the residue and atomic level is made explicit through structural adjacency in the representation.

For image recognition and classification, it is necessary to pick out characteristic properties and ignore irrelevant variations. One approach to image classification is on the basis of shape. Although the visual representation provides one approach to shape determination, the spatial representation allows for a hierarchical, topological representation for shape. This approach is particularly useful in applications where images are subject to a large number of transformations. For example, a human body can be configured many ways depending on the positions of the arms, legs, and so forth. Although it is impossible to store a separate representation for every possible configuration, it is

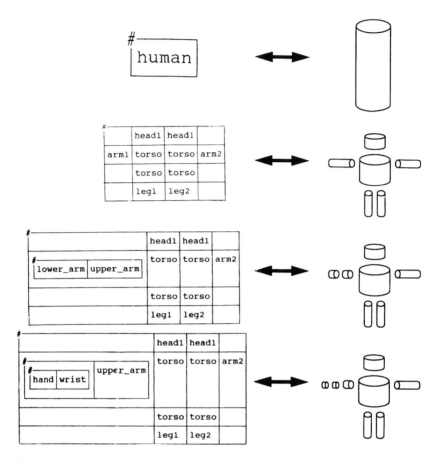

Figure 7.9
Spatial representation for topological shape description.

possible to represent a body using a symbolic array that makes explicit
the parts of the body and the relations among parts that remain constant under allowable transformations. Figure 7.9 illustrates such a
spatial representation. Combined with a primitive shape descriptor
(such as generalized cylinder), the spatial representation provides for
multidimensional shape descriptors as proposed by Marr (1982).

The spatial representation can be thought of as descriptive
because it can be expressed as a propositional representation, where
the predicates are spatial relationships and the arguments are concrete,
imaginable objects. Although information in the spatial representation can be expressed as propositions, the representations are not

computationally equivalent, that is, the efficiency of the inference mechanisms is not the same. The spatial structure of images has properties not possessed by deductive propositional representations. As pointed out by Lindsay (1988, p. 231), these properties help avoid the "combinatorial explosion by correct but trivial inferences that must be explicitly represented in a propositional system." Lindsay also argued that the spatial image representations (symbolic representations in our case) support nondeductive inference using built-in constraints on the processes that construct and access them. Consider, for example, the spatial representation of the map of Europe. To retrieve the information about what countries are north of Germany, we need only search a small portion of the symbolic array. Alternatively, in a propositional approach, the spatial relations would be stored as axioms such as

north-of(Britain,Portugal), *north-of(France,Spain)*, *north-of(Holland, Belgium)* . . . ,

and general rules such as

north-of$(X, Y) \land$ *north-of*$(Y, Z) \rightarrow$ *north-of*(X, Z).

To determine what countries are north of Germany using this representation involves considering all axioms plus recursive calls to the general rule. Thus, although the information embodied in the spatial representation is derivable from propositional knowledge, the indexing of this information using an array data structure can make spatial reasoning more efficient.

Another advantage of symbolic arrays, with respect to propositional representations, concerns temporal reasoning. Any cognitive system, natural or artificial, should be able to deal with a dynamic environment in which a change in a single item of knowledge might have widespread effects. The problem of updating a system's representation of the state of the world to reflect the effects of actions is known as the *frame problem* (Raphael, 1971). Representing an image as a symbolic array has advantages when considering this problem. Consider, for example, changing the position of a country in our map of Europe. In a propositional representation we would have to consider all of the effects that this would have on the current state. Using the symbolic array to store the map, we need only delete the country from its previous position and insert it in the new one. Because spatial relationships are interpreted, not logically inferred, from image representations, we eliminate some of the problems associated with nonmonotonicity in domains involving spatial and/or temporal reasoning. There still remains, however, the problem of dealing with truth maintenance if we desire to preserve relations as changes are made.

The representation scheme provides the ability to extract propositional information from symbolic arrays and to create or manipulate symbolic arrays with respect to propositional information. It should be noted, though, that the spatial representation does not provide the full expressive power of first-order logic: We cannot express quantification or disjunction. For example, it is not possible to represent an image of Europe that denotes the fact that Britain is either north of *or* south of Portugal. But mental images cannot express such information either. The representation scheme can be integrated with a logic representation through Nlog, a logic programming environment based on the theory of nested arrays (Glasgow, Fortier, and Allen, 1991). In this environment, the spatial information extracted through imagery processes can be used as propositions in logical deductions.

Primitive Functions for Computational Imagery

Approaches to knowledge representation are distinguished by the operations performed on the representations. Thus, the effectiveness of our scheme can be partially measured by how well it facilitates the implementation of imagery-related processes. In this section we review some of the primitive imagery functions that have been defined for the scheme. We also discuss how these functions provide the building blocks for more complex processes.

In his computational model for imagery, Kosslyn (1980) considered three basic categories of image processes: procedures for image generation (mapping deep representations into visual representations), procedures for evaluating a visual image, and procedures for transforming an image. Although we attempt to capture much of the functionality of the procedures described by Kosslyn, and in fact can categorize our operations similarly, the nature of our representations imply great difference in the implementations. For example, we define operations for both visual and spatial reasoning of three-dimensional images. Also, because our images can be organized hierarchically, we have defined functions that allow us to depict parts of an image at varying levels of abstraction using embedded arrays. When considering spatial functions, we were also influenced by the work of Kritchevsky (1988), who defined (but did not implement) a classification scheme for elementary, spatial functions that include operations for spatial perception, spatial memory, spatial attention, spatial mental operations, and spatial construction. As well as attempting to capture much of the functionality derived from cognitive studies of behavior, we have been influenced by our desire to incorporate our tools in reasoning systems for knowledge-based system development. Thus, we have been concerned with issues such as efficiency and reusability of our primitive functions.

The implementation of the imagery functions assumes global variables corresponding to the current states of long-term and working memory. The primitive functions modify these states by retrieving images from memory, transforming the contents of working memory or storing new (or modified) images in long-term memory.

We consider the primitive functions for imagery in three classes corresponding to the three representations: deep, visual, and spatial. Functions for deep and visual memory have been considered previously in research areas such as semantic memory, vision, computational geometry, and graphics. Thus, we provide a brief overview of these classes and concentrate on the more novel aspect of our research, the functions for spatial reasoning. We also discuss the processes involved in transforming one representation into another, a powerful feature of our knowledge representation scheme. Note that the proposed functions have been specified using array theory and implemented in the programming language Nial.

Long-Term Memory Functions The frame concept was initially proposed as a model for analogy-driven reasoning (Minsky, 1975). In the context of imagery, this type of reasoning involves the understanding of an image in a new context based on previously stored images. The functions for the deep representation of imagery are exactly those of the Nial Frame Language (Hache, 1986). In this language, imagery frames contain information describing images or classes of images, where knowledge is organized into slots that represent the attributes of an image.

Like most frame languages, the Nial frame language uses a semantic network approach to create configurations of frame taxonomies. The hierarchical network approach supports AKO links for implementing an inheritance mechanism within the frame structure. Frames in the language are implemented and manipulated as nested association lists of slots and values. Creating a generic or instance frame for an image requires assigning values to its slots, which is achieved using the function *fdefine*. Information is modified, added to, or deleted from an existing frame using the *fchange*, *fput*, and *fdelete* operators. Knowledge is retrieved (directly or through inheritance) from frames using the *fget* function. These and many other frame functions are implemented as part of the Nial AI Toolkit (Jenkins, et al., 1988).

The decomposition of images into their components is an important concept of computational imagery. This is achieved through a PARTS slot that contains the meaningful parts of an image and their relative location. Because the spatial representation of an image is stored relative to a particular axis, an instance frame may also contain an ORIENTATION slot. As described later, the PARTS and ORIENTATION slots allow for reconstruction of the spatial representation of an image.

Functions for Visual Reasoning Functions for visual reasoning have been studied extensively in areas such as machine vision and graphics. Similar to previous work, we consider visual images as surface or occupancy representations that can be constructed, transformed, and analyzed.

The occupancy array representation for the visual component of imagery can be constructed in a number of ways, depending on the domain of application. For example, the visual representation can be stored as generalized shape descriptions and regenerated at varying levels of resolution. They may also be reconstructed from geometric information stored in the deep representation.

Imagery functions for manipulating occupancy arrays include *rotate*, *translate*, and *zoom*, which change the orientation, location, or size of a visual image. Functions for retrieving *volume* and *shape* are also being implemented. Whereas many of these functions are generic, domain-specific functions can also be implemented for a particular application. For example, when considering molecular scenes we are concerned with a class of shape descriptors that correspond to the shape of molecular fragments at varying levels of abstraction (e.g., residues, secondary structure, molecule, etc.)

Functions for Spatial Reasoning   Whereas functions for visual and memory-based reasoning have been studied previously, the primitive functions for spatial imagery are more unique to our representation. The importance of spatial reasoning is supported by research in a number of areas, including computer vision, task planning, navigation for mobile robots, spatial databases, symbolic reasoning, and so on (Chen, 1990). Within the imagery context we consider spatial reasoning in terms of a knowledge representation framework that is general enough to apply to various problem domains. We also consider the relationship of spatial image representations to visual and deep representations.

As mentioned earlier, the functions for computational imagery are implemented assuming a global environment consisting of a frame knowledge base and the current working-memory representation. Generally, the working-memory representation consists of a single symbolic array (for spatial reasoning) or an occupancy array (for visual reasoning). One exception to this case is when we are using the spatial array to browse an image by focusing and unfocusing attention on particular subimages. In this case we need to represent working memory as a stack, where we push images onto the stack as we focus and pop images from the stack as we unfocus. Table 7.1 presents a summary of some of the functions for spatial imagery. We specify these functions as mappings with parameters corresponding to deep memory (DM), working memory (WM), image name (N) and relative or absolute location (L).

In order to reason with images, it is necessary to provide functions that allow us to interpret the spatial representations in terms of propositions within a given domain. For example, consider the three-term series problem: *John is taller than Mary, Sam is shorter than Mary, who is tallest?* It has been suggested that people represent and solve

Table 7.1
Primitive Functions for Spatial Reasoning

Name	Mapping	Description
retrieve	$DM \times N \rightarrow WM$	Reconstruct spatial image
put	$WM \times N \times N \times L \rightarrow WM$	Place one image component relative to another
find	$WM \times N \rightarrow L$	Find location of component
delete	$WM \times N \rightarrow WM$	Delete image component
move	$WM \times N \times L \rightarrow WM$	Move image component to new location
turn	$WM \times Direction \rightarrow WM$	Rotate image 90° in specified direction
focus	$WM \times N \rightarrow WM$	Replace specified subimage with its spatial representation
unfocus	$WM \rightarrow WM$	Return to original image
store	$WM \times DM \times N \rightarrow DM$	Stores current image in long-term memory
adjacent	$WM \times N \rightarrow N^*$	Determine adjacent image components

such a problem using an array where the spatial relationships correspond to the relative heights (Huttenlocker, 1968):

John	Mary	Sam

As discussed earlier, describing and solving such a problem using a propositional approach involves an exhaustive search of all the axioms describing the relation. The symbolic array representation allows direct access to such information using a domain-specific array theory function *tallest*, which returns the first element of the array:

tallest is operation A $\{first\ A\}$.

If our array is representing a map domain, we could similarly define domain-specific functions for *north-of, east-of, bordering-on*, and so forth.

Cognitive theories for pattern recognition support the need for *attention* in imagery, where attention is defined as the ability to concentrate tasks on a component (or components) of an image. The concept of attention is achieved using the spatial representation by defining a global variable that corresponds to a region of attention (and possibly an orientation) in a spatial representation of an image and implementing functions that implicitly refer to this region. For example, we have defined functions that initialize a region of attention (*attend*), shift attention to a new region (*shift*), retrieve the components in the region of attention (*at-attend*), focus on region of attention to retrieve detail (*focus-attend*), and so on. These functions are particularly useful for applications where we wish to describe and reason about a scene from an internal, rather than external, perspective. Consider, for example, a motion-planning application where the spatial representation reflects the orientation and current location of the moving body.

Complex Functions for Imagery   Using the primitive functions for computational imagery we can design processes corresponding to more complex imagery tasks. For example, a function for visual pattern matching can be defined using the *rotation* and *translation* functions to align two visual representations of images, and a primitive *compare* function to measure the similarity between these occupancy arrays.

To retrieve properties of an image, it may be necessary to focus on details of subimages. For example, we may wish to determine all the regions of countries on the border of an arbitrary country *X*. This can easily be determined by applying the *focus* function to the countries *adjacent* to country *X* and then determining the *content* of these subimages. This can be expressed as the array theory function definition *border*, where the body of the definition is enclosed by the curly brackets:

border is operation X {content (EACH focus) adjacent X}.

A key feature of our approach to knowledge representation for imagery is the underlying array theory semantics, which allows us to consider all representations as array data structures and implement functions that transform one representation of an image to another. Figure 7.10 illustrates the transformations supported by the scheme. Although the implementation of functions used for storage, retrieval, and interpretation may be complex and domain specific, the primitive functions for imagery provide a basis for their implementation. For

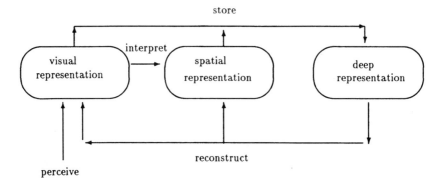

Figure 7.10
Stages of image representation.

further details of the use of imagery for image interpretation in the domain of molecular scene analysis see Glasgow, Fortier, and Allen (1991).

Contributions of Computational Imagery

In the introduction we proposed three goals for our research in computational imagery: the cognitive science goal, the AI goal, and the applications goal. Combined, these goals attempt to address the fundamental question: *What are the underlying processes involved in mental imagery, and how can corresponding computational processes be efficiently implemented and used to solve real-world problems?* We do not believe that the three goals can be approached independently. The representations and functionality of computational imagery are motivated by empirical results from cognitive science, as well as the pragmatic needs of applications in AI. Also, the tools that have been developed for computational imagery can be used to implement and test cognitive theories and thus increase our understanding of mental imagery. In this section we discuss the major contributions of computational imagery to each of the prescribed goals.

Cognitive Science Goal

A primary objective of research in cognitive science is to study and explain how the mind works. One aspect of work in this area is the theory of computability. If a model is computable, then it is usually comprehensible, complete, and available for analysis; theories that are implemented can be checked for sufficiency and used to simulate new predictive results. In a discussion of the issues of computability of cognitive theories for imagery, Kosslyn (1980) expressed frustration with existing implementation tools:

> There is a major problem with this approach however; the program will not run without numerous "kluges," numerous ad hoc manipulations required by the realities of working with a digital computer and a programming language like ALGOL or LISP. (p. 137)

Kosslyn went on to state that:

> The ideal would be a precise, explicit language in which to specify the theory and how it maps into the program. (p. 138)

Array theory, combined with the primitive functions and representations for computational imagery, provides such a meta-language. Moreover, it allows us to represent an image either visually or spatially, and provides for the implementation and testing of alternative, and possibly conflicting, models for mental imagery.

Consider the problem of mental rotation. Although empirical observations conclude that rotation involves an object representation being moved through intermediate orientations (Shepard and Cooper, 1982), a still unresolved issue is the actual content of the representation used. One obvious representation is a visual depiction of the object that preserves detailed three-dimensional shape information. An alternative approach is one in which the object is represented as vectors corresponding to the major axes of the object (Just and Carpenter, 1985). This type of representation can be considered as spatial in nature: It preserves connectivity of parts but discards surface information about the image. Furthermore, whereas some researchers argue that images encode size (e.g., Kosslyn, 1980), others claim that mental images preserve information about relative positions but not size (e.g., Kubovy and Podgorny, 1981). This conflict, as possibly others, could be attributed to the different representations used by subjects in the different experimental tasks. Using the primitives of computational imagery and array theory, such theories could be simulated and analyzed. Although we are not interested in entering into the imagery debate, we suggest that such simulations could contribute to discussions in this area. As another example, consider that Pylyshyn's (1981) main criticism of depictive theories of imagery is that they confuse physical distance in the world with the representation of distance in the head. The visual representation for computational imagery does, in fact, attach a real distance to the representation, in terms of the number of cells in the array depicting the image. The spatial representation, on the other hand, does not preserve distance information. Thus, the distinct representations could be used to model conflicting theories of image scanning.

The use of abstract representations for storing and manipulating three-dimensional images has been supported by research in cognition. Attneave (1974) suggested that humans represent three-dimensional objects using an internal model that at some abstract level is structurally isomorphic to the object. This isomorphism provides a "what–where" connection between the visual perception of an object and its location in space. A similar connection exists between the visual and spatial representations for imagery.

The human brain is often compared to an information-processing system where computations can either be serial or parallel. Ullman (1984) suggested that there may be several forms of parallelism involved in mental imagery. One form is spatial parallelism, which corresponds to the same operations being applied concurrently to different spatial locations in an image. Functional parallelism occurs when different operations are applied simultaneously to the same location. Funt (1983) also argued that many spatial problems are amenable to parallel processing. In developing a parallel computational model for the rotation problem, Funt was able to simulate the linear-time behavior corresponding to the human solution of the problem.

As well as allowing for multiple representations for testing cognitive theories, the array theory underlying computational imagery also provides both sequential and parallel constructs for specifying the processes involved in imagery. For example, the *EACH* transformer of array theory is a primitive second-order function that applies an operation to all of the arguments of an array, that is, $EACH$ $f[A_1, \ldots, A_n] = [f(A_1), \ldots, f(A_n)]$. Thus, we could specify a spatial parallel operation such as *EACH focus*, which would simultaneously reconstruct all of the subimages in a given image. Functional parallelism can be captured using the *atlas* notation of array theory. An atlas is a list of functions that may be applied in parallel to an array. For example, the expression $[f_1, f_2, \ldots, f_n]$ A specifies simultaneous application to the functions $f_1, \ldots, f_n$ to array A. Using the atlas construct and the functions of computational imagery we can specify such spatial parallelism as [*turn, move*], which expresses the simultaneous updating of working and deep memory to reflect the translation and rotation of an image.

A full study of the relationship between parallel processing in mental imagery and computational parallelism is a topic for future research. It has previously been demonstrated that the constructs of array theory are powerful enough to express a wide gambit of concurrent processing (Glasgow, et al., 1989). It may then be possible to analyze the limitations of parallel processing in cognitive tasks by analyzing the limitations when specifying these in array theory; if we cannot express a parallel algorithm for a task, then perhaps it is inherently sequential, cognitively as well as computationally.

A detailed discussion of the relationship between mind and computer was presented by Jackendoff (1989), who addressed the issue of studying the mind in terms of computation. More specifically, Jackendoff suggested that to do so involves a strategy that divides cognitive science into studies of structure and processing. Our functional approach to computational imagery is complimentary to this philosophy; image representations are array data structures, which can be considered distinctly from the array functions that operate on them. Jackendoff also supported the possibility of different levels of visual representation with varying expressive powers.

In summary, the underlying mathematics for computational imagery satisfies Kosslyn's ideal by providing a precise and explicit language for specifying theories of mental imagery. Visual and spatial representations are implemented as arrays and manipulated using the primitive functions of computational imagery, which themselves are expressed as array theory operations. Finally, the primitives of array theory and computational imagery have been directly mapped into Nial programs, which run without any "kluges" or "ad hoc manipulations." Note that the theory can also provide the basis for other implementations of computational imagery, as illustrated by the Lisp implementation of Thagard and Tanner (1991).

AI Goal

AI research is concerned with the discovery of computational tools for solving hard problems that rely on the extensive use of knowledge. Whereas traditional approaches to knowledge representation have been effective for linguistic reasoning, they do not always embody the salient visual and spatial features of an image. Also, they do not allow for an efficient implementation of the operations performed on this information, such as comparing shapes and accessing relevant spatial properties.

Whereas representations and operations for visual reasoning have previously been studied in imagery, as well as other areas such as computer vision and graphics, there has been little attention given to knowledge representations for spatial reasoning. We suggest that the proposed scheme for representing and manipulating spatial images has several advantages over visual or propositional representations. First, the spatial structure imposed by symbolic arrays supports efficient, nondeductive inferencing. Furthermore, the symbolic array representation for images can deal more easily with dynamic environments.

The symbolic array representation for computational imagery has also provided the basis for analogical reasoning in spatial problems (Conklin and Glasgow, 1992; Glasgow, 1991). A thesis of this work is that the structural aspects of images, in particular the spatial relations among their parts, can be used to guide analogical access for spatial reasoning. Preliminary results in the conceptual clustering of chess game motifs has illustrated that computational imagery can be applied to the area of image classification. Currently, we are extending this work to include classification of molecular structures based on spatial analogies (Conklin, et al., 1992).

Applications Goal

Since the time of Aristotle, imagery has been considered by many as a major medium of thought. Einstein stated that his abilities did not lie in mathematical calculations but in his visualization abilities (Holton, 1971). Similarly, the German chemist Kekulé stated that it was spontaneous imagery that led him to the discovery of the structure of benzene (MacKenzie, 1965). Mental simulations provide insights that contribute to effective problem-solving techniques. Thus, it is only natural to use the representations and functions of computational imagery to develop knowledge-based systems that incorporate the imagery problem-solving paradigm. One such system is an application to the problem of molecular scene analysis (Glasgow, Fortier, and Allen, 1991), which combines tools from the areas of protein crystallography and molecular database analysis, through a framework of computational imagery.

In determining structures, crystallographers relate the use of visualization or imagery in their interpretation of electron density maps of a molecular scene. These maps contain features that are analyzed in terms of the expected chemical constitution of the crystal. Thus, it is natural for crystallographers to use their own mental recall of known molecular structures, or of fragments thereof, to compare with, interpret, and evaluate the electron density features. Because molecular scenes can be represented as three-dimensional visual or spatial images, this mental pattern recognition process can be implemented using the primitive functions of computational imagery.

In molecular scene analysis, we attempt to locate and identify the recognizable molecular fragments within a scene. As in Marr's (1982, p. 3) definition of computational vision, it is the "process of discovering what is present in the world, and where it is." The integrated methodology for molecular scene analysis is being implemented as a knowledge-based system, through the development of five independent, communicating processes: (1) retrieval and reconstruction of visual representation of anticipated motifs from the long-term memory (deep representation) of molecular images; (2) enhancement and segmentation of the visual representation of the three-dimensional electron density map molecular scene; (3) visual pattern matching of the segmented image features with the retrieved visual motifs; (4) analysis and evaluation of the hypothesized, partially interpreted spatial representation of the perceived image; and (5) resolution and reconstruction of the molecular image. These processes are applied iteratively, resulting in progressively higher resolution images, until ultimately, a fully interpreted molecular scene is reconstructed.

The organization of the comprehensive information of crystal and molecular structures into a deep representation is crucial to the overall strategy for molecular scene analysis. This representation stores concepts and instances of molecular scene in terms of their structural and conceptual hierarchies. A serious problem in this domain, and in general, is to find appropriate visual and spatial depictions. This involves determining what features (visual or spatial) we wish to preserve in each of the representations. Initial algorithms have been developed to construct visual representations that depict the surface structure of an image and spatial representations that preserve bonding and symmetry information. Whether these are the most appropriate structures for all our reasoning in the domain is still an open question.

A full implementation of the knowledge-based system for molecular scene analysis is an ambitious and on-going research project. To date, we have been encouraged by preliminary results in the development of a long-term memory model (deep representation) for molecular scenes and the implementation of some of the essential tasks of molecular imagery. These tasks include transforming geometric information into spatial and visual representations, evaluation of partially interpreted images, classification and retrieval of images, and visual and spatial comparison of molecular scenes.

Although molecular scene analysis shares many features with visual scene analysis, it also differs in many ways. Both tasks involve segmentation of perceived images, retrieval and reconstruction of image templates, and pattern matching for object classification. The problem of molecular scene analysis is more tractable, however. Molecular images are perceived in three dimensions, thus eliminating the bottleneck of early vision routines. As well, the molecular domain is highly constrained: Molecular interactions and symmetry constraints impose hard restrictions on the image representations. Finally, there exists a wealth of knowledge about molecular scenes and molecular interactions in existing crystallographic databases. Using machine-learning techniques, we hope, ultimately, to generalize, correlate, and classify this information.

Although molecular scene analysis is only one of many potential applications for computational imagery, we feel that it is important to apply our reasoning paradigm to a complex problem that involves extensive imagery abilities when carried out by humans. Because of the experience embodied in existing crystallographic databases and algorithms, the availability of experts in the field and the natural constraints that exist in the domain, we believe that the important and real problem of molecular image reconstruction is an ideal test case for the concepts and implementations of computational imagery. It also suggests that the multiple representations of the scheme provide the framework for a complete computational model for the complex reasoning tasks involved in scene analysis.

Other potential applications for imagery-based systems include haptic perception and medical imaging. Literature in haptic perception provides evidence for an interdependence between haptic perception and visual imagery (Katz, 1989). Of special interest, are applications such as motion planning and game playing, which combine spatial and temporal reasoning. As suggested earlier, the spatial representation for computational imagery facilitates nondeductive reasoning, thus precluding many of the nonmonotonicity problems involved in deductive approaches in these areas. Preliminary work in imagery and machine learning has demonstrated that the spatial representation for imagery can be used to depict and reason about structural motifs in a chess game (Conklin and Glasgow, 1992). As well, the representations for computational imagery have been used to describe the role of visual thinking in such complex domains as atomic theory development (Thagard and Hardy, 1992).

Discussion

This article introduces the concept of computational imagery, which treats imagery as a problem-solving paradigm in AI. By proposing a knowledge representation scheme that attempts to capture the fundamental principles of mental imagery, we provide a foundation for implementing systems relying on imagery-based reasoning.

Aside from related research in perception and early work in frame representations, the AI community has given little attention to the topic of imagery. Thus, we rely on relevant theories of cognition to provide initial guidance for our research. We are also driven by the need to apply the scheme to real-world applications. The representation scheme is not intended to be a model of mental imagery; we do not claim that in human working memory two "mind's eyes" exist that process visual and spatial representations identical to the ones we have implemented. What we do suggest is that the internal image representations are informationally equivalent to representations involved in our scheme, that is, information in one representation is inferable from the other (Larkin and Simon, 1987).

The knowledge representation scheme for computational imagery includes three image representations, each appropriate for a different kind of information processing. A set of primitive functions, corresponding to the fundamental processes involved in mental imagery, has been designed using the mathematics of array theory and implemented in the functional array language Nial. These functions provide the building blocks for more complex imagery-related processes.

The most relevant previous contribution to imagery is the work of Kosslyn (1980), who proposed a computational theory for mental imagery. In that theory, images have two components: a surface representation (a quasipictorial representation that occurs in a visual buffer), and a deep representation for information stored in long-term memory. Like Kosslyn, we consider a separate long-term memory model for imagery, that encodes visual information descriptively. Unlike Kosslyn, we consider the long-term memory to be structured according to the decomposition and conceptual hierarchies of an image domain. Thus, we use a semantic network model, implemented using frames, to describe the properties of images. The long-term memory model in Kosslyn's theory is structured as sets of lists of propositions, stored in files.

The surface representation in Kosslyn's theory has been likened to spatial displays on a cathode ray tube screen; an image is displayed by selectively filling in cells of a two-dimensional array. Our scheme for representing images in working memory is richer in two important ways. First, we treat images as inherently three dimensional, although two-dimensional images can be handled as special cases. As pointed out by Pinker (1988), images must be represented and manipulated as patterns in three dimensions, which can be accessed using either an object-centered or a world-centered coordinate system. Second, we consider two working-memory representations, corresponding to the visual and spatial components of mental imagery. Just as the long-term memory stores images hierarchically, the visual and spatial representations use nested arrays to depict varying levels of resolution or abstraction of an image. Although the functionality of many of the primitive operations for computational imagery were initially motivated by the processes defined by Kosslyn's theory, their implementation varies greatly because of the nature of the image representations.

Possibly the most important distinction between our approach to computational imagery and Kosslyn's computational theory is the underlying motivation behind the two pieces of work. Kosslyn's model was initially developed to simulate and test a particular theory for mental imagery. Whereas computational imagery can be used to specify and implement cognitive theories, its development was based on the desire to construct computer programs to solve hard problems that require visual and spatial reasoning. Thus, efficiency and expressive power, not predictive and explanatory power, are our main concerns.

As a final illustration of the knowledge representation scheme, consider the island map used by Kosslyn (1980) to investigate the processes involved in mental image scanning. Figure 7.11 presents a visual depiction of such a map, as well as a spatial representation that preserves the properties of closeness (expressed as adjacency) and relative location of the important features of the island. It does not attempt to preserve relative distance. Consider answering such questions as: *What is the shape of the island? Is the beach or the tree closer to the hut?* These properties can be retrieved using the visual representation of the map. For example, we could analyze the surface of the island and compare this with known descriptions in the deep representation to retrieve shape information. Now consider the queries: *What is north of the tree? What is the three-dimensional structure of the hut?* Although it may be possible to derive this information from the visual representation, it would be a costly process. Using the symbolic array representation, however, we can easily access and retrieve spatial information using an efficient constrained search procedure. Although it may be argued that it is also initially costly to construct the spatial representation, the process of determining the structure of this representation can be carried out once, and then the results stored in the deep representation for later use.

More detailed information can be accessed from the spatial representation using the *focus* function to construct and inspect spatial images at lower levels of the structural hierarchy. For this particular example, there is not sufficient information to determine all of the three-dimensional features of the hut from the two-dimensional visual depiction. Using the computational imagery paradigm, which incorporates inheritance in the deep representation, we can construct

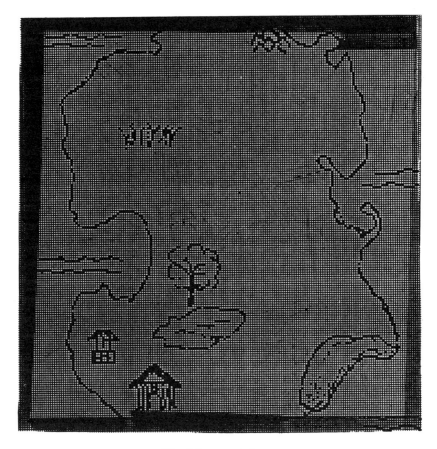

Visual Representation

Figure 7.11
Visual and spatial representation of Kosslyn's (1980) island map.

the three-dimensional symbolic array using information stored in the
generic frame for the concept "hut" to fill in missing details.

   It is worth noting here that the spatial representation is not just
a low-resolution version, or approximation, of the visual representation of an image. As well as capturing the structural hierarchy of an
image, the symbolic array may discard, not just approximate, irrelevant visual information. For example, in particular molecular applications we are primarily concerned with bonding information, which
is made explicit using adjacency in a three-dimensional symbolic array.
Visual and spatial properties such as size, distance, relative location

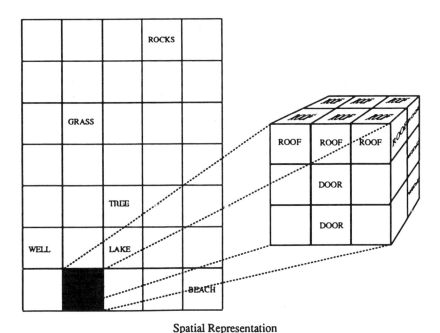

Spatial Representation

Figure 7.11 (continued)

(i.e., *above, behind, left-of,* etc.) may not be important for such applications and thus are not preserved.

Another approach to visual reasoning was presented by Funt (1980), who represented the state of the world as a diagram, and actions in the world as corresponding actions in the diagram. Similar to Kosslyn, Funt used two-dimensional arrays to denote visual images. A more recent model describes how visual information can be represented within the computational framework of discrete symbolic representations in such a way that both mental images and symbolic thought processes can be explained (Chandrasekaran and Narayanan, 1990). Although this model allows a hierarchy of descriptions, it is not spatially organized.

One way of evaluating our approach to computational imagery is in terms of the fundamental principles of mental imagery, as described in Finke (1989). In particular, the scheme was designed around the principle of *implicit encoding*, which states that imagery is used to extract information that was not explicitly stored in long-term memory. We retrieve information such as shape and size using the visual representation and information pertaining to the relative locations of objects in an image using the spatial representation for working memory. The principle of *perceptual equivalence* is captured by our assumption that perception and imagery share common representations. In fact, the processes involved in transforming a visual representation to a spatial representation are just those of scene analysis: taking a raw, uninterpreted image (visual representation) and identifying the subcomponents and their relative positions (spatial representation). The spatial representation captures the principle of *spatial equivalence*, because there is a correspondence between the arrangement of the parts of a symbolic array of an image, and the arrangement of the actual objects in the space. Note, though, that Finke argued for a continuous space of mental images, wheras the spatial representation assumes a discrete space. The principle of *structural equivalence* is preserved by the deep and the spatial representations, which capture the hierarchical organization of images. Furthermore, images in our representation scheme can be reorganized and reinterpreted. The scheme captures the functionality required of the principle of *transformational equivalence* by providing primitive array functions that can be used to manipulate both the visual and spatial representations of images.

When questioned on the most urgent unresolved difficulties in AI research, Sloman (1985) replied:

I believe that when we know how to represent shapes, spatial structures and spatial relationships, many other areas of AI will benefit, since spatial analogies and spatial modes of reasoning are so pervasive. (pp. 386–387)

Experimental results suggest that people use mental imagery for spatial reasoning. Thus, by facilitating an efficient implementation of the processes involved in mental imagery, computation imagery provides a basis for addressing the difficulties suggested by Sloman and developing AI systems that rely on representing, retrieving, and reasoning about visual and spatial properties of images.

Acknowledgments

The research described in this article was supported by grants from the Intelligent Robotics and Information Systems Federal Network

Center of Excellence, the Information Technology Research Center of Ontario, and the Natural Science and Engineering Research Council of Canada. We would like to acknowledge crystallographers Suzanne Fortier and Frank Allen for their collaboration and contributions in the area of molecular scene analysis.

References

Allen, F. H., Bergerhoff, G., and Sievers, R. (Eds.). (1987). *Crystallographic databases*. Chester, England: IUCr.

Anderson, J. R. (1978) Arguments concerning representations for mental imagery. *Psychological Review, 85*, 249–277.

Attneave, F. (1974). Apparent movement and the what-where connection. *Psychologica, 17*, 108–120.

Atwood, G. E. (1971). An experimental study of visual imagination and memory. *Cognitive Psychology, 2*.

Baddeley, A. D., and Lieberman, K. (1980). Spatial working memory. In R. Nickerson (Ed.), *Attention and performance* (Vol. 8, pp. 521–617). Hillsdale, NJ: Erlbaum.

Bauer, R. M., and Rubens, A. B. (1985). Agnosia. In K. M. Heilman and E. Valenstein (Eds.), *Clinical neuropsychology* (pp. 187–241). New York: Oxford University Press.

Biederman, I. (1987). Recognition by components: A theory of human image understanding. *Psychological Review, 94*, 115–147.

Block, N. (Ed.). (1981). *Imagery*. Cambridge, MA: MIT Press.

Brooks, L. R. (1968). Spatial and verbal components in the act of recall. *Canadian Journal of Psychology, 22*, 349–368.

Chandrasekaran, B., and Narayanan, N. H. (1990). Integrating imagery and visual representations. *Proceedings of the 12th Annual Conference of the Cognitive Science Society* (pp. 670–677). Hillsdale, NJ: Erlbaum.

Chen, S. (Ed.). (1990). *Advances in spatial reasoning* (Vols. 1 and 2). Norwood, NJ: Ablex.

Collins, A. M., and Quillian, M. P. (1969). Retrieval time from semantic memory. *Journal of Verbal Learning and Verbal Behavior, 8*, 240–247.

Conklin, D., Fortier, S., Glasgow, J. I., and Allen, F. A. (1992). Discovery of spatial concepts in crystallographic databases. *Proceedings of the Machine Discovery Workshop* (pp. 111–116).

Conklin, D., and Glasgow, J. I. (1992). Spatial analogy and subsumption. In D. Sleeman and P. Edwards (Eds.), *Machine Learning: Proceedings of the Ninth International Conference ML* (92) (pp. 111–116). San Mateo, CA: Morgan Kaufmann.

De Renzi, E. (1982). *Disorders of space exploration and cognition*. New York: Wiley.

Farah, M. J. (1988a). Is visual imagery really visual? Overlooked evidence from neuropsychology. *Psychological Review, 95*, 307–317.

Farah, M. J. (1988b). The neuropsychology of mental imagery: Converging evidence from brain-damaged and normal subjects. In J. Stiles-Davis, M. Kritchevsky, and U. Bellugi (Eds.), *Spatial cognition—Brain bases and development* (pp. 33–56). Hillsdale, NJ: Erlbaum.

Finke, R. A. (1989). *Principles of mental imagery*. Cambridge, MA: MIT Press.

Finke, R. A., Pinker, S., and Farah, M. J. (1989). Reinterpreting visual patterns in mental imagery. *Cognitive Science, 13*, 51–78.

Finke, R. A., and Slayton, K. (1988). Explorations of creative visual synthesis in mental imagery. *Memory and Cognition, 16*, 252–257.

Funt, B. V. (1980). Problem solving with diagrammatic representations. *Artificial Intelligence, 13*, 201–230.

Funt, B. V. (1983). A parallel-process model of mental rotation. *Cognitive Science, 7*, 67–73.

Glasgow, J. I. (1990). Artificial intelligence and imagery. In S. M. Humphrey and B. H. Kwasnick (Eds.), *Advances in classification research: Proceedings of the 1st ASIS SIG/CRF Classification Workshop*. Learned Information, Inc. for the American Society for Information Science.

Glasgow, J. I. (1991). Imagery and classification. In S. M. Humphrey (Ed.), *Advances in classification research and application*. Medford, NJ: Learned Information.

Glasgow, J. I., and Browse, R. (1985). Programming languages for artificial intellgence. *Computers and Mathematics with Applications, 11*, 431–448.

Glasgow, J. I., Fortier, S., and Allen, F. H. (1991). Crystal and molecular structure determination through imagery. *Proceedings of the Seventh Conference on Artificial Intelligence* (pp. 98–105).

Glasgow, J. I., Jenkins, M. A., Blevis, E., and Feret, M. (September, 1991). Logic programming with arrays. *IEEE Transactions on Knowledge and Data Engineering, 3* (3), 307–319.

Glasgow, J. I., Jenkins, M. A., McCrosky, C., and Meijer, H. (1989). Expressing parallel algorithms in Nial. *Parallel Computing, 11*, 331–347.

Hache, L. (1986). *The Nial frame language*. Unpublished master's thesis, Queen's University, Kingston, Canada.

Hinton, G. (1979). Some demonstrations of the effects of structural descriptions in mental imagery. *Cognitive Science, 3*, 231–250.

Holton, G. (1971). On trying to understand scientific genius. *American Scholar, 41*, 95–119.

Huttenlocker, J. (1968). Constructing spatial images: A strategy in reasoning. *Psychological Review, 4*, 277–299.

Intons-Peterson, M. J. (1983). Imagery paradigms: How vulnerable are they to experimenters' expectations? *Journal of Experimental Psychology: Human Perception and Performance, 9,* 394–412.

Israel, D. J. (1987). Some remarks on the place of logic in knowledge representation. In N. Cercone and G. McCalla (Eds.), *The knowledge frontier* (pp. 80–91). New York: Springer Verlag.

Jackendoff, R. (1989). *Consciousness and the computational mind.* Cambridge, MA: MIT Press.

Jannsen, W. H. (1976). Selective interference during the retrieval of visual images. *Quarterly Journal of Experimental Psychology, 28,* 535–539.

Jenkins, M. A., Glasgow, J. I., Blevis, E., Chau, R., Hache, E., and Lawson, E. (1988). The Nial AI toolkit. *Annual Proceedings of Avignon '88 Eighth International Workshop on Expert Systems and their Applications, 2,* 37–52.

Jenkins, M. A., Glasgow, J. I., and McCrosky, C. (1986). Programming styles in Nial. *IEEE Software, 86,* 46–55.

Jenkins, M. A., and Jenkins, W. H. (1985). *The Q'Nial Reference Manual.* Kingston, Canada: Nial Systems Ltd.

Just, M. A., and Carpenter, P. A. (1985). Cognitive coordinate systems: Accounts of mental rotation and individual differences in spatial ability. *Psychological Review, 92,* 137–172.

Katz, D. (1989). *The world of touch.* Hillsdale, NJ: Erlbaum.

Kosslyn, S. M. (1980). *Image and mind.* Cambridge, MA: Harvard University Press.

Kosslyn, S. M. (1987). Seeing and imagining in the cerebral hemispheres: A computational approach. *Psychological Review, 94,* 148–175.

Kosslyn, S. M., and Pomerantz, J. P. (1977). Imagery, propositions, and the form of internal representations. *Cognitive Science, 9,* 52–76.

Kritchevsky, M. (1988). The elementary spatial functions of the brain. In J. Stiles-Davis, M. Krithchevsky, and U. Bellugi (Eds.), *Spatial cognition—brain bases and development.* Hillsdale, NJ: Erlbaum.

Kubovy, M., and Podgorny, P. (1981). Does pattern matching require the normalization of size and orientation? *Perception and Psychophysics, 30,* 24–28.

Larkin, J., and Simon, H. A. (1987). Why a diagram is (sometimes) worth ten thousand words. *Cognitive Science, 10,* 65–99.

Levine, D. N., Warach, J., and Farah, M. J. (1985). Two visual systems in mental imagery: Dissociation of "what" and "where" in imagery disorders due to bilateral posterior cerebral lesions. *Neurology, 35,* 1010–1018.

Levine, M., (1978). A knowledge-based computer vision system. In A. Hanson and E. Riseman (Eds.), *Computer vision systems* (pp. 335–352). New York: Academic.

Lindsay, R. K. (1988). Images and inference. *Cognition, 29,* 229–250.

MacKenzie, N. (1965). *Dreams and dreaming.* London: Aldus Books.

Marr, D. (1982). *Vision: A computational investigation in the human representation of visual information.* San Francisco: Freeman.

Marr, D., and Nishihara, H. K. (1978). Representation and recognition of the spatial organization of three dimensional shapes. *Proceedings of the Royal Society, B200,* 269–294.

Marschark, M., Richman, C. L., Yuille, J. C., and Hunt, R. (1987). The role of imagery in memory: On shared and distinctive information. *Psychological Bulletin, 102,* 28–41.

McDermott, D. V., and Davis, E. (1984). Planning routes through uncertain territory. *Artificial Intelligence, 22,* 107–156.

Minsky, M. (1975). A framework for representing knowledge. In P. Winston (Ed.), *The Psychology of computer vision* (pp. 211–277). New York: McGraw Hill.

Mishkin, M., Ungerleider, L. G., and Macko, K. A. (1983). Object vision and spatial vision: Two cortical pathways. *Trends in Neuroscience, 6,* 414–417.

More, T. (1981). Notes on diagrams, logic and operations of array theory. In P. Bjorke and O. Franksen (Eds.), *Structures and operations in engineering and management systems.* Trondheim, Norway: Tapir Publishers.

Paivio, A. (1975). Perceptual comparisons through the mind's eye. *Memory and Cognition, 3,* 635–647.

Papadias, D., and Glasgow, J. I. (1991). A knowledge representation scheme for computational imagery. *Proceedings of the 13th Annual Conference of the Cognitive Science Society.* Hillsdale, NJ: Erlbaum.

Pinker, S. (1984). Visual cognition: An introduction. *Cognition, 18,* 1–63.

Pinker, S. (1988). A computational theory of the mental imagery medium. In M. Denis, J. Engelkamp, and J. T. E. Richardson (Eds.), *Cognitive and Neuropsychological Approaches to Mental Imagery* (pp. 17–36). Dordrecht/Boston/Lancaster: Martinus Nijhorff.

Pylyshyn, Z. W. (1973). What the mind's eye tells the mind's brain: A critique of mental imagery. *Psychological Bulletin, 80,* 1–24.

Pylyshyn, Z. W. (1981). The imagery debate: Analogue media versus tacit knowledge. *Psychological Review, 88,* 16–45.

Raphael, B. (1971). The frame problem in problem-solving systems. In X. Findler and X. Meltzer (Eds.), *Artificial intelligence and heuristic programming* (pp. 159–169). Edinburgh: Edinburgh University Press.

Ratcliff, G. (1982). Disturbances of spatial orientation associated with cerebral lesions. In X. Potegal (Ed.), *Spatial abilities: Development and physiological foundations* (pp. 301–331). New York: Academic.

Reed, S. K. (1974). Structural descriptions and the limitations of visual images. *Memory and Cognition, 2,* 329–336.

Shepard, R. N., and Cooper, L. A. (1982). *Mental images and their transformations*. Cambridge, MA: MIT Press.

Sloman, A. (1985). Artificial intelligence: Where are we. In Bobrow and Hayes (Eds.), *Artificial Intelligence*, *25*(1), 386.

Standing, L. (1973). Learning 10,000 pictures. *Quarterly Journal of Experimental Psychology*, *25*, 207–222.

Thagard, P., and Hardy, S. (1992). Visual thinking in the development of Dalton's atomic theory. In J. Glasgow and R. Hadley (Eds.), *Proceedings of AI '92* (pp. 30–37).

Thagard, P., and Tanner, C. (1991). *Lisp implementation for computational imagery* [Computer program]. Princeton, NJ: Princeton University.

Ullman, S. (1984). Visual routines. In S. Pinker (Ed.), *Visual Cognition* (pp. 97 159). Cambridge, MA: MIT Press.

Winston, P. H. (1975). Learning structural descriptions from examples. In P. H. Winston (Ed.), *Psychology of computer vision*. New York: McGraw-Hill.

The Architecture of Mind: A Connectionist Approach

David E. Rumelhart

Cognitive science has a long-standing and important relationship to the computer. The computer has provided a tool whereby we have been able to express our theories of mental activity; it has been a valuable source of metaphors through which we have come to understand and appreciate how mental activities might arise out of the operations of simple-component processing elements.

I recall vividly a class I taught some fifteen years ago in which I outlined the then-current view of the cognitive system. A particularly skeptical student challenged my account with its reliance on concepts drawn from computer science and artificial intelligence with the question of whether I thought my theories would be different if it had happened that our computers were parallel instead of serial. My response, as I recall, was to concede that our theories might very well be different, but to argue that that wasn't a bad thing. I pointed out that the inspiration for our theories and our understanding of abstract phenomena always is based on our experience with the technology of the time. I pointed out that Aristotle had a wax tablet theory of memory, that Leibniz saw the universe as clockworks, that Freud used a hydraulic model of libido flowing through the system, and that the telephone-switchboard model of intelligence had played an important role as well. The theories posited by those of previous generations had, I suggested, been useful in spite of the fact that they were based on the metaphors of their time. Therefore, I argued, it was natural that in our generation—the generation of the serial computer—we should draw our insights from analogies with the most advanced technological developments of our time. I don't now remember whether my response satisfied the student, but I have no doubt that we in cognitive science have gained much of value through our use of concepts drawn from our experience with the computer.

In addition to its value as a source of metaphors, the computer differs from earlier technologies in another remarkable way. The computer can be made to *simulate* systems whose operations are very different from the computers on which these simulations run. In this way we can use the computer to simulate systems with which we *wish* to have experience and thereby provide a source of experience that can be drawn upon in giving us new metaphors and new insights into how mental operations might be accomplished. It is this use of the computer that the connectionists have employed. The architecture that we are exploring is not one based on the von Neumann architecture of our current generation of computers but rather an architecture based on considerations of how brains themselves might function. Our strategy has thus become one of offering a general and abstract model of the computational architecture of brains, to develop algorithms and procedures well suited to this architecture, to simulate these procedures and architecture on a computer, and to explore them as hypotheses about the nature of the human information-processing system. We say that such models are *neurally inspired*, and we call computation on such a system *brain-style computation*. Our goal in short is to replace the computer metaphor with the brain metaphor.

8.1   Why Brain-Style Computation?

Why should a brain-style computer be an especially interesting source of inspiration? Implicit in the adoption of the computer metaphor is an assumption about the appropriate level of explanation in cognitive science. The basic assumption is that we should seek explanation at the *program* or *functional* level rather than the implementational level. It is thus often pointed out that we can learn very little about what kind of program a particular computer may be running by looking at the electronics. In fact we don't care much about the details of the computer at all; all we care about is the particular program it is running. If we know the program, we know how the system will behave in any situation. It doesn't matter whether we use vacuum tubes or transistors, whether we use an IBM or an Apple, the essential characteristics are the same. This is a very misleading analogy. It is true for computers because they are all essentially the same. Whether we make them out of vacuum tubes or transistors, and whether we use an IBM or an Apple computer, we are using computers of the same general design. When we look at essentially different architecture, we see that the architecture makes a good deal of difference. It is the architecture that determines which kinds of algorithms are most easily carried out on the machine in question. It is the architecture of the machine that determines the essential nature of the program itself. It is thus reasonable that we should begin by asking what we know about the architecture of the brain and how it might shape the algorithms underlying biological intelligence and human mental life.

The basic strategy of the connectionist approach is to take as its fundamental processing unit something close to an abstract neuron. We imagine that computation is carried out through simple interactions among such processing units. Essentially the idea is that these processing elements communicate by sending numbers along the lines that connect the processing elements. This identification already provides some interesting constraints on the kinds of algorithms that might underlie human intelligence.

The operations in our models then can best be characterized as "neurally inspired." How does the replacement of the computer metaphor with the brain metaphor as model of mind affect our thinking? This change in orientation leads us to a number of considerations that further inform and constrain our model-building efforts. Perhaps the most crucial of these is time. Neurons are remarkably slow relative to components in modern computers. Neurons operate in the time scale of milliseconds, whereas computer components operate in the time scale of nanoseconds—a factor of 10^6 faster. This means that human processes that take on the order of a second or less can involve only a hundred or so time steps. Because most of the processes we have studied—perception, memory retrieval, speech processing, sentence comprehension, and the like—take about a second or so, it makes sense to impose what Feldman (1985) calls the "100-step program" constraint. That is, we seek explanations for these mental phenomena that do not require more than about a hundred elementary sequential operations. Given that the processes we seek to characterize are often quite complex and may involve consideration of large numbers of simultaneous constraints, our algorithms *must* involve considerable parallelism. Thus although a serial computer could be created out of the kinds of components represented by our units, such an implementation would surely violate the 100-step program constraint for any but the simplest processes. Some might argue that although parallelism is obviously present in much of human information processing, this fact alone need not greatly modify our world view. This is unlikely. The speed of components is a critical design constraint. Although the brain has *slow* components, it has *very many* of them. The human brain contains billions of such processing elements. Rather than organize computation with many, many serial steps, as we do with systems whose steps are very fast, the brain must deploy many, many processing elements cooperatively and in parallel to carry out its activities. These design characteristics, among others, lead, I believe, to a general organization of computing that is fundamentally different from what we are used to.

A further consideration differentiates our models from those inspired by the computer metaphor—that is, the constraint that all the knowledge is *in the connections*. From conventional programmable computers we are used to thinking of knowledge as being stored in the state of certain units in the system. In our systems we assume that only very short-term storage can occur in the states of units; long-term storage takes place in the connections among units. Indeed it is the connections—or perhaps the rules for forming them through experience—that primarily differentiate one model from another. This is a profound difference between our approach and other more conventional approaches, for it means that almost all knowledge is *implicit* in the structure of the device that carries out the task rather than *explicit* in the states of units themselves. Knowledge is not directly accessible to interpretation by some separate processor, but it is built into the processor itself and directly determines the course of processing. It is acquired through tuning of connections as these are used in processing, rather than formulated and stored as declarative facts.

These and other neurally inspired classes of working assumptions have been one important source of assumptions underlying the connectionist program of research. These have not been the only considerations. A second class of constraints arises from our beliefs about the nature of human information processing considered at a more abstract, computational level of analysis. We see the kinds of phenomena we have been studying as products of a kind of constraint-satisfaction procedure in which a very large number of constraints act simultaneously to produce the behavior. Thus we see most behavior not as the product of a single, separate component of the cognitive system but as the product of large set of interacting components, each mutually constraining the others and contributing in its own way to the globally observable behavior of the system. It is very difficult to use serial algorithms to implement such a conception but very natural to use highly parallel ones. These problems can often be characterized as *best-match* or *optimization* problems. As Minsky and Papert (1969) have pointed out, it is very difficult to solve best-match problems serially. This is precisely the kind of problem, however, that is readily implemented using highly parallel algorithms of the kind we have been studying.

The use of brain-style computational systems, then, offers not only a hope that we can characterize how brains actually carry out certain information-processing tasks but also solutions to computational problems that seem difficult to solve in more traditional computational frameworks. It is here where the ultimate value of connectionist systems must be evaluated.

In this chapter I begin with a somewhat more formal sketch of the computational framework of connectionist models. I then follow with a general discussion of the kinds of computational problems that connectionist models seem best suited for. Finally, I will briefly review the state of the art in connectionist modeling.

The Connectionist Framework

There are seven major components of any connectionist system:

- a *set of processing units*;
- a *state of activation* defined over the processing units;
- an *output function* for each unit that maps its state of activation into an output;
- a *pattern of connectivity* among units;
- an *activation rule* for combining the inputs impinging on a unit with its current state to produce a new level of activation for the unit;
- a *learning rule* whereby patterns of connectivity are modified by experience;
- an *environment* within which the system must operate.

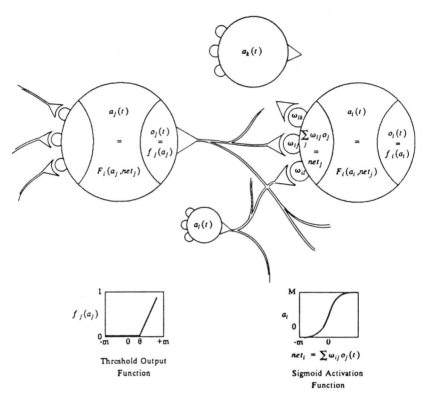

Figure 8.1
The basic components of a parallel distributed processing system.

Figure 8.1 illustrates the basic aspects of these systems. There is a set of processing units, generally indicated by circles in my diagrams; at each point in time each unit u_i has an activation value, denoted in the diagram as $a_i(t)$; this activation value is passed through a function f_i to produce an output value $o_i(t)$. This output value can be seen as passing through a set of unidirectional connections (indicated by lines or arrows in the diagrams) to other units in the system. There is associated with each connection a real number, usually called the *weight* or *strength* of the connection, designated w_{ij}, which determines the affect that the first unit has on the second. All of the inputs must then be combined, and the combined inputs to a unit (usually designated the *net input* to the unit) along with its current activation value determine its new activation value via a function F. These systems are viewed as being plastic in the sense that the pattern of interconnections is not fixed for all time; rather the weights can undergo modification as a function of experience. In this way the system can evolve. What a unit represents can change with experience, and the system can come to perform in substantially different ways.

A Set of Processing Units   Any connectionist system begins with a set of processing units. Specifying the set of processing units and what they represent is typically the first stage of specifying a connectionist model. In some systems these units may represent particular conceptual objects such as features, letters, words, or concepts; in others they are simply abstract elements over which meaningful patterns can be defined. When we speak of a distributed representation, we mean one in which the units represent small, featurelike entities we call *microfeatures*. In this case it is the pattern as a whole that is the meaningful level of analysis. This should be contrasted to a *one-unit–one-concept* or *localist* representational system in which single units represent entire concepts or other large meaningful entities.

All of the processing of a connectionist system is carried out by these units. There is no executive or other overseer. There are only relatively simple units, each doing its own relatively simple job. A unit's job is simply to receive input from its neighbors and, as a function of the inputs it receives, to compute an output value, which it sends to its neighbors. The system is inherently parallel in that many units can carry out their computations at the same time.

Within any system we are modeling, it is useful to characterize three types of units: *input*, *output*, and *hidden* units. Input units receive inputs from sources external to the system under study. These inputs may be either sensory inputs or inputs from other parts of the processing system in which the model is embedded. The output units send signals out of the system. They may either directly affect motoric systems or simply influence other systems external to the ones we are modeling. The hidden units are those whose only inputs and outputs are within the system we are modeling. They are not "visible" to outside systems.

The State of Activation   In addition to the set of units we need a representation of the state of the system at time t. This is primarily specified by a vector $\mathbf{a}(t)$, representing the pattern of activation over the set of processing units. Each element of the vector stands for the activation of one of the units. It is the pattern of activation over the set of units that captures what the system is representing at any time. It is useful to see processing in the system as the evolution, through time, of a pattern of activity over the set of units.

Different models make different assumptions about the activation values a unit is allowed to take on. Activation values may be continuous or discrete. If they are continuous, they may be unbounded or bounded. If they are discrete, they may take binary values or any of a small set of values. Thus in some models units are continuous and may take on any real number as an activation value. In other cases they may take on any real value between some minimum and maximum such as, for example, the interval $[0, 1]$. When activation values are restricted to discrete values, they most often are binary. Sometimes they are restricted to the values 0 and 1, where 1 is usually taken to mean that the unit is active and 0 is taken to mean that it is inactive.

Output of the Units   Units interact by transmitting signals to their neighbors. The strength of their signals and therefore the degree to which they affect their neighbors are determined by their degree of activation. Associated with each unit u_i is an output function $f_i(a_i(t))$, which maps the current state of activation to an output signal $o_i(t)$. In some of our models the output level is exactly equal to the activation level of the unit. In this case f is the identity function $f(x) = x$. Sometimes f is some sort of threshold function so that a unit has no affect on another unit unless its activation exceeds a certain value. Sometimes the function f is assumed to be a stochastic function in which the output of the unit depends probabilistically on its activation values.

The Pattern of Connectivity   Units are connected to one another. It is this pattern of connectivity that constitutes what the system knows and determines how it will respond to any arbitrary input. Specifying the processing system and the knowledge encoded therein is, in a connectionist model, a matter of specifying this pattern of connectivity among the processing units.

In many cases we assume that each unit provides an additive contribution to the input of the units to which it is connected. In such cases the total input to the unit is simply the weighted sum of the separate inputs from each of the individual units. That is, the inputs from all of the incoming units are simply multiplied by a weight and summed to get the overall input to that unit. In this case the total pattern of connectivity can be represented by merely specifying the weights for each of the connections in the system. A positive weight represents an excitatory input, and a negative weight represents an inhibitory input. It is often convenient to represent such a pattern of connectivity by a weight matrix $\mathbf{W}$ in which the entry w_{ij} represents the strength and sense of the connection from unit u_j to unit u_i. The weight w_{ij} is a positive number if unit u_j excites unit u_i; it is a negative number if unit u_j inhibits unit u_i; and it is 0 if unit u_j has no direct connection to unit u_i. The absolute value of w_{ij} specifies the *strength of the connection*.

The pattern of connectivity is very important. It is this pattern that determines what each unit represents. One important issue that may determine both how much information can be stored and how much serial processing the network must perform is the *fan-in* and *fan-out* of a unit. The fan-in is the number of elements that either excite or inhibit a given unit. The fan-out of a unit is the number of units affected directly by a unit. It is useful to note that in brains these numbers are relatively large. Fan-in and fan-out range as high as 100,000 in some parts of the brain. It seems likely that this large fan-in and fan-out allows for a kind of operation that is less like a fixed circuit and more statistical in character.

Activation Rule We also need a rule whereby the inputs impinging on a particular unit are combined with one another and with the current state of the unit to produce a new state of activation. We need function $\mathbf{F}$, which takes $\mathbf{a}(t)$ and the net inputs, $\text{net}_i = \sum_j w_{ij} o_j(t)$, and produces a new state of activation. In the simplest cases, when $\mathbf{F}$ is the identity function, we can write $\mathbf{a}(t+1) = \mathbf{W}\mathbf{o}(t) = \mathbf{net}\,(t)$. Sometimes $\mathbf{F}$ is a threshold function so that the net input must exceed some value before contributing to the new state of activation. Often the new state of activation depends on the old one as well as the current input. The function $\mathbf{F}$ itself is what we call the activation rule. Usually the function is assumed to be deterministic. Thus, for example, if a threshold is involved it may be that $a_i(t) = 1$ if the total input exceeds some threshold value and equals 0 otherwise. Other times it is assumed that **F** is stochastic. Sometimes activations are assumed to decay slowly with time so that even with no external input the activation of a unit will simply decay and not go directly to zero. Whenever $a_i(t)$ is assumed to take on continuous values, it is common to assume that **F** is a kind of sigmoid function. In this case an individual unit can *saturate* and reach a minimum or maximum value of activation.

Modifying Patterns of Connectivity as a Function of Experience
Changing the processing or knowledge structure in a connectionist system involves modifying the patterns of interconnectivity. In principle this can involve three kinds of modifications:

1. development of new connections;
2. loss of existing connections;
3. modification of the strengths of connections that already exist.

Very little work has been done on (1) and (2). To a first order of approximation, however, (1) and (2) can be considered a special case of (3). Whenever we change the strength of connection away from zero to some positive or negative value, it has the same effect as growing a new connection. Whenever we change the strength of a connection to zero, that has the same effect as losing an existing connection. Thus we have concentrated on rules whereby *strengths* of connections are modified through experience.

Virtually all learning rules for models of this type can be considered a variant of the *Hebbian* learning rule suggested by Hebb (1949) in his classic book *Organization of Behavior*. Hebb's basic idea is this: If a unit u_i receives an input from another unit u_j, then, if both are highly active, the weight w_{ij} from u_j to u_i should be *strengthened*. This idea has been extended and modified so that it can be more generally stated as

$$\delta w_{ij} = g(a_i(t), t_i(t))h(o_j(t), w_{ij}),$$

where $t_i(t)$ is a kind of *teaching* input to u_i. Simply stated, this equation says that the change in the connection from u_j to u_i is given by the product of a function $g(\ )$ of the activation of u_i and its teaching input t_i and another function $h(\ )$ of the output value of u_j and the connection strength w_{ij}. In the simplest versions of Hebbian learning, there is no teacher and the functions g and h are simply proportional to their first arguments. Thus we have

$$\delta w_{ij} = \varepsilon a_i o_j,$$

where ε is the constant of proportionality representing the learning rate. Another common variation is a rule in which $h(o_j(t), w_{ij}) = o_j(t)$ and $g(a_i(t), t_i(t)) = \varepsilon(t_i(t) - a_i(t))$. This is often called the *Widrow-Hoff*, because it was originally formulated by Widrow and Hoff (1960), or the *delta rule*, because the amount of learning is proportional to the *difference* (or delta) between the actual activation achieved and the target activation provided by a teacher. In this case we have

$$\delta w_{ij} = \varepsilon(t_i(t) - a_i(t))o_j(t).$$

This is a generalization of the *perceptron* learning rule for which the famous *perception convergence theorem* has been proved. Still another variation has

$$\delta w_{ij} = \varepsilon a_i(t)(o_i(t) - w_{ij}).$$

This is a rule employed by Grossberg (1976) and others in the study of *competitive learning*. In this case usually only the units with the strongest activation values are allowed to learn.

Representation of the Environment   It is crucial in the development of any model to have a clear representation of the environment in which this model is to exist. In connectionist models we represent the environment as a time-varying stochastic function over the space of input patterns. That is, we imagine that at any point in time there is some probability that any of the possible set of input patterns is impinging on the input units. This probability function may in general depend on the history of inputs to the system as well as outputs of the system. In practice most connectionist models involve a much simpler characterization of the environment. Typically the environment is characterized by a stable probability distribution over the set of possible input patterns independent of past inputs and past responses of the system. In this case we can imagine listing the set of possible inputs to the system and numbering them from 1 to M. The environment is then characterized by a set of probabilities p_i for $i = 1, \ldots, M$. Because each input pattern can be considered a vector, it is sometimes useful to characterize those patterns with nonzero probabilities as constituting *orthogonal* or *linearly independent* sets of vectors.

To summarize, the connectionist framework consists not only of a formal language but also a perspective on our models. Other qualitative and quantitative considerations arising from our understanding of brain processing and of human behavior combine with the formal system to form what might be viewed as an aesthetic for our model-building enterprises.

Computational Features of Connectionist Models

In addition to the fact that connectionist systems are capable of exploiting parallelism in computation and mimicking brain-style computation, connectionist systems are important because they provide good solutions to a number of very difficult computational problems that seem to arise often in models of cognition. In particular they are good at solving constraint-satisfaction problems, implementing content-addressable memory-storage systems, and implementing best match; they allow for the automatic implementation of similarity-based generalization; they exhibit graceful degradation with damage or information overload; and there are simple, general mechanisms for learning that allow connectionist systems to adapt to their environments.

Constraint Satisfaction   Many cognitive-science problems are usefully conceptualized as constraint-satisfaction problems in which a solution is given through the satisfaction of a very large number of mutually interacting constraints. The problem is to devise a computational algorithm that is capable of efficiently implementing such a system. Connectionist systems are ideal for implementing such a constraint-satisfaction system, and the trick for getting connectionist networks to solve difficult problems is often to cast the problem as a constraint-satisfaction problem. In this case we conceptualize the connectionist network as a *constraint network* in which each unit represents a hypothesis of some sort (for example, that a certain semantic feature, visual feature, or acoustic feature is present in the input) and in which each connection represents constraints among the hypotheses. Thus, for example, if feature B is expected to be present whenever feature A is present, there should be a positive connection from the unit corresponding to the hypothesis that A is present to the unit representing the hypothesis that B is present. Similarly if there is a constraint that whenever A is present B is expected *not* to be present, there should be a negative connection from A to B. If the constraints are weak, the weights should be small. If the constraints are strong, then the weights should be large. Similarly the inputs to such a network can also be thought of as constraints. A positive input to a particular unit means that there is evidence from the outside that the relevant feature is present. A negative input means that there is evidence from the outside that the feature is not present. The stronger the input, the greater the evidence. If such a network is allowed to run, it will eventually *settle* into a locally optimal state in which as many as possible of the constraints are satisfied, with priority given to the strongest constraints. (Actually, these systems will find a *locally* best solution to this constraint satisfaction problem. *Global* optima are more difficult to find.) The procedure whereby such a system *settles* into such a state is called *relaxation*. We speak of the system *relaxing* to a solution. Thus a large class of connectionist models contains constraint satisfaction models that settle on locally optimal solutions through the process of relaxation.

Figure 8.2 shows an example of a simple 16-unit constraint network. Each unit in the network represents a hypothesis concerning a vertex in a line drawing of a Necker cube. The network consists of two interconnected subnetworks—one corresponding to each of the two global interpretations of the Necker cube. Each unit in each network is assumed to receive input from the region of the input figure—the cube—corresponding to its location in the network. Each unit in figure 8.2 is labeled with a three-letter sequence indicating whether its vertex is hypothesized to be front or back (F or B), upper or lower (U or L), and right or left (R or L). Thus, for example, the lower-left unit of each subnetwork is assumed to receive input from the lower-left vertex of the input figure. The unit in the left network represents the hypothesis that it is receiving input from a lower-left vertex in the front surface of the cube (and is thus labeled FLL),

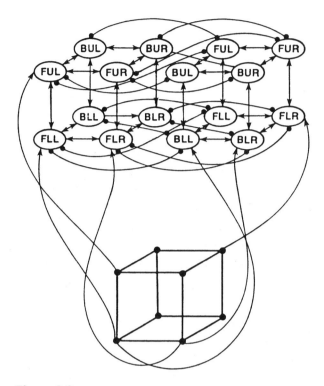

Figure 8.2
A simple network representing some constraints involved in perceiving a
Necker cube.

whereas the one in the right subnetwork represents the hypothesis
that it is receiving input from a lower-left vertex in the back surface
(BLL). Because there is a constraint that each vertex has a single
interpretation, these two units are connected by a strong negative
connection. Because the interpretation of any given vertex is constrained by the interpretations of its neighbors, each unit in a subnetwork is connected positively with each of its neighbors within the
network. Finally there is the constraint that there can be only one
vertex of a single kind (for example, there can be only one lower-left
vertex in the front plane FLL). There is a strong negative connection
between units representing the same label in each subnetwork. Thus
each unit has three neighbors connected positively, two competitors
connected negatively, and one positive input from the stimulus. For
purposes of this example the strengths of connections have been

arranged so that two negative inputs exactly balance three positive inputs. Further it is assumed that each unit receives an excitatory input from the ambiguous stimulus pattern and that each of these excitatory influences is relatively small. Thus if all three of a unit's neighbors are on and both of its competitors are on, these effects would entirely cancel out one another; and if there were a small input from the outside, the unit would have a tendency to come on. On the other hand if fewer than three of its neighbors were on and both of its competitors were on, the unit would have a tendency to turn off, even with an excitatory input from the stimulus pattern.

In the preceding paragraph I focused on the individual units of the networks. It is often useful to focus not on the units, however, but on entire *states* of the network. In the case of binary (on-off or 0-1) units, there is a total of 2^{16} possible states in which this system could reside. That is, in principle each of the 16 units could have either value 0 or 1. In the case of continuous units, in which each unit can take on any value between 0 and 1, the system can in principle take on any of an infinite number of states. Yet because of the constraints built into the network, there are only a few of those states in which the system will settle. To see this, consider the case in which the units are updated asynchronously, one at a time. During each time slice one of the units is chosen to update. If its net input exceeds 0, its value will be pushed toward 1; otherwise its value will be pushed toward 0.

Imagine that the system starts with all units off. A unit is then chosen at random to be updated. Because it is receiving a slight positive input from the stimulus and no other inputs, it will be given a positive activation value. Then another unit is chosen to update. Unless it is in direct competition with the first unit, it too will be turned on. Eventually a coalition of neighboring units will be turned on. These units will tend to turn on more of their neighbors in the same subnetwork and turn off their competitors in the other subnetwork. The system will (almost always) end up in a situation in which all of the units in one subnetwork are fully activated and none of the units in the other subnetwork is activated. That is, the system will end up interpreting the Necker cube as either facing left or facing right. Whenever the system gets into a state and stays there, the state is called a *stable state* or a *fixed point* of the network. The constraints implicit in the pattern of connections among the units determine the set of possible stable states of the system and therefore the set of possible interpretations of the inputs.

Hopfield (1982) has shown that it is possible to give a general account of the behavior of systems such as this one (with symmetric weights and asynchronous updates). In particular Hopfield has shown that such systems can be conceptualized as minimizing a global measure, which he calls the *energy* of the system, through a method of *gradient descent* or, equivalently, maximizing the constraints satisfied through a method of *hill climbing*. In particular Hopfield has shown that the system operates in such a way as to always move from a state that satisfies fewer constraints to a state that satisfies more constraints, where the measure of constraint satisfaction is given by

$$G(t) = \sum_i \sum_j w_{ij} a_i(t) a_j(t) + \sum_i \text{input}_i(t) a_i(t).$$

Essentially the equation says that the overall goodness of fit is given by the sum of the degrees to which each pair of units contributes to the goodness plus the degree to which the units satisfy the input constraints. The contribution of a pair of units is given by the product of their activation values and the weights connecting them. Thus if the weight is positive, each unit wants to be as active as possible— that is, the activation values for these two units should be pushed toward 1. If the weight is negative, then at least one of the units should be 0 to maximize the pairwise goodness. Similarly if the input constraint for a given unit is positive, then its contribution to the total goodness of fit is maximized by being the activation of that unit toward its maximal value. If it is negative, the activation value should be decreased toward 0. Of course the constraints will generally not be totally consistent. Sometimes a given unit may have to be turned on to increase the function in some ways yet decrease it in other ways. The point is that it is the sum of all of these individual contributions that the system seeks to maximize. Thus for every state of the system —every possible pattern of activation over the units—the pattern of inputs and the connectivity matrix **W** determine a value of the goodness-of-fit function. The system processes its input by moving upward from state to adjacent state until it reaches a state of maximum goodness. When it reaches such a *stable state* or *fixed point*, it will stay in that state and it can be said to have "settled" on a solution to the constraint-satisfaction problem or alternatively, in our present case, "settled into an interpretation" of the input.

It is important to see then that entirely *local* computational operations, in which each unit adjusts its activation up or down on the basis of its net input, serve to allow the network to converge toward states that maximize a *global* measure of goodness or degree of constraint satisfaction. Hopfield's main contribution to the present analysis was to point out this basic fact about the behavior of networks with symmetrical connections and asynchronous update of activations.

To summarize, there is a large subset of connectionist models that can be considered constraint-satisfaction models. These networks can be described as carrying out their information processing by climbing into states of maximal satisfaction of the constraints implicit in the network. A very useful concept that arises from this way of viewing these networks is that we can describe that behavior of these networks not only in terms of the behavior of individual units but also in terms of properties of the network itself. A primary concept for understanding these network properties is the *goodness-of-fit landscape* over which the system moves. Once we have correctly described this landscape, we have described the operational properties of the system—it will process information by moving uphill toward goodness maxima. The particular maximum that the system will find is determined by where the system starts and by the distortions of the space induced by the input. One of the very important descriptors of a goodness landscape is the set of maxima that the system can find, the size of the region that feeds into each maximum, and the height of the maximum itself. The states themselves correspond to possible interpretations, the peaks in the space correspond to the best interpretations, the extent of the foothills or skirts surrounding a particular peak determines the likelihood of finding the peak, and the height of the peak corresponds to the degree to which the constraints of the network are actually met or alternatively to the goodness of the interpretation associated with the corresponding state.

Interactive Processing   One of the difficult problems in cognitive science is to build systems that are capable of allowing a large number of knowledge sources to usefully interact in the solution of a problem. Thus in language processing we would want syntactic, phonological, semantic, and pragmatic knowledge sources all to interact in the construction of the meaning of an input. Reddy and his colleagues (1973) have had some success in the case of speech perception with the Hearsay system because they were working in the highly structured domain of language. Less structured domains have proved very difficult to organize. Connectionist models, conceptualized as constraint-satisfaction networks, are ideally suited for the blending of multiple-knowledge sources. Each knowledge type is simply another constraint, and the system will, in parallel, find those figurations of values that best satisfy all of the constraints from all of the knowledge sources. The uniformity of representation and the common currency of interaction (activation values) make connectionist systems especially powerful for this domain.

Rapid Pattern Matching, Best-Match Search, Content-Addressable Memory   Rapid pattern matching, best-match search, and content-addressable memory are all variants on the general best-match problem (compare Minsky and Papert 1969). Best-match problems are especially difficult for serial computational algorithms (it involves exhaustive search), but as we have just indicated connectionist systems can readily be used to find the interpretation that best matches a set of constraints. It can similarly be used to find stored data that best match some target. In this case it is useful to imagine that the network consists of two classes of units, with one class, the *visible* units, corresponding to the content stored in the network, and the remaining, *hidden* units are used to help store the patterns. Each visible unit corresponds to the hypothesis that some particular feature was present in the stored pattern. Thus we think of the content of the stored data as consisting of collections of features. Each hidden unit corresponds to a hypothesis concerning the *configuration* of features present in a stored pattern. The hypothesis to which a particular hidden unit corresponds is determined by the exact *learning rule* used to store the input and the characteristics of the ensemble of stored patterns. Retrieval in such a network amounts to turning on some of the visible units (a retrieval probe) and letting the system settle to the best interpretation of the input. This is a kind of pattern completion. The details are not too important here because a variety of learning rules lead to networks with the following important properties:

• When a previously stored (that is, familiar) pattern enters the memory system, it is amplified, and the system responds with a stronger version of the input pattern. This is a kind of recognition response.
• When an unfamiliar pattern enters the memory system, it is dampened, and the activity of the memory system is shut down. This is a kind of unfamiliarity response.
• When part of a familiar pattern is presented, the system responds by "filling in" the missing parts. This is a kind of recall paradigm in which the part constitutes the retrieval cue, and the filling in is a kind of memory-reconstruction process. This is a content-addressable memory system.
• When a pattern similar to a stored pattern is presented, the system responds by distorting the input pattern toward the stored pattern. This is a kind of assimilation response in which similar inputs are assimilated to similar stored events.
• Finally, if a number of similar patterns have been stored, the system will respond strongly to the central tendency of the stored patterns, even though the central tendency itself was never stored. Thus this sort of memory system automatically responds to prototypes even when no prototype has been seen.

These properties correspond very closely to the characteristics of human memory and, I believe, are exactly the kind of properties we want in any theory of memory.

Automatic Generalization and Direct Representation of Similarity

One of the major complaints against AI programs is their "fragility." The programs are usually very good at what they are programmed to do, but respond in unintelligent or odd ways when faced with novel situations. There seem to be at least two reasons for this fragility. In conventional symbol-processing systems similarity is indirectly represented and therefore are generally incapable of generalization, and most AI programs are not self-modifying and cannot adapt to their environment. In our connectionist systems on the other hand, the content is directly represented in the pattern and similar patterns have similar effects—therefore generalization is an automatic property of connectionist models. It should be noted that the degree of similarity between patterns is roughly given by the inner product of the vectors representing the patterns. Thus the dimensions of generalization are given by the dimensions of the representational space. Often this will lead to the right generalizations. There are situations in which this will lead to inappropriate generalizations. In such a case we must allow the system to *learn* its appropriate representation. In the next section I describe how the appropriate representation can be learned so that the correct generalizations are automatically made.

Learning A key advantage of the connectionist systems is the fact that simple yet powerful learning procedures can be defined that allow the systems to adapt to their environment. It was work on the learning aspect of these neurally inspired models that first led to an interest in them (compare Rosenblatt, 1962), and it was the demonstration that the learning procedures for complex networks could never be developed that contributed to the loss of interest (compare Minsky and Papert 1969). Although the *perceptron convergence procedure* and its variants have been around for some time, these learning procedures were limited to simple one-layer networks involving only input and output units. There were no hidden units in these cases and no internal representation. The coding provided by the external world had to suffice. Nevertheless these networks have proved useful in a wide variety of applications. Perhaps the essential character of such networks is that they map similar input patterns to similar output patterns. This is what allows these networks to make reasonable generalizations and perform reasonably on patterns that have never before been presented. The similarity of patterns in the connectionist system is determined by their overlap. The overlap in such networks is determined outside the learning system itself—by whatever produces the patterns.

The constraint that similar input patterns lead to similar outputs can lead to an inability of the system to learn certain mappings from input to output. Whenever the representation provided by the outside world is such that the similarity structure of the input and output patterns is very different, a network without internal representations (that is, a network without hidden units) will be unable to perform the necessary mappings. A classic example of this case is the exclusive-or (XOR) problem illustrated in table 8.1. Here we see that those patterns that overlap least are supposed to generate identical output values. This problem and many others like it cannot be performed by networks without hidden units with which to create their own

Table 8.1
XOR Problem

Input Patterns		Output Patterns
00	→	0
01	→	1
10	→	1
11	→	0

Table 8.2
XOR with Redundant Third Bit

Input Patterns		Output Patterns
000	→	0
010	→	1
100	→	1
111	→	0

internal representations of the input patterns. It is interesting to note that if the input patterns contained a third input taking the value 1 whenever the first two have value 1, as shown in table 8.2, a two-layer system would be able to solve the problem.

Minsky and Papert (1969) have provided a careful analysis of conditions under which such systems are capable of carrying out the required mappings. They show that in many interesting cases networks of this kind are incapable of solving the problems. On the other hand, as Minsky and Papert also pointed out, if there is a layer of simple perceptronlike hidden units, as shown in figure 8.3, with which the original input pattern can be augmented, there is always a recoding (that is, an internal representation) of the input patterns in the hidden units in which the similarity of the patterns among the hidden units can support any required mapping from the input to the output units. Thus if we have the right connections from the input units to a large enough set of hidden units, we can always find a representation that will perform any mapping from input to output through these hidden units. In the case of the XOR problem, the addition of a feature that detects the conjunction of the input units changes the similarity structure of the patterns sufficiently to allow the solution to be learned. As illustrated in figure 8.4, this can be done with a single hidden unit.

Output Patterns

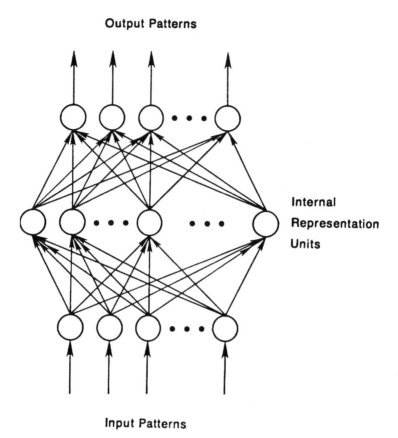

Internal Representation Units

Input Patterns

Figure 8.3
A multilayer network in which input patterns are *recoded* by internal representation units.

The numbers on the arrows represent the strengths of the connections among the units. The numbers written in the circles represent the thresholds of the units. The value of $+1.5$ for the threshold of the hidden unit ensures that it will be turned on only when both input units are on. The value 0.5 for the output unit ensures that it will turn on only when it receives a net positive input greater than 0.5. The weight of -2 from the hidden unit to the output unit ensures that the output unit will not come on when both input units are on. Note that from the point of view of the output unit the hidden unit is treated as simply another input unit. It is as if the input patterns consisted of three rather than two units.

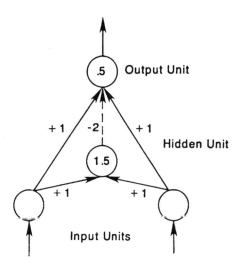

Figure 8.4
A simple XOR network with one hidden unit.

The existence of networks such as this illustrates the potential power of hidden units and internal representations. The problem, as noted by Minsky and Papert, is that whereas there is a very simple guaranteed learning rule for all problems that can be solved without hidden units, namely, the perceptron convergence procedure (or the variation reported originally by Widrow and Hoff 1960), there has been no equally powerful rule for learning in multilayer networks.

It is clear that if we hope to use these connectionist networks for general computational purposes, we must have a learning scheme capable of learning its own internal representations. This is just what we (Rumelhart, Hinton, and Williams 1986) have done. We have developed a generalization of the perceptron learning procedure, called the *generalized delta rule*, which allows the system to learn to compute arbitrary functions. The constraints inherent in networks without self-modifying internal representations are no longer applicable. The basic learning procedure is a two-stage process. First, an input is applied to the network; then, after the system has processed for some time, certain units of the network are informed of the values they ought to have at this time. If they have attained the desired values, the weights are unchanged. If they differ from the target values, then the weights are changed according to the difference between the actual value the units have attained and the target for those units. This difference becomes an error signal. This error signal must then be sent back to those units that impinged on the output. Each such unit receives an error measure that is equal to the error in all of the units to which it connects times the weight connecting it to the output unit. Then, based on the error, the weights into these "second-layer" units are modified, after which the error is passed back another layer. This process continues until the error signal reaches the input units or until it has been passed back for a fixed number of times. Then a new input pattern is presented and the process repeats. Although the procedure may sound difficult, it is actually quite simple and easy to implement within these nets. As shown in Rumelhart, Hinton, and Williams 1986, such a procedure will always change its weights in such a way as to reduce the difference between the actual output values and the desired output values. Moreover it can be shown that this system will work for any network whatsoever.

Minsky and Papert (1969, pp. 231–232), in their pessimistic discussion of perceptrons, discuss *multilayer machines*. They state that

The perceptron has shown itself worthy of study despite (and even because of!) its severe limitations. It has many features that attract attention: its linearity; its intriguing learning theorem; its clear paradigmatic simplicity as a kind of parallel computation. There is no reason to suppose that any of these virtues carry over to the many-layered version. Nevertheless, we consider it to be an important research problem to elucidate (or reject) our intuitive judgment that the extension is sterile. Perhaps some powerful convergence theorem will be discovered, or some profound reason for the failure to produce an interesting "learning theorem" for the multilayered machine will be found.

Although our learning results do not *guarantee* that we can find a solution for all solvable problems, our analyses and simulation results have shown that as a practical matter, this error propagation scheme leads to solutions in virtually every case. In short I believe that we have answered Minsky and Papert's challenge and *have* found a learning result sufficiently powerful to demonstrate that their pessimism about learning in multilayer machines was misplaced.

One way to view the procedure I have been describing is as a parallel computer that, having been shown the appropriate input/output exemplars specifying some function, programs itself to compute that function in general. Parallel computers are notoriously difficult to program. Here we have a mechanism whereby we do not actually have to know how to write the program to get the system to do it.

Graceful Degradation   Finally connectionist models are interesting candidates for cognitive-science models because of their property of graceful degradation in the face of damage and information overload. The ability of our networks to learn leads to the promise of computers that can literally learn their way around faulty components because every unit participates in the storage of many patterns and because each pattern involves many different units, the loss of a few components will degrade the stored information, but will not lose it. Similarly such memories should not be conceptualized as having a certain fixed capacity. Rather there is simply more and more storage interference and blending of similar pieces of information as the memory is overloaded. This property of graceful degradation mimics the human response in many ways and is one of the reasons we find these models of human information processing plausible.

8.2   The State of the Art

Recent years have seen a virtual explosion of work in the connectionist area. This work has been singularly interdisciplinary, being carried out by psychologists, physicists, computer scientists, engineers, neuroscientists, and other cognitive scientists. A number of national and international conferences have been established and are being held each year. In such environment it is difficult to keep up with the rapidly developing field. Nevertheless a reading of recent papers indicates a few central themes to this activity. These themes include the study of learning and generalization (especially the use of the backpropagation learning procedure), applications to neuroscience, mathematical properties of networks—both in terms of learning and the question of the relationship among connectionist style computation and more conventional computational paradigms—and finally the development of an implementational base for physical realizations of connectionist computational devices, especially in the areas of optics and analog VLSI.

Although there are many other interesting and important developments, I conclude with a brief summary of the work with which I have been most involved over the past several years, namely, the study of learning and generalization within multilayer networks. Even this summary is necessarily selective, but it should give a sampling of much of the current work in the area.

Learning and Generalization

The backpropagation learning procedure has become possibly the single most popular method for training networks. The procedure has been used to train networks on problem domains including character recognition, speech recognition, sonar detection, mapping from spelling to sound, motor control, analysis of molecular structure, diagnosis of eye diseases, prediction of chaotic functions, playing backgammon, the parsing of simple sentences, and many, many more areas of application. Perhaps the major point of these examples is the enormous range of problems to which the backpropagation learning procedure can usefully be applied. In spite of the rather impressive breadth of topics and the success of some of these applications, there are a number of serious open problems. The theoretical issues of primary concern fall into three main areas: (1) The architecture problem—are there useful architectures beyond the standard three-layer network used in most of these areas that are appropriate for certain areas of application? (2) The scaling problem—how can we cut down on the substantial training time that seems to be involved for the more difficult and interesting problem application areas? (3) The generalization problem—how can we be certain that the network trained on a subset of the example set will generalize correctly to the entire set of exemplars?

Some Architecture

Although most applications have involved the simple three-layer back propagation network with one input layer, one hidden layer, and one output layer of units, there have been a large number of interesting architectures proposed—each for the solution of some particular problem of interest. There are, for example, a number of "special" architectures that have been proposed for the modeling

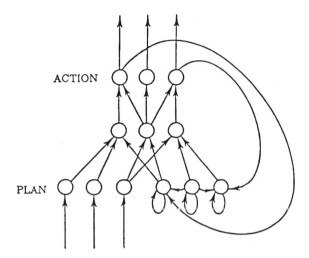

Figure 8.5
A recurrent network of the type developed by Jordan (1986) for learning to perform sequences.

of such sequential phenomena as motor control. Perhaps the most important of these is the one proposed by Mike Jordan (1986) for producing sequences of phonemes. The basic structure of the network is illustrated in figure 8.5. It consists of four groups of units: *Plan units*, which tell the network which sequence it is producing, are fixed at the start of a sequence and are not changed. *Context units*, which keep track of where the system is in the sequence, receive input from the output units of the systems and from themselves, constituting a memory for the sequence produced thus far. *Hidden units* combine the information from the plan units with that from the context units to determine which output is to be produced next. *Output units* produce the desired output values. This basic structure, with numerous variations, has been used successfully in producing sequences of phonemes (Jordan 1986), sequences of movements (Jordan 1989), sequences of notes in a melody (Todd 1989), sequences of turns in a simulated ship (Miyata 1987), and for many other applications. An analogous network for *recognizing* sequences has been used by Elman (1988) for processing sentences one at a time, and another variation has been developed and studied by Mozer (1988). The architecture used by Elman is illustrated in figure 8.6. This

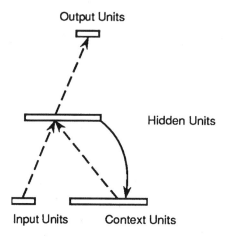

Figure 8.6
A recurrent network of the type employed by Elman (1988) for learning to recognize sequences.

network also involves three sets of units: *input units*, in which the sequence to be recognized is presented one element at a time; a set of *context units* that receive inputs from and send inputs to the hidden units and thus constitute a memory for recent events; a set of *hidden units* that combine the current input with its memory of past inputs to either name the sequence, predict the next element of the sequence, or both.

Another kind of architecture that has received some attention has been suggested by Hinton and has been employed by Elman and Zipser (1987), Cottrell, Munro, and Zipser (1987), and many others. It has become part of the standard toolkit of backpropagation. This is the so-called method of autoencoding the pattern set. The basic architecture in this case consists of three layers of units as in the conventional case; however, the input and output layers are identical. The idea is to pass the input through a small number of hidden units and reproduce it over the output units. This requires the hidden units to do a kind of nonlinear-principle components analysis of the input patterns. In this case that corresponds to a kind of extraction of critical features. In many applications these features turn out to provide a useful compact description of the patterns. Many other architectures are being explored. The space of interesting and useful architecture is large and the exploration will continue for many years.

The Scaling Problem

The scaling problem has received somewhat less attention, although it has clearly emerged as a central problem with backpropagationlike learning procedures. The basic finding has been that difficult problems require many learning trials. For example, it is not unusual to require tens or even hundreds of thousands of pattern presentations to learn moderately difficult problems—that is, those whose solution requires tens of thousands to a few hundred thousand connections. Large and fast computers are required for such problems, and it is impractical for problems requiring more than a few hundred thousand connections. It is therefore a matter of concern to learn to speed up the learning so that it can learn more difficult problems in a more reasonable number of exposures. The proposed solutions fall into two basic categories. One line of attack is to improve the learning procedure either by optimizing the parameters dynamically (that is, change the learning rate systematically during learning) or by using more information in the weight-changing procedure (that is, the so-called second-order backpropagation in which the second derivatives are also computed). Although some improvements can be attained through the use of these methods, in certain problem domains the basic scaling problem still remains. It seems that the basic problem is that difficult problems require a large number of exemplars, however efficiently each exemplar is used. The other view grows from viewing *learning* and *evolution* as continuous with one another. On this view the fact that networks take a long time to learn is to be expected because we normally compare their behavior to organisms that have long evolutionary histories. On this view the solution is to start the system at places that are as appropriate as possible for the problem domain to be learned. Shepherd (1989) has argued that such an approach is critical for an appropriate understanding of the phenomena being modeled.

A final approach to the scale problem is through modularity. It is possible to break the problem into smaller subproblems and train subnetworks on these subproblems. Networks can then finally be assembled to solve the entire problem after all of the modules are trained. An advantage of the connectionist approach in this regard is that the original training needs to be only approximately right. A final round of training can be used to learn the interfaces among the modules.

The Generalization Problem

One final aspect of learning that has been looked at is the nature of generalization. It is clear that the most important aspect of networks is not that they learn a set of mappings but that they learn the function implicit in the exemplars under study in such a way that they respond properly to those cases not yet observed. Although there are many cases of successful generalization (compare the learning of spelling with phoneme mappings in Sejnowski and Rosenberg's Nettalk (1987), there are a number of cases in which the networks do not generalize correctly (compare Denker, et al. 1987). One simple way to understand this is to note that for most problems there are enough degrees of freedom in the network that there are a large number of genuinely different solutions to the problems, and each solution constitutes a different way of generalizing to the unseen patterns. Clearly not all of these can be correct. I have proposed a hypothesis that shows some promise in promoting better generalization (Rumelhart 1988). The basic idea is this: The problem of generalization is essentially the induction problem. Given a set of observations, what is the appropriate principle that applies to all cases? Note that the network at any point in time can be viewed as a specification of the inductive hypothesis. I have proposed that we follow a version of Occam's razor and select the *simplest, most robust* network that is consistent with the observations made. The assumption of robustness is simply an embodiment of a kind of continuity assumption that small variations in the input patterns should have little effect on the output and on the performance of the system. The simplicity assumption is simply—of all networks that correctly account for the input data—to choose that net with the fewest hidden units, fewest connections, most symmetries among the weights, and so on. I have formalized this procedure and modified the backpropagation learning procedure so that it prefers simple, robust networks and, all things being equal, will select those networks. In many cases it turns out that these are just the networks that do the best job generalizing.

References

Cottrell, G. W., Munro, P. W., and Zipser, D. 1987. Learning internal representations from grey-scale images: An example of extensional programming. In *Proceedings of the Ninth Annual Meeting of the Cognitive Science Society*. Hillsdale, NJ: Erlbaum.

Denker, J., Schwartz, D., Wittner, B., Solla, S., Hopfield, J., Howard, R., and Jackel, L. 1987. Automatic learning, rule extraction, and generalization. *Complex Systems* 1:877–922.

Elman, J. 1988. *Finding Structure in Time*. CRL Tech. Rep. 88–01, Center for Research in Language, University of California, San Diego.

Elman, J., and Zipser, D. 1987. *Learning the Hidden Structure of Speech*. Rep. no. 8701. Institute for Cognitive Science, University of California, San Diego.

Feldman, J. A. 1985. Connectionist models and their applications: Introduction. *Cognitive Science* 9:1–2.

Grossberg, S. 1976. Adaptive pattern classification and universal recoding: Part I. Parallel development and coding of neural feature detectors. *Biological Cybernetics* 23:121–134.

Hebb, D. O. 1949. *The Organization of Behavior*. New York: Wiley.

Hinton, G. E., and Sejnowski, T. 1986. Learning and relearning in Boltzmann machines. In D. E. Rumelhart, J. L. McClelland, and the PDP Research Group. *Parallel Distributed Processing: Explorations in the Microstructure of Cognition. Volume 1: Foundations*. Cambridge, MA: MIT Press, A Bradford Book.

Hopfield, J. J. 1982. Neural networks and physical systems with emergent collective computational abilities. *Proceedings of the National Academy of Sciences, USA* 79:2554–2558.

Jordan, M. I. 1986. Attractor dynamics and parallelism in a connectionist sequential machine. In *Proceedings of the Eighth Annual Meeting of the Cognitive Science Society*. Hillsdale, NJ: Erlbaum.

Jordan, M. I. 1989. Supervised learning and systems with excess degrees of freedom. In D. Touretzky, G. Hinton, and T. Sejnowski, eds. *Connectionist Models*. San Mateo, CA: Morgan Kaufmann.

Minsky, M., and Papert, S. 1969. *Perceptrons*. Cambridge, MA: MIT Press.

Miyata, Y. 1987. *The Learning and Planning of Actions*. Ph.D. thesis, University of California, San Diego.

McClelland, J. L., Rumelhart D. E., and the PDP Research Group. 1986. *Parallel Distributed Processing: Explorations in the Microstructure of Cognition. Volume 2: Psychological and Biological Models*. Cambridge, MA: MIT Press, A Bradford Book.

Mozer, M. C. 1988. *A Focused Book-Propagation Algorithm for Temporal Pattern Recognition*. Rep. no. 88–3, Departments of Psychology and Computer Science, University of Toronto, Toronto, Ontario.

Reddy, D. R., Erman, L. D., Fennell, R. D., and Neely, R. B. 1973. The Hearsay speech understanding system: An example of the recognition process. In *Proceedings of the International Conference on Artificial Intelligence.* pp. 185–194.

Rosenblatt, F. 1962. *Principles of Neurodynamics.* New York: Spartan.

Rumelhart, D. E. 1988. *Generalization and the Learning of Minimal Networks by Backpropagation.* In preparation.

Rumelhart, D. E., Hinton, G. E., and Williams, R. J. (1986). Learning internal representations by error propagation. In D. E. Rumelhart, J. L. McClelland, and the PDP Research Group. *Parallel Distributed Processing: Explorations in the Microstructure of Cognition. Volume 1: Foundations.* Cambridge, MA: MIT Press, A Bradford Book.

Rumelhart, D. E., McClelland, J. L., and the PDP Research Group 1986. *Parallel Distributed Processing: Explorations in the Microstructure of Cognition. Volume 1: Foundations.* Cambridge, MA: MIT Press, A Bradford Book.

Sejnowski, T., and Rosenberg, C. 1987. Parallel networks that learn to pronounce English text. *Complex Systems* 1:145–168.

Shepherd, R. N. 1989. Internal representation of universal regularities: A challenge for connectionism. In L. Nadel, L. A. Cooper, P. Calicover, and R. M. Harnish, eds. *Neural Connections, Mental Computation.* Cambridge, MA: MIT Press, A Bradford Book.

Smolensky, P. 1986. Information processing in dynamical systems: Foundations of harmony theory. In D. E. Rumelhart, J. L. McClelland, and the PDP Research Group. *Parallel Distributed Processing: Explorations in the Microstructure of Cognition. Volume 1: Foundations.* Cambridge, MA: MIT Press, A Bradford Book.

Todd, P. 1989. A sequential network design for musical applications. In D. Touretzky, G. Hinton, and T. Sejnowski, eds. *Connectionist Models.* San Mateo, CA: Morgan Kaufmann.

Widrow, G., and Hoff, M. E. 1960. Adaptive switching circuits. In *Institute of Radio Engineers, Western Electronic Show and Convention, Convention Record, Part 4.* pp. 96–104.

The Structure of Emotions

Keith Oatley

Man is a synthesis of the infinite and the finite, of the temporal and the eternal, of freedom and necessity.
Søren Kierkegaard.

Body and Mind

We live in two worlds: a finite world of embodiment in time, place, and biological nature and an infinite world of imagination, language, and culture. It is perhaps the transition from the nineteenth to the twentieth century that prompts the substitution of "nature" and "culture" for Kierkegaard's "finite" and "infinite." Despite the rather old-fashioned tone of Kierkegaard's aphorism, the problems of synthesis of these two worlds could scarcely be more apt to a discussion of the structure of human emotions.

As to nature: Emotions are concerned with the bodily, with facts, with our limitations. Often emotions occur as a kind of necessity, outside voluntary control. As to culture: Emotions are concerned with our imagination, with plans and aspirations, which continually change and are limitless. Emotions arise with the meeting of these two worlds of nature and culture. This chapter is concerned with exploring and understanding this meeting.

Scenes of Emotion

Here, from Leo Tolstoy's *Anna Karenina* (1980/1877) is a scene of emotion: Anna and her husband, Alexis Alexandrovitch, are watching a cavalry officers' race when one of the riders falls (Tolstoy, 1980/1877):

The officer brought the news that the rider was unhurt but that the horse had broken its back.

On hearing this Anna quickly sat down and hid her face behind her fan. Karenin saw that she was crying, and that she was unable to keep back either her tears or her sobs that were making her bosom heave. He stepped forward so as to screen her, giving her time to recover.

"For the third time I offer you my arm," he said. (p. 210)

Then, later in the carriage on the way home:

"Perhaps I was mistaken," said he. "In that case I beg your pardon."

"No, you were not mistaken," she said slowly, looking despairingly into his cold face. "You were not mistaken. I was, and cannot help being, in despair. I listen to you, but I am thinking of him. I love him, I am his mistress, I cannot endure you; I am afraid of you, and I hate you." (p. 212)

Tolstoy depicts here the clash of nature and culture: When the accident happened, "a change came over Anna's face which was positively improper. She quite lost self-control" (p. 209). She was unable to restrain her show of concern for her lover, Vronsky, who was riding in the race. When she heard that he was alive after his fall, she was still less able to act voluntarily. She was caught up in emotions, in events of nature, precipitated by the fact of her lover's near death. At the same time, the meaning of this event in the lives of Anna and her husband is a product of culture, of their aspirations, of the rules and expectations of marriage, and the implications of having an adulterous affair in that part of Russian aristocratic society.

Karenin says he is sorry if he was wrong. He had tried to prevent others seeing his wife's emotion following her lover's fall, and suggested that they leave. He apologizes because he has had suspicions of her fidelity previously, and she had mockingly rebuffed them, making him feel ridiculous. He apologizes because he wants, against the evidence, to believe his wife faithful. He wants to be, and be seen to be, an irreproachable member of society. It is for Anna's public show of concern for her lover that he has reproached her.

In the terms of the nineteenth-century novel, emotions are depicted. Anna weeps—from relief that her lover is not killed. Karenin declares sorrow that inadequately masks jealousy clinging to a shred of hope: "Perhaps I was mistaken.... If so, I beg your pardon" (p. 212). Karenin's apology is more formal than one might expect in the conversation of husbands and wives—but he is formal and becomes more so when angry. He finds it easier to reproach Anna for public indiscretion than to talk of any regrets he might have at the loss of her love. In any case, he makes an apology. On it, and on what is said next, hang the future of Karenin's and Anna's lives, individually and with each other. Around this moment between Karenin's apology and Anna's reply the novel turns. Anna expresses hatred, rebuffing him after her forbearance and then her deceit: "No, you were not mistaken," said Anna.... "I love him. I am afraid of you, and I hate you" (p. 212).

Two common conventions of the nineteenth-century European novel are that plots turn on such moments of emotion and that the emotions are not straightforward but are expressed in subtle ways. Though emotions may affect us strongly, often their meanings are not obvious. The insights of the great novelists include the light they throw on the meanings of emotions. Tolstoy's Anna struggles with herself in her life with Karenin. Then her ardent nature finds an object in Vronsky. Karenin is not an emotional man. Even in this moment of severe disappointment, he can only express his emotions with a coldness of face and an overformality of manner.

What Is an Emotion?

What is an emotion? This is the title of a famous paper by William James (1884)—and, indeed, it is a good question.

We all might agree that Anna, as she is sobbing, is undergoing an emotion, but to define emotion is difficult. Some argue that it is impossible. Mandler (1984) observes that there is no commonly or even superficially acceptable definition of the term, and, he adds, too many psychologists fail to understand this. Emotion may merely be an ordinary language usage that points to a quite heterogeneous set of phenomena. Though we may all agree on some states as examples of emotion, we may disagree about others.

Fehr and Russell (1984) asked 200 subjects to write down examples of emotion terms for 1 minute. In their analysis, Fehr and Russell treated syntactic variants of a term as the same, for example, "anxious," "anxiety," and "anxiously" all counted as the same term. They found that 196 such terms were mentioned by at least two people. Some seem obviously good examples of emotions, like "happiness," the most common and mentioned by 152 subjects. But what about "hurt," with 16 mentions, "lust" with 8, "stress" with 4, "thinking" with 3, and "insecurity" with 2?

These examples are quite varied; the full list of 196 terms is even more so. Is it possible to make sense out of such emotional vocabularies? James (1890) thought not:

> If one should seek to name each particular one of them [emotions] of which the human heart is the seat, it is plain that the limit to their number would lie in the introspective vocabulary of the seeker, each race of men having found names for some shade of feeling which other races have left undiscriminated. If we should seek to break the emotions, thus enumerated, into groups, according to their affinities, it is again plain that all sorts of groupings would be possible, according as we chose this character or that as a basis, and that all groupings would be equally real and true. (p. 485)

James thought the answer to his question would lie elsewhere. His answer was that emotions are perceptions of bodily states. Because indefinitely many such perceptions are possible, just as there are indefinitely many perceptions of the outside world, there is an infinite number of emotions and they will be variously described.

This chapter is based on the theory that emotion is a coherent concept, and that emotions are mental states that can be defined, that can be talked about in ordinary language, and that have functions. Two competing proposals will be compared with this theory. One proposal I will call the heterogeneity argument. James's theory is an example. The heterogeneity theory holds that emotion terms arise from folk theories in ordinary language, but they have no coherent psychological status. Instead, bodily changes and physiology should be investigated and related to eliciting events using natural scientific methods. This theory states that emotions are vestiges of our animal and infantile history that tend to distort adult mental functions.

James proposed that folk theories have no relation to any future scientific account, but that there are such things as emotions: They are perceptions of bodily events. A more extreme version of the heterogeneity argument is that when we have a scientific account of physiological and perceptual processes, scientific discourse will not include emotion terms at all, except perhaps as a shorthand or in passing (cf. Churchland, 1986). Today we no longer discuss personality or disease in terms of humors. Saying that someone is melancholy or phlegmatic has an archaic sound. A yet more radical variant of the heterogeneity argument might be put as follows. The failure of universally accepted theories of emotion to emerge despite more than a century's research may indicate that the very enterprise of trying to create even such theories as James's is mistaken.

James's "What is an emotion?" may have misled us. Just because it sounds like a question does not mean that it has an answer, any more than does "Why is the Moon made of cream cheese?" Draper has put it as follows: Hypotheses of the form "All emotions are X" invite counterexamples, and that for the theories so far advanced in the psychological literature these are not difficult to think of. So, for James's theory that emotions are perceptions of bodily states, one could ask: What about emotions that occur when listening to music? It was to combat such an argument that James developed the idea of the coarse emotions that involve strong bodily perturbations. Thus only some emotions are covered by his theory.

According to the radical heterogeneity argument, examples can always be found that will not be covered by any possible unifying proposal. This is because, as Draper continues, it may make no more sense to ask what an emotion is than to ask what intelligence is. Emotion, like intelligence, is a term used variously to indicate aspects of the functioning of the whole cognitive system. It is not a property of any specific subsystem or a description of a specific kind of process.

An Answer to William James's Question

In contrast to these arguments of heterogeneity, I propose that emotions are mental states with coherent psychological functions and that they are recognizable by empirical and theoretical criteria. When these criteria are applied, apparent heterogeneities and ambiguities disappear. Emotions can be described scientifically in a way that corresponds recognizably to emotions as referred to in ordinary language. We should continue to refer to emotions as mental states, just as we talk about seeing and hearing even though more than a hundred years of research has taught us much more about them than is known to a layperson.

What, then, are emotions from this viewpoint? And how do they differ from bodily states like feeling cold or from personality traits like shyness? An emotion is a distinctive mental state that normally occurs in identifiable eliciting conditions. It has distinctive parts and recognizable consequences. I describe these rather generally at first, indicating typical emotions, and then extend the analysis to all emotions.

Eliciting Conditions of Emotions

Emotions occur in distinctive circumstances, but the events that elicit them are not purely physical. Rather, they are psychological. By physical, I mean that when a stimulus is applied it has a reliable effect, irrespective of to whom it is applied or the recipient's evaluations. For instance, if someone is put in a cold environment, bodily changes, such as shivering, occur. Pursuing this kind of argument, Ekman, Friesen, and Simons (1985) have shown that startle is not an emotion. It is a reflex reaction with stereotyped characteristics that can be triggered reliably by a physical stimulus, a loud, sharp sound.

Emotions are not elicited in this way. There is no physical situation that will reliably initiate particular emotions, because emotions depend on evaluations of what has happened in relation to the person's goals and beliefs. For instance, I may suddenly feel frightened if the vehicle in which I am traveling seems to be heading for an accident. I evaluate a perception in relation to my concerns for safety, though not necessarily consciously. This may be the common experience in such situations. But a person confident that an accident would not occur, perhaps the one who is driving, or the one who is unconcerned about personal safety at that moment, may not feel fear.

We do, however, think of emotions as more or less appropriate to circumstances. So it world be strange not to feel fear in response to a believable threat of torture. Clinicians often categorize the anxiety of patients as abnormal when they can see no reason for it. So we expect people to feel sadness at a loss, anger at being thwarted, happiness at meeting a friend, and so on. The relation is not always simple, though, and novelists who chronicle events that elicit emotions often comment on how appropriate the emotions are to those events (cf. also De Sousa, 1987).

The Two Components of an Emotion

Action Readiness   If we ask what the core of an emotion is, the best answer based on our present state of knowledge is that it is a mental state of readiness for action (Frijda, 1986), or a change of readiness. Such a change of readiness is normally based on an evaluation of something happening that affects important concerns (e.g., Lazarus, 1966; Frijda, 1986; Roberts, 1988). This evaluation need not be made consciously.

An emotion tends to specify a range of options for action. When frightened, we evaluate a situation in relation to a concern for safety and become ready to freeze, fight, or flee. We stop what we are doing and check for signs of danger (Gray, 1982). In an emotional state we are pressed toward a small range of actions in a compulsive way. In fear, it may seem impossible to act except in ways to make ourselves feel safer. When angry, we are prompted to attack. When sad, we may not feel able to do anything very much.

Phenomenological Tone   This description of emotions as states of action readiness points to an underlying function of emotion. Emotions also have a distinctive phenomenological tone, of which we may be conscious. Each emotion can typically be felt as different from contrasting emotions and from nonemotions: Sadness feels different from happiness and from states like deductive reasoning or sleepiness. Sometimes we may not be consciously aware of an emotion, though others can see signs of it in our behavior. Sometimes emotions seem inchoate, and we do not quite know how we feel.

The conscious feeling of an emotion, of sadness, fear, or the like, is not identical with the evaluation or the state of readiness. An underlying mental state is the core of an emotion. In common with most mental states, only limited aspects of it are conscious. Mechanisms of generating the action readiness are not conscious. In Western culture, however, it is common (wrongly) to identify the underlying mental state of an emotion with its conscious feeling, for example, "I *feel* sad," as if the conscious feeling were the whole emotion.

The Usual Accompaniments of Emotions

As well as the underlying mental state and its associated feeling tone, emotions are typically accompanied by one or more of the following.

Conscious preoccupation.   Emotions have attentional properties. They often include a preoccupying and even compulsive inner dialogue. When in an emotional state, we may find it difficult to stop thinking about the issue. When angry, for example, we may dwell on thoughts of revenge.

Bodily disturbance.   An emotion is typically accompanied by a bodily disturbance involving the autonomic nervous system and other physiological processes. In anger, skin temperature tends to rise; in fear, it may fall, and the face becomes pale.

Expressions. Emotions are often outwardly expressed by recognizable facial gestures, bodily postures, and tones of voice that are not entirely voluntary. For instance, happiness typically involves smiling, particular patterns of muscle movements around the eyes, and a lightness and spontaneity of speaking.

Action Consequences of Emotions

The consequences of an emotion are that we may act, perhaps somewhat involuntarily. So Anna acts by speaking to her husband: "No, you were not mistaken," she said. . . . "I love him. I am afraid of you, and I hate you" (p. 212). Such speech acts, like all actions, may change the world. Anna is at the beginning of a sequence of actions of withdrawing from her husband.

Typical Emotions

A fully developed, typical emotion is a kind of readiness elicited by some event that impinges on a person's concerns. It will have a tone that is experienced consciously and it will include accompaniments of conscious preoccupation, bodily disturbance, and expression. It will also issue in some course of action prompted by the emotion.

   In certain episodes of emotion, however, an eliciting condition, a feeling tone, some of the accompaniments, or an action consequence may not occur or may not be noticed. In other words, ordinary instances of emotions may differ from the typical emotion just described by lacking one or more of these features. In a study in which subjects kept structured diaries of episodes of emotion, Oatley and Duncan (1992) found that 77% of emotions of happiness, sadness, anger, and fear included a subjective inner feeling of emotion, 77% included a bodily sensation, 81% were accompanied by involuntary thoughts, and 90% involved a consciously recognized action or an urge to act emotionally. Most episodes of emotion included all these features, but in some one or several features were absent.

The Emotion Process

Frijda's (1986) conceptualization of emotions is similar to that described here, and he discusses thoroughly the evidence for his formulation. He has proposed that emotions are processes of the following kind:

event coding→appraisal→significance evaluation→action
readiness→action

Each step is itself complex. For instance, appraisal involves comparing the coded event with the person's concerns, evaluation involves diagnosing what can be done about it, and so on. Some steps may have conscious accompaniments, and the action that occurs may include emotional expressions, physiological changes, and physical actions on the world.

A difference between Frijda's account and that offered here is that Frijda argues that an emotion is not a state but a whole process from event coding to action. I argue that it is more straightforward to see emotion as a mental state of readiness based on an evaluation and with a specific phenomenological tone, but to distinguish this for purposes of analysis from eliciting conditions, from accompaniments, and from action sequences. These are minor divergences.

We often recognize an emotion in others, says Frijda, like this:

> At some moments when observing behavior that behavior seems to come to a stop. Effective interaction with the environment halts and is replaced by behavior that is centered, as it were, around the person himself, as in a fit of weeping or laughter, anger or fear. (1986, p. 2)

Tolstoy depicts just such an event. Anna ceased to concentrate on the race, and stopped behaving in the way that one does when watching a sporting event. It was on seeing this that her husband tried to shield her display from others who might guess at its significance.

The Duration and Intensity of Emotions

As well as qualitative features emotions have quantitative dimensions, specifically of time and intensity. An emotion may start suddenly or slowly and decay either fast or slowly. The interval between an eliciting event and the start of an emotion may vary. At any moment an emotion will have a specific intensity, which can be measured by facial, physiological, or phenomenological indices.

Emotional expressions of the face and the physiological perturbations of emotions last typically for seconds or minutes (Ekman, 1984). People's subjective experiences of episodes of emotion can last for much longer. Frijda et al. (1991) had people draw graphs of the time course of emotion episodes. The shapes of such graphs were rather variable, and there was often periodic fluctuation of intensity, as the emotion returned in waves. Frijda et al. found that it was not unusual for emotions to last for several hours and that a few bridged across a period of sleep into the following day. They use these observations to argue that emotion is a process. In the diary study of Oatley and Duncan (1992), 33% of episodes of happiness, sadness, or anger lasted 5 minutes or less, 34% lasted 5 to 30 minutes, and 33% lasted longer than 30 minutes. The diary method and the method used by Frijda et al., however, are insensitive to more fleeting emotions.

Informally the picture is this: Depending on factors such as the importance of the concern involved, an emotion may rise to a peak and perhaps fade after some minutes or hours or until the issue is resolved interpersonally or in some other way. Intensity may wane and then increase in further waves, or an emotion may be replaced by another emotion focused on a different aspect of the issue that elicited the original emotion. The duration of an emotion, a few minutes to several hours of preoccupation with an emotional event, corresponds to an emotion occurring at a point of transition. Emotions are changes in action readiness, and other cognitive changes accompany them. If an emotion lasts a long time it is because the transition that is occurring is not just a switch from one state to another. The starting up of new plans and other cognitive reprogramming that may be involved can have extensive implications that occupy a person mentally for some time.

People do experience emotional states that last for days, weeks, months, and even years, as the sadness that follows bereavement. Emotional states that last for more than a few hours are referred to as *moods*, particularly when the subject is unaware of how the state started. Moods tend to be of lower intensity, perhaps punctuated by waves of more distinct emotion. So, for the purposes of description, we see emotions as discrete states of some intensity, typically noticeable to the self or to others or from recording of autonomic nervous system indices, and lasting for finite periods.

Moods are emotional in that, like episodes of emotion, they are based on exactly the same kinds of readiness. Moods are, however, longer lasting background states that, rather than being associated with changes and interruptions, resist further changes and interruptions. They do not have the compulsiveness of an emotion episode— other actions may be superimposed upon them. Thus, we may see Anna's sobbing as indicating a discrete involuntary emotion, and her outburst at Karenin as another. But the state of longing in which she later waits to see her lover Vronsky again after returning home is best thought of as a mood, during which she would no doubt do things quite unrelated to it.

The Functions of Emotions

The account given so far has been descriptive. Even though emotions have been identified as types of readiness for action, why should this be important for understanding mental life? The most fundamental question for a psychological understanding of emotions is "What are their functions?" The answer that I propose is based on the idea that most human action has many simultaneous aims but limited resources. It takes place in a world that is imperfectly known and in conjunction with other people. Emotions function in the management of action when all the consequences of such action cannot be fully foreseen.

In cognitive psychology it is axiomatic that actions do not occur singly or haphazardly. They occur in ordered sequences and achieve purposes. An ordered sequence of actions that achieves a purpose is known as a plan. So it is to the principles of planned action that we should look to understand the functions of emotions.

Simple Plans

Plots and Plans

The plot of a story or play is a sequence of actions, a *plan*, of one or several protagonists. The cognitive representation of a plan can be thought of as follows:

Goal (preconditions)→actions→effects

This is to be read as: A goal (when the right preconditions exist) prompts a series of actions that in turn produce effects in the world.

A goal is an aim, or as Frijda puts it, a concern. It is a description of a possible state of the world represented symbolically in a cognitive system. I will use the term *goal* in a way that is neutral as to whether or not it is conscious. A goal-directed system works to achieve a correspondence between the world and the goal by changing the world through an ordered series of actions, a plan. Preconditions are states of the world that affect whether and how a plan can be accomplished. Again, I will use the term *plan* in a way that is neutral as to how conscious it is.

Marriage is a plan, a long-term one requiring two actors to carry it out jointly. In our society, marriage is the very paradigm of a joint plan eagerly adopted. Into its course unforeseen circumstances intrude. For Karenin, in Tolstoy's novel, the plan of marriage was meant to accomplish, among other goals, a faultless display of respectworthy adult life that would support his role as an important person with a public position. By becoming married, Anna had entered into the joint plan with Karenin and pursued a goal that was somewhat similar to his. Only when her lover was in danger did emotions cause her to bungle an aspect of it. Her show of emotion revealed that she was simultaneously conducting another plan, with another goal that was incompatible with the first. A juncture occurred at which her two plans collided. At this point the possible outcomes of each were evaluated very differently than before.

Emotions emerge at just such significant junctures in plans. The re-evaluations that occur are communicated to oneself and somewhat involuntarily to others. European novels of the nineteenth century are representations of the ways in which emotions occur in the course of our most serious life plans. At the same time, emotions are communicated to readers who identify with one or more of the characters, and in so doing may activate experiences of their own. The implication is that in such novels each reader may reflect on issues of action in relation to others.

Novels and plays have been able to depict and transmit emotions because they have plots. Within psychology, however, emotions may have been difficult to understand partly because the psychological structures corresponding to plots, namely, plans and narrative accounts, in some ways have been neglected.

The Hierarchical Arrangement of Plans

In a conscious plan some effects of actions are imagined in advance and can form the basis of an intention. Here is another passage from *Anna Karenina*, describing a plan of a single actor. Early in the book, Vronsky drives to the train station to meet his mother, who is arriving in Moscow from St. Petersburg. The train arrives, and a guard tells him what compartment Countess Vronsky is in.

Vronsky followed the guard to the carriage, and had to stop at the entrance of the compartment to let a lady pass out.

The trained insight of a Society man enabled Vronsky with a glance to decide that she belonged to the best Society. He apologised for being in her way and was about to enter the carriage, but felt compelled to have another look at her. (p. 60)

A basic formulation of cognitive science is that the structure of plans can be represented as a hierarchy or tree. Hierarchy was postulated by Miller, Galanter, and Pribram (1960) as the major principle of plans. A plan is an organization of action similar to a computer program. It has an overall goal, to be achieved by fulfilling a set of subgoals. Miller, Galanter, and Pribram speak of a goal as a kind of image of how the world might be, so that action can then be devoted to making the world like the image. In turn, each goal can evoke lower-level goals and so on down a hierarchical tree that terminates in actions.

Using this formulation, we can express some of Vronsky's plan as in Figure 9.1. The top-level goal is to meet his mother. Tolstoy describes the action as involving various subgoals: drive to station, chat with Oblonsky (whom Vronsky meets by chance), wait for train, and board train. Terminal nodes of this tree are actions such as ask porter about train.

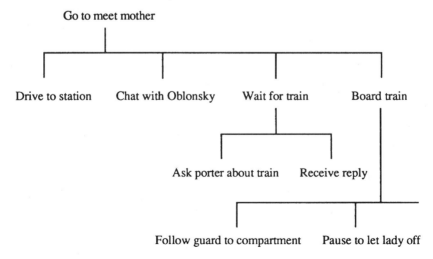

Figure 9.1
Fragment of a hierarchical plan tree representing a sequence of actions from Tolstoy's *Anna Karenina*. (Modified from Oatley, 1988.)

A novelist assumes that only a few elements need be mentioned, often in terms of subgoals and actions: Vronsky drives to the station, chats with Oblonsky, asks the porter when the train will come, follows the guard to his mother's compartment, and so on. We, the readers, use these cues to build from our own knowledge a mental model of the scene and a plan tree of an actor corresponding to that in Figure 9.1. A mental model is a means of simulating states of the world; a plan tree represents a sequence of actions made meaningful by the goals they accomplish. From such a model and such a plan tree we fill in the gaps in the narrative.

The Cognitive Psychology of Plans

To meet one's mother at a station is to enact a plan. Vronsky imagines a state of affairs: meeting his mother. He also has a model of himself. This includes the knowledge that he can act to achieve such a state of affairs. One formulation would be that by operating with his mental models (involving, perhaps, times, routes, places) he assembles a series of subgoals, and hence the actions he will perform, to achieve the overall goal. After assembling the plan in the simulation space of his mind, he can act, directing himself, as it were, by reading off the actions in sequence. This idea of the planning hierarchy captures a principle of what we mean by acting intentionally. It also allows us to connect this fundamental piece of human cognition with computational accounts of action.

The analysis given in Figure 9.1 has actions like asking and receiving a reply as primitives at that level of detail. Part of the interest for psychologists is the idea that a plan tree can be applied at any level of detail. A similar hierarchy could be constructed in which muscle movements of the mouth and throat are the primitives in a hierarchy that specifies the articulation of certain sounds when speaking. At a yet finer level a hierarchy based on primitives of individual muscle fiber contractions could be constructed. The idea of hierarchical organization has often been invoked in brain research as an organizing principle, as evidenced by the common use of such terms as higher and lower brain functions. Computer programs are constructed in the same way. Programs in high-level programming languages are implemented as programs in lower-level languages.

Goals in Narrative   At the level of detail shown in Figure 9.1, human actors can talk about their goals and subgoals. To give a reason for an action or subgoal is like reading off the goal at the next highest node. For instance, Vronsky might say: "I waited because I wanted a train which had not yet arrived." The subgoal was not achieved immediately because the precondition of the train's arrival was not yet fulfilled. For the next higher level of analysis (not shown in Figure 9.1), higher goals are referred to. Tolstoy informs us about them: In novels, such goals constitute "character": Vronsky meets his mother not because he loves her, but because, "in accordance with the views of the set he lived in, and as a result of his education, he could not imagine himself treating her in any but one altogether submissive and respectful" (p. 60).

So we begin to understand that Vronsky acts partly to fulfill goals set by convention and propriety. In the wake of his ambivalence about these, in the scene at the station, a potentially conflicting plan is hinted at, with a goal of a quite different kind. The first nuance of a sexual plan is implied. Anna is the woman at whom he takes another look as he goes to enter the railway carriage. This is their first meeting.

Mental Models   A plan implies forethought. Craik (1943) proposed that thinking consists of translating perceptual information into the terms of a model of the world, then operating on this model, and finally doing a retranslation into terms of the world again, for example, into actions. Models allow the representation of effects of actions without inappropriate, expensive, or dangerous consequences that wrong actions might have in the real world.

Search in Constructing Plans   The idea of a plan itself has been modeled in artificial intelligence programs. To plan means to search for courses of action in a simulated model world. To construct a plan means starting up a model of the world and searching sequences of actions until a path from the current state to the goal is discovered. Typical planning programs search backward from the goal because this makes it easier to keep account of the reasons, that is, the goals, for each action. When a solution is discovered—the sequence of

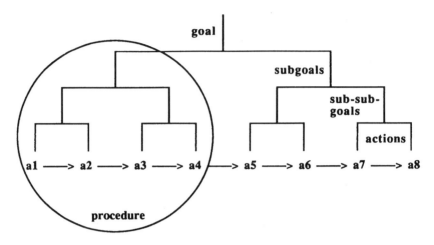

Figure 9.2
A simple plan: a sequence of actions a1 to a8 organized to achieve sub-sub-goals, which are organized to achieve subgoals, and the whole organized to achieve an overall goal. The circle encloses a separable procedure that achieves a sub-goal.

actions that connects the goal to the starting point—it is remembered. Then this stored sequence can be unreeled in the opposite direction in the actual world.

Procedures   Plans are often decomposed into parts each of which achieves a subgoal. In computation such parts are procedures. A computer program is a simple hierarchical plan. If it is to be understood or developed it needs to be composed of procedures. Figure 9.2 illustrates such a hierarchical structure of a plan, with subgoals at each level, dominating lower-level goals downward to primitive actions. Procedures, such as the one circled, result from decomposing a complex plan into parts that can be more readily understood. Each procedure is relatively self-contained, and each is relatively free of side effects. Procedures can be nested together so that one procedure, higher in the hierarchy, can call other subprocedures with as many levels of embedding as necessary.

When it is run, then, the action sequence in Figure 9.2, a1 to a8, is orchestrated by procedures invoking one another in the hierarchy—the overt action of a plan, then, depends on unseen inner structure. The virtue of composing plans from procedures is that procedures can be tested and developed on their own and then the problems of assembling them can be tackled.

Plans and Technical Skills

All this is, in a sense, familiar to the European or American mind. The idea of rational planning to achieve a goal is indeed a conception expounded nearly two and a half thousand years ago that has profoundly influenced the Western tradition. One of the accomplishments of this tradition of Socrates, Plato, and Aristotle was to formalize the idea of *techne*, meaning a craft or skill, and to apply it to all sorts of situations. *Techne* is the skilled application of plans, for giving speeches, for navigating ships, for curing diseases, and so on. *Techne* requires reliable knowledge, *episteme*, or, as cognitive scientists might now say, an accurate model of the world. *Episteme* is technical knowledge that allows plans to be constructed, and *techne* is a simple plan (like that in Figure 9.2) for achieving a defined goal or "good," as classical writers called it. Technical knowledge is exportable to other people, but it is usually applicable only to a single domain. So a person can learn the skill of rhetoric but may know only how to organize information to give a speech, a navigator can learn about stars and coastlines, a doctor about diseases.

The classical philosophers distinguished means and ends. As in an artificial intelligence plan, the planning phase involves first considering the goal and then the steps to achieve it. Enacting a plan takes place in the reverse order: Actions are followed by the goal. The Greeks described the hierarchical organization of skills whereby the finished product of one craft becomes the raw material of another: Chunks of marble produced from the quarry become blocks shaped by the mason that become the components arranged by an architect.

Techne is perhaps the most successful of all ideas in the history of ideas. On its applications the world in which we now live depends. It is embodied in technology based on procedures of science that produce reliable *episteme*. The computer is a device by which means can be related to ends. It is itself a means that can undertake a *techne* like skilled people. And, for the first time, because its processes are open to investigation, we can compare artificial knowledge-based systems achieving plans with our own less accessible mental operations. The cognitive conception of a simple plan as a hierarchy of subgoals that might be accomplished by a single robot actor forms an all-important kernel of understanding action. It is indeed the fundamental principle of cognitive science that accomplishing an intended action involves a plan based on a model and organized in this way. It is, moreover, the kernel that is needed for understanding emotions.

How, exactly, does the idea of emotions as changing readiness for action connect with this principle of planned action? The connection is that the principle of planning takes us some way toward understanding human action, but not far enough. Despite the idea of *techne* being such a good one, even the early philosophers had to restrain their enthusiasm in trying to apply it to everything. Are there aspects of human life where the principle of planning does not fit? Plato, in *The Republic*, argues, for instance, that though justice is a good (a goal), attaining it is not a technical matter. Aristotle, in the *Nicomachean Ethics*, is even more skeptical of the universal applicability of *techne*. A *techne* of ethics would require a universal metric against which the results of all personal and political actions could be measured in order to make rational choices in relation to some single top-level goal. If some subgoals are incompatible with others, however, no such *techne* of ethics can exist (Nussbaum, 1986). In *Anna Karenina*, we, too, may wonder whether Anna's uncontrollable sobbing at the races, or even Vronsky's actions as he goes to meet his mother at the station, are really the results of simple plans that involved exact goals or a complete model of the world, in the way that artificial intelligence plans do.

The idea of goals and operations in a mental model world provides a fundamental principle, as Aristotle might say, the *logos*, of human action. Yet human actions, including conducting a love affair or meeting one's mother at the station, are clearly different from anything yet programmed in a computer. To understand issues of human intention, the simple idea of a plan as described so far is necessary, but not sufficient. In an attempt to explain ordinary human action, we must augment the basic theory. As we do so, we discover that it is no accident that a simple technical plan such as a computer program has nothing emotional about it. As we introduce the augmentations to basic planning theory, we find we must also consider the function of emotions in human action.

References

Churchland, Patricia S. (1986). *Neurophilosophy*. Cambridge, MA: MIT Press.

Craik, K. J. W. (1943). *The nature of explanation*. Cambridge: Cambridge University Press.

De Sousa, R. (1987). The rationality of emotions. In A. O. Rorty (Ed.), *Explaining emotions*. Berkeley: University of California Press.

Ekman, P. (1984). Expression and the nature of emotion. In K. Scherer and P. Ekman (Eds.), *Approaches to emotion*. Hillsdale, NJ: Erlbaum.

Ekman, P., Friesen, W. V., and Simons, R. V. (1985). Is the startle reaction an emotion? *Journal of Personality and Social Psychology, 49*, 1416–1426.

Fehr, B., and Russell, J. A. (1984). Concept of emotion viewed from a prototype perspective. *Journal of Experimental Psychology: General, 113*, 464–486.

Frijda, N. H. (1986). *The emotions*. Cambridge: Cambridge University Press.

Frijda, N. H., Mesquita, B., Sonnemans, J., and van Goozen, S. (1991). The duration of affective phenomena or emotions, sentiments and passions. In K. T. Strongman (Ed.), *International Review of Studies on Emotion, Vol. 1*. Chichester: Wiley.

Gray, J. A. (1982). *The neuropsychology of anxiety: An enquiry into the functions of the septo-hippocampal system*. Oxford: Oxford University Press.

James, W. (1884). What is an emotion? *Mind, 9*, 188–205.

James, W. (1890). *The principles of psychology*. New York: Holt.

Lazarus, R. S. (1966). *Psychological stress and the coping process*. New York: McGraw-Hill.

Mandler, G. (1984). *Mind and body: Psychology of emotions and stress*. New York: Norton.

Miller, G. A., Galanter, E., and Pribram, K. H. (1960). *Plans and the structure of behavior*. New York: Holt, Rinehart and Winston.

Nussbaum, M. C. (1986). *The fragility of goodness: Luck and ethics in Greek tragedy and philosophy*. Cambridge: Cambridge University Press.

Oatley, K. (1988). Plans and the communicative function of emotions: A cognitive theory. In V. Hamilton, G. H. Bower, and N. H. Frijda (Eds.), *Cognitive perspectives on emotion and motivation. NATO ASI Series D, No. 44*. Dordrecht: Kluwer.

Oatley, K., and Duncan, E. (1992). Structured diaries for emotions in daily life. In K. T. Strongman (Ed.), *International Review of Studies on Emotion, Vol. 2*. Chichester: Wiley.

Roberts, R. C. (1988). What is an emotion: A sketch. *Philosophical Review, 97*, 183–209.

Tolstoy, L. (1980). *Anna Karenina*. Trans. L. Maude and A. Maude. Oxford: Oxford University Press. The world's classics. (Original published 1877.)

A Unified Theory of Consciousness?

Owen Flanagan

10.1 Prospects for a Theory of Consciousness

Some naturalists are skeptical about the prospects for a theory of consciousness. This is not because they are new mysterians. It is because they think that 'consciousness' names a heterogeneous hodge-podge and because they do not believe that one can develop a theory for a hodge-podge (P. S. Churchland 1983, 1988; Wilkes 1988a, 1988b). Consciousness includes sensations, perceptions, moods, emotions, propositional-attitude states, and large narrative structures. Dreams are experienced, as are other altered states of consciousness, many psychotic states, and so on. At a fine-grained level we will want to individuate types within these larger types, so that, for example, there will be a different experiential type for each sensory modality (touch, olfaction, vision, and so on). And one can easily imagine the need to divide these subtypes into more fine-grained types, for example, seeing red versus seeing blue.

The claim that 'consciousness' names a heterogeneous set of phenomena is absolutely right. 'Consciousness' is a superordinate category term. But I don't see that the subcategories that constitute it, taken together or individually, show signs of being a hodge-podge, and therefore I don't share the conviction that the search for a theory of consciousness is an idle fantasy.

Wilkes (1988b, 33) thinks that "conscious phenomena" are more like the arbitrary set consisting of "all the words with 'g' as the fourth letter" than they are like a superordinate category ('metal', 'mammal', 'fish') or like a subcategory of such a superordinate category ('gold', 'whale', 'flounder'). Her argument turns on the conviction that for a superordinate category to be nonarbitrary, it must display a certain coherence, but that "conscious phenomena" fail to display the required coherence. "What sort of coherence? Well, even though most of the interesting laws may concern only the subclasses, there might be some laws at least that are interestingly—nontrivially—true of all the subclasses; or even if this is not so, the laws that concern the subclasses may have significant structural analogy or isomorphism" (Wilkes 1988b, 33–34).

Contrary to Wilkes, I think that the evidence suggests that conscious phenomena display coherence. First, despite the truth of the heterogeneity thesis, all conscious mental events share the property of being conscious, of being in awareness, of there being something it is like to be in one of the relevant states. Second, whereas the subsets that make up a hodge-podge make it up precisely because they lack any interesting systematic connection to each other, all conscious phenomena bear the interesting systematic relation of being phenomena of mind.

The shared phenomenological property and the fact that conscious phenomena are properties, states, and events of the mind suggest that conscious mental life constitutes a category suitable for marking a set of phenomena in need of scientific explanation. To be sure, the theory of consciousness will be an interest-relative subset of our overall science of the mind. In this respect, our theory of consciousness may well turn out like our theory of memory. 'Memory' is a superordinate category. It divides first into long-term and short-term memory. Long-term memory is usually divided into declarative or explicit memory and nondeclarative or implicit memory. Declarative memory is memory for facts and events; nondeclarative memory covers acquired skills and habits, priming effects, habituation, classical conditioning, and subliminal learning. The neural substrate differs for these different types of memory, as do the psychological generalizations that describe them (Squire and Zola-Morgan 1991). The theory of memory consists of a classification scheme and of all the well-founded psychological and neurophysiological generalizations about the events so classified. In terms of underlying neurophysiology, it might be that short-term memory has more in common with the semantic representation of single words than short-term memory does with declarative long-term memory. This interesting commonality would be revealed in the larger systematic structure of the general theory of mind. But it would not undermine the fact that for the theorist interested in memory, there exists a set of well-founded generalizations about different types of memory that does not include the well-founded generalizations about semantic representation. These will be part of a different theory, the theory of semantic representation. The point is that there is a clear and coherent sense in which there is a theory of memory, a theory of all the different types of memory. This is true despite the fact that this theory crosscuts in important ways our theories of perception, learning, and consciousness. For example, declarative memories are subject to conscious recall in a way that nondeclarative memories typically are not.

Like the superordinate categories of perception, memory, and learning, the category of consciousness might play a coherent, nonarbitrary role in the science of the mind. There are a variety of ways it could play such a role. Suppose that there is some underlying physical property P that is necessary and sufficient for all experiences. If this is so, then just as $E = mc^2$, so consciously experiencing = being in state P, and therefore, it is a truth of nature that if some organism is in state P, then that organism is consciously aware of something. New mysterianism actually frames things in this way, that is, as if from "the God's eye point of view" there is some property P (beyond our cognitive powers to discover) that subserves all experience.

Or, to imagine a somewhat weaker relation, it is possible that a single brain property P, say the 40-hertz oscillation patterns I've mentioned several times, plays the role for all experiences that the virus plays that subserves the variety of conditions, differing widely in severity and symptomatology, that we call the common cold. The cold virus is not sufficient for a cold—the body might beat back the virus—but it is necessary for a cold. Likewise, 40-hertz oscillation patterns might be necessary for conscious experiences. Not sufficient, but necessary. The point is that the property of conscious awareness could conceivably turn out to be type-identical with some neural feature or there could turn out to be necessary connections between certain neural properties and conscious states even if there are no strict type identities.

Genes provide an illuminating model of a superordinate type defined by certain shared properties whose subtypes nonetheless have heterogeneous realizations and causal powers. Genes hold in their DNA the key to life. The property of being alive is realized, as far as we know, only in systems with DNA (although there are RNA viruses). But different types of genes have distinctive structures and distinctive roles in the etiology of phenotypic traits. The idea that the neural properties subserving visual awareness might be different from those subserving consciously planned action is no more incoherent than the actual fact that the genes subserving eye color are different from those subserving cystic fibrosis or Huntington's disease. If we think in terms of the superordinate category of the gene, then the right thing to say is that a heterogeneous set of properties supervene on a common type of thing, genes. If we think in terms of the sub-types, that is, in terms of specific kinds of genes, then we will say that heterogeneous phenotypic traits have their roots in heterogeneous gene types. Depending on the level of analysis we choose, heterogeneous properties can be legitimately viewed as subserved by the same superordinate type or by different subtypes.

In all probability there is a large set of neural connections capable of subserving different kinds of conscious experience. Perhaps they share some interesting and ubiquitous micro properties, such as the 40-hertz oscillation patterns. Perhaps they do not. No one yet knows one way or the other. But if there exists some single brain property P that is necessary and sufficient, or just necessary, for all conscious experience, then there exists a lawlike link between property P and all conscious experiences. Even if there is no ubiquitous property P subserving conscious states of every kind, there may be different property sets $\{P_1, P_2, \ldots, P_n\}$ that ground the type identity of certain kinds of experience, for example, color perception or sweet sensations or hearing a high note. If different sets of brain properties subserve different types of conscious experiences, then there exist generalizations linking the neural with the phenomenological. There may well be certain types of phenomenal experience that, despite being realized in the brain, do not map in remotely clean ways onto neural types, even for the same person over time. If so, this will be an important discovery.

There exists an important class of cases where phenomenal similarity is not subserved by similarity at the micro level. For example, the phenomenal property of wetness is multiply realized. After all, H_2O is wet, and heavy water D_2O is wet. Perhaps consciousness is such that at the phenomenal level there is the shared property but this shared property is subserved by all manner of different types of brain processes. I have already acknowledged this possibility. I don't see that it harms the prospects for a theory of consciousness as I have been conceiving it. But one might imagine cases where phenomenal similarity is unsupported by similarities at lower levels. If this is so, it might be used to argue that the shared property of being experienced may be superficial, even if it is nonarbitrary.

Patricia Churchland reminds us how the commonsense concept of fire has fared as science has progressed: "'Fire' was used to classify not only burning wood, but also the activity on the sun and various stars (actually fusion), lightning (actually electrically induced incandescence), the Northern lights (actually spectral emission), and fireflies (actually phosphorescence). As we now understand matters, only some of these things involve oxidation, and some processes which do involve oxidation, namely rusting, tarnishing, and metabolism, are not on the 'Fire' list" (1988, 285). Churchland concludes that "the case of fire illustrates both how the intuitive classification can be re-drawn, and how the new classification can pull together superficially diverse phenomena once the underlying theory is available." This is true and important. Our commonsense concept of consciousness is open to revision, to being redrawn. Indeed, it would be very surprising if different kinds of consciousness were not realized in different ways. The individuation of conscious events at the neural level will undoubtedly entail tracing complex neural maps originating at different points on the sensory periphery and traversing all sorts of different neural terrain. This will be true even if all the events mapped share a physical property, such as having the same oscillatory frequency. We should also expect the neural underpinnings of certain kinds of conscious states to be essential components of certain nonconscious states but not of other kinds of conscious states. For example, it might be that the areas of the brain that light up during ordinary visual awareness or when we are solving problems in geometry also light up when we turn over during sleep but never light up when we are listening to music with our eyes closed. And perhaps there is a deep reason why the relevant area lights up in the conscious and nonconscious cases in which it lights up. Imagine that the area is a necessary component of all spatial analysis, so it is activated when one is wide awake and trying to prove the Pythagorean theorem and when one is sound asleep but computing information about edges and distances in order to keep from falling out of bed. In cases like this the theory of consciousness is interwoven, as it must be, with theories of unconscious processing.

But such results would in no way undermine the idea that conscious phenomena are legitimate explananda for which to build theory and are possibly legitimate explanantia with which to build theory. It is to be expected that the development of the science of the mind will reveal deep and surprising things about the phenomena with the shared property of being experienced. Such discoveries might include the discovery that there are greater similarities in certain respects between certain phenomena that possess the shared property and those which do not than among all those with the shared phenomenal property. The neural spatial analyzer would be such an example. But this could happen even as important generalizations are found among all or most of the disparate events that possess the shared property.

The critics suspect that 'conscious phenomena' names a hodge-podge or is too superficial to play a useful role in explanation or prediction. The evidence suggests otherwise. Indeed, the evidence suggests that conscious phenomena will not merely serve up phenomena to be explained by the science of the mind but may also play an explanatory role. There are credible grounds for believing that some interesting generalizations will implicate consciousness in causal roles. For example, there are important functional differences between people with phenomenal awareness in certain domains and those without. Suitably motivated individuals with normal sight naturally carry out voluntary actions toward seen things. When thirsty, we step over to the water fountain we see to our right. However, blind-sighted individuals who are identically motivated and who process information about the very same things in the visual field do not naturally or efficiently carry out suitable actions toward the "seen" things. There are also the differential abilities of amnesiacs to form integrated self-concepts and to create and abide by a consistent narrative model of the self. And persons incapable of experiencing certain qualia, for example, color-blind people, show all sorts of functional differences from non-color-blind people. Check out their wardrobes.

This evidence suggests that there are true counterfactual generalizations in the domain of consciousness. Some of these generalizations will relate phenomena at the psychological level, for example, persons with qualia of kind q do x in circumstances c, but persons without qualia q (who are otherwise identical) fail to do x in c. Other generalizations will link psychological processes with brain processes. Here are three from a multitude of possible examples. (1) Persons with damage to the speech centers, and in particular to the left brain interpreter, will have trouble generating a narrative model of the self. (2) Persons with certain kinds of frontal-lobe damage will have trouble formulating plans and intentions; other kinds of frontal-lobe damage will obstruct links between consciously formulated action plans and actually carrying out the intentions. (3) Rats, cats, and humans all possess four types of taste receptors. In rats the pathway subserving bitter tastes "shows a narrower range of evocable activity (it is less discriminating) than it does in humans. In cats, it shows a wider range of activity (it is more discriminating)" (P. M. Churchland 1989, 105). This explains why rats eat anything and cats are finicky eaters. And as Paul Churchland says, it also gives us some insight into what it is like to be a rat (or a cat).

Since these sorts of generalizations already exist and have been corroborated, it follows that there are laws that conscious mental life answers to. To be sure, the laws are pitched to the heterogeneous multiplicity of events and processes that possess the shared property of being experienced. But I see no reason to say that they are not part of an emerging theory of consciousness, one basic insight of which is that consciousness is heterogeneous.

Physics deals with an extraordinary variety of heterogeneous entities and processes. But no one is tempted to think that there cannot be a physical theory. We do not infer the impossibility of a unified field theory from the heterogeneity of the known physical forces. We do not think celestial mechanics is suspect because of the heterogeneity of the composition, size, and gravitational force of bodies in our solar system. Nor do we think that the astronomical

variety of subatomic particles, within the three main classes, forecloses
the possibility of quantum theory. A theory of consciousness will in
the end be part of a unified theory of the mind. This is compatible
with the theory making generalizations suited to whatever deep local
idiosyncracies exist. Physics tells us that bodies at extremely far distances from each other traveling at close to the speed of light are
subject to regularities very different from objects moving around our
little spherelike home. It would be no more surprising and no more
damaging to the success of the science of the mind if it tells us that
visual consciousness obeys very different laws and is subserved by
different neural mechanisms from conscious reflection on one's love
life. In fact, this is exactly what we expect.

Some think that it is important to distinguish the question of
whether there can be a scientific theory of some phenomena from the
question of whether there can be a unified theory of those phenomena. I doubt that the distinction is especially clear, or even if it is, that
it is especially important. It seems to me that there can be a scientific
theory of conscious phenomena in a relatively straightforward sense.
Conscious phenomena constitute legitimate explananda, and conscious events play explanatory roles in certain well-grounded generalizations. Gathering together whatever scientific truths there are
about this set of phenomena will constitute the theory of consciousness. It will amount to gathering together all the interesting truths
about the class of phenomena that possess the shared feature of being
experienced. Such a theory will cut across our theories of perception,
memory, and learning. It will be replete with information about the
neural substrate upon which phenomenal experiences supervene and
about various kinds of nonconscious processes that are essential components of conscious phenomena. The theory of consciousness will
be part of the larger, more systematic theory of the mind as a whole,
and it is capable of taking on whatever depth the facts require. This
much will confer two sorts of unity. First, the theory of consciousness
will be about a set of phenomena that we find interesting in its own
right and that we can mark fairly perspicuously by the shared phenomenal property. Second, the theory and the uncovered generalizations have a unity conferred by the fact that they are truths about a
unified biological system, the human mind. The products of a scav-
enger hunt constitute a heap, an arbitrary set, because they are gath-

ered from locations that have no interesting intersystemic relations. But facts gathered about aspects of the mind are facts about a complex integrated system. The truths about perception or memory or consciousness have a unity that derives from there being truths about salient kinds of activity of a unified mental system that is the product of evolutionary processes. Things are different with fire. Gathering together all the now accepted truths about fire will produce a theory in one sense, but it will have less integrity than the theory of consciousness, for there is no single system, certainly not a biologically evolved one, in which the heterogeneous kinds of fire occur, unless it is the whole universe itself.

There is perhaps a stronger sort of theoretical unity. A theory or a science can be unified in this stronger sense if there are certain important laws that govern all the types in its domain. Physics is often said to be unified, or on its way to unity, in this sense. But it is unclear why one of the least mature sciences should be judged against our most mature science. It may be that all conscious phenomena are governed by a small set of laws, and more generally that mental phenomena are governed by an even smaller but more inclusive set of laws. It is too early to tell. But it seems to me a mistake to hold up an idealized model of physics and hold that there must be a small set of deep laws that govern a domain for the domain to be a coherent domain of scientific inquiry. And in any case, even if we operate with this ideal, there is no way of knowing in advance of long-term inquiry which domains might satisfy the ideal and which domains most likely cannot.

There must be truths about consciousness, since consciousness exists, is a natural phenomenon, and is in need of explanation. So there can be a theory of consciousness. What sort of unity the theory will possess and what interrelations it will have to other theories within the overall science of the mind we do not yet know. The best strategy is to get on with the hard work of providing the right fine-grained analysis of conscious mental life and see where it leads. It will be our proudest achievement if we can demystify consciousness. Consciousness exists. It would be a mistake to eliminate talk of it because its semantic past is so bound up with ghostly fairy tales or because it names such a multiplicity of things. The right attitude, it seems to me, is to deliver the concept from its ghostly past and provide it with a credible naturalistic analysis. I have tried to say a bit about how this might be done, indeed, about how it is already being done.

10.2   A Brief Recapitulation

The constructive naturalistic theory I have sketched pictures consciousness as a name for a heterogeneous set of events and processes that share the property of being experienced. Consciousness is taken to name a set of processes, not a thing or a mental faculty. The theory is neo-Darwinian in that it is committed to the view that the capacity to experience things evolved via the processes responsible for the development of our nervous system: migration, mutation, genetic drift, natural selection, and free riding. The theory denies that consciousness is as consciousness seems at the surface. Consciousness has a complex structure. Getting at this complex structure requires coordination of phenomenological, psychological, and neural analyses. The theory is neurophilosophical in that it tries to mesh a naturalistic metaphysic of mind with our still sketchy but maturing understanding of how the brain works. The most plausible hypothesis is that the mind is the brain, a Darwin machine that is a massively well-connected system of parallel processors interacting with each other from above and below and every which way besides. It is no wonder that meaning holism is true, that we somehow solve the frame problem, and that my belief that snow is white is realized quite possibly in a somewhat different way in my brain than the same belief is realized in yours. Finally, the theory claims to provide an explanation of the gap between the first-person way in which conscious mental life reveals itself and the way it is, or can be described, from an objective point of view. Mind and brain are one and the same thing seen from two different perspectives. The gap between the subjective and the objective is an epistemic gap, not an ontological gap. Indeed, it is precisely the fact that individuals possess organismic integrity that explains why subjectivity accrues first-personally.

Conscious inessentialism, the doctrine that consciousness is not essential to the analysis of human mentality, can be set to one side when the task is, as I have framed it, to sketch a naturalistic theory of consciousness consistent with our natures as biological creatures with nervous systems of a certain kind. There are possible creatures that are identical to us at the level of observable input-output relations but that lack inner lives altogether. We are not like this. Consciousness is essential to human nature and to the human mind.

The epiphenomenalist suspicion should be taken seriously, but it should not overwhelm us. Some conscious processes are akin to the ineffectual functionary who is always the last to know. But other conscious processes and models, including the self that is the center of narrative gravity, figure crucially in cognition and in the overall conduct of our lives.

New mysterianism, the doctrine that consciousness is part of the natural order, though it nonetheless can never be understood as such, is belied by the degree of understanding that constructive naturalism has already given to us. Thinking that consciousness is terminally mysterious is easy to fall for if we set impossibly high standards on explanation and intelligibility. But if we require "perfect intelligibility" for the consciousness-brain problem, then we should require such standards before we declare a solution to any interesting problem relating two seemingly disparate phenomena. The trouble is that abiding by such high standards would mean that we know nothing about any interesting natural process, for example, the origin and nature of life, the existence of the subatomic world, and so on. If we operate with more sensible standards of intelligibility, several credible stories can already be told to explain how such things as sensory qualia supervene on certain patterns of neural activity. Just as ordinary water *is* H_2O and is *caused* by H_2O, so too are experiences of colors, tastes, and smells identical to and caused by activity patterns in certain brain pathways. Higher-level sorts of consciousness also supervene on brain processes. But whether they do so by satisfying even roughly hewn type-identity conditions is something we do not yet know.

The idea that a mind's "I" stands behind all experience as a very condition of its possibility is an illusion. My consciousness is mine; it is uniquely personal. But this is not because some mind's "I" or some immutable transcendental ego shadows my experience. It is because of my organic nature, because of the way thoughts hang together in evolved human beings. The self emerges. It is a complex construct that we are eventually able to represent in language and in thought. The self that is the center of narrative gravity provides grounds for identity and self-respect. Conscious representation of this self is one type of self-consciousness. Such self-consciousness is nothing mysterious. It is realized in the brain. But the narrative represented is the joint production of the organism and the complex social world in which she lives her life. Presumably, it would be idle labor to look for type-identical neural maps of the self-representations of different individuals. This is not because self-representation is not neurally realized. It is because the phenomenological particularity of self-represented identity suggests neural particularity. Self-representation is a good candidate for activity that, despite being realized in the brain, is probably realized in very complex and multifarious ways. Our theories of self-representation may therefore profitably proceed with a certain explanatory autonomy from the level of neural analysis.

Despite its extraordinary difficulty, the problem of consciousness is beginning to yield. One will not see the entry points if one plays ostrich and puts one's head in the sand, having declared the whole thing beyond us. But if one looks to naturalistically informed work in the philosophy of mind, to neuroscience and neuropsychology, and to certain segments of psychology and cognitive science, one will see the sort of work I have described here, and one will be less reticent about undertaking the project of making consciousness reveal its secrets. Understanding consciousness with the conscious mind is a wonderful, giddy idea, yet it is also a genuine possibility.

References

Churchland, Patricia S. 1983. "Consciousness: The Transmutation of a Concept." *Pacific Philosophical Quarterly* 64:80–93.

Churchland, Patricia S. 1988. "Reduction and the Neurobiological Basis of Consciousness." In Marcel and Bisiach 1988.

Churchland, Paul M. 1989. *A Neurocomputational Perspective: The Nature of Mind and the Structure of Science*. Cambridge: MIT Press.

Marcel, A., and Bisiach, E. (eds.) (1988). *Consciousness in Contemporary Science*. New York: Oxford University Press.

Squire, L., and S. Zola-Morgan. 1991. "The Medial Temporal Lobe Memory System." *Science* 253:1380–1386.

Wilkes, K. V. 1988a. *Real People: Personal Identity without Thought Experiments*. Oxford: Oxford University Press.

Wilkes, K. V. 1988b. "_____, Yishi, Duh, Um, and Consciousness." In Marcel and Bisiach 1988.

On Seeing Robots

Alan Mackworth

Good Old Fashioned Artificial Intelligence and Robotics (GOFAIR) relies on a set of restrictive Omniscient Fortune Teller Assumptions about the agent, the world and their relationship. The emerging Situated Agent paradigm is challenging GOFAIR by grounding the agent in space and time, relaxing some of those assumptions, proposing new architectures and integrating perception, reasoning and action in behavioral modules. GOFAIR is typically forced to adopt a hybrid architecture for integrating signal-based and symbol-based approaches because of the inherent mismatch between the corresponding on-line and off-line computational models. It is argued that Situated Agents should be designed using a unitary on-line computational model. The Constraint Net model of Zhang and Mackworth satisfies that requirement. Two systems for situated perception built in our laboratory are described to illustrate the new approach: one for visual monitoring of a robot's arm, the other for real-time visual control of multiple robots competing and cooperating in a dynamic world.

11.1   Introduction

The title of this chapter, "On Seeing Robots," leaves substantial scope for playful exploration. The simple ambiguity is, of course, between describing robots that see their worlds and systems that see robots. These categories are not exclusive: I also combine them and discuss robots that see robots and even robots that see themselves. Furthermore, the title is designed to echo, and pay homage to, a classic vision paper entitled "On Seeing Things" by Max Clowes [1] as I have done once before [2]. But the context, the arguments and the conclusions are new; the comparison is used explicitly here to show the difference between the classical approach and an emerging situated approach to robotic perception. The most important reading of the title is that the paper is about how *we* see robots; it is about the computational paradigms, the assumptions, the architectures and the tools we use to design and build robots.

11.2   Good Old Fashioned Artificial Intelligence and Robotics

The phrase Good Old Fashioned Artificial Intelligence (GOFAI) was introduced by Haugeland [3] to characterize the classical symbol manipulation approach to AI. In GOFAI intelligence is identified with reasoning and reasoning with rule-based manipulation of symbolic structures. Given the fact that syntactic proof theory and Tarskian semantic model theory can be placed in isomorphic correspondence, a GOFAI system can be said to reason about the real world. How it senses the world and how it acts in the world, if at all, are secondary concerns delegated to separate perception and action modules. We extend GOFAI here to Good Old Fashioned AI and Robotics (GOFAIR) to characterize the idea of building a robotic system with a perception front end that translates from signal to symbol, a GOFAI system as the meat in the sandwich and a motor back end that carries out actions in the world. So a GOFAIR system consists of three modules for perception, reasoning and action, respectively. (This characterization of a GOFAIR robot is, of course, an unfair but useful caricature.) The paradigmatic environment that a GOFAIR robot inhabits is the blocks world. Clowes [1] and many others [4] provided the tools to build perceptual systems that translated arbitrary images of that world to symbolic descriptions for the purposes of reasoning and planning. Planning for a GOFAIR robot, using the situation calculus or the simplified STRIPS representation, models actions as changes to a global world model, maintained as a set of sentences, to produce a plan. In GOFAIR (but not in general as we shall see) a plan is just a list of actions which if executed would change the world into its desired state, provided that the world were as modelled, the action models were correct and that nothing else intervened. It is possible to make explicit some of the meta-assumptions about the agent and its world implicit in much of the GOFAIR research strategy [5]:

• **Assumption IR (Individuals and Relations)**   All that is useful for an agent can be described in terms of individuals and relations amongst individuals.
• **Assumption BK (Belief Is Knowledge)**   An agent's beliefs about the world are true and justified.
• **Assumption DK (Definite Knowledge)**   An agent's knowledge of the world is definite and positive.

- **Assumption CK (Complete Knowledge)**   The agent's knowledge of the world is complete. This requires that everything relevant about the world be known to the agent. This Closed World Assumption allows the agent to assume safely that a fact is false if it cannot infer that it is true.
- **Assumption SE (Static Environment)**   The environment is static unless an agent changes it.
- **Assumption OA (One Agent)**   There is only one agent in the world.
- **Assumption DW (Deterministic World)**   Given a complete and definite description of the world the agent can predict all the effects of an action.
- **Assumption DSA (Discrete Sequential Actions)**   Actions are discrete and they are carried out sequentially.

These assumptions are very restrictive. OA rules out other agents acting cooperatively to help the agent, competitively to frustrate the agent's plans or neutrally, as nature might do. OA also means that the agent does not have to react in real time to changes in the world. DW rules out non-deterministic actions, such as tossing a coin. BK, DK and CK mean that the agent is really omniscient—it has definite knowledge of everything relevant to achieving its goals. Assumption DSA rules out the need to consider continuous events such as processes, and the possibility of performing actions concurrently, which would require reasoning about the duration and termination of actions. By making all these assumptions explicit we can consider relaxing them independently, as needed.

To realize the force of these assumptions let us consider a world in which they are all violated. Suppose we want to build a robot to play soccer. Quite apart from all the difficult robotics and perception problems involved, we have substantial challenges in representation for planning and action. OA is violated: There are cooperating agents on the robot's team, competing agents on the other team, and neutral agents such as the referee and the weather. DW is violated: It is not possible to predict precisely where the ball will go when it is kicked, even if all the relevant factors are known. Each of BK, DK and CK is violated. Moreover, DSA is violated: Continuous events such as a player running to a position, or the ball moving through the air, occur concurrently.

Our idealizations and simple worlds can lead us astray. The collective force of these assumptions is that, in GOFAIR, we postulate a world in which all the effects of an action are knowable before the action is taken in the world. In homage to this powerful consequence, we dub them the Omniscient Fortune Teller Assumptions (OFTA).

A further radical consequence of the OFTA is that they dictate that perception is unnecessary for intelligent action except as it is needed to determine the initial state of the world. They allow an agent to retreat into its head constructing, by reason alone, a plan as an action sequence which is then played as a motor command tape. In other words, planning is reduced to finding a straight-line program without conditionals or loops. Some of the OFTA are now being relaxed (see, for example, the work on reactive planning [6]) but they still permeate the way we design our agents. They have sanctioned the divorce of reasoning from perception and action. There is an interesting analogy here with motor control in robotics. The off-line approach to straight-line planning is directly analogous to open loop dead reckoning control. They both embody the assumption of perfect knowledge of the consequences of all actions. The OFTA, and not the frame problem which follows from them, is the real difficulty here. Just as dead reckoning fails for navigation, the unacceptable consequences of the OFTA have forced a crisis for GOFAIR which presages a paradigm shift. In the period of extraordinary science provoked by the impending collapse of a paradigm there are many contenders for the new paradigm [7]. Some believe that a normal process of relaxing some of the OFTA assumptions will succeed; others that nothing short of a revolution will work. Either way, it is worth spending some time and effort to understand and make explicit the foundations of GOFAIR to see if they are all rotten or just a little shaky and in need of shoring up.

11.3   Situated Agents

The attempt, in the GOFAIR paradigm, to establish perception, reasoning and action as semi-autonomous disciplines has yielded useful mathematical and computational results but has also led to sterility. That strategy has failed to produce the coherent analytical science necessary for the synthetic engineering activity of building intelligent agents. Unlike Gaul, intelligence is not divisible into three parts. The perception, reasoning and action modules of GOFAIR not only can't be built but also do not correspond to natural scientific domains with clean interfaces and limited interaction amongst them. Perception, reasoning and action correspond only to labels that we use to carica- ture aspects of the agent's behavior. Brooks [8] has correctly pointed out that the traditional divide-and-conquer AI approach to robotics, by slicing intelligence into perception, reasoning and action, has pursued a strategy that does not scale up. This, incidentally, implies that any research program based on that division will be sterile. But, although this reduction does not carry through, that's no excuse for abandoning reductionist scientific activity and retreating to holistic philosophizing. Alternate reductionist strategies are available, such as focussing on hierarchies of behavior units, each of which can embody elements of perception, reasoning and action, as in the subsumption architecture [9]. I accept Brooks' diagnosis of the problem but not his prescription for the solution [10]. It is clear though that closer coupling of perception and action, intermediated by reasoning when necessary, in embedded behavioral modules is the correct general approach. As discussed later in this paper, an alternative decomposi- tion strategy is the Constraint Net model of intelligent systems [11], that allows formal characterization and implementation techniques.

Neither AI nor robotics (nor, for that matter, computational vision or any other subdiscipline of either field) can proceed auto- nomously. The version of divide-and-conquer that we have been playing, namely, functional decomposition, is not now the best strategy. The best payoff in the next few years will come from approaches that design, analyze and build integrated agents. This requirement for *cognitive integration*, the tight coupling of perception, reasoning and action, should dominate our research strategy. This is a non-trivial requirement: as I'll argue later, it follows as a consequence that systems must be designed and implemented in a single unitary framework.

By abandoning the OFTA, we see that the agent cannot main- tain a faithful world model by reasoning alone. (From this it does not follow, *pace* Brooks, that we should abandon reason [12] or repre- sentation [13]!) Indeed, it cannot maintain a completely faithful world model by any means. Actions have many possible unpredict- able outcomes and real worlds cannot be exhaustively modelled. But, ranges and likelihoods of outcomes can be characterized and real worlds can be partially modelled. Risk-taking under uncertainty is a necessary aspect of intelligent behavior. Perception is not exhaustive; it is purposive, model-based, situated, incremental and multi-modal. Perceptual actions are planned and carried out to acquire knowledge. A blind person's cane tapping strategy illustrates the coupling of perception, reasoning and action: each subserves the others.

Plans are robot programs. Straight-line code is only their simplest form. However, we must learn the automatic programming lesson. Even in the predictable, disembodied world inside a computer, automatic programming has proven an elusive goal. Automatic planning in the world of a robot is much harder. But planning, in its fully generality, is not a necessary component of an intelligent agent; however, responding appropriately to changes in the world is always necessary.

The claim is that AI and robotics will be integrated only if AI researchers stop focussing on disembodied, solipsistic reasoners and if roboticists accept the need for richer, more adequate methodologies to describe the world. Nonstandard logical approaches based on theory formation, dialectical reasoning, argument structures, belief as defeasible knowledge, situated automata and constraint-based model-theoretic approaches are all promising but they must consider perception and action as playing roles in the theory beyond simply providing truth values for atomic propositions. Overthrow the tyrannical reasoner! For example, Reiter and Mackworth [14, 15] have provided a logical framework for depiction that allows reasoning about a world and images of that world, characterizing the interpretations of an image as the logical models of the description of the image, the scene and the image-scene mapping. This allows the coupling of perception and reasoning through a common logic-based language.

The critiques and rejection, by some, of the GOFAIR paradigm have given rise to what we shall call the Situated Agent (SA) approaches of Rosenschein and Kaebling [16,17], Agre and Chapman [18, 19], Smith [20], Brooks [12], Ballard [21], Winograd and Flores [22], Lavignon and Shoham [23], Zhang and Mackworth [24] and many others. The collection of SA approaches is sometimes also known loosely as Nouvelle AI. It is hard to define the SA approach succinctly; emerging paradigms can often only be defined in retrospect. Indeed, the various approaches hardly constitute a mutually consistent and coherent school; but, they do represent a movement. Perhaps a way to convey the flavor of the difference is that in GOFAIR *ad hoc* is a term of abuse (used, say, to describe a system without a Tarskian semantics); in SA, on the other hand, *ad hoc*, meaning literally "to this," is an indexical—a great compliment. In short, a situated agent is a real physical system grounded and embedded in a real world, here and now, acting and reacting in real-time.

Situated agents clearly indulge not only in situated action and, perhaps, in situated reasoning but also in situated perception [21, 25]. Another shift in moving from GOFAIR to SA is from a single agent in a static world to multiple agents in a dynamic world which, for our purposes, entails also a shift from static perception to dynamic perception. So one theme of this paper is *situated dynamic perception*.

Some of the connotations of the shift from GOFAIR to SA can be elicited by the shift from "Seeing Things" to "Seeing Robots": the ultimately situated agent sees not randomly-arrayed, unexpected "things" but a coherent, dynamic evolving scene resulting, in part, from its own movements and actions. This shift is most dramatically and effectively conveyed when the robot sees parts of its own body.

11.4 Back to the Future

Feedback control theory, using the perceived effects of actions to control future actions in order to achieve a desired purpose, has led to an array of mathematical and engineering triumphs. Moreover, hierarchical feedback control theory has shown us how to achieve stable behaviors for a wide variety of complex systems, by closing feedback loops between the agent and the world at every level of the hierarchical structure. This is achieved despite the stubborn reality of phenomena, such as joint backlash, friction and flexible links, that are hard to model tractably. So far, however, hierarchical feedback control has mostly been used to control agents where the environmental description is impoverished: an *n*-dimensional vector of scalars. We need to apply the key insight of hierarchical feedback control but use descriptively richer languages and methodology to model the environment and the agent itself.

Occam's Razor requires that our most fundamental research goal should be to base the new paradigm on a unitary theory. Ideally such a theory will be mathematical in nature but will lead to appropriate computational formalisms. We already know that it must include standard control theory as a special case.

An alternative to a unitary theory is the approach, taken by many, of building hybrid systems with signal-based low-level systems and symbol-based high-level GOFAIR systems. The hybrid approach is esthetically repellent and pragmatically cumbersome; moreover, it has had limited experimental success.

The root problem with the hybrid approach is a complete mismatch of the nature of the two underlying computational paradigms [24]. The GOFAIR symbol-manipulating systems are based on *off-line* computational models such as virtual machines for Lisp or Prolog. In essence these are all in the off-line Turing Machine paradigm of computation. An off-line model computes its output as a mathematical *function* of its inputs. There is no notion that the inputs arrive over time. The signal-manipulating systems, though, are based on *on-line* models. An on-line model, such as a circuit, computes an output trace (a function of time, on a discrete, dense or event-based time structure, to a domain of values) as a *transduction* of its input traces. This fundamental mismatch ensures that the oft-discussed signal-symbol interface is hard, if not impossible, to specify coherently, let alone build.

Notice, in particular, that the off-line approach pervades GOFAIR. Planning, for example, is seen as an atemporal activity; it involves reasoning *about* actions in time but it does not occur *in* time. The recent flurry of activity in 'anytime' planning is an acknowledgment of this discrepancy. Vision is conceived as implementing a mathematical *function* whose input is the retinal stimulation and whose output is, variously, a description of the image, a viewer-centred description of the visible surfaces or a world-centred description. Deconstruction of GOFAIR along these lines is instructive, and perhaps necessary, if we are to escape the pervading off-line assumptions.

One of the requirements we place on a unitary paradigm is that it subsume, for example, signal processing, control systems, analog and digital circuit models, and dynamical systems, most generally. (This is indeed a tall order.) All of these paradigms assume an on-line computational model; they are also all of a venerable vintage. And yet the impression created by GOFAIR is that we have left these frameworks behind, or beneath, us. On the contrary, we must revisit them, include them and situate them in the symbolic paradigm; this requires substantial generalization of both the traditional signal-based and the traditional symbol-based approaches. (If this analysis is correct this move back to the future will indeed be ironic, and painful, both for GOFAIR and for Nouvelle AI; each is rather fond of thinking of itself as the *avant garde*.) The unitary approach will only succeed, following this line of argument, if that generalization is a single on-line computational model.

One such model is embodied in the Constraint Net (CN) approach that Ying Zhang and I have developed. CN is a model for robotic systems software implemented as modules with I/O ports [26]. A module performs a transduction from its input traces to its output traces, subject to the principle of causality: an output value at any time can depend only on the input values before, or at, that time. The language has a formal semantics based on the least fixpoint of sets of equations [11]. In applying it to a robot operating in a given environment one separately specifies the behaviour of the robot plant, the robot control program and the environment. The total system can then be shown to have various properties, such as safety and liveness, based on provable properties of its subsystems. This approach allows one to specify formally, and verify, models of embedded control systems. Our goal is to develop it as a practical tool for building real, complex, sensor-based robots. It can be seen as a development of Brooks' subsumption architecture [8] that enhances its modular advantages while avoiding the limitations of the augmented finite state machine approach.

A robot situated in an environment is modeled as three machines: the robot plant, the robot control and the environment. Each is modeled separately as a dynamical system by specifying a CN with identified input and output ports. The robot is modeled as a CN consisting of a coupling of its plant CN and its control CN by identifying corresponding input and output ports. Similarly the robot CN is coupled to the environment CN to form a closed robot-enviroment CN.

The CN model is realized as an on-line distributed programming language with a formal algebraic denotational semantics and a specification language, a real-time temporal logic, that allows the designer to specify and prove properties of the situated robot by proving them of the robot-environment CN. So far, we have been able to specify, design, verify and implement systems for a robot that can track other robots [26], a robot that can escape from mazes and a two-handed robot that assembles objects [24], an elevator system [27] and a car-like robot that can plan and execute paths under non-holonomic constraints. Although CN can carry out traditional symbolic computation on-line, such as solving Constraint Satisfaction Problems and path planning, notice that much of the symbolic reasoning and theorem-proving may be outside the agent, in the mind of the designer. GOFAIR does not make this distinction, assuming that such symbolic reasoning occurs explicitly in, and only in, the mind of the agent.

11.5   Situated Perception

Whether or not Situated Agents in general, or Constraint Nets in particular, emerge as the focus of the next paradigm, the choice of target problem domain is key for moving beyond GOFAIR. It must require for its solution cognitive integration. It should require experimental and theoretical progress in techniques for perception, reasoning, and action but be within their grasp, so to speak. It should be useful with objective criteria for success, perhaps competing with another baseline technology. It should allow us to acknowledge the difficulty of automatic planning. It should allow for situated perception, that is, perception in a specific environmental context of the relevant environmental variables. Given all that, it should also be as simple, and exciting, as possible.

One target domain with these characteristics is telerobotics. Telerobotics is a further development beyond teleoperation. In teleoperation a human controls some remote device in a master-slave relationship. Telerobotics incorporates some autonomous robotic control with high-level human supervision. Such a system should have an internal model of the environment and a model of itself. Mulligan, Lawrence and I have designed and built a model-based vision system that allows a telerobot to see and monitor its own limbs, allowing us to supplement or, perhaps, replace traditional joint sensors for position control. By incorporating a 3D model of a telerobot's manipulator we used model-based techniques to determine the joint angles of the manipulator. It offers a cheap, fast and reliable solution to the problem of joint angle feedback [28]. Related work on visual feedback for robotics has been successful for highly constrained tasks such as table tennis [29] and throwing and juggling a ball [30] or requires special marks on the arm, special sensors or special lighting [31]. We now have a prototype system that can monitor the joint angles of the boom, stick and bucket of an excavator. We have completed a redesign, and a second prototype implementation, for a system with real-time performance at 10 Hz using parallel and distributed algorithms on image analysis boards and a Transputer system.

As the robot moves its limbs the perceptual system uses visual and proprioceptive information to provide updates to its internal self-model. A GOFAIR blocks world hand-eye system has to hide its arm before looking at the scene. Surely one of the first perceptual tasks for a robot or a telerobot must be to understand images of its own moving body parts. Once it has achieved that, then visually-guided grasping and coordinated manipulation become possible. It suggests using visual feedback to supplement or replace the traditional inverse kinematic and setpoint methods for path planning and path following which, again, can be seen as an extension of the off-line planning method for robot action. It is consistent with our ideas on distributed robotic architectures in Constraint Nets. So this is a truly situated robot: situated in the spatial context of its own body.

What we have done may be seen as a step towards achieving one of the goals set out earlier, namely, integrating control-theoretic and knowledge-based approaches. A robot manipulator is typically controlled by representing its configuration as a vector of joint angles. Individual servo loops for each joint allow precise control of the manipulator. In our model-based vision systems we are using an articulated, 3D model of the limb, a richer description than a vector of joint angles, to represent the proximal environment. But we envision using the perceptual data to close servo loops, allowing for the control of the movement of the limb continuously during an action.

This approach achieves the necessary tight coupling of perception, reasoning and action. The system is purposive, model-based, incremental and multisensory. Telerobotics, as an integrating application domain, has the advantage over building completely autonomous robots in that we can incrementally automate aspects of the total system's behavior while maintaining functionality. This gives us a common framework for the design of systems for a spectrum of applications ranging from human-controlled manipulators operating in constrained environments to autonomous agents in less structured environments. An agent's behavior must be specified and controlled at many levels: for example, at the joint level, at the end effector level and at the task level. At the lower levels that specification is in terms of set points and parameter vectors, at the higher levels as symbolic task descriptions. There are operational criteria for success: we cannot finesse reality by hiding in the OFTA. In order to satisfy those criteria, it must achieve cognitive integration.

To investigate another world in which the OFTA do not hold, Dinesh Pai and I have started the Dynamo (Dynamics and Mobile Robots) Project in our laboratory. We are experimenting with multiple mobile robots under visual control. The basic Dynamo testbed consists of fleets of radio-controlled vehicles that receive commands from a remote computer. Using a parallel and distributed SIMD/MIMD integrated environment, vision programs are able to monitor the position and orientation of each robot at 60 Hz; planning and control programs can generate and send motor commands out at 50 Hz. This approach allows umbilical-free behaviour and very rapid, lightweight fully autonomous robots. As far as we know, it is a unique and successful approach to all the tradeoffs involved in mobile robot design. In a related project we also plan to mount sensors, including television cameras, on-board the robots and transmit the data back to off-board computers. As with other experiments in mobile robotics, such as [32, 33], our aim is to integrate theory and practice, as well as symbolic reasoning and control algorithms. So in a real sense these robots can see themselves and their environment, so they can monitor the effects of their own actions and the actions of others.

A long term goal is to have teams of robots engaged in cooperative and competitive behaviour. In particular, we have chosen soccer playing as one of the tasks. Our initial experiments have been successful. With Rod Barman, Stewart Kingdon, Michael Sahota and Ying Zhang, we have developed and tested path planning and motion

Figure 11.1
Two soccer players compete in the Dynamo project. The striker on the right is shooting at the goal on the left.

control algorithms that allow a player to get to the ball and to shoot it at the goal, while a goalie tries to stop it, as shown in Figure 11.1. Some of this work is based on the Constraint Net formulation outlined above. That formulation is particularly useful here since we have written a simulation of the dynamics of the player as a constraint net and developed planning and control algorithms in CN. The Dynamo testbed will force us to develop and experiment with algorithms at all behavioral levels. Current work in the field typically adopts a hybrid scheme, grafting symbolic AI algorithms onto numerical, or fuzzy, control schemes with the problems resulting from the underlying off-line/on-line computational mismatch described earlier. We intend further practical and theoretical development of CN as a language for writing robot programs in this environment. An important hypothesis to be tested is that this single uniform on-line framework is adequate for expressing plans at all levels.

11.6 Conclusions

We have looked at robots looking at the world, at other robots and at themselves. We have also looked inside robots to examine their architecture and embedded assumptions. GOFAIR robots, based on the Omniscient Fortune Teller Assumptions and hybrid off-line/on-line computational models, are being challenged by Situated Agents, embedded in time and space. The Constraint Net approach models the robot and its world symmetrically as coupled dynamical systems.

CN is an appropriate formalism for the new paradigm since it allows analysis of the interaction of the robot embedded in its specific world; moreover, it is allows us to develop practical tools based on a unitary on-line distributed computational framework. Two systems for situated perception were described as benchmark challenges for the new approach to seeing robots.

Acknowledgments

I am grateful to Rod Barman, Craig Boutilier, Randy Goebel, Stewart Kingdon, Jim Little, Keiji Kanazawa, Peter Lawrence, David Lowe, Jane Mulligan, Dinesh Pai, David Poole, Ray Reiter, Michael Sahota, Bob Woodham and Ying Zhang for help with this. This work is supported, in part, by the Canadian Institute for Advanced Research, the Natural Sciences and Engineering Research Council of Canada and the Institute for Robotics and Intelligent Systems Network of Centres of Excellence.

References

[1] M. B. Clowes, "On seeing things," *Artificial Intelligence*, vol. 2, pp. 79–116, 1971.

[2] A. K. Mackworth, "On seeing things again," in *Proc. 8th International Joint Conf. on Artificial Intelligence* (Karlsruhe, West Germany), pp. 1187–1191, 1983.

[3] J. Haugeland, *Artificial Intelligence: The Very Idea*. Cambridge, Mass: MIT Press, 1985.

[4] A. K. Mackworth, "How to see a simple world: an exegesis of some computer programs for scene analysis," in *Machine Intelligence 8* (E. W. Elcock and D. Michie, eds.), pp. 510–540, New York, NY: John Wiley & Sons, 1977.

[5] D. L. Poole, A. K. Mackworth, and R. G. Goebel, *Computational Intelligence: A Logical Approach*. Vancouver, B.C.: Dept. of Computer Science, University of British Columbia, 1992. (339 pp.).

[6] T. M. Mitchell, "Becoming increasingly reactive," in *AAAI-90*, (Boston, MA), pp. 1051–1058, 1990.

[7] T. S. Kuhn, *The structure of scientific revolutions*. Chicago: University of Chicago Press, 1962.

[8] R. A. Brooks, *A robot that walks: emergent behaviors from a carefully evolved network*. Cambridge, MA: Massachusetts Institute of Technology, 1988.

[9] R. A. Brooks, "A robust layered control system for a mobile robot," *IEEE Transactions on Robotics and Automation*, vol. 2, pp. 14–23, 1987.

[10] A. K. Mackworth, "Building robots," in *Proc. Vision Interface '92*, (Vancouver, BC), pp. 187–188, Canadian Information Processing Society, May 1992. Invited.

[11] Y. Zhang and A. K. Mackworth, "Constraint nets: A semantic model for real-time embedded systems," Tech. Rep. TR 92-10, UBC, Vancouver, B.C., May 1992.

[12] R. A. Brooks, "Intelligence without reason," in *IJCAI-91*, (Sydney, Australia), pp. 569–595, Aug. 1991.

[13] R. A. Brooks, "Intelligence without representation," *Artificial Intelligence*, vol. 47, pp. 139–160, 1991.

[14] R. Reiter and A. K. Mackworth, "A logical framework for depiction and image interpretation," *Artificial Intelligence*, vol. 41, pp. 125–155, 1990.

[15] A. K. Mackworth, "The logic of constraint satisfaction," *Artificial Intelligence*, vol. 58, pp. 3–20, 1992.

[16] S. J. Rosenschein and L. P. Kaelbling, "The synthesis of machines with provable epistemic properties," in *Proc. Conf. on Theoretical Aspects of Reasoning about Knowledge* (Joseph Halpern, ed.), pp. 83–98, Los Altos, CA: Morgan Kaufmann, 1986.

[17] L. P. Kaelbling and S. J. Rosenschein, "Action and planning in embedded agents," in *Designing Autonomous Agents: Theory and Practice from Biology to Engineering and Back* (P. Maes, ed.), pp. 35–48, Cambridge, MA: MIT Press, 1990.

[18] P. E. Agre and D. Chapman, "Pengi: An implementation of a theory of activity," in *AAAI-87*, (Seattle, WA), pp. 268–272, 1987.

[19] D. Chapman, "Vision instruction and action," Tech. Rep. MIT AI TR-1085, MIT, Cambridge, MA, June 1990.

[20] B. C. Smith, "The owl and the electric encyclopedia," *Artificial Intelligence*, vol. 47, pp. 251–288, 1991.

[21] D. H. Ballard, "Reference frames for active vision," in *Proceedings IJCAI-89*, (Detroit, MI), pp. 1635–1641, 1989.

[22] T. Winograd and F. Flores, *Understanding Computers and Cognition*. Reading, MA: Addison-Wesley, 1986.

[23] J. Lavignon and Y. Shoham, "Temporal automata," Tech. Rep. STAN-CS-90-1325, Stanford University, Stanford, CA, 1990.

[24] Y. Zhang and A. K. Mackworth, "Will the robot do the right thing?" Tech. Rep. TR 92-31, UBC, Vancouver, B.C., Nov. 1992.

[25] I. D. Horswill and R. A. Brooks, "Situated vision in a dynamic world: Chasing objects," in *AAAI-88*, (St. Paul, MN), pp. 796–800, 1988.

[26] Y. Zhang and A. K. Mackworth, "Modeling behavioral dynamics in discrete robotic systems with logical concurrent objects," in *Robotics and Flexible Manufacturing Systems*, pp. 187–196, Elsevier Science Publishers B.V., 1992.

[27] Y. Zhang and A. K. Mackworth, "Design and analysis of embedded real-time systems: An elevator case study," Tech. Rep. TR 93-4, UBC, Vancouver, B.C., Feb. 1993.

[28] I. J. Mulligan, A. K. Mackworth, and P. D. Lawrence, "A model-based vision system for manipulator position sensing," in *Proc. IEEE Workshop on Interpretation of 3D Scenes*, (Austin, TX), pp. 186–193, 1989.

[29] R. L. Andersson, *A Robot Ping-Pong Player: Experiment in Real-Time Intelligent Control*. Cambridge, MA: MIT Press, 1988.

[30] E. W. Aboaf, A. K. Drucker, and C. B. Atkeson, "Task-level robot learning: Juggling a tennis ball more accurately," in *Proc. IEEE Int. Conf. on Robotics and Automation*, pp. 1290–1295, 1989.

[31] J. M. Hollerbach, "A review of kinematic calibration," in *The Robotics Review I* (O. Khatib and J. J. Craig and T. Lozano-Perez, ed.), pp. 207–242, Cambridge, MA: MIT Press, 1989.

[32] O. Amidi and C. Thorpe, "Integrated mobile robot control," in *SPIE Mobile Robots V*, pp. 504–523, 1990.

[33] T. Skewis and V. Lumelsky, "Experiments with a mobile robot operating in a cluttered unknown environment," in *Proc. 1992 IEEE Int. Conf. on Robotics and Automation* (Nice, France), pp. 1482–1487, May 1992.

What Your Computer Really Needs to Know, You Learned in Kindergarten

E. H. Durfee

Research in distributed AI has led to computational techniques for providing AI systems with rudimentary social skills. This paper gives a brief survey of distributed AI, describing the work that strives for social skills that a person might acquire in kindergarten, and highlighting important unresolved problems facing the field.

Introduction

In the pursuit of artificial intelligence (AI), it has become increasingly clear that intelligence, whatever it is, has a strong social component [Bobrow, 1991; Gasser, 1991]. Tests for intelligence, such as the Turing test, generally rely on having an (assumedly) intelligent agent evaluate the agent in question by interacting with it. For an agent to be intelligent under such criteria, therefore, it has to be able to participate in a society of agents.

Distributed AI (DAI) is the subfield of AI that has, for over a decade now, been investigating the knowledge and reasoning techniques that computational agents might need in order to participate in societies. Distributed AI researchers have come from a particularly diverse set of backgrounds, ranging from distributed computing systems to discourse analysis, from formalisms for representing nested beliefs in agents to cognitive studies of human performance in organizations, from solving inherently distributed problems in applications such as communication network management to analyzing the evolution of cooperation in populations of artificial systems. The wealth of the field of DAI lies in its interdisciplinary nature, generating a melting pot of ideas from people with widely different perspectives who share a common goal of realizing in computers many of the social capabilities that we take for granted in people.

In studying these capabilities, it is helpful to consider how people become socialized. In our modern culture, one important socialization step happens when a child enters school. In his book *All I Really Need to Know I Learned in Kindergarten*, Robert Fulghum lists sixteen things he learned in kindergarten that, he claims, form a core of knowledge and skills that he has used throughout life [Fulghum, 1986]. Now, while this list is anecdotal, I would argue that it is not by chance that the majority of the items he lists, ten of the sixteen, deal with social knowledge and skills.

In fact, these ten items in Fulghum's list have strong correspondence to exactly the issues that DAI researchers confront. In this paper, therefore, I will use Fulghum's points to structure my brief survey of the field. My goals are twofold. First, while I cannot give in this small space as thorough a treatment of the field as can be found elsewhere [Bond and Gasser, 1988; Durfee *et al.*, 1989; Durfee *et al.*, 1991; Gasser and Huhns, 1989; Huhns, 1987], I do want to provide pointers to more detailed descriptions of individual research projects. Second I want to use Fulghum's points as a way of clustering work together with perhaps a little bit different a spin. This helps highlight open and unresolved issues within DAI, and hopefully might give the DAI melting pot another little stir.

Share Everything

When resources like information, knowledge, and authority are distributed among agents, agents might need to share to accomplish their tasks. Task sharing and result sharing have been investigated in DAI [Smith and Davis, 1981]. In task sharing, an agent with a task that it cannot achieve will try to pass the task, either whole or in pieces, to agent(s) that can perform the task(s). Generally, task passing is done through some variation of contracting. As developed in the Contract Net protocol [Smith, 1980], the agent that needs help assigns tasks to other agents by first announcing a task to the network, then collecting bids from potential contractors, and then awarding the task to the most suitable bidder(s). Note that both the initial agent (manager) and the eventual contractor(s) have a say in the assignment: a contractor chooses whether to bid or not (and how much), and a manager chooses from among bidders. Tasks are thus shared through *mutual selection*.

Whereas task sharing is generally used to break apart and distribute pieces of large tasks, result sharing takes the opposite view. Specifically, some problems are inherently distributed, such as monitoring the global stock market, or national aircraft traffic. The challenge with these problems is getting agents, who have small local views, to share enough information to formulate a complete solution. This style of distributed problem solving has been termed functionally accurate, cooperative [Lesser and Erman, 1980; Lesser and Corkill, 1981; Lesser, 1991]. At any given time, an agent might use its local view to generate partial solutions that are, in fact, incompatible with the solutions of other agents. However, given enough sharing of information, and strong assumptions about agent homogeneity (that if agents have the same information they will derive the same solutions), complete solutions will emerge eventually.

Of course, the wholesale exchange of every partial solution among all agents is far from an appealing prospect. Substantial work, much of which we will see in later sections, has gone into ways of being more selective of what is sent and when. For example, in DARES [Conry *et al.*, 1990; MacIntosh *et al.*, 1991] a network of theorem proving agents, each of which begins with a subset of the complete set of axioms, will request partial solutions (axioms) from each other when they are stuck or otherwise making poor progress. A request can specify characteristics of axioms that could be useful, to avoid exchanging useless information.

Sharing is clearly a useful approach, but it makes some very strong assumptions that are certainly not universally embraced. In particular, it generally assumes a common language for tasks and/or results that has identical semantics at each agent. Researchers concerned with modeling people recognize that people cannot be assumed to ever attribute precisely identical semantics to a language. However, the counterargument is that computers *can* be programmed to have precisely identical semantics (so long as they cannot modify themselves). Moreover, as evidenced in human coordination, identical semantics is not critical, so long as satisfactory coordination can arise.

Play Fair

In both task sharing and result sharing, agents are assumed to want to help each other. The contracting approach generally assumes that any agent that can do a task and is not otherwise committed will be happy to take on a task. Similarly, in result sharing, agents voluntarily pass around information without any expectations in return. Benevolence on the parts of these agents stems from an underlying assumption of many coordination approaches: that the goal is for the system to solve the problem as best it can, so the agents have a shared, often implicit, global goal that they all are unselfishly committed to achieving. Load is to be balanced so that each agent will perform its fair share of the task.

Some researchers argue that shared goals, and the resultant *benevolence assumption* [Rosenschein *et al.*, 1986], are artificial and contrived. Autonomous agents cannot be instilled with common goals, but instead must arrive at cooperation based on being selfish. However, other researchers argue that, first of all, the agents we are building are artificial, and so can be built with common goals if desired. Moreover, common goals even among adversaries seem to be prevalent: opposing teams on the field have a shared goal of having a fair competition.

Thus, even having the agents share a common, high-level goal will not guarantee compatibility among their actions and results. For example, even though specialists in the fields of marketing, design, and manufacture might share the goal of making a quality, profitable car, they still might disagree on how best to achieve that goal because each interprets that goal using different knowledge and preferences. Participating in a team like this requires negotiation and compromise. While contracting demonstrates rudiments of negotiation due to mutual selection [Smith and Davis, 1983], a broad array of more sophisticated techniques have emerged in this area, including using cases and utility theory to negotiate compromises [Sycara, 1988; Sycara, 1989], characterizing methods for resolving different impasse types [Klein, 1991; Lander *et al.*, 1991; Sathi and Fox, 1989], proposing alternative task decompositions given resource constraints [Durfee and Lesser, 1991], and using the costs of delay to drive negotiation [Kraus and Wilkenfeld, 1991].

Don't Hit People

As discussed above, distributed problem solving generally assumes that, at some level, agents implicitly or explicitly have some commonality among their goals. This assumption is really a result of the perspective taken: that the focus of the exercise is the distributed problem to be solved. Rather than look at DAI systems from the perspective of the global problem, many researchers have looked at it instead from the perspective of an individual. Given its goals, how should an individual take actions, coordinate, and communicate if it happens to be in a multiagent world?

Following the same spirit as in the influential work of Axelrod on the evolution of cooperation among self-interested agents [Axelrod, 1984], a number of DAI researchers have taken the stance of seeing an agent as a purely selfish, utility-maximizing entity. Given a population of these agents, what prevents agents from constantly fighting among themselves?

Surprisingly, cooperation can still emerge under the right circumstances even among selfish agents, as Axelrod's initial experiments showed. The rationale for this result can be found in different forms in the DAI literature. One approach is to consider what agents can know about other agents. Rosenschein and his colleagues have considered different levels of rationality that agents can use to view each other [Rosenschein et al., 1986]. With strong rationality assumptions, an agent that might separately consider a nasty action could reason that, since I assume that the other agents are just like me, we will all take the same action. With that deduction, the agents might jointly take cooperative actions, as shown in the prisoner's dilemma. Moreover, given the ability to communicate, rational agents can strike deals even in adversarial situations [Zlotkin and Rosenschein, 1991].

Another strong motivation for agents being "nice" is that agents might encounter each other repeatedly, and so they might be punished for past transgressions. An agent might thus determine that its long-term payoff will be better if it does not antagonize another. This intuition has been captured [Gmytrasiewicz et al., 1991a; Vane and Lehner, 1990], and has introduced the game theoretic definition of cooperation—as what agents will do if they expect to interact infinitely many times—into DAI.

Put Things Back Where You Found Them

Agents that share a world must contend with the dynamics that each introduces to the others. Given realistic assumptions about uncertainty in communication and observation, it will generally be the case that the agents can never be assured to have completely "common knowledge" about aspects of the world they share, including what each other knows and believes [Halpern and Moses, 1984].

Several strategies to deal with this dilemma have been studied. One strategy is to have each agent take situated actions, essentially treating other agents as generators of noise who change the world in (possibly) unpredictable ways and with whom coordination is either impossible or not worthwhile. We'll get back to this strategy in a later section. Another strategy is to have agents try to make minimal changes to the world so as to not violate the expectations of others. For example, the work by Ephrati and Rosenschein [Ephrati and Rosenschein, 1992] examines how an agent that is acting in the world can choose its actions so as to achieve a state of the world that it believes another agent expects. This is a more sophisticated variation of putting things back where you found them so that others can find them later.

Rather than trying to maintain the world in a somewhat predictable state, the agents can instead communicate about changes to the world, or of their beliefs about the world. In this strategy, agents that need to maintain consistent beliefs about some aspects of the world use communication to propagate beliefs as they change nonmonotonically, performing distributed truth maintenance [Bridgeland and Huhns, 1990; Doyle and Wellman, 1990; Huhns and Bridgeland, 1991; Mason and Johnson, 1989]. More generally, agents can use communication to ensure that their expectations, plans, goals, etc. satisfy constraints [Conry *et al.*, 1991; Yokoo *et al.*, 1990]. Of course, making such communication decisions requires planning the impact of each communication action [Cohen and Perrault, 1979] and modeling joint commitments to activities [Levesque *et al.*, 1990].

Finally, some research has assumed that agents should communicate to improve consistency in how they expect to interact, but should permit some inconsistency. In essence, the agents should balance how predictable they are to each other (to improve consistency) with the need to respond to changing circumstances [Durfee and Lesser, 1988]. At some point, it is better to settle for some degree of inconsistency than to expend the resources on reaching complete agreement. This idea has been a fundamental part of the partial global planning approach to coordination, its extensions, and its relatives [Carver *et al.*, 1991; Decker *et al.*, 1990; Durfee, 1988; Durfee and Lesser, 1991; Durfee and Montgomery, 1991].

Clean Up Your Own Mess

Like putting things back, cleaning up your own mess emphasizes taking responsibility for an area of the shared, multiagent space. Some DAI researchers have approached the problem of coordination from the perspective of organization theory and management science, which sees each agent as playing one or more roles in the collective endeavor. Organizations arise when the complexity of a task exceeds the bounds of what a single agent can do [Fox, 1981; Malone, 1987; March and Simon, 1958]. Within an organization, it is important that each agent know what its own role is and what the roles of other relevant agents are.

Organizational structuring has been employed as a technique for reducing the combinatorics of the functionally accurate, cooperative paradigm [Corkill and Lesser, 1983]. The essence of this approach is that each agent has common knowledge of the organization, including its own interests and the interests of others. When it has or generates information that could be of interest to another agent, it can send that information off. While playing its role in the organization, an agent is free to take any actions that are consistent with its role. Thus, organizations provide a flexible coordination mechanism when roles are defined broadly enough, although incoherence can arise if the roles are defined too broadly [Durfee *et al.*, 1987].

Don't Take Things That Aren't Yours

Conflict avoidance has been a fundamental objective of DAI systems. Because goal interaction has also been at the forefront of AI planning research, it is not surprising that the initial meeting ground between planning and DAI was in the area of synchronizing the plans being carried out at different agents to ensure proper sequencing of actions to avoid having the actions of one agent clobber the goals already achieved by another. Among the efforts in this area have been techniques by which a single agent can collect and synchronize the plans of multiple agents [Cammarata *et al.*, 1983; Georgeff, 1983] and by which multiple agents can generate their plans and insert synchronization in a distributed fashion [Corkill, 1979].

Similarly, resource contention has been critical in scheduling applications. Identifying and resolving constraint violations in allocating and scheduling resources has continued to be of interest in DAI [Adler *et al.*, 1989; Conry *et al.*, 1991; Sycara *et al.*, 1991].

While important, there is more to cooperation than only avoiding conflicts. Even when there is no conflict, coordination could still be beneficial, leading agents to take actions that mutually benefit each other even though they could have acted alone. But deciding how to search for such beneficial interactions, and how much effort to exert in this search, is a difficult problem [Durfee and Montgomery, 1991; von Martial, 1990].

Say You're Sorry When You Hurt Someone

If we had to decide from scratch how to interact whenever we encountered another person, we would never get anything done. Fortunately, most encounters are of a routine sort, and so we can fall back on fairly complete plans and expectations for interaction. I use the term "protocol" to represent the expectations that agents use to structure an interaction. We have seen already some examples of protocols, most notably the contract net in which agents use specific message types for communication, along with expectations about the impact of a message (that a task announcement will elicit a bid, for example).

Most DAI research has rested on providing agents with explicit, predesigned, unambiguous communication protocols. Agents will often exchange expressions in first-order logic, or exchange frames representing plans or goals, or exchange some other structured messages with assurance that others will know how to treat them. Given that we can construct agents as we desire, assuming not only a common language but also a common protocol to structure how the language will be used is not unreasonable.

However, a number of researchers both within DAI and without have been investigating more deeply questions of how communication decisions might be made when explicit protocols are not assumed, based on the intentions and capabilities of the agents involved [Cohen and Levesque, 1990; Grosz and Sidner, 1990; Werner, 1989; Singh, 1991]. As an example of such an approach, a selfish utility-maximizing agent will not necessarily want to communicate based on some predefined protocol (although it might have advantages), but instead might want to consider what messages it could possibly send and, using models of how the impacts of the messages on others might affect interaction, choose to send a message that is expected to increase its utility [Gmytrasiewicz *et al.*, 1991b]. In fact, agents might intentionally choose to lie to each other [Zlotkin and Rosenschein, 1990]. One exciting opportunity for further research is investigating how protocols and truth-telling can arise through repeated communication among individuals, much as cooperation can arise among the actions of selfish agents engaged in repeated encounters.

Flush

Just as apologizing for hurting someone is an expected protocol when it comes to communication actions, so also is flushing an expected protocol for interacting through a reusable (but not shared!) resource in the environment. We might term such protocols for noncommunicative interaction *conventions*. For example, we follow conventions to drive on a particular side of the road, to hold the door for others, to clasp a hand extended for a handshake, and so on.

Because conventions seem to be, in some sense, something shared among agents in a population, they have much in common with organizational structures which similarly guide how agents should act when interacting with others. Unlike organizational structures, however, in which different agents have different roles, conventions carry the connotation of being laws that everyone must obey. Recent work has been directed toward the automatic generation of such social laws [Shoham and Tennenholtz, 1992]. With such laws, agents can reduce the need for explicit coordination, and instead can adopt the strategy (mentioned previously) of taking situated actions, with the restriction that the actions be legal.

Important, and so far little explored, questions arise when agents must act in concert with little or no prearranged organization or laws, however. For example, what happens if people that had expected to stick together suddenly find themselves separated? What should they decide to do in order to find each other? Most likely, they will try to distinguish particular unique locations for finding each other (the car, the lobby, . . .) that each believes the other will distinguish too. The same ideas are being considered now in DAI, with questions arising as to how such distinguished places, or *focal points*, can be found by an artificial agent [Kraus and Rosenschein, 1991].

When You Go Out into the World, Watch for Traffic, Hold Hands, and Stick Together

Unlike the previous bits of coordination knowledge, which had to do with how to behave in your own group, this suggestion shows us a bigger world, comprised both of friends (with whom you stick) and enemies (traffic). This highlights a fundamental aspect of cooperative activity: That cooperation often emerges as a way for members of a team to compete effectively against non-members. In turn, this means that organizations don't simply begin full grown, but instead they emerge as individuals form dependencies among each other as a means to compete against outside individuals more effectively.

The idea of organizations emerging and evolving, while acknowledged in early DAI work, has only recently been given due attention. Based on sociological ideas, Gasser's work has emphasized the dynamics of organizations [Gasser *et al.*, 1989], and in joint work with Ishida has explored techniques for organizational self-design [Gasser and Ishida, 1991]. Research on computational ecologies [Hogg and Huberman, 1991; Kephart *et al.*, 1989] has similarly been concerned with how agent populations will evolve to meet the needs of a changing environment.

Eventually, Everything Dies

This is my paraphrase for one of Fulghum's points. From a DAI perspective, I see its meaning as reminding us of one of the primary motivations for DAI, or for group activity in general. That is, you cannot count on any one individual to succeed. The chances of success are improved by distributing responsibility, and reliance, across a number of agents so that success can arise even if only a subset of them succeed.

The fact that populations of agents change emphasizes the open nature of DAI systems, where a (relatively) static organizational structure will be ineffective due to the dynamically changing composition of the agent population. The open system's view maintains that agents take responsibility for themselves, and that they form commitments dynamically [Hewitt and Inman, 1991; Gasser, 1991]. Much of this work is based on the influential ACTORs formalism [Hewitt, 1977; Kornfeld and Hewitt, 1981; Ferber and Carle, 1991].

Conclusion

A goal of AI is to endow computer systems with capabilities approaching those of people. If AI is to succeed in this goal, it is critical for AI researchers to attend to the social capabilities that, in a very real sense, are what give people their identities. In this paper, I have used a list of important knowledge and skills learned in kindergarten as a vehicle for illustrating some of the social capabilities that computers will need. I have described some of the work in DAI that has explored computational theories and techniques for endowing computers with these capabilities, and I have also tried to convey the diversity of perspectives and opinions even among those doing DAI about appropriate assumptions and about what problems are the important ones to solve. As I see it, all of the problems are important, and we have a long and exciting road ahead of us to build a computer system with the same social graces as a kindergarten graduate.

Acknowledgment

This work was supported, in part, by the National Science Foundation under Presidential Young Investigator award IRI-9158473.

References

[Adler *et al.*, 1989] Mark R. Adler, Alvah B. Davis, Robert Weihmayer, and Ralph Worrest. Conflict-resolution strategies for nonhierarchical distributed agents. In [Gasser and Huhns, 1989].

[Axelrod, 1984] Robert Axelrod. *The Evolution of Cooperation*. Basic Books, 1984.

[Bobrow, 1991] Daniel G. Bobrow. Dimensions of interaction: A shift of perspective in artificial intelligence. *AI Magazine* 12(3):64–80, Fall 1991.

[Bond and Gasser, 1988] Alan H. Bond and Les Gasser. *Readings in Distributed Artificial Intelligence*. Morgan Kaufmann Publishers, San Mateo, CA, 1988.

[Bridgeland and Huhns, 1990] David Murray Bridgeland and Michael N. Huhns. Distributed truth maintenance. In *Proceedings of the National Conference on Artificial Intelligence*, pages 72–77, July 1990.

[Cammarata *et al.*, 1983] Stephanie Cammarata, David McArthur, and Randall Steeb. Strategies of cooperation in distributed problem solving. In *Proceedings of the Eighth International Joint Conference on Artificial Intelligence*, pages 767–770, Karlsruhe, Federal Republic of Germany, August 1983. (Also in [Bond and Gasser, 1988].).

[Carver *et al.*, 1991] Norman Carver, Zarko Cvetanovic, and Victor Lesser. Sophisticated cooperation in FA/C distributed problem solving systems. In *Proceedings of the National Conference on Artificial Intelligence*, July 1991.

[Cohen and Levesque, 1990] P. R. Cohen and H. J. Levesque. Rational interaction as the basis for communication. In P. R. Cohen, J. Morgan, and M. E. Pollack, editors, *Intentions in Communication*. MIT Press, 1990.

[Cohen and Perrault, 1979] Philip R. Cohen and C. Raymond Perrault. Elements of a plan-based theory of speech acts. *Cognitive Science*, 3(3):177–212, 1979.

[Conry *et al.*, 1990] Susan E. Conry, Douglas J. MacIntosh, and Robert A. Meyer. DARES: A Distributed Automated REasoning System. In *Proceedings of the National Conference on Artificial Intelligence*, pages 78–85, July 1990.

[Conry *et al.*, 1991] S. E. Conry, K. Kuwabara, V. R. Lesser, and R. A. Meyer. Multistage negotiation for distributed constraint satisfaction. *IEEE Transactions on Systems, Man, and Cybernetics*, 21(6), December 1991.

[Corkill and Lesser, 1983] Daniel D. Corkill and Victor R. Lesser. The use of meta-level control for coordination in a distributed problem solving network. In *Proceedings of the Eighth International Joint Conference on Artificial Intelligence*, pages 784–756, Karlsruhe, Federal Republic of Germany, August 1983.

[Corkill, 1979] Daniel D. Corkill. Hierarchical planning in a distributed environment. In *Proceedings of the Sixth International Joint Conference on Artificial Intelligence*, pages 168–175, Cambridge, Massachusetts, August 1979.

[Decker *et al.*, 1990] Keith S. Decker, Victor R. Lesser, and Robert C. Whitehair. Extending a blackboard architecture for approximate processing. *The Journal of Real-Time Systems*, 2(1/2):47–79, 1990.

[Doyle and Wellman, 1990] Jon Doyle and Michael P. Wellman. Rational distributed reason maintenance for planning and replanning of large-scale activities (preliminary report). In *Proceedings of the 1990 DARPA Workshop on Innovative Approaches to Planning, Scheduling, and Control*, pages 28–36, November 1990.

[Durfee and Lesser, 1988] Edmund H. Durfee and Victor R. Lesser. Predictability versus responsiveness: Coordinating problem solvers in dynamic domains. In *Proceedings of the National Conference on Artificial Intelligence*, pages 66–71, August 1988.

[Durfee and Lesser, 1991] Edmund H. Durfee and Victor R. Lesser. Partial global planning: A coordination framework for distributed hypothesis formation. *IEEE Transactions on Systems, Man, and Cybernetics*, 21(5):1167–1183, September 1991.

[Durfee and Montgomery, 1991] Edmund H. Durfee and Thomas A. Montgomery. Coordination as distributed search in a hierarchical behavior space. *IEEE Transactions on Systems, Man, and Cybernetics*, 21(6), December 1991.

[Durfee et al., 1987] Edmund H. Durfee, Victor R. Lesser, and Daniel D. Corkill. Coherent cooperation among communicating problem solvers. *IEEE Transactions on Computers*, C-36(11):1275–1291, November 1987. (Also in [Bond and Gasser, 1988].).

[Durfee et al., 1989] Edmund H. Durfee, Victor R. Lesser, and Daniel D. Corkill. Cooperative distributed problem solving. In Avron Barr, Paul R. Cohen, and Edward A. Feigenbaum, editors, *The Handbook of Artificial Intelligence*, volume IV, chapter XVII, pages 83–137. AddisonWesley, 1989.

[Durfee et al., 1991] Edmund H. Durfee, Victor R. Lesser, and Daniel D. Corkill. Distributed problem solving. In S. Shapiro, editor, *The Encyclopedia of Artificial Intelligence, Second Edition*. John Wiley & Sons, 1991.

[Durfee, 1988] Edmund H. Durfee. *Coordination of Distributed Problem Solvers*. Kluwer Acadmic Publishers, 1988.

[Ephrati and Rosenschein, 1992] Eithan Ephrati and Jeffrey S. Rosenschein. Constrained intelligent action: Planning under the influence of a master agent. In *Proceedings of the National Conference on Artificial Intelligence*, July 1992.

[Ferber and Carle, 1991] Jacques Ferber and Patrice Carle. Actors and agents as reflective concurrent objects: A MERING IV perspective. *IEEE Transactions on Systems, Man, and Cybernetics*, 21(6), December 1991.

[Fox, 1981] Mark S. Fox. An organizational view of distributed systems. *IEEE Transactions on Systems, Man, and Cybernetics*, 11(1):70–80, January 1981. (Also in [Bond and Gasser, 1988].).

[Fulghum 1986] Robert Fulghum. *All I Really Need to Know I Learned in Kindergarten*. Random House, New York, 1986.

[Gasser and Huhns, 1989] Les Gasser and Michael N. Huhns, editors. *Distributed Artificial Intelligence*, volume 2 of *Research Notes in Artificial Intelligence*. Pitman, 1989.

[Gasser and Ishida, 1991] Les Gasser and Toru Ishida. A dynamic organizational architecture for adaptive problem solving. In *Proceedings of the National Conference on Artificial Intelligence*, pages 185–190, July 1991.

[Gasser et al., 1989] Les Gasser, Nicolas Rouquette, Randall W. Hill, and John Lieb. Representing and using organizational knowledge in DAI systems. In [Gasser and Huhns, 1989].

[Gasser, 1991] Les Gasser. Social conception of knowledge and action: DAI foundations and open systems semantics. *Artificial Intelligence*, 47(1–3):107–138, 1991.

[Georgeff, 1983] Michael Georgeff. Communication and interaction in multi-agent planning. In *Proceedings of the National Conference on Artificial Intelligence*, pages 125–129, Washington, D.C., August 1983. (Also in [Bond and Gasser, 1988].).

[Gmytrasiewicz et al., 1991a] Piotr J. Gmytrasiewicz, Edmund H. Durfee, and David K. Wehe. A decision-theoretic approach to coordinating multiagent interactions. In *Proceedings of the Twelfth International Joint Conference on Artificial Intelligence*, August 1991.

[Gmytrasiewicz et al., 1991b] Piotr J. Gmytrasiewicz, Edmund H. Durfee, and David K. Wehe. The utility of communication in coordinating intelligent agents. In *Proceedings of the National Conference on Artificial Intelligence*, pages 166–172, July 1991.

[Grosz and Sidner, 1990] B. J. Grosz and C. Sidner. Plans for discourse. In P. R. Cohen, J. Morgan, and M. E. Pollack, editors, *Intentions in Communication*. MIT Press, 1990.

[Halpern and Moses, 1984] Joseph Y. Halpern and Yoram Moses. Knowledge and common knowledge in a distributed environment. In *Third ACM Conference on Principles of Distributed Computing*, 1984.

[Hewitt and Inman, 1991] Carl Hewitt and Jeff Inman. DAI betwixt and between: From "intelligent agents" to open systems science. *IEEE Transactions on Systems, Man, and Cybernetics*, 21(6), December 1991.

[Hewitt, 1977] Carl Hewitt. Viewing control structures as patterns of passing messages. *Artificial Intelligence*, 8(3):323–364, Fall 1977.

[Hogg and Huberman, 1991] Tad Hogg and Bernardo A. Huberman. Controlling chaos in distributed systems. *IEEE Transactions on Systems, Man, and Cybernetics*, 21(6), December 1991.

[Huhns and Bridgeland, 1991] Michael N. Huhns and David M. Bridgeland. Multiagent truth maintenance. *IEEE Transactions on Systems, Man, and Cybernetics*, 21(6), December 1991.

[Huhns, 1987] Michael Huhns, editor. *Distributed Artificial Intelligence*. Morgan Kaufmann, 1987.

[Kephart et al., 1989] J. O. Kephart, T. Hogg, and B. A. Huberman. Dynamics of computational ecosystems: Implications for DAI. In [Gasser and Huhns, 1989].

[Klein, 1991] Mark Klein. Supporting conflict resolution in cooperative design systems. *IEEE Transactions on Systems, Man, and Cybernetics*, 21(6), December 1991.

[Kornfeld and Hewitt, 1981] William A. Kornfeld and Carl E. Hewitt. The scientific community metaphor. *IEEE Transactions on Systems, Man, and Cybernetics*, SMC-11(1):24–33, January 1981. (Also in [Bond and Gasser, 1988].).

[Kraus and Rosenschein, 1991] Sarit Kraus and Jeffrey S. Rosenschein. The role of representation in interaction: Discovering focal points among alternative solutions. In Y. Demazeau and J.-P. Muller, Editors, *Decentralized AI*. North Holland, 1991.

[Kraus and Wilkenfeld, 1991] Sarit Kraus and Jonathan Wilkenfeld. The function of time in cooperative negotiations. In *Proceedings of the Twelfth International Joint Conference on Artificial intelligence*, August 1991.

[Lander et al., 1991] Susan E. Lander, Victor R. Lesser, and Margaret E. Connell. Knowledge-based conflict resolution for cooperation among expert agents. In D. Sriram, R. Logher, and S. Fukuda, editors, *Computer-Aided Cooperative Product Development*. Springer Verlag, 1991.

[Lesser and Corkill, 1981] Victor R. Lesser and Daniel D. Corkill. Functionally accurate, cooperative distributed systems. *IEEE Transactions on Systems, Man, and Cybernetics*, SMC-11(1):81–96, January 1981.

[Lesser and Erman, 1980] Victor R. Lesser and Lee D. Erman. Distributed interpretation: A model and experiment. *IEEE Transactions on Computers*, C-29(12): 1144–1163, December 1980. (Also in [Bond and Gasser, 1988].)

[Lesser, 1991] Victor R. Lesser. A retrospective view of FA/C distributed problem solving. *IEEE Transactions on Systems, Man, and Cybernetics*, 21(6), December 1991.

[Levesque et al., 1990] Hector J. Levesque, Philip R. Cohen, and Jose H. T. Nunes. On acting together. In *Proceedings of the National Conference on Artificial Intelligence*, pages 94–99, July 1990.

[MacIntosh et al., 1991] Douglas J. MacIntosh, Susan E. Conry, and Robert A. Meyer. Distributed automated reasoning: Issues in coordination, cooperation, and performance. *IEEE Transactions on Systems, Man, and Cybernetics*, 21(6), December 1991.

[Malone, 1987] Thomas W. Malone. Modeling coordination in organizations and markets. *Management Science*, 33(10):1317–1332, 1987. (Also in [Bond and Gasser, 1988].).

[March and Simon, 1958] James G. March and Herbert A. Simon. *Organizations*. John Wiley & Sons, 1958.

[Mason and Johnson, 1989] Cindy L. Mason and Rowland R. Johnson. DATMS: A framework for distributed assumption based reasoning. In [Gasser and Huhns, 1989].

[Rosenschein et al., 1986] Jeffrey S. Rosenschein, Matthew L. Ginsberg, and Michael R. Genesereth. Cooperation without communication. In *Proceedings of the National Conference on Artificial Intelligence*, pages 51–57, Philadelphia, Pennsylvania, August 1986.

[Sathi and Fox, 1989] Arvind Sathi and Mark S. Fox. Constraint-directed negotiation of resource reallocations. In [Gasser and Huhns, 1989].

[Shoham and Tennenholtz, 1992] Yoav Shoham and Moshe Tennenholtz. On the synthesis of useful social laws for artificial agents societies (preliminary report). In *Proceedings of the National Conference on Artificial Intelligence*, July 1992.

[Singh, 1991] Munindar Singh. Towards a formal theory of communication for multiagent systems. In *Proceedings of the Twelfth International Joint Conference on Artificial Intelligence*, August 1991.

[Smith and Davis, 1981] Reid G. Smith and Randall Davis. Frameworks for cooperation in distributed problem solving. *IEEE Transactions on Systems, Man, and Cybernetics*, SMC-11(1):61–70, January 1981. (Also in [Bond and Gasser, 1988].).

[Smith and Davis, 1983] Reid G. Smith and Randall Davis. Negotiation as a metaphor for distributed problem solving. *Artificial Intelligence*, 20:63–109, 1983.

[Smith, 1980] Reid G. Smith. The contract net protocol: High-level communication and control in a distributed problem solver. *IEEE Transactions on Computers*, C-29(12):1104–1113, December 1980.

[Sycara et al., 1991] K. Sycara, S. Roth, N. Sadeh, and M. Fox. Distributed constrained heuristic search. *IEEE Transactions on Systems, Man, and Cybernetics*, 21(6), December 1991.

[Sycara, 1988] Katia Sycara. Resolving goal conflicts via negotiation. In *Proceedings of the National Conference on Artificial Intelligence*, pages 245–250, August 1988.

[Sycara, 1989] Katia P. Sycara. Multiagent compromise via negotiation. In [Gasser and Huhns, 1989].

[Vane and Lehner, 1990] R. R. Vane and P. E. Lehner. Hypergames and AI in automated adversarial planning. In *Proceedings of the 1990 DARPA Planning Workshop*, pages 198–206, November 1990.

[von Martial, 1990] Frank von Martial. Interactions among autonomous planning agents. In Y. Demazeau and J.-P.Muller, editors, *Decentralized AI*, pages 105–119. North Holland, 1990.

[Werner, 1989] Eric Werner. Cooperating agents: A unified theory of communication and social structure. In [Gasser and Huhns, 1989].

[Yokoo et al., 1990] Makoto Yokoo, Toru Ishida, and Kazuhiro Kuwabara. Distributed constraint satisfaction for DAI problems. In *Proceedings of the 1990 Distributed AI Workshop*, Bandara, Texas, October 1990.

[Zlotkin and Rosenschein, 1990] Gilad Zlotkin and Jeffrey S. Rosenschein. Blocks, lies, and postal freight: Nature of deception in negotiation. In *Proceedings of the 1990 Distributed AI Workshop*, October 1990.

[Zlotkin and Rosenschein, 1991] Gilad Zlotkin and Jeffrey S. Rosenschein. Cooperation and conflict resolution via negotiation among autonomous agents in noncooperative domains. *IEEE Transactions on Systems, Man, and Cybernetics*, 21(6), December 1991.

13

The Third Contender: A Critical Examination of the Dynamicist Theory of Cognition

Chris Eliasmith

In a recent series of publications, dynamicist researchers have proposed a new conception of cognitive functioning. This conception is intended to replace the currently dominant theories of connectionism and symbolicism. The dynamicist approach to cognitive modeling employs concepts developed in the mathematical field of dynamical systems theory. They claim that cognitive models should be embedded, low-dimensional, complex, described by coupled differential equations, and non-representational. In this paper I begin with a short description of the dynamicist project and its role as a cognitive theory. Subsequently, I determine the theoretical commitments of dynamicists, critically examine those commitments and discuss current examples of dynamicist models. In conclusion, I determine dynamicism's relation to symbolicism and connectionism and find that the dynamicist goal to establish a new paradigm has yet to be realized.

13.1   Introduction

Since the emergence of connectionism in the 1980s, connectionism and symbolicism have been the two main paradigms of cognitive science (Bechtel and Abrahamsen, 1991). However, in recent years, a new approach to the study of cognition has issued a challenge to their dominance: that new approach is called *dynamicism*. There have been a series of papers and books (Globus, 1992; Robertson *et al.*, 1993; Thelen and Smith, 1994; van Gelder, 1995; van Gelder and Port, 1995) that have advanced the claim that cognition is not best understood as symbolic manipulation or connectionist processing, but rather as complex, dynamical interactions of a cognizer with its environment. Dynamicists have criticized both symbolicism and connectionism and have decided to dismiss these theories of cognition and instead wish to propose a "radical departure from current cognitive theory," one in which "there *are* no structures" and "there *are* no rules" (Thelen and Smith, 1994, p. xix, italics added).

Dynamicism arose because many powerful criticisms which the symbolicist and connectionist paradigms leveled at one another remained unanswered (Bechtel and Abrahamsen, 1991; Fodor and McLaughlin, 1990; Fodor and Pylyshyn, 1988; Smolensky, 1988); it seems there must be a better approach to understanding cognition. But, more than this, there are a number of issues which dynamicists feel are inadequately addressed by either alternative approach. Dissatisfaction with the symbolicist *computational hypothesis* and the *connectionist hypothesis*, because of their different emphases and conceptions of time, architecture, computation and representation, have led dynamicists to forward their own *dynamicist hypothesis*.

Symbolicism is most often the approach against which dynamicists rebel (van Gelder and Port, 1995). Dynamicists have offered a number of clear, concise reasons for rejecting the symbolicist view of cognition. The symbolicist stance is well exemplified by the work of Newell, Chomsky, Minsky and Anderson (van Gelder and Port, 1995, p. 1). However, Newell and Simon (1976) are cited by van Gelder as having best identified the *computationalist hypothesis* with the following *Physical Symbol System Hypothesis* (see Newell, 1990, pp. 75–77; van Gelder and Port, 1995, p. 4):

Natural cognitive systems are intelligent in virtue of being physical symbol systems of the right kind.

Similarly, though for more obscure reasons, dynamicists wish to reject the connectionist view of cognition. Churchland and Sejnowski espouse a commitment to the connectionist view with the hypothesis that "emergent properties are high-level effects that depend on lower-level phenomena in some systematic way" (Churchland and Sejnowski, 1992, p. 2). As a result, they are committed to a low-level neural-network type of architecture to achieve complex cognitive effects (Churchland and Sejnowski, 1992, p. 4). These same commitments are echoed by another connectionist, Smolensky, in his version of the *connectionist hypothesis*[1] (1988, p. 7):

The intuitive processor is a subconceptual connectionist dynamical system that does not admit a complete, formal, and precise conceptual-level description.

Or, to rephrase:

Natural cognitive systems are dynamic neural systems best understood as subconceptual networks.

However, dynamicists wish to reject both of these hypotheses in favor of an explicit commitment to understanding cognition as a dynamical system. Taken at its most literal, the class of *dynamical systems* includes any systems which change through time. Clearly such a definition is inadequate, since both connectionist networks and symbolicist algorithms are dynamic in this sense (Guinti (1991) as cited in van Gelder, 1993). Thus, dynamicists wish to delineate a specific *type* of dynamical system that is appropriate to describing cognition. This is exactly van Gelder's contention with his version of the *Dynamicist Hypothesis* (1995, p. 4):

Natural cognitive systems are certain kinds of dynamical systems, and are best understood from the perspective of dynamics.

The hypothesis suggests the heavy reliance of dynamicism on an area of mathematics referred to as *dynamical systems theory*. The concepts of dynamical systems theory are applied by dynamicists to a description of cognition. Mathematical ideas such as *state space, attractor, trajectory,* and *deterministic chaos* are used to explain the internal processing which underlies an agent's interactions with the environment. These ideas imply that the dynamicist should employ systems of differential equations to represent an agent's cognitive trajectory through a state space. In other words, cognition is explained as a multidimensional space of all possible thoughts and behaviors that is traversed by a path of thinking followed by an agent under certain environmental and internal pressures, all of which is captured by sets of differential equations (van Gelder and Port, 1995). Dynamicists believe that they have identified what *should* be the reigning paradigm in cognitive science, and have a mandate to prove that the dynamicist conception of cognition is the correct one to the exclusion of symbolicism and connectionism.

13.2   Dynamicism as a Cognitive Theory

Through their discussion of the *dynamicist hypothesis*, dynamicists identify those "certain kinds" of dynamical systems which are suitable to describing cognition. Specifically, they are: "state-determined systems whose behavior is governed by differential equations.... Dynamical systems in this strict sense always have variables that are evolving continuously and simultaneously and which at any point in time are mutually determining each other's evolution" (van Gelder and Port, 1995, p. 5)—in other words, systems governed by coupled non-linear differential equations. Thus the *dynamicist hypothesis* has determined that a dynamicist model must have a number of component behaviors, they must be: deterministic; generally complex; described with respect to the independent variable of time; of low dimensionality; and intimately linked (van Gelder, 1995; van Gelder and Port, 1995). Before discussing what each of these component behaviors mean to the dynamicist view of cognition, we need to examine briefly the motivation behind the dynamicist project— dynamic systems theory.

13.2.1 Dynamical Systems Theory

The branch of mathematics called *dynamical systems theory* describes the natural world with essentially geometrical concepts. Concepts commonly employed by dynamicists include: *state space, path* or *trajectory, topology,* and *attractor.* The *state space* of a system is simply the space defined by the set of all possible states that the system could ever pass through. A *trajectory* plots a particular succession of states through the state space and is commonly equated with the *behavior* of the system. The *topology* of the state space describes the "attractive" properties of all points of the state space. Finally, an *attractor* is a point or path in the state space towards which the trajectory will tend when in the neighborhood of that attractor. Employing these concepts, dynamicists can attempt to predict the behavior of a cognitive system if they are given the set of governing equations (which will define the state space, topology and attractors) and a state on the trajectory. The fact that dynamical systems theory employs a novel set of metaphors for thinking about cognition is paramount. Black's emphatic contention that science must start with metaphor underlines the importance of addressing new metaphors like those used by dynamicists (Black, 1962). These metaphors may provide us with a perspective on cognition that is instrumental in understanding some of the problems of cognitive science.

13.2.2 Determinism and Complexity

The practical and theoretical advantages of dynamical systems theory descriptions of cognition are multitude. The most obvious advantage is that dynamical systems theory is a proven empirical theory. Thus, the differential equations used in formulating a description of a cognitive system can be analysed and (often) solved using known techniques. One result of having chosen this mathematical basis for a description of cognition is that dynamicists are bound to a deterministic view of cognition (see section 13.2; Bogartz, 1994, pp. 303–304).

As well, the disposition of dynamical descriptions to exhibit complex and chaotic behavior is generally considered by dynamicists as an advantage. Dynamicists convincingly argue that human behavior, the target of their dynamical description, is quite complex and in some instances chaotic (van Gelder, 1995; Thelen and Smith, 1994).

13.2.3 Time

Dynamical systems theory was designed to describe continuous temporal behaviors; thus the dynamicist commitment to this theory provides for a natural account for behavioral continuity. Though the question of whether or not all intelligent behavior is continuous or discrete is a matter of great debate among psychologists (Miller, 1988; Molenaar, 1990), dynamical systems models possess the ability to describe both. So, relying on the assumption that behavior is "pervaded by *both* continuities and discrete transitions" (van Gelder and Port, 1995, p. 14) as seems reasonable (Churchland and Sejnowski, 1992; Egeth and Dagenbach, 1991; Luck and Hillyard, 1990; Schweicker and Boggs, 1984), dynamicism is in a very strong position to provide good cognitive models based on its theoretical commitments.

Fundamentally, dynamicists believe that the other approaches to cognition "leave time out of the picture" (van Gelder and Port, 1995, p. 2). They view the brain as continually changing as it intersects with information from its environment. There are no representations, rather there are "state-space evolution[s] in certain kinds of non-computational dynamical systems" (van Gelder and Port, 1995, p. 1). The temporal nature of cognition does not rely on "clock ticks" or on the completion of a particular task, rather it is captured by a *continual* evolution of interacting system parts which are always reacting to, and interacting with the environment and each other. These temporal properties can be captured with relatively simple sets of differential equations.

13.2.4 Dimensionality

In order to avoid the difficult analyses of high-dimensional dynamical systems, dynamicists have claimed that accurate descriptions of cognition are achievable with low-dimensional descriptions. The aim of dynamicists is to "provide a *low-dimensional* model that provides a scientifically tractable description of the same qualitative dynamics as is exhibited by the high-dimensional system (the brain)" (van Gelder and Port, 1995, p. 28).

The dimension of a dynamical systems model is simply equal to the number of parameters in the system of equations describing a model's behavior. Thus, a low-dimensional model has few parameters and a high-dimensional model has many parameters. The dimensionality of a system refers to the size of its state space. Therefore, each axis in the state space corresponds to the set of values a particular parameter can have.

The low dimensionality of dynamicist systems is a feature which contrasts the dynamicist approach with that of the connectionists. By noting that certain dynamical systems can capture very complex behavior with low-dimensional descriptions, dynamicists have insisted that complex *cognitive* behavior should be modeled via this property. Thus, dynamicists avoid the difficult analyses of high-dimensional systems, necessary for understanding connectionist systems. However, it also makes the choice of equations and variables very difficult (see section 13.3.3).

13.2.5 Coupling

The linked, or *coupled*, nature of a system of equations implies that changes to one component (most often reflected by changes in a system variable) have an immediate effect on other parts of the system. Thus, there is no representation passing between components of such a system; rather the system is linked via the inclusion of the same parameter in multiple equations. The ability of such systems of equations to model "cognitive" behaviors has prompted theorists, like van Gelder, to insist that the systems being modeled similarly have no need of representation (van Gelder and Port, 1995; van Gelder, 1995). In a way, "coupling" thus replaces the idea of "representation passing" for dynamicists.

13.2.6 Embeddedness

Dynamicist systems also have a special relation with their environment in that they are not easily distinguishable from their surroundings: "In this vision, the cognitive system is not just the encapsulated brain; rather, since the nervous system, body, and environment are all constantly changing and simultaneously influencing each other, the true cognitive system is a single unified system embracing all three" (van Gelder, 1995, p. 373). Since the environment is also a dynamical system, and since it is affecting the cognitive system and the cognitive system is affecting it, the environment and cognitive system are strongly coupled. Such *embeddedness* of the cognitive system makes a precise distinction between the system and the system's environment very difficult—in other words, the system boundaries are obscure. But this fact, dynamicists claim, is not only a good reflection of how things really are, it is a unique strength of the dynamicist approach (van Gelder and Port, 1995, p. 25). Coupling amongst not only the equations describing a cognizing system, but also between those describing the environment and those describing the system results in complex "total system" behaviors.

13.3   A Critical Examination of Dynamicism

13.3.1   The Dynamicist Project

The power of dynamical systems theory to provide useful descriptions of natural phenomena has been demonstrated through its application to many non-cognitive phenomena on various scales, ranging from microscopic fluid turbulence and cell behavior, to macroscopic weather patterns and ecosystems. Still, the questions remains: Why should we apply these tools to a cognitive system? Why should we accept the claim that "cognitive phenomena, like so many other kinds of phenomena in the natural world, are the evolution over time of a self-contained system governed by differential equations" (van Gelder and Port, 1995, p. 6)?

A dynamicist advances this claim because of the embeddedness and obvious temporal nature of cognitive systems (van Gelder and Port, 1995, p. 9). The omnipresence of embedded, temporal cognitive systems lead van Gelder and Port to conclude that dynamical descriptions of cognition are not only necessary, but also sufficient for an understanding of mind: "... whenever confronted with the problem of explaining how a natural cognitive system might interact with another system which is essentially temporal, one finds that the relevant aspect of the cognitive system itself *must* be given a dynamical account" (van Gelder and Port, 1995, p. 24, italics added). This strong commitment to a particular form of modeling has resulted in the dynamicists claiming to posit a new "paradigm for the study of cognition" (van Gelder and Port, 1995, p. 29)—not, notably, an extension to either of connectionism or symbolicism, but a *new paradigm*. Thus, the dynamicists are insisting that there is an inherent value in understanding cognition as dynamical *instead of* connectionist or symbolicist (van Gelder and Port, 1995).

One of the greatest strengths of the mathematics of dynamical systems theory is its inherent ability effectively to model complex temporal behavior. It is a unanimous judgment among the proponents of all three paradigms that the temporal features of natural cognizers must be adequately accounted for in a good cognitive model (Churchland and Sejnowski, 1992; Newell, 1990; van Gelder and Port, 1995). Not only do dynamicists address the temporal aspect of cognition, they make this aspect *the most important*. The reasons for espousing this theoretical commitment are obvious: We humans exist in time; we act in time; and we cognize in time—*real* time. Therefore, dynamical systems theory, which has been applied successfully in other fields to predict complex temporal behaviors, should be applied to the complex temporal behavior of cognitive agents. Whether or not we choose to subscribe to the dynamicist commitment to a particular type of dynamical model, they convincingly argue that we cannot remove temporal considerations from our models of cognition—natural cognition is indeed inherently temporal in nature.

Dynamicists have often pointed to their temporal commitment as the most important (van Gelder and Port, 1995, p. 14). Unfortunately, it is not clear that dynamicists have a monopoly on good temporal cognitive models. In particular, connectionists have provided numerous convincing models of sensorimotor coordination, sensorimotor integration and rhythmic behaviors, such as swimming, in which they "embrace *time*" (Churchland, 1992, p. 337). If dynamicists do *not* have this monopoly, it will be difficult to argue convincingly that dynamicism should properly be considered a new paradigm.

13.3.2 Dynamical Systems Metaphors

The intuitive appeal of a dynamical systems theory description of many systems' behaviors is quite difficult to resist. It simply makes sense to think of the behavior of cognitive systems in terms of an "attraction" to a certain state (e.g., some people seem to be disposed to being happy). However, can such metaphorical descriptions of complex systems actually provide us with new insights, integrate previously unrelated facts, or in some other way lead to a deeper understanding of these systems? In other words, can dynamical descriptions be more than metaphorical in nature?

In order to answer this question in the affirmative, we must be able to show the potential for new predictions and explanations. The dynamicist analogy between cognition and dynamical systems theory (see section 13.2) is compelling, but is it predictive and explanatory? We cannot allow ourselves to accept new concepts and theories which do not deepen our understanding of the system being modeled: "[even though] dynamical concepts and theory are seductive, we may mistake translation for explanation" (Robertson *et al.*, 1993, p. 119).

Philosopher of science Mary Hesse has noted that theoretical models often rely on this sort of analogy to the already familiar (1988, p. 356):

[Theoretical models] provide explanation in terms of something already familiar and intelligible. This is true of all attempts to reduce relatively obscure phenomena to more familiar mechanisms or to picturable non-mechanical systems. . . . Basically, the theoretical model exploits some other system (such as a mechanism or a familiar mathematical or empirical theory from another domain) that is already well known and understood in order to explain the less well-established system under investigation.

Clearly, this tack is the one that dynamicists have taken. They are attempting to address the obscure and poorly-understood phenomena of cognition in terms of the more familiar mathematical theory of dynamical systems, which has been successfully applied to complex mechanical and general mathematical systems.

However, simply providing an analogy is not enough (Robertson *et al.*, 1993, p. 119):

> There is a danger, however, in this new fascination with dynamic theory. The danger lies in the temptation to naively adopt a new terminology or set of metaphors, to merely redescribe the phenomena we have been studying for so long, and then conclude that we have explained them.

In science it is necessary to provide a *model*. A model is no longer simply a resemblance, but rather a precise description of the properties of the system being modeled. The more important properties of the source that are exactly demonstrated by the model, the better the model. So, to differentiate between model and analogy in science, one can determine if the mapping of these important properties is explicit, leaving no room for interpretation; if so, one is dealing with a model. In this sense, a model can be thought of as "a kind of controlled metaphor" (Beardsley, 1972, p. 287).[2] Thus, where an analogy may consist of the statement: "The atom is like the solar system"— leaving room for the listener to fill in the details, and possibly to infer wrongly that the orbits of electrons and planets are similar—a model would consist of a picture, physical prototype, or mathematical description in which each element of the source would be explicitly represented by some particular aspect of the model. In other words, a model presents a precisely constrained analogy.

An excellent example of the mistake of considering analogical application of dynamical systems theory and concepts to be a valid model can be found in Abraham *et al.* (1994). Specifically, their dynamical descriptions of behavior apply the concepts of dynamical systems theory to a Jungian analysis of human behavior. However, applying these concepts in such a metaphorical manner simply seems to relate the phenomena in a new way. There is no rigor added to their model simply because the chosen metaphor is mathematical. They have provided a metaphor, not a model. Barton duly notes that in the paper describing one such dynamical model of a Jungian hypothesis, Abraham *et al.* "imply a level of measurement precision we don't have in clinical psychology" (Barton, 1994, p. 12).

Often, clinical psychologists applying dynamics to their field ignore the differences between their field and the rigorous ones from which dynamical systems theory arose: "One way that the distinction between fields is set aside is when authors use rigorous terminology from nonlinear dynamics to refer to psychological variables that are multidimensional and difficult to quantify" (Barton, 1994, p. 12). For example, some psychologists have equated the dynamical concept of chaos with overwhelming anxiety, others with creativity, and still others with destructiveness (Barton, 1994). These diverse applications of the concept of chaos are clearly more metaphorical than rigorous, and bear little resemblance to the definitions used in precise dynamical systems theory models.

For this reason, these is no real *explanation* provided by such psychological applications of dynamical systems theory to the phenomenology or intentionality of cognition. These supposed "models" are simply metaphorical *descriptions*, they advance no new insights in clinical psychology. They do not reveal any details about what is being described (i.e., cognition). There are no consistent and explicit mappings between dynamical systems theory and human behavior. We have clearly not been presented with anything resembling Beardsley's desirable "controlled metaphor" (Beardsley, 1972, p. 287).

From the standpoint of cognitive models, there is not a lot of value in such descriptions. We cannot generate a rigorous explanatory model, nor produce computational simulations from metaphor, so we are not able to discover if the models are predictive. This is a serious failure for any scientific model (Cartwright, 1991; Hesse, 1972; Koertge, 1992; cf. Le Poidevin, 1991). Of course, it is possible haphazardly to generate a model which produces data that seem appropriate, but since we have no explicit map between the concepts of clinical psychology and those of dynamical systems theory, the data are meaningful only in their mathematical context, not in a cognitive one.

Even in the most rigorous of dynamical models, such as the Skarda and Freeman (1987) model of the rabbit olfactory bulb, extending dynamical systems theory concepts beyond the metaphorical still proves difficult: "Given this broad picture of the dynamics of this neural system we can sketch a metaphorical picture of its multiple stable states in terms of a phase portrait" (Skarda and Freeman, 1987,

p. 166). Despite the application of non-linear differential equations in their model, when it comes time to show how the model relates to cognition, a metaphorical description is employed.

The concepts of dynamical systems theory provide an interesting method of thinking about cognitive systems, but they have not yet been shown to be successfully transferable to rigorous definitions of human behavior or cognition. The "haziness" of clinical psychology does not allow for quantification of mechanisms in dynamical systems theory terms. Furthermore, even some physiological processes do not seem to lend themselves to precise quantitative dynamicist descriptions that are able to provide the predictive or explanative powers expected of good models (cf. van Geert, 1996).

13.3.3 Dimensionality and Parameter Estimation

In providing any dynamical systems theoretic model, one must provide a set of differential equations. These equations consist of constants and parameters (or variables). In a simple equation describing the motion of a pendulum, an example of a parameter would be the current arm angle, which changes as the pendulum swings, whereas a constant is exemplified by the gravitational field which remains constant no matter the position of the pendulum.

One reason that it has been so difficult for dynamicists to provide good cognitive models is that they have been unable to meet the challenge of identifying and quantifying the parameters sufficiently for a dynamical model. It is extremely difficult, if not impossible, simply to examine a complex cognitive system and select which behaviors are appropriately mapped to parameters to be used in a dynamical model (Robertson *et al.*, 1993, p. 142):

The central dilemma faced by any experimentalist hoping to apply dynamic systems theory is ignorance, in particular, ignorance of the state variables.

This is a common problem in investigating complex natural nonlinear systems: "Not only are investigators rarely able to completely characterize all the variables that affect a complex system, but they must isolate a system well enough to cut through what Morrison (1991) called a 'sea of noise'" (Barton, 1994, p. 10). Dynamicists must realize that the natural systems they wish to model (i.e., cognitive systems) are among the most complex systems known.

When it is difficult to define or even distinguish individual cognitive behaviors (and thus parameters), and similarly challenging to find the signal of interest in ambient noise, it is common practice for dynamicists to define *collective parameters* (also referred to as order parameters) (Thelen and Smith, 1994). A collective parameter is one which accounts for macroscopic behaviors of the system. In other words, many behaviors which *could* be identified with unique system parameters are "collected" into a group, and the overall behavior of that group is represented by a single system parameter: the collective parameter. Consequently, assigning a meaning or particular interpretation to a collective variable becomes very difficult to justify. Barton (1994) attributes this practice to a confusion of techniques between levels of analysis. Clearly, if the meaning of a parameter cannot be determined, it becomes next to impossible to test a model, or to verify hypotheses derived from observing the behavior of the model. In other words, having identified a parameter which controls a macroscopic behavior of an equation describing a system, does not mean that the parameter can be interpreted in the context of the system being described.[3] Thus, it is difficult to determine if such a parameter provides an explanation of the mechanisms at work in the system or what, precisely, the relation between the parameter and the original system is.

However, dynamicists have a mandate to "provide a *low-dimensional* model that provides a scientifically tractable description of the same qualitative dynamics as is exhibited by the high-dimensional system (the brain)" (van Gelder and Port, 1995, p. 28). The only feasible way to generate low-dimensional models of admittedly high-dimensional systems is to use collective parameters. Thus, dynamicists must reconsider their criteria of accepting only low-dimensional models as being valid models of cognition.

By adopting a purely dynamicist approach and thus necessitating the use of collective parameters, it becomes impossible to identify the underlying mechanisms that affect behavior. In contrast, connectionism provides a reasonably simple unit (the neuron or node) to which behavior can ultimately be referred. Similarly, symbolicism provides fundamental symbols to which we can appeal. In both of these instances, understanding global behavior is achieved through small steps, modeling progressively more complex behavior and allowing a "backtrace" when necessary to explain a behavior. With dynamical equations, on the other hand, no such progression can be made. The model is general to such an extent as to lose its ability to explain from where the behaviors it is producing are coming.

13.3.4 System Boundaries

Perhaps the best solution to the difficulties involved in using collective parameters is simply not to use them. Unfortunately, this solution does not help to avoid an important new problem, one which is a consideration for dynamicist models that used collective parameters as well: the problem of systems boundaries.

Dynamicists claim that through their critique of the current state of cognitive science, they are challenging a conceptual framework which has been applied to the problem of cognition since the time of Descartes. Rather than a Cartesian distinction between the cognizer and its environment, dynamicists hold that "the human agent as essentially embedded in, and skillfully coping with, a changing world" (van Gelder and Port, 1995, p. 39) (see section 13.2). Thus, dynamicists feel that it is unnatural to distinguish a cognitive system from its environment.

To begin, let us assume that we are attempting to construct a dynamicist model with a number of parameters, let us say n of them. Thus, we will need an n-tuple that we can use (we hope) to characterize completely the behavior of the system we are modeling. Of course, these n parameters are contained in coupled, non-linear, differential equations. As an example let us assume we are to model a human cognizer; let us think for a moment about the complexity of the model we are attempting to construct.

The human brain contains approximately one trillion connections (Pinel, 1993). Furthermore, the number of parameters *affecting* this system seems almost infinite. Remember, we must account for not only the cognitive system itself, but all environmental factors as there are no discernible system boundaries on the cognitive system. The environment, which must be coupled to our human cognizer, consists not only of other provably chaotic systems like weather, ocean currents, and species populations but billions of other brains (let alone the artificial systems we interact with every day, or the planets, moons, stars, etc.). Having put ourselves in the place of the dynamicist it seems we have the impossible task of characterizing a nearly limitless system. Thus we will, for argument sake, assume the number of parameters is large, but also finite. This same result could be arrived at by using collective parameters (see section 13.3.3).

So, we now have a large, finite n-tuple of parameters for the equations describing our complex system. Is such a coupled non-linear differential equation description of human behavior of any value? Using even the most advanced numerical methods, and the most powerful computers, such a problem would probably be unsolvable. So, let us assume infinite computing power. Let us thus be guaranteed that we can solve our system of equations. However, before we can solve our system, we must ask: what can we use for initial conditions?

Is it feasible for us to be able to measure n starting conditions for our model, with any kind of precision? Unlikely, but let us assume once more, that we have n initial conditions of sufficient accuracy. What kind of answer can we expect? Of course, we will get an n-dimensional trajectory through an n-dimensional state space. How can we possibly interpret such output? At this point, it seems that an interpretation of such a trajectory becomes, if not impossible, meaningless. There is absolutely no way to either 'un-collect' parameters, or to find out exactly what it means for the system to move through the trillion dimensional (to be conservative) state space.

As our attempt to construct a dynamicist model progresses, it becomes more and more difficult to continue justifying further assumptions. However, such assumptions are necessary in light of the dynamicist hypothesis and its commitments to a "certain type" of dynamical model which is both low-dimensional and completely embedded in its environment. Perhaps these commitments should be reexamined.

13.3.5 Representation
An important distinction between dynamicism and either symbolicism or connectionism is the dynamicists' unique view of representation; to be a truly dynamicist model, there should be *no representation*. In contrast, symbolicist models are fundamentally dependent on symbolic representations, so clearly they are inadequate. Similarly,

connectionists represent concepts (via either distributed representation or local symbolic representation) in their simplified networks. But dynamicists decry the use of representation in cognitive models (Globus, 1992; Thelen and Smith, 1994; van Gelder, 1993, 1995).

In a criticism of connectionism, Globus concludes: "It is the processing of representations that qualifies simplified nets as computational (i.e., symbolic). In realistic nets, however, it is not the representations that are changed; it is the self-organizing *process* that changes via chemical modulation. Indeed, it no longer makes sense to talk of 'representations'" (Globus, 1992, p. 302). Similarly, van Gelder insists: "it is the concept of *representation* which is insufficiently sophisticated" (van Gelder, 1993, p. 6) for understanding cognition. Again, Thelen and Smith pronounce: "We are not building representations at all!" (Thelen and Smith, 1994, p. 338). However, it is never mentioned what it *would* "make sense" to talk of, or what *would* be "sophisticated" enough, or what dynamicists *are* "building." Notably, the dynamicist assertion that representation is *not* necessary to adequately explain cognition is strongly reminiscent of the unsuccessful behaviorist project.

In the late 1950s there was extensive debate over the behaviorist contention that representation had no place in understanding cognition. One of the best known refutations of this position was given by Chomsky in his 1959 review of B. F. Skinner's book *Verbal behavior.* Subsequently, behaviorism fell out of favor as it was further shown that the behaviorist approach was inadequate for explicating even basic animal learning (Thagard, 1992, p. 231). The reason for the behaviorist failure was its fundamental rejection of representation in natural cognizers.

Dynamicists have advanced a similar rejection of representation as important to cognition. Consequently, they fall prey to the same criticism that was forwarded over three decades ago. Furthermore, the early work of researchers like Johnson-Laird, Miller, Simon and Newell firmly established a general commitment to representation in cognitive science inquiries (Thagard, 1992, p. 233). There have been no alternatives offered by dynamicists which would fundamentally disturb this commitment.

Thus, it is not easy to deny convincingly that representation plays an important role in cognition. It seems obvious that human cognizers use representation in their dealings with the world around them. For example, people seem to have the ability to rotate and examine objects in their head. It seems they are manipulating a representation (Kosslyn, 1980, 1994). More striking perhaps is the abundant use of auditory and visual symbols by human cognizers every day to communicate with one another. Exactly where these ever-present communicative representations arise in the dynamicist approach is uncertain. It will evidently be a significant challenge, if not an impossibility, for dynamicists to give a full account of human cognition, without naturally accounting for the representational aspects of thinking. Though dynamicists can remind us of the impressive behaviors exhibited by Brooks's (1991) dynamical robots, it is improbable that the insect-like reactions of these sorts of systems will scale to the complex interactions of mammalian cognition.

13.3.6 Examples of Dynamicist Models

To understand better the outcome of the theoretical difficulties discussed in the previous sections, we will now examine three examples that dynamicists have cited as being good dynamicist models. These models are not only considered to be examples of application of the dynamicist hypothesis, but are considered by dynamicists to be exemplars of their project.

13.3.6.1 Cyclical Motor Behavior Model

Though a number of dynamicist models have been proposed by clinical psychologists, many have not been cited as paradigmatic. Because of the difficulties involved in developing convincing, non-metaphorical models of psychological phenomena, even dynamicist proponents tend to shy away from praising these abundant models.

Physiological psychologists, in contrast, have developed far more precise models. Robertson *et al.* (1990) outlined a model for CM (cyclicity in spontaneous motor activity in the human neonate) using a dynamical approach. It seems that such quantifiable physiological behavior should lend itself more readily to a non-metaphorical dynamical description than perhaps clinical psychology would, allowing the psychophysiologist to avoid the poor conceptual mappings of clinical psychologists.

Indeed, Robertson *et al.* gathered reams of data on the cyclic motor activity apparent in human children. Because of the availability of this empirical data, this dynamicist CM model is one of the few able to begin to breach the metaphor/model boundary (Thelen and Smith, 1994, p. 72) which proves impenetrable to many (see section 13.3.2). However, it is another matter to be able to understand and interpret the data in a manner which sheds some light on the mechanisms behind this behavior.

Robertson *et al.*, after "filtering" the observed state space, obtained a dynamicist model with desirably few degrees of freedom which seemed to be able to model the stochastic process of CM. However, upon further investigation, the only conclusions that could be drawn were: "We clearly know very little about the biological substrate of CM" (Robertson *et al.*, 1993, p. 147). In the end, there is no completed dynamicist model presented, though various versions of the model which do *not* work are discounted. So, Robertson *et al.* have employed dynamicist models to constrain the solution, but not to provide new insights. In their closing remarks, they note (Robertson *et al.*, 1993, p. 147):

We are therefore a long way from the goal of building a dynamical model of CM in which the state variables and parameters have a clear correspondence with psychobiological and environmental factors.

In other words, a truly dynamicist model is still a future consideration.

13.3.6.2 Olfactory Bulb Model

The olfactory bulb model by Skarda and Freeman is one of the few well-developed models that dynamicists claim as their own. Many authors, including van Gelder, Globus, Barton, and Newman have cited this work as strong evidence for the value of dynamical systems modeling of cognition. Upon closer examination, however, it becomes clear that this model is subject to important theoretical difficulties. Furthermore, it is not even evident that this dynamicist exemplar is indeed a truly dynamicist model.

In Skarda and Freeman's (1987) article "How brains make chaos in order to make sense of the world," a dynamical model for the olfactory bulb in rabbits was outlined and tested to some degree.

They advanced a detailed model of the neural processing underlying the ability to smell. This model relies on a complex dynamical system description which may alternate between chaotic activity and more orderly trajectories, corresponding to a learning phase or a specific scent respectively. They hypothesized that chaotic neural activity serves as an essential ground state for the neural perceptual apparatus. They concluded that there is evidence of the existence of important sensory information in the spatial dimension of electroencephalogram (EEG) activity and thus there is a need for new physiological metaphors and techniques of analysis.

Skarda and Freeman observed that their model-generated output was statistically indistinguishable from the background EEGs of resting animals. This output was achieved by setting a number of feedback gains and distributed delays "in accordance with our understanding of the anatomy and physiology of the larger system" (Skarda and Freeman, 1987, p. 166) in the set of differential equations that had been chosen to model the olfactory bulb. Notably, the behavior of the system can be greatly affected by the choice of certain parameters, especially if the system is potentially chaotic (Abraham and Shaw, 1992). It is thus uncertain whether the given model is providing an accurate picture of the behavior, or whether it has been molded by a clever choice of system parameters into behaving similarly to the system being modeled.

Even assuming that the model is not subject to this objection, a further criticism can be directed at its predictive or correlative properties. Although the model accounts quite well for a number of observed properties, "it does not correspond with the actual EEG patterns in the olfactory lobe" (Barton, 1994, p. 10). The consequences of this inaccuracy seem quite severe. For, if both the model, and what is *being* modeled are indeed chaotic systems (i.e., very sensitive to initial conditions), but they are not the *same* chaotic system, and if there are any inaccuracies in their initial conditions,[4] then the divergence of the state spaces of the model and the real system will be enormous within a short time frame. Consequently, the model will not be robust and will be difficult to use in a predictive role.

Finally, the authors themselves see their paper and model as showing that "the brain may indeed use computational mechanisms like those found in connectionist models" (Skarda and Freeman, 1987, p. 161). Furthermore, they realized that: "Our model supports the line of research pursued by proponents of connectionist or parallel distributed processing (PDP) models in cognitive science" (Skarda and Freeman, 1987, p. 170). Dynamicists, however, wish to rest their cognitive paradigm on the shoulders of this model. Ironically, the model is simply not a dynamicist model; the architecture is very much like a connectionist network, only with the slightly less typical addition of inhibition and far more complex transfer functions at each node. These facts make it rather curious that it is touted as a paradigmatically important dynamical systems model. The model's similarities with connectionism make it quite difficult to accept the assertion that this type of dynamical model is the seed of a new paradigm in cognitive modeling.

13.3.6.3 Motivational Oscillatory Theory The model which has been touted by van Gelder (1995) as an exemplar of the dynamicist hypothesis is the Motivational Oscillatory Theory (MOT) modeling framework by James Townsend (1992; see also Busemeyer and Townsend, 1993). In this case, unlike the Skarda and Freeman model, MOT does indeed provide dynamicist models, though simplified versions. However, it is also evident that the model provided falls victim to the theoretical criticisms already advanced (see sections 13.3.2–5).

The most evident difficulty in the MOT model relates to the correct choice of systems parameters (see sections 13.3.3 and 13.3.4). Admittedly, for dynamicist models, "changing a parameter of [the] dynamical system changes its total dynamics" (van Gelder, 1995, p. 357). Thus, it is extremely important to be able to correctly select these parameters. However, the MOT model does not seem to have any reliable way of doing so (Townsend, 1992, pp. 221–222):

A closely allied difficulty [i.e., allied to the difficulty of setting initial conditions]—in fact, one that interacts with setting the initial conditions—is that of selecting appropriate parameter values. Unlike physics, where initial conditions and parameter values are usually prescribed by the situation, usually in psychology, the form of the functions is hypothesized in a "reasonable way." However, we often have little idea as to the "best" numbers to assign, especially for parameters.

The devastating result of this difficulty is that the model needs new descriptions for each task. In other words, it becomes impossible to apply the model more than once without having to rethink its system parameters. It seems that this points to the likelihood of the model being molded by a clever choice of parameters, not to the ability of the model to predict the trajectory of a class of behaviors.

Furthermore, this model is an admittedly simple one (Townsend, 1992, p. 219), which makes it rather disconcerting that it is necessary to fix the system manually when it is not behaving correctly (Townsend, 1992, p. 223). This presents a great limitation because the expected complexity and dimension of a truly dynamicist model is immense (see section 13.3.4). Such manual fixing and redescription of each task would surely be impossible in a full-scale model.

The admissions that: "[MOT] appears very simple indeed but is nevertheless nonlinear, and at this time, we do not have a complete handle on its behavior" (Townsend, 1992, p. 220) does not bode well for the dynamicist project. If it is not possible to have a handle on the behavior of the simplest of models, and the dynamicist hypothesis calls for massively complex models, what chance do you have of ever achieving the goal of a truly dynamicist model?

13.4 The Place of Dynamicism

Dynamicists tend to be quite succinct in presenting their opinion of what the relation between dynamicism and the other two approaches should be, and are not shy about their project to replace current cognitive approaches: "we propose here a radical departure from current cognitive theory," (Thelen and Smith, 1994, p. xix). The dynamicist project to supersede both connectionism and symbolicism has given them reason to assess critically the theoretical commitments of both paradigms. Dynamicists have effectively distinguished themselves from the symbolicist approach and, in doing so, have provided various persuasive critical arguments (Globus, 1992; Thelen and Smith, 1994; van Gelder, 1995; van Gelder and Port, 1995). However, dynamicists are not nearly as successful in their attempts to differentiate themselves from connectionists. When they manage to do so, they encounter their greatest theoretical challenges; e.g., providing a non-representational account of cognition. For this reason, deciding the place of dynamicism in the space of cognitive theories reduces to deciding its relation to connectionism. If dynamicism does not include connectionism in its class of acceptable cognitive models, or if it is not a distinct cognitive approach, there is no basis for accepting the dynamicist hypothesis as defining a new paradigm.

Critics may claim that a dynamical systems approach to cognition is simply not new—as early as 1970, Simon and Newell were discussing the dynamical aspects of cognition (Simon and Newell, 1970, p. 273). In 1991, Giunti showed that the symbolicist Turing Machine *is* a dynamical system (van Gelder, 1993), so it could be concluded that there is nothing to gain from introducing a separate dynamicist paradigm for studying cognition. However, Turing Machines and connectionist networks have *also* been shown to be computationally equivalent, yet these approaches are vastly disparate in their methods, strengths, and philosophical commitments (Fodor and Pylyshyn, 1988, p. 10). Similarly, though Turing Machines are dynamical in the strictest mathematical sense, they are none the less serial and discrete. Hence, symbolicist models do not behave in the same ideally-coupled, dynamical and continuous manner as dynamicist systems are expected to. Dynamicist systems can behave either continuously or discretely, whereas Turing Machines are necessarily discrete. Furthermore, they are not linked in the same way to their environment, and the types of processing and behavior exhibited are qualitatively different. For these reasons, dynamicists believe that their approach will give rise to fundamentally superior models of cognition. Biological evidence and the symbolicists' practical difficulties lend support to many of the dynamicists criticisms (Newell, 1990; Churchland and Sejnowski, 1992; van Gelder and Port, 1995).

However, Smolensky's (1988) claim that connectionism presents a dynamical systems approach to modeling cognition can not be similarly dismissed. Connectionist nets *are* inherently coupled, non-linear, parallel dynamical systems. These systems are self-organizing and evolve based on continuously varying input from their environment. Still, dynamicists claim that connectionist networks are limited in ways that a *truly* dynamical description is not.

However, differentiating between connectionist networks and dynamical systems models is no easy task: connectionists often assert that a connectionist network "is a dynamical system" (Bechtel and

Abrahamsen 1991; cf. Churchland, 1992). Frequently, dynamicists themselves admit that connectionist networks are indeed "continuous nonlinear dynamical systems" (van Gelder and Port, 1995, p. 26). Smolensky outlined the many ways in which a connectionist network *is* a dynamical system—he encapsulated the essence of dynamical systems in their relation to cognition and connectionism (Smolensky, 1988). Churchland and Sejnowski have gone further, discussing limit cycles, state spaces, and many other dynamical properties of nervous systems and have included purely dynamical analyses in their connectionist discussions of natural cognitive systems (Churchland and Sejnowski, 1992, p. 396).

The relationship between connectionism and dynamicism is undeniably more intimate than that between either of these approaches and symbolicism. Nevertheless, dynamicists wish to subordinate connectionism to their cognitive approach (van Gelder and Port, 1995, p. 27). Dynamicists fundamentally reject the connectionist commitment to computationalism, representationalism, and high-dimensional dynamical descriptions.

Critiques of connectionism from dynamicists do not seem to present any sort of united front. Some dynamicists note the lack of realism in some networks (Globus, 1992). Others reject connectionism not because of a "failure in principle" but because of "a failure of spirit" (Thelen and Smith, 1994, p. 41). Still others reject connectionism as being high-dimensional and too committed to symbolicist ideas: ideas like representation (see section 13.3.5).

The lack of realism in networks is often due to the limitations of current computational power. Networks as complex as those found in the human brain are infeasible to simulate on present-day computers. The complexity of real networks does not represent a qualitatively distinct functioning, rather just the end-goal of current connectionist models. Thus, claims consonant with "simplified silicon nets can be thought of as computing but biologically realistic nets are non computational" (Globus, 1992, p. 300) are severely misleading. The chemical modulation of neurotransmitter synthesis, release, transport, etc., is simply a more complicated *process*, not a qualitatively different method of functioning. As Globus (1992) later admits, connectionist networks "severely stretch" the concept of computation in the direction of dynamical systems theory. Currently, most, if not all, types of dynamical behavior have been exhibited by various connectionist networks, including chaos, catastrophe, phase change, oscillation, attraction, etc. (Churchland, 1992; Meade and Fernandez, 1994). Thus, it is a very safe assumption that the distinctions between real and simplified networks which Globus advances are ones which will, with time and improved processing power, become obsolete.

The claim that connectionism is simply a "failure in spirit" does nothing to advance the dynamicist cause; it simply reminds us where (perhaps) connectionist modeling should be headed. The final two criticisms of connectionism as being high-dimensional and representational have been addressed in sections 13.3.3–5. It is not clear from this discussion that either of these properties is a hindrance to connectionism. Rather, denying them provides great theoretical difficulty for dynamicism. What is clear, however, is that dynamicism does not include connectionism in its class of acceptable cognitive models. Maybe, then, dynamicism and connectionism are completely distinct cognitive approaches.

Van Gelder urges us to accept that connectionist networks are too limited a way to think about dynamical systems. He claims that "many if not most connectionists do not customarily conceptualize cognitive activity as state-space evolution in dynamical systems, and few apply dynamical systems concepts and techniques in studying their networks" (van Gelder, 1993, p. 21). However, there are a great number of influential connectionists, including the Churchlands, Pollack, Meade, Traub, Hopfield, Smolensky and many others who have addressed connectionist networks in exactly this manner.

There does not seem to be any lack of examples of the application of dynamical systems descriptions to networks (Churchland and Sejnowski, 1992; Pollack, 1990; Smolensky, 1988). In one instance, Kauffman (1993) discusses massively parallel Boolean networks in terms of order, complexity, chaos, attractors, etc. In fact it seems the only viable way to discuss such large (i.e., 100,000 unit) networks is by appealing to the overall dynamics of the system and thoroughly apply dynamical systems concepts, descriptions and analysis (Kauffman, 1993, p. 210).

Van Gelder insists that dynamical descriptions of connectionist networks is where connectionists should be headed; many connectionists would no doubt concur. However, he goes on to conclude that connectionism "is little more than an ill-fated attempt to find a half-way house between the two worldviews [i.e., dynamicism and symbolicism]" (van Gelder and Port, 1995, p. 27). Rather, it seems connectionism may be the only viable solution to a unified cognitive theory, since cognition seems to be neither solely representational/ symbolic nor non-representational/dynamical. Connectionism is able to naturally incorporate both dynamical and representational commitments into one theory. In any case, all that van Gelder has really accomplished is to cast a dynamical systems theory description of cognition into the role of a normative goal for connectionism— he has not provided a basis for claiming to have identified a new paradigm.

The fundamental disagreement between connectionists and dynamicists seems to be whether or not connectionist networks are satisfactory for describing the class of dynamical systems which describes human cognition. By claiming that connectionist networks are "too narrow" in scope, van Gelder wishes to increase the generality of the dynamicist hypothesis, excluding high-dimensional, neuron-based connectionist networks. However, connectionist networks naturally exhibit *both* high-level and low-level dynamical behaviors, providing room for van Gelder's desired generality while not sacrificing a unit to which behavior can be referred. In other words, the mechanism of cognition remains comprehensible in connectionist networks and does not fall prey to the difficulties involved with collective parameters (see section 13.3.3). The fact that connectionist networks are amenable to high-level dynamical descriptions makes it hardly surprising that differentiating between connectionist networks and dynamical systems is no easy task. Frequently, dynamicists realize: "indeed, neural networks, which are themselves typically continuous non-linear dynamical systems, constitute an excellent medium for dynamical modeling" (van Gelder and Port, 1995, p. 26). Furthermore, in Smolensky's paper "On the proper treatment of connectionism," he has outlined some of the many ways in which a connectionist network *is* a dynamical system (1988, p. 6):

The state of the intuitive processor at any moment is precisely defined by a vector of numerical values (one for each unit). The dynamics of the intuitive processor are governed by a differential equation. The numerical parameters in this equation constitute the processor's program or knowledge. In learning systems, these parameters change according to another differential equation.

As Smolensky explicitly noted, a connectionist network represents the state of the system at any particular time by the activity of all units in the network. These units are naturally interpretable as axes of a state space. Their behaviors can be effectively described at a general level in dynamical systems theory terms. Such systems *are* nonlinear, differentially describable, self-organizing and dynamical as they trace a path through their high-order state space. The behavior of these networks is *exactly* describable by the state space and the system's trajectory, as in any typical dynamical system. In other words, the tools provided by dynamical systems theory are directly applicable to the description of the behavior of connectionist networks. Examples of strange attractors, chaos, catastrophe, etc. are all found in connectionist networks, and such concepts have been used to analyse these networks. These qualities lend such systems all the desirable traits of dynamicism (e.g., natural temporal behavior, amenability to general descriptions) but they remain connectionist and thus representational, computational, and high-dimensional.

So, dynamicism does not include connectionism in its class of models, as some of their theoretical commitments are incompatible. Neither, however, is dynamicism a distinct cognitive approach as important aspects (and the least controversial) of the dynamicist hypothesis are naturally addressed by connectionist networks. Thus, the dynamicist hypothesis has not provided a foundation on which to build a new paradigm. What it has provided, however, are reasons to intensify a particular type of connectionist modeling, one which uses the tools of dynamical systems theory to understand the functioning of connectionist networks.

13.5   Conclusion

It is undeniable that brains are dynamical systems. Cognizers are situated agents, exhibiting complex temporal behaviors. The dynamicist description emphasizes our ongoing, real-time interaction with the world. For these reasons, it seems that dynamical systems theory has far greater appeal for describing some aspects of cognition than classical computationalism.

However, by restricting dynamicist descriptions to low-dimensional systems of differential equations which must rely on collective parameters, the dynamicist has created serious problems in attempting to apply these models to cognition. In general it seems that dynamicists have a difficult time keeping arbitrariness from permeating their models. There are no clear ways of justifying parameter settings, choosing equations, interpreting data, or creating system boundaries. The dynamicist emphasis on collective parameter models makes interpretation of a system's behavior confounding; there is no evident method for determining the 'meaning' of a particular parameter in a model.

Similarly, though dynamicists present interesting instances when it seems representation may be inappropriate (e.g., motor control, habitual behavior, etc.) it is difficult to understand how dynamicists intend to explain the ubiquitous use of representation by human cognizers while maintaining a complete rejection of representation. This project failed with the behaviorists, and it is not clear why it should succeed now.

It is difficult to accept that dynamical models can effectively stand as their own class of cognitive models. The difficulties which arise at the proposed level of generality seem insurmountable, no matter the resources available. They seem to offer exciting new ways of understanding these systems and of thinking intuitively about human behavior. However, as a rigorous descriptive model of either, the purely dynamical description falls disappointingly short. At most, dynamicists offer new metaphors and interesting discussion, but shaky models. However, at the very least they offer a compelling normative direction for cognitive science (cf. Aslin, 1993).

Despite the power and intuitive appeal of dynamical systems theory, the dynamicist interpretation of how this field of mathematics should be applied to cognitive modeling is neither trivial nor obviously preferable to connectionism and symbolism, as dynamicists would have us believe. However, dynamical systems theory can contribute invaluably to the description, discussion and analysis of cognitive models. Possibly more cognitive scientists should realize "Our brains are dynamical, not incidentally or in passing, but essentially, inevitably, and to their very core" (Churchland and Sejnowski, 1992, p. 187).

Acknowledgments

Special thanks to Cameron Shelley, Paul Thagard and Jim Van Evra for helpful comments on earlier drafts of this paper.

Notes

1. Smolensky actually refers to this hypothesis as the *subsymbolic hypothesis* to address the distinction between local and distributed connectionist commitments. However, Churchland and Sejnowksi reject local connectionist networks as biologically unrealistic (Churchland and Sejnowski, 1992, pp. 179–182) and so this form of the hypothesis is suitable for our purposes.

2. In contrast to an explicitly controlled metaphor, Beardsley describes to the use of a *normal* metaphor: "But of course the (normal) metaphorical description, as its implications are pursued, can be checked at each step, and we need not feel committed to all of its implications merely because it has a general appropriateness. So the metaphorical description may least misleadingly, perhaps, be considered as an aid to thought rather than a special mode of thinking" (Beardsley, 1972, p. 287).

3. It has been noted by an anonymous reviewer that a number of dynamics-oriented researchers explicitly remark on the importance of providing component referents for collective variables and others derive these variables from low-level behaviors. For example, Thelen and Smith (1994) note that Edelman "provide(s) a neural account of the more macroscropic (sic) dynamic principles of behavioral development" (p. 143). As well, Kauffman derives collective variables from complex binary networks (see section 4.0). However, in van Gelder's characterization of dynamicism, derivation or grounding of collective variables is not mentioned as criteria for "good" collective variables. Furthermore, in practice, many collective variables are neither derived nor are their neural correlates mentioned (see Clark *et al.*, 1993; Robertson, *et al.*, 1993; Abraham *et al.*, 1994).

4. Which there are theoretically guaranteed to be, given that the systems are chaotic (Gleick, 1987).

References

Abraham, F., Abraham, R., and Shaw, C. D. (1994). Dynamical systems for psychology. In R. Vallacher and A. Nowak (Eds.), *Dynamical systems in social psychology*. San Diego: Academic Press.

Aslin, R. N. (1993). Commentary: The strange attractiveness of dynamics systems to development. In L. B. Smith and E. Thelen (Eds.), *A dynamic systems approach to development: Applications* (pp. 385–400). Cambridge, MA: MIT Press.

Barton, S. (1994). Chaos, self-organization, and psychology. *American Psychologist, 49*, 5–14.

Beardsley, M. (1972). Metaphor. In *The encyclopedia of philosophy* (pp. 284–298). New York: Macmillan and The Free Press.

Bechtel, W., and Abrahamsen, A. (1991). *Connectionism and the mind: An introduction to parallel processing in networks*. Cambridge, MA: Basil Blackwell.

Bogartz, R. S. (1994). The future of dynamic systems models in developmental psychology in the light of the past. *Journal of Experimental Child Psychology, 58,* 289–319.

Brooks, R. (1991). Intelligence without representation. *Artificial Intelligence, 47,* 139–159.

Busemeyer, J. R., and Townsend, J. T. (1993). Decision field theory: A dynamic-cognitive approach to decision making in an uncertain environment. *Psychological Review, 100,* 432–459.

Cartwright, N. (1991). Fables and models I. *Proceedings of the Aristotelian Society Supplement, 65,* 55–68.

Clark, J. E., Truly, T. L., and Phillips, S. J. (1993). On the development of walking as a limit-cycle system. In L. B. Smith and E. Thelen (Eds.), *A dynamic systems approach to development: Applications* (pp. 71–94). Cambridge, MA: MIT Press.

Chomsky, N. (1959). A review of B. F. Skinner's *Verbal Behavior. Language, 35,* 26–58.

Churchland, P. S., and Sejnowski, T. (1992). *The computational brain.* Cambridge, MA: MIT Press.

Egeth, H. E., and Dagenbach, D. (1991). Parallel versus serial processing in visual search: Further evidence from subadditive effects of visual quality. *Journal of Experimental Psychology: Human Perception and Performance, 17,* 551–560.

Fodor, J., and Pylyshyn Z. (1988). Connectionism and cognitive architecture: A critical analysis. *Cognition, 28,* 3–71.

Fodor, J., and McLaughlin, B. (1990). Connectionism and the problem of systematicity: Why Smolensky's solution doesn't work. *Cognition, 35,* 183–204.

Gleick, J. (1987). *Chaos: Making a new science.* New York: Viking.

Globus, G. G. (1992). Toward a noncomputational cognitive neuroscience. *Journal of Cognitive Neuroscience, 4,* 299–310.

Hesse, M. (1972). Models and analogies in science. In *The encyclopedia of philosophy,* (pp. 354–359). New York: Macmillan and The Free Press.

Hesse, M. (1988). Theories, family resemblances and analogy. In *Analogical reasoning* (pp. 317–340). Boston: Kluwer.

Kauffman, S. A. (1993). *The origins of order: Self-organization and selection in evolution.* Oxford: Oxford University Press.

Koertge, N. (1992). Explanation and its problems. *British Journal of the Philosophy of Science, 43,* 85–98.

Kosslyn, S. M. (1980). *Image and mind.* Cambridge, MA: Harvard University Press.

Kosslyn, S. M. (1994). *Image and brain: The resolution of the imagery debate.* Cambridge, MA: MIT Press.

Le Poidevin, R. (1991). Fables and models II. *Proceedings of the Aristotelian Society Supplement, 65,* 69–82.

Luck, S. J., and Hillyard, S. A. (1990). Electrophysiological evidence for parallel and serial processing during visual search. *Perception and Psychophysics, 48,* 603–617.

Meade, A. J., and Fernandez, A. A. (1994). Solution of nonlinear ordinary differential equations by feedforward neural networks. *Mathematical and Computer Modelling, 20,* 19–44.

Miller, J. O. (1988). Discrete and continuous models of human information processing: Theoretical distinctions and empirical results. *Acta Psychologica, 67,* 191–257.

Molenaar, P. C. M. (1990). Neural network simulation of a discrete model of continuous effects of irrelevant stimuli. *Acta Psychologica, 74,* 237–258.

Morrison, F. (1991). *The art of modeling dynamic systems.* New York: Wiley.

Newell, A. (1990). *Unified theories of cognition.* Cambridge, MA: Harvard University Press.

Newell, A., and Simon, H. A. (1976). Computer science as empirical enquiry: Symbols and search. *Communications of the Association for Computing Machinery, 19,* 113–126.

Pinel, J. P. (1993). *Biopsychology.* Boston: Allyn & Bacon.

Pollack, J. (1990). Recursive distributed representation. *Artificial Intelligence, 46,* 77–105.

Robertson, S. S., Cohen, A. H. and Mayer-Kess, R. G. (1993). Behavioural chaos: Beyond the metaphor. In L. B. Smith and E. Thelen (Eds.), *A dynamic systems approach to development: Applications,* (pp. 120–150). Cambridge, MA: MIT Press.

Schweicker, R., and Boggs, G. J. (1984). Models of central capacity and concurrency. *Journal of Mathematical Psychology, 28,* 223–281.

Simon, H. A., and Newell, A. (1970). Information-processing in computer and man. In *Perspectives on the computer revolution.* Englewood Cliffs: Prentice-Hall.

Skarda, C. A., and Freeman, W. J. (1987). How brains make chaos in order to make sense of the world. *Behavioral and Brain Sciences, 10,* 161–195.

Smolensky, P. (1988). On the proper treatment of connectionism. *Behavioral and Brain Sciences, 11,* 1–23.

Thagard, P. (1992). *Conceptual revolutions.* Princeton: Princeton University Press.

Thelen, E., and Smith, L. B. (1994). *A dynamic systems approach to the development of cognition and action.* Cambridge, MA: MIT Press.

Townsend, J. T. (1992). Don't be fazed by PHASER: Beginning exploration of a cyclical motivational system. *Behavior Research Methods, Instruments, & Computers, 24,* 219–227.

Van Geert, P. (1996). The dynamics of Father Brown. Essay review of "A dynamic systems approach to the development of cognition and action." *Human Development, 39,* 57–66.

Van Gelder, T. (1993). What might cognition be if not computation? *Cognitive Sciences Indiana University Research Report, 75.*

Van Gelder, T. (1995). What might cognition be, if not computation? *Journal of Philosophy, 91,* 345–381.

Van Gelder, T., and Port, R. (1995). It's about time: An overview of the dynamical approach to cognition. In *Mind as motion: Explorations in the dynamics of cognition.* Cambridge, MA: MIT Press.

Notes on the Contributors

John R. Anderson is Walter VanDyke Bingham Professor of Cognitive Psychology and Computer Science at Carnegie Mellon University.
Ruth M. J. Byrne is lecturer in the psychology department at Trinity College, Dublin.
E. H. Durfee is Associate Professor of Electrical Engineering and Computer Science at the University of Michigan.
Chris Eliasmith is in the program in Philosophy/Neuroscience/Psychology at Washington University in St. Louis.
Owen Flanagan is Professor of Philosophy at Duke University.
Dedre Gentner is Professor of Psychology at Northwestern University.
Janice Glasgow is Professor of Computing and Information Science at Queen's University in Ontario.
Philip N. Johnson-Laird is Stuart Professor of Psychology at Princeton University.
Alan Mackworth is Professor of Computer Science at the University of British Columbia.
Arthur B. Markman is Assistant Professor of Psychology at Columbia University.
Douglas L. Medin is Professor of Psychology at Northwestern University.
Keith Oatley is Professor of Applied Psychology at the Ontario Institute for Studies in Education/University of Toronto.
Dimitri Papadias is Assistant Professor of Computer Science at the Hong Kong University of Science and Technology.
Steven Pinker is Professor of Brain and Cognitive Sciences at MIT.
David E. Rumelhart is Professor of Psychology at Stanford University.
Herbert A. Simon is Richard King Mellon University Professor of Computer Science and Psychology at Carnegie Mellon University.

Index